Intelligence Scienc
Study on Educing In
Phase 1 Advi

D0292380

Robert A. Fein, Ph.D.
Chair of the Study and Member, Intelligence Science Board

Paul Lehner, Ph.D.
Senior Study Team Member, MITRE Corporation

Bryan Vossekuil
Senior Study Team Member, Counterintelligence Field Activity

Members of Government Experts Committee on Educing Information

David Becker	Defense Intelligence Agency
John Berglund	Department of Homeland Security
Brian Boetig	Federal Bureau of Investigation
Michael Gelles, Psy.D	Naval Criminal Investigative Service
Michael Kremlacek	U.S. Army Intelligence
Robert McFadden	Counterintelligence Field Activity
C.A. Morgan III, M.D.	Intelligence Technology Innovation Center
Kenneth Rollins, Ph.D.	Joint Personnel Recovery Agency
Scott Shumate, Psy.D.	Counterintelligence Field Activity
Andre Simons	Federal Bureau of Investigation
John Wahlquist	National Defense Intelligence College

Members of Intelligence Science Board Senior Advisory Group on Educing Information

Randall Fort
Vice President, Goldman Sachs

Dr. Paul Gray
Professor of Electrical Engineering and President Emeritus, MIT

About the Intelligence Science Board

Mission

The Intelligence Science Board was chartered in August 2002 and advises the Office of the Director of National Intelligence and senior Intelligence Community leaders on emerging scientific and technical issues of special importance to the Intelligence Community. The mission of the Board is to provide the Intelligence Community with outside expert advice and unconventional thinking, early notice of advances in science and technology, insight into new applications of existing technology, and special studies that require skills or organizational approaches not resident within the Intelligence Community. The Board also creates linkages between the Intelligence Community and the scientific and technical communities.

Impact

Board members initiate studies and assessments in topic areas where they believe that the Board's interdisciplinary expertise and experience could benefit the Intelligence Community. In addition, the Board responds to tasking from the Associate Director of National Intelligence for Science and Technology and from the heads of elements of the Intelligence Community. All ISB tasks are mutually agreed to by the ISB and by the Associate Director of National Intelligence for Science and Technology. The Board's procedures for developing and communicating its findings and advice will remain as flexible and informal as is possible, consistent with the mission.

Membership

The Board is composed of approximately 25 members whose range of expertise encompasses the physical and biological sciences, information technology and communications, information policy, and the law, among others.

EDUCING INFORMATION

Interrogation: Science and Art

Foundations for the Future

Intelligence Science Board
Phase 1 Report

DISCARD

CENTER FOR STRATEGIC INTELLIGENCE RESEARCH

NDIC PRESS

National Defense Intelligence College
Washington, DC
December 2006

The National Defense Intelligence College supports and encourages research on intelligence issues that distills lessons and improves Intelligence Community capabilities for policy-level and operational consumers

Educing Information: Interrogation: Science and Art—Foundations for the Future, Intelligence Science Board.

The National Defense Intelligence College is pleased to present this work of the Intelligence Science Board on Educing Information. "Educing information" refers to information elicitation and strategic debriefing as well as to interrogation. Essays were prepared with the guidance of Dr. Robert Fein and other Board advisors. Works by authors who were employees of the Department of Defense when the essays were first created were reviewed and cleared for unrestricted public release by the Department of Defense's Office of Security Review. This book has benefited from reviews by authoritative professionals in government and academia. The College appreciates the editorial contributions made by those reviewers, and especially the detailed comments by Margaret S. McDonald of the Mitre Corporation. The Foreword and Commentaries included in the book were invited by the editor and are not part of the Intelligence Science Board Report itself.

Russell.Swenson@dia.mil, Editor and Director
Center for Strategic Intelligence Research
National Defense Intelligence College

Library of Congress Control Number   2006932276
ISBN   1-932946-17-9

Table of Contents

Acknowledgments v

Foreword, *Robert Destro* vii

Prologue, *Robert A. Fein* xi

Commentaries, *Pauletta Otis, John Wahlquist* xv

About the Authors xxvii

Introduction, *Robert A. Fein* 1

Scientific Papers

1. The Costs and Benefits of Interrogation in
   the Struggle Against Terrorism
   Robert Coulam 7

2. Approaching Truth: Behavioral Science Lessons on
   Educing Information from Human Sources
   Randy Borum 17

3. Research on Detection of Deception:
   What We Know vs. What We Think We Know
   Gary Hazlett 45

4. Mechanical Detection of Deception: A Short Review
   Kristin E. Heckman and Mark D. Happel 63

5. KUBARK Counterintelligence Interrogation Review:
   Observations of an Interrogator – Lessons Learned and
   Avenues for Further Research
   Steven M. Kleinman 95

6. Custodial Interrogations: What We Know,
   What We Do, and What We Can Learn from
   Law Enforcement Experiences
   Ariel Neuman and Daniel Salinas-Serrano 141

7. Barriers to Success: Critical Challenges in
   Developing a New Educing Information Paradigm
   Steven M. Kleinman 235

8. Negotiation Theory and Practice:
   Exploring Ideas to Aid Information Eduction
   Daniel L. Shapiro 267

9. Negotiation Theory and Educing Information:
   Practical Concepts and Tools
   M. P. Rowe 285

10. Options for Scientific Research on Eduction Practices
   Paul Lehner. 303

11. Educing Information Bibliography (Annotated)
   Theresa Dillon. 311

Index. 329

Acknowledgments

Many individuals and organizations contributed to Phase 1 of the Study on Educing Information (EI). I deeply appreciate the participation and encouragement of these experts from government, the academic community, and other organizations.

The staff of the Study on EI, as well as numerous consultants, assisted immensely and immeasurably in its work. Others provided specialized and invaluable knowledge, editorial assistance, and moral and intellectual support throughout.

The authors of the scientific papers responded to requests, tasks, and deadlines with disciplined scholarship and grace. Staff from the NDIC Press worked skillfully, and patiently, to turn the study report into a book.

To each and all I express my thanks.

Robert Fein

Foreword

Robert A. Destro*

Educing Information is a profoundly important book because it offers both professionals and ordinary citizens a primer on the "science and art" of both interrogation and intelligence gathering. Because this is a book written by and for intelligence professionals, it starts exactly where one might expect it to start – with Dr. Robert Coulam's superb discussion of the costs and benefits of various approaches to interrogation. For those who are (like me) unschooled in the art and science of intelligence gathering, careful study of the table of contents is perhaps the best way to decide which of the papers would provide the most convenient portal through which to enter a realm that is, by the admission of the authors themselves, both largely unexplored and enormously important to our national security. Steven M. Kleinman's excellent paper on the "KUBARK Counterintelligence Interrogation Review" provided just the historical and theoretical background I needed to feel comfortable with the other papers. This book "works" either way.

Wherever one starts or ends this book, certain conclusions are inescapable. The first is that there is ample room for inter- and multi-disciplinary research and collaboration. Each of the papers included in *Educing Information* provides at least one, if not many, important "Foundations for the Future." I look forward to participating in that process.

The second conclusion is that it is going to take a lot of hard work to convince other disciplines that the Intelligence Community is not making the case for interdisciplinary clean-up of what Dr. Robert Fein's "Prologue" calls "traditional police-state methods of extracting information from their prisoners." Even a cursory reading of the papers in this book points to the enormous opportunities for research and human rights protection that will flow from a systematic, and entirely legitimate, set of inquiries into the realm of information gathering.

I fear, however, that the authors and editors may have compounded the problem when they decided to characterize "interrogation" as "educing information." Though "educing information" may sound a bit more benign than the far more robust-sounding image created by the concept of "interrogation," it is not nearly benign enough to overcome the public relations problem that led to the choice of the phrase in the first place.[1] We lawyers call this process "characterization"

---

*Professor of Law and Director, Interdisciplinary Program in Law & Religion, Columbus School of Law, The Catholic University of America, Washington, D.C. B.A. 1972, Miami University, Oxford, Ohio; J.D., 1975, Boalt Hall School of Law, The University of California, Berkeley. Commissioner, United States Commission on Civil Rights, 1983-1989.

[1] Editor's Note: As pointed out by Robert Fein in the Introduction to this book, the term "Educing Information," although not yet in common usage, encompasses information "elicitation" and "strategic debriefing" as well as interrogation. Robert Destro's comments highlight the swift undercurrents that attend the topic at hand, and that can easily enlist adversarial stratagems. Professor Destro is not associated with the Intelligence Science Board.

in some contexts, and either "categorization" or "classification" in others. The advocate selects the characterization that seems to serve immediate purpose and constructs the argument from there. The problem is that others will be doing precisely the same thing – and, in this case, those "others" are likely to be the lawyers and human rights advocates that advise the legislators who in turn control intelligence research budgets.

Professor Kathleen Sullivan, Dean of Stanford University Law School, has observed that, in constitutional law:

> Categorization is the taxonomist's style – a job of classification and labeling. When categorical formulas operate, all the important work in litigation is done at the outset. Once the relevant right and mode of infringement have been described, the outcome follows, without any explicit judicial balancing of the claimed right against the government's justification for the infringement. Balancing is more like grocer's work (or Justice's) – the judge's job is to place competing rights and interests on a scale and weigh them against each other. Here the outcome is not determined at the outset, but depends on the relative strength of a multitude of factors. These two styles have competed endlessly in contemporary constitutional law; neither has ever entirely eclipsed the other.[2]

Thus, it is not enough simply to choose a benign-sounding term like "educing." Any lawyer or human rights advocate will understand both how and why the re-characterization was selected, and force the original discussion of how one "balances" the "need to know" against human rights concerns. There is no point in hiding the fact that we are talking about "interrogation," and, to be honest, reasonable minds might differ on whether the term "educing" sounds all that "benign" in the first place.

All who are interested in the work product and ethics of the Intelligence Community should understand that the road ahead is going to be a long one. Like many, if not most, Americans I learned what I "know" about the "interrogation of bad guys" (both male and female) by watching prime-time television. Law school was (and remains) even less informative with respect to such questions. Most lawyers and judges learn the "art" (but not the "science") of cross-examination of a hostile witness from either a mentor or a supervisor after embarking on the practice of law, and supplement that "training" by watching courtroom dramas recommended by their peers. It is going to take a sustained period of intensive inter-disciplinary cooperation to clean up the rather sordid images of "interrogation" that have become the stuff of movies and prime-time television.

There is a real need for "outreach" and professional collaboration here. Lawyers, judges, legislators, and human rights advocates know little to nothing about either the "science or art" of intelligence gathering, but all of them know

---

[2] Kathleen M. Sullivan, "Post-Liberal Judging: The Roles of Categorization and Balancing," 63 *U. Colo. L. Rev.* 293, 293-294 (1992).

that the interrogation of adverse parties in litigation is essential to the litigation or Congressional hearing process. We freely admit (among ourselves) that "discovery" (our term for "educing information") is often a grueling, time-consuming, and expensive process, but many see absolutely nothing wrong with hiding the costs – and the results – from the general public. We teach our law students quite a lot about the law governing the custodial interrogation of criminal suspects, but not too much about the theory and practice discussed in Ariel Neuman and Daniel Salinas-Serrano's fine paper on custodial interrogation in the law enforcement context. We pride ourselves on our commitment to both human rights and the preservation of rule of law, but work in a profession that decries the loss of civility brought about by the hard-hitting (and sometimes unethical), adversarial litigators we see every night on television.

These are your critics. They are a tough audience with quite a lot to learn *from you.* Human rights advocates and civil rights litigators view themselves as "private attorneys general" whose role is to litigate in defense of individual rights, and they view the courts as the only branch of government capable of striking what now-retired Justice Sandra Day O'Connor called "sensible balances" between the rights of the individual and the needs of organized society. Courts and legislatures cannot strike those "sensible balances" without first acquiring a thorough grounding in the "science and art" of your profession. *Educing Information* is a welcome "first installment" on that effort.

And what are we to make of "public opinion"? Unfortunately, that is a relatively easy question. Prime-time television increasingly offers up plot lines involving the incineration of metropolitan Los Angeles by an atomic weapon or its depopulation by an aerosol nerve toxin. The characters do not have the time to reflect upon, much less to utilize, what real professionals know to be the "science and art" of "educing information." They want results. Now. The public thinks the same way. They want, and rightly expect, precisely the kind of "protection" that only a skilled intelligence professional can provide. Unfortunately, they have no idea how such a person is supposed to act "in real life."

Is there a theme here? Yes, a simple one. Prime time television is not just entertainment. It is "adult education." We should not be surprised when the public (and many otherwise law-abiding lawyers) applaud when an actor threatens the "hostile *du jour*" with pain or mayhem unless he or she answers a few, pointed questions before the end of the episode. The writers craft the script using "extreme" measures because they assume, as our own government has, that police-state tactics studied for defensive purposes can be "reverse engineered" and morphed into cost-effective, "offensive" measures.

Though eminently understandable, such reactions are incredibly short-sighted and profoundly unethical. We don't need just any answers, we need good answers. Our health and safety, and our posterity, depend on it.

Don't expect *Educing Information* to become required reading among the Hollywood screen writer set anytime soon, but it certainly should be. All of us could learn quite a lot.

Prologue

U.S. Experience and Research in Educing Information: A Brief History

Robert A. Fein, Ph.D.

MIS-Y Program

In World War II, the United States military developed a secret "offensive" program, called MIS-Y, designed to obtain intelligence from captured adversaries. This "educing information" program (though it was not described as such at the time) was designed to obtain intelligence from senior German officials, officers, and scientists in U.S. custody. The prisoners were taken to a facility at Fort Hunt, VA, specially developed for educing information. Each internee was carefully screened to ensure that he was likely to have information critical to national security before being sent to Fort Hunt.

Each Fort Hunt internee was paired with a trained interrogator, selected because of his language ability, knowledge of subject matter, and perceived ability to relate to the source. Rooms where detainees ate, slept, washed, recreated, and talked were wired for sound. In addition, collaborators were placed in the prison population. The German officers, scientists, and officials were monitored on a 24-hour basis; information was also collected from them while they were in formal interrogation sessions, while they conversed with their roommates and "colleagues," and at other times. The information was analyzed on an ongoing basis, with dossiers of the internees updated regularly. Intelligence was developed and disseminated to military commands and organizations. The MIS-Y program ended with the conclusion of WWII.

Research on Interrogation Techniques

World events in the post-war period shifted U.S. government attention to the techniques that other countries might apply against U.S. personnel. The rise of the Soviet Union as a world power and the birth of the People's Republic of China led to widespread concern about Soviet and Chinese interrogation capacities. These concerns were highlighted by a number of Communist show trials and the public confessions of a few captured U.S. servicemen during the Korean War.

A national debate ensued at the conclusion of hostilities in Korea. How could one understand U.S. servicemen who "confessed" to dropping bombs filled with germs on civilian populations (events that did not occur)? Were these men traitors or had they been "brainwashed" (a term popularized by Edward Hunter in 1951)? The general U.S. public and researchers alike wondered whether the Russians and/or the Chinese (possibly building on behavioral conditioning techniques developed by scientists such as Ivan Pavlov) had developed scientific technologies for interrogation. What kinds of "mind control" techniques were being employed behind the Iron and Bamboo Curtains?

Concerns about communist interrogation methods led to substantial U.S. government research programs in the 1950s into the nature of practices utilized by the Soviets and the Chinese. These studies were essentially "defensive" in nature. Their goal was to learn about the interrogation behaviors of adversaries in order to equip U.S. servicemen with needed defensive capacities.

Noted social scientists and physicians who were affiliated with the military and the intelligence community (including Arthur Biderman, Robert J. Lifton, Edgar Schein, Lawrence Hinkle, Jr., and Harold Wolff) conducted studies of servicemen who had been prisoners of the Communist Chinese and examined the experience of persons subjected to Soviet interrogations. Respected professional organizations such as the Group for the Advancement of Psychiatry sponsored scientific meetings at which topics relating to interrogation were explored and discussed. Articles in distinguished professional journals (such as the American Medical Association's *Archives of Neurology and Psychiatry*) described Soviet and Chinese interrogation methods and techniques in detail. Several scholarly books were published on interrogation, such as *The Manipulation of Human Behavior* (a series of essays that explored scientific knowledge about interrogation) and *Coercive Persuasion* (a study of servicemen captured by the Chinese).

The overwhelming conclusion of these studies was that the Soviets and the Chinese were using traditional police-state methods of extracting information from their prisoners. Hinkle and Wolff noted in 1957:

> in no case is there reliable evidence that neurologists, psychiatrists, psychologists or other scientifically trained personnel have designed or participated in these police procedures. There is no evidence that drugs, hypnosis or other devices play any significant role in them. The effects produced are understandable in terms of the methods used. There is no reason to dignify these methods by surrounding them with an aura of scientific mystery, or to denote them by terms such as "menticide" or "brain washing" which imply that they are scientifically organized techniques of predictable effectiveness.[3]

---

[3] Lawrence E. Hinkle, Jr. and Harold G. Wolff, "The Methods of Interrogation and Indoctrination Used by the Communist State Police," *Bulletin of the NY Academy of Medicine*, 33 (9): 609-610.

Efforts to Improve Interrogation Practices

At the same time as researchers and scientists were studying interrogation from a defensive perspective, officials in the Central Intelligence Agency (CIA) began a series of explorations about "offensive" interrogation. Throughout the 1950s and into the 1960s, the CIA sponsored studies designed to explore how drugs (LSD, for example), sensory deprivation, and hypnosis might be used as techniques to elicit information. Some of this work was used in developing the *KUBARK Counterintelligence Interrogation Manual*, written in 1963 and publicly released in the late 1990s. The CIA research, much of it conducted through the MKULTRA program, became the subject of concern within the CIA, the Intelligence Community, the Congress, and the public. Although most documents concerning the program's work reportedly were destroyed in 1972, Congressional hearings in 1977 put a spotlight on the research and led to widespread criticism.

Publicity and concerns about the MKULTRA program cast a pall on efforts to conduct systematic inquiry in areas of human intelligence gathering, including interrogation, during the 1970s, 1980s, and 1990s. Most interrogation training in that period, including that provided by the military, was designed to equip soldiers (primarily young enlisted men) with a rudimentary set of skills and techniques that would permit them to gather basic tactical information from captured Soviet soldiers on and about the battlefield. The techniques for interrogation were promulgated in Army Field Manuals, such as FM 34-52. The seventeen or so authorized techniques in the Army manuals are believed to have been developed in the period immediately following World War II.

Although the U.S. government later engaged in interrogation activities to a limited extent in the first Gulf War and in Bosnia, there was little government-supported research in these areas. Additionally, there was little opportunity for U.S. interrogators to practice and hone their skills. For example, soldiers who were trained and certified as interrogators might complete their military service without ever conducting an interrogation.

With the attacks of 11 September 2001, and the initiation of the Global War on Terrorism, the Intelligence Community plunged into activities that, of necessity, involved efforts to obtain information from persons in U.S. custody who at least initially appeared uncooperative. At holding facilities in Afghanistan, Cuba, Iraq, and perhaps other sites, active duty military personnel, reservists, intelligence officers, law enforcement agents, contracted interrogators, and others worked to glean information and create intelligence that might help prevent terrorist attacks and contribute to national security. Since there had been little or no development of sustained capacity for interrogation practice, training, or research within intelligence or military communities in the post-Soviet period, many interrogators were forced to "make it up" on the fly. This shortfall in advanced, research-based interrogation methods at a time of intense pressure from operational commanders to produce actionable intelligence from high-value targets may have contributed significantly to the unfortunate cases of abuse that have recently come to light. Perhaps in the future, EI professionals and researchers can develop knowledge that will inform and improve both practice and policy in these critical areas of national security.

Commentaries

Educing Information: The Right Initiative at the Right Time by the Right People

Pauletta Otis, Ph.D.*

Revelations surrounding the interrogation and treatment of Muslim males at Abu Ghraib in Iraq and at Guantanamo Bay in Cuba shocked the public and provoked the collective conscience. How could this happen? What are the rules in this "time of terror?" Do rules always apply? Whose rules? How should the "potential and suspected" terrorist be treated? What if,... just what if, he had information that would save lives? International terrorists, propelled by unreasonable religious motives, and inflicting mass causalities on the innocent, are not unprecedented in human history.

Although politicians, scholars, and theologians have been quick to condemn harsh methods, the Intelligence Community has a need to know whether any particular method of obtaining information actually works. Yet the scholarly and scientific community has not systematically studied eduction for 45 years. The present study is a good beginning toward redressing that oversight, and is remarkable for its honesty, clarity, and objectivity.

This publication does not specifically address ethical, moral, religious, or legal questions, but instead focuses on "What works?" Dr. Robert Coulam clearly enumerates incentives for "getting it right": upholding ethical concerns and the rule of law, increasing international support, reducing the danger to troops and others at risk of capture, avoiding legal problems for U.S. troops and officials, maintaining U.S. leadership on human rights, avoiding the creation of more enemies, and maintaining the integrity of the military. The research reported in the book comes across as focused and disciplined. It concentrates on the problem of educing information from human sources held in prison or other confined situations. It does not address "field interrogation." Field interrogations that depend on swift movement of both military units and prisoners are not well documented. The evidence we do have about field interrogation is anecdotal and not subject to scientific investigation and validation.

*Pauletta Otis, Ph.D. has been a Faculty Member at the National Defense Intelligence College and now works with the U.S. Marine Corps' Center for Advanced Operational Cultural Learning. As both scholar and citizen, Dr. Otis has focused on the use of military force to prevent systematic violations of human rights during wartime, including the treatment of prisoners of war, or detainees, under jus ad bellum and jus en bello conditions. Editors Note: Dr. Otis's remarks review the historical use of torture and the infliction of pain by the politically powerful to gain information from the weak, putting into greater eduction the value of principles and procedures that now guide U.S. practices in information "eduction," and reinforcing the need for systematic research in the field. Dr. Otis is not associated with the Intelligence Science Board.

Previous literature reflects three historical ways in which individuals and populations with little power are made to interact with those who are in power, where those in power have as their purpose the control or acquisition of information. The common element has been "pain": (1) pain used as punishment, (2) pain used for religious or ideological confession, and (3) pain used to elicit "truthful" information and/or intelligence.

Pain administered publicly as *punishment* has been used for its demonstration effect: It is designed to deter opposition, control populations, and display the power of the government, or of rulers. Individuals have been punished to deter others from proscribed acts; entire groups have been executed in painful, public ways in order to maintain control over empires. Of course, the effect of such a public spectacle has depended on the character of the viewing audience. The public might find it simply fascinating. Some well-known examples include Aztec flaying, Roman circuses, group beheadings by Genghis Khan, and public tortures known to the Hindu dynasties in early India. It is said that Nero enjoyed watching people being thrown off the city walls; the Nazis took pictures of their victims for later viewing; and drawing and quartering as well as hanging in medieval England were accepted public spectacle. Most recently and instructively, the number of people who tried to access pictures of Abu Ghraib prisoner mistreatment numbered in the millions within 48 hours after they were posted.[4] Evidently, public fascination with the infliction of pain on others is not merely an historical phenomenon.

The second focus of literature is on the use of pain to elicit *confession*. Between the 12th and 14th centuries, punishment was given a religious quality by associating it with purification before a Supreme Being, or God.[5] The individuals inflicting pain were only instruments in the hands of the Almighty, performing a service for the targeted individual. It was reasoned that if the tortured individual suffered sufficiently on this earth, he would not have to undergo the sufferings of eternal damnation. The purification of each individual helped society in turn by exorcising the evil from within it – the cancer could not spread. Infliction of physical pain was rationalized, justified, and blessed by the more powerful in a society and even by God Himself.

The use of pain to elicit *truth* in these centuries and those to follow was focused on truth as an ideological belief system congruent with church and political authority. The church was considered to have failed if the heretic refused to confess and recant. Only *after* the religious confession and ruling might the accused be turned over to the political/secular government for punishment and public execution, called "releasing" the prisoner to (non-ecclesiastical) authority. The secular authorities then applied punishment – ranging from public humiliation

---

[4] Luc Boltanski, *Distant Suffering*, trans. Graham Burchell (Cambridge, UK: Cambridge University Press, 1999) provides insight into why people choose to watch the sufferings of others.

[5] Purification through self-flagellation, fasting, and denial of bodily needs has been accepted practice in the Middle East for time immemorial. The concept was known from India to Spain, and was manifested in traditional, indigenous religions as well as in Islam, Christianity, and Judaism

to public execution. This saved the poor soul from eternal damnation and only incidentally reinforced the power of religious and secular authorities.[6]

The 13th century saw the proliferation of "how to" manuals for religious persons to help illuminate motives and circumstances, and to aid in evaluating the magnitude of an offense, as well as how to overcome the obstacles of fear, shame, presumption, despair, and denial in order to elicit a good confession. The earliest manual, *Processus inquisitionis* (1248-49), was relatively simple, but the manuals grew in size, complexity and sophistication. Nicholas Eymerich, Inquisitor General of Aragon (1350s), enumerates various ruses the inquisitor can use to elicit the truth. These approaches reappear in the KUBARK Manual (1963).

In addition, specific guidance regarding "evasive discourse" or how to tell when suspects are not telling the truth, is found in the 13th-century manuals. Nicholas Eymerich wrote of "ten ways in which heretics seek to hide their errors." They are: equivocation, adding a condition to the original question, redirecting questions, feigned astonishment, twisting the meaning of words, changing the subject, self-justification, feigned illness, feigning stupidity or madness, and the use of sanctity or the "holier than thou" method.[7] Eymerich addresses the nature of intimidation and of foot-dragging, of tool-breaking and petty sabotage, of playing one off against another; the differences between men and women, social connections, and occupations, as well as how to overcome "evasion and deception."

Although these three approaches to the control or acquisition of information have developed sequentially, they are often overlapping, and frequently congruent. To some extent, the U.S. Intelligence Community is "stuck" with this history.

	PURPOSE	AUTHORITY	VENUE	TECHNIQUE	RESULT	EDUCTOR
PUNISHMENT	Group repression	Empire	Public	Physical brutality	Fear to elicit obedience	Autocrat
CONFESSION	Cleanse;define in-group and out-group	Church and state	Private, secret, then public	Mental and physical	Promote loyalty and group cohesion	Zealot
TRUTH	Information, Intelligence to prevent further violence	State	Secret	Mental	Useful and timely information	Professional interrogator

Evolution of Information Elicitation by Authorities in the Common Era
Source: Compiled by author.

---

[6] Maureen Flynn, "Mimesis of the Last Judgment: the Spanish auto de fe," *Sixteenth Century Journal* 22 (2), (Summer 1991): 281-297

[7] Found in James V. Given, *Inquisition and Medieval Society: Power, Discipline and Resistance in Languedoc* (Ithaca, NY: Cornell University Press, 1997).

The pre-history of the United States includes well-known instances of the use of pain by officialdom against those less powerful. The Salem witchcraft trials used water and burning to elicit confession. The trials ended only when they were deemed ineffective and counterproductive. The documents that brought the U.S. into being were conceived with awareness of the European history noted above, and were a product of learning from it. The Founders' clear purpose was to protect human dignity by restraining government from the abuse of power.

As public support for church-related governance diminished in the 19th and 20th centuries in favor of codified public law, the rules about use of pain to elicit information were consistently tightened to protect individual rights and liberties within the domestic law enforcement community. However, the needs of the U.S. military and Intelligence Community have been different from those of domestic law enforcement, and the history of the use of pain to elicit information and intelligence is yet to be written. Suffice to say, manuals and laws have suggested ways of educing information and have also provided information to teach how to resist mental and physical pressure.

If there was any case whereby harsh interrogation practices would seem justified, it may have been World War II. The world was aware of the atrocities of the Nazi regime and "eye for an eye" seemed to be the rule of the day. The actual record is somewhat surprising: The Western world was so repulsed by the Nazi spectacle that the "high ground" seemed the safest. In fact, the most successful British interrogator was reputedly "Old Tin Eye," Lieutenant Colonel Robert Stephens at Camp 020, Latchmere House at Ham, on the edge of London. According to his biographer, Alan Judd, his success was a result of thorough preparation by the interrogators, linguistic fluency, and the right mixture of firmness in questioning and sympathy in handling. Violence of any sort was forbidden. The interrogators who worked at Camp 020 knew the difference between "talking" and "truth." [8]

After World War II, the domestic law enforcement community and the U.S. military community took slightly differing views on educing information. FBI and state and local officials were pressured to abide by the rule of law and encouraged to apply two principles: (1) that an individual is innocent until proven guilty and (2) that civil rights are inherent in Constitutional Law. The "enemy within" was to be interrogated as a citizen and therefore had certain rights. The "enemy without"– the Communist threat – presented a different picture. The political turbulence of the 1950s produced new efforts at finding out about the Communists, discovering how to resist brainwashing, and investigating technological and chemical shortcuts in interrogation. The FBI and the CIA handled these issues and produced a good number of reports, among which was the KUBARK Manual. However, for the Department of Defense it was still something of a puzzle as to whether "foreigners," especially those found in combat areas, were to be accorded legal rights and due process. The international community and DOD developed a set

---

[8] Oliver Hoare, *Camp 020: MI5 and the Nazi Spies: The Official History of MI5's Wartime Interrogation Centre* (Richmond, Surrey, UK: Public Record Office, 2000).

of principles and rules to guide the treatment of enemies that were quite specific. The bottom line was that domestic law enforcement developed one set of rules and guidelines; those who dealt with military security were left with only the Law of Armed Combat, which is based on rules pertaining to conventional warfare and therefore difficult to apply to genocide, international crime, and/or terrorism.

Chris Mackey and Greg Miller, in *The Interrogators: Inside the Secret War Against Al Queda*, discuss the development of U.S. intelligence and interrogation capabilities during and after World War II. "In July 1940, a month after German troops entered Paris, the army issued its first field manual on interrogation, or more specifically, on the "examination of enemy personnel, repatriates, documents and material." The 28-page manual described and warned interrogators to observe the Geneva Conventions' ban on coercion. There was no mention of anything resembling the distinct approaches outlined in today's interrogation manuals. Indeed, about the only guidance it offered on method was that "a cigarette or a cup of coffee will frequently elicit more accurate and important information than threats." [9] In 1942, the U.S. Army opened its first centralized intelligence training center at Camp Ritchie, Maryland; its first priority was to train interrogators and the students learned personality analysis, ways of influencing people and making friends (the Dale Carnegie approach applied to war prisoners.)

Since the early 1950s, the U.S. military has trained professional interrogators and taught specific ways of "educing" information from unwilling sources. It was assumed that the information needed was of a military-engagement type – assuming "conventional warfare" (although realizing that Vietnam clearly falls out of this category). The methods used were a combination of those developed from the oral histories of professional interrogators from World War II, the Korean Conflict, and Vietnam. The other component was the list of ways of conducting interrogation as described in KUBARK and mostly Army training documents such as Field Manual 34-52 (1992). Some of the training, especially at SERE (Survival, Evasion, Resistance and Escape) schools, was highly creative and designed to help soldiers resist interrogation and torture. The infamous "dog on a leash" tactic was ostensibly created to show that "nothing can take away your dignity."

This background brings us to the present work on *Educing Information, Interrogation: Science and Art,* which has four chapters devoted to an overview and analysis of U.S. interrogators, techniques, and procedures since World War II. The authors review what we think we know, yet wonder about what we really do not know. Further, the authors note that although some interrogators are formally trained in the techniques, there is no evidence that those techniques actually do what they are supposed to do.

Chapters 5 and 6 of this book describe how current eduction is conducted and note that although there is no valid scientific research to back the conclusion,

---

[9] Chris Mackey and Greg Miller, *The Interrogators: Inside the Secret War Against Al Queda* (New York: Little, Brown and Company, 2004), 27.

most professionals believe that pain, coercion, and threats are counterproductive to the elicitation of good information. The authors cite a number of psychological and behavioral studies to buttress the argument, but are forced to return to the statement: "more research is necessary."

Chapter 6 addresses "Custodial Interrogations: What We Know, What We Do, and What We Can Learn from Law Enforcement Experiences." It is well written but disillusioning. If the Intelligence Community expects to learn what law enforcement officials do actually *know* and have scientific evidence for, they are in for disappointment. The interrogation processes as depicted on the TV program *Law and Order* and the like, and that there work clearly and cleanly, are a fantasy. The authors clearly state, as do others, that there is no particular evidence that supports current interrogation (eduction) techniques and that "more research is necessary."

Chapters 7 through 10 provide a number of good suggestions about how to go about doing research and finding out "what works." A promising suggestion is to study eduction as a negotiation process with wins, losses, and tradeoffs for each party. This model may prove fruitful – but the authors of this report also repeatedly point out that more research is necessary.

The importance of this book and its topic are hard to overstate: Our interests in Iraq and Afghanistan will be enhanced by its spurring us on to better ways of educing information; developments following from this baseline document can give us hope that relationships with allies and friends will be stabilized; the American public will be satisfied that its core values are supported internationally; the concerns of the U.S. Congress will be assuaged; and bureaucratic infighting will be dampened by reliable research. Just as important is the certification by the authors of this volume that eduction of information aims for truth and justice; we do not intend to exert arbitrary power over others. The United States will be able to do the "right thing for the right reason at the right time."

Notably, things are already in motion to discover "better ways of doing business." The U.S. Army has a new field manual (FM 2-22.3) to guide the full range of human intelligence collection operations. The Army also recently stood up the 201st Military Intelligence Battalion at Fort Sam Houston, Texas. It is the first of four interrogation battalions to be created and will specialize in detainee screening and interrogation. It is to be hoped that the Army will make *Educing Information* required reading.

The topic of educing information has significant historical baggage, but it also continues to carry national and global importance. The Intelligence Community is well served by this report. When the Intelligence Community, acting through its individual practitioners who know and understand ground truth, who appreciate the consequences of getting it wrong, and who have respect for the American public, notes and internalizes a document like this, it deserves respect and admiration. Some interrogators may take the message of this book as personal criticism and bastions of bureaucracy may be threatened, but the realm of global security will be better for the clear thinking and courageous writing.

Educing Information: Interrogation—Science and Art

John A. Wahlquist*

"The goal of the interrogation process is to develop the truth."[10] This simple statement captures the spirit that animates *Educing Information: Interrogation: Science and Art.* The "truth" awaiting development in this case is what we think we know and what we really know about educing information (EI), a politically neutral term that encompasses often highly controversial human intelligence collection activities such as interrogation, strategic debriefing, and elicitation. In his article, "Approaching Truth: Behavioral Science Lessons on Educing Information from Human Sources," Dr. Randy Borum explains: *"Almost no empirical studies in the social and behavioral sciences directly address the effectiveness of interrogation in general practice, or of specific techniques in generating accurate and useful information from otherwise uncooperative persons* (emphasis in the original)."

As a practitioner and student of educing information, I share Dr. Borum's surprise and concern over the lack of rigorous scientific examination of educing information fundamentals. What this means is that the effectiveness of existing interrogation techniques has been accepted without sufficient scrutiny. Under these circumstances, any resulting ineffectiveness is attributed to improper execution of the techniques rather than inherent flaws in the techniques themselves. Similarly, detecting deception, a key ingredient in evaluating the usefulness of information obtained through interrogation, is popularly and even professionally considered simply the natural result of properly applying the "right" techniques. While many such techniques apparently have an anecdotal basis, most have not been subjected to recent and thorough scientific analysis. In the worst case some actually may be counterproductive to uncovering the truth. It is to highlight these issues, at a time when information obtained from human sources is increasingly important to protecting vital national security interests, that the Intelligence Science Board sponsored its educing information study.

Despite a dearth of recent systematic studies on the theory and practice of interrogation, historical accounts, primarily anecdotal, have dealt with this issue in considerable detail. Some of the best documented are "how-to" interrogation

*Mr. John A. Wahlquist is a Faculty Member at the National Defense Intelligence College and a member of the Government Experts Committee for the Intelligence Science Board Study on Educing Information. As a member of the Iraq Survey Group in Baghdad (2004-2005), he headed Team Huwaysh, consisting of interrogator-debriefers and subject matter experts, dedicated to debriefing Iraqi detainee 'Abd-al-Tawab Al Mullah Huwaysh, Saddam Husayn's former fourth-ranking Deputy Prime Minister and Minister of Military Industrialization. Previously Mr. Wahlquist served as Defense Attaché to Oman and Deputy Director of Intelligence at U.S. Central Command. Editor's Note: Mr. Wahlquist's comments are not necessarily those of the Intelligence Science Board which he supported as a member of the Government Experts Committee.

[10] John E. Reid and Associates, "Critics Corner: Defending the Reid Technique of Interrogation," at *http://www.reid.com/educational_info/critictechniquedefend.html*, accessed 18 August 2006.

manuals compiled by 13th- century Franciscan and Dominican friars and designed to assist parish priests in obtaining truthful and complete confessions from lay church members. These confession handbooks "explained how to guide the penitent through his or her examination of conscience, how to illuminate motives and circumstances, and thus how to evaluate the magnitude of an offense, and how to overcome obstacles…to a good confession."[11]

The methods promoted in the handbooks, when refined by Roman Catholic inquisitors, evolved into more complicated and sophisticated techniques for interrogating suspected heretics. For example, the *Practica inquisitionis heretice pravitatis*, written in 1323 by Bernard Gui, inquisitor of Toulouse, explains that interrogation methods used must be linked to the types of heresy encountered and then "offers suggestions on the best strategy to pursue in interrogating" members of six specific heretical sects.[12] A later inquisitor, Nicholas Eymerich of Aragon, likely drawing on Gui's account, "describes [in his treatise *Directorium inquisitorum*] ten ways in which heretics try to hide their beliefs" followed by a detailed set of interrogation "ruses the inquisitor can use to elicit the truth." Anticipating modern-day interrogation guides such as CIA's "KUBARK Counterintelligence Interrogation" manual and U.S. Army Field Manual 34-52, Eymerich suggests the interrogator use "manipulative and deceptive behavior" to obtain a confession.[13] Another text, *De inquisitione hereticorum,* takes a more direct approach, recommending that "reluctant witnesses might be persuaded to confess by threatening them with death or telling them that other witnesses had already implicated them." [14]

Not surprisingly, the inquisitors also believed that imprisonment, often for long periods under cruel conditions including solitary confinement, was likely their most effective interrogation technique, surpassing the utility of torture. Bernard Gui described "imprisonment as an integral component of the inquisitor's interrogation strategy…. [C]oupled if necessary, with hunger, shackles, and torture…[it] could…loosen the tongues of even the most obdurate."[15] In practice, such methods may have posed a dilemma for Gui and his fellow inquisitors, who zealously sought truthful confessions not only to root out heresy itself but also to save the immortal souls of the heretics – a dilemma over how to ensure the veracity of forced confessions. An account of the conditions in one notorious 13th century inquisitorial prison and their impact on the "truth" paints a grim picture:

> Some of these cells are dark and airless, so that those lodged there cannot tell if it is day or night…. In other cells there are kept miserable wretches laden with shackles…. These cannot

---

[11] Quotation from Jean Delumeau, *Sin and Fear: The Emergence of a Western Guilt Culture, 13th-18th Centuries,* translated by Eric Nicholson (New York: St. Martin's Press, 1990), 199-200, as presented in James B. Given, *Inquisition and Medieval Society*: Power, Discipline, & Resistance in Languedoc (Ithaca, NY: Cornell University Press, 1997), 45.

[12] Given, 46.

[13] Given, 47.

[14] Given, 45.

[15] Given, 54.

move, but defecate and urinate on themselves. Nor can they lie down except on the frigid ground.... And thus coerced they say that what is false is true, choosing to die once rather than to endure more torture. As a result of these false and coerced confessions not only do those making confessions perish, but so do the innocent people named by them.... [M]any of those who are newly cited to appear [before the inquisitors], hearing of the torments and trials of those who are detained...assert that what is false is true; in which assertions they accuse not only themselves but other innocent people, that they may avoid the above mentioned pains.... Those who thus confess afterward reveal to their close friends that those things that they said to the inquisitors are not true, but rather false, and they confessed out of imminent danger. [16]

Sadly, the conditions described above, although 800 years in the past, are direct antecedents of conditions experienced by Iraqi prisoners confined in Abu Ghraib prison during 2003 and 2004, and perhaps by other prisoners in U.S. custody. The results of interrogations conducted under these conditions were just as unreliable as those in the 13th century. Why, in the 21st century, with all our accumulated knowledge about how human beings think and interact and function, are we still repeating costly medieval mistakes? "The problem," according to Dr. Robert Coulam, "is that...there is little systematic knowledge available to tell us 'what works' in interrogation. We do not know what methods or processes of interrogation best protect the nation's security (emphasis in the original)." In essence, this is why *Educing Information: Interrogation: Science and Art* in is so important and timely. Its conclusions demonstrate that the entire field of educing information needs critical reexamination; there are no easy answers or generic solutions when it comes to understanding these highly complex behaviors.

Especially pertinent, since it confounds conventional wisdom and much of historical practice, is Dr. Borum's finding that "There is little or no research to indicate whether [coercive] techniques succeed.... [B]ut the preponderance of reports seems to weigh against their effectiveness.... Psychological theory...and related research suggest that coercion or pressure can actually *increase* a source's resistance and determination not to comply (emphasis in the original)." Regarding behavioral indicators of veracity, Dr. Gary Hazlett concludes "*We do not really know what we think we know.* Overall, knowledge of behavioral indicators that might assist in the detection of deception is very limited (emphasis in the original)." Wide-ranging mechanical and chemical approaches to educing information, once thought to be a promising panacea, have not lived up to earlier expectations. Over seventy years after the introduction of the so-called "lie-detector," Drs. Kristin Heckman and Mark Happel contend that "despite the polygraph's shortcomings, there is currently no viable technical alternative to polygraphy."

---

[16] Given, 64, extracted from Jean-Marie Vidal, *Un Inquisiteur jugé par ses "victimes": Jean Galand et les Carcassonnais (1285-1286)* (Paris, 1903).

Study of historical documents, such as CIA's infamous "KUBARK" manual, written in 1963 and declassified in 1997, provides examples of both the pitfalls of past thinking and practices, as well as important insights into the relationship between interrogator and subject. Drawing on his detailed review of the "KUBARK" manual and his extensive experience as an interrogator, Steven Kleinman explains that "interrogation is defined both by its intensely interpersonal nature and intractably shaped by the unique personalities of the interrogator and the source.... [E]ach interrogation is unique and therefore one must be cautious in trying to apply a strategic template that would prove effective in each case." Likewise, the lengthy comparative study of interrogation in law enforcement, conducted by Ariel Neuman and Daniel Salinas-Serrano, notes that "all agencies underscored the general caution that no single interrogation technique works with every suspect, and indeed that every suspect is different." In practice, however, Neuman and Salinas-Serrano found that law enforcement interrogation techniques and training "takes a 'one-size-fits-all' approach and fails...to adapt the techniques to differences in age, ethnicity, or culture of the suspect." Similarly, law enforcement interrogators are not necessarily specially selected and trained for that role. Rather, interrogation is viewed as one of several general skills in which every police investigator is expected to be competent. Lastly, although law enforcement personnel "heavily emphasize rapport-building as the main tool for interrogators, it appears," Neuman and Salinas-Serrano assert, "that without some underlying *fear* interrogations will rarely succeed (emphasis added)."

According to Dr. Paul Lehner, "Experience and lessons learned offer a necessary, but insufficient, basis for determining the effectiveness of eduction practices. A program of scientific research on eduction practices is both necessary and highly feasible." The *Educing Information* anthology offers some provocative alternatives for rethinking the art and science of educing information and subjecting eduction practices to systematic evaluation. In separate articles, Drs. Daniel Shapiro and M.P. Rowe recommend the use of negotiation theory to tailor alternative interrogation strategies and guide empirical research on the relationship between interrogators and sources. The goal, Dr. Rowe suggests, "would be not just to evaluate tactics 'today,' or in a single time period, but for *continuous improvement* of EI (emphasis added)."

A key consideration in moving to what Steven Kleinman calls the "*third generation* of doctrine and practice for educing information (emphasis in the original)," is overcoming three barriers to success linguistic and cultural, scientific and technical, and interpersonal and intrapersonal. History, Kleinman argues, is an appropriate guide to developing a future strategy. In the latter years of World War II, *first generation* approaches to educing information that depended primarily on physical force (but were of marginal value in supplying useful information) gave way among Allied and Axis interrogators alike to a more sophisticated *second generation* strategy, "a systematic, outcome-oriented approach to interrogation that relied far more on finesse than on force." However, with the onset of the Cold War, the focus in the United States changed to developing defensive strategies to help service members counteract coercive interrogation methods encountered in Korea and Vietnam. Important lessons learned about the usefulness of non-coercive, "strategic interrogation" techniques were forgotten. Today, Kleinman maintains, "a considerable portion of 'what we know' about interrogation–including approach methodology, the detection of deception, and reading body language – is...largely unsubstantiated....adulterated by the principles of coercive interrogation drawn from studies of Communist methodologies." As a result, "evidence of the employment of coercive methods by U.S. interrogators has appeared with alarming frequency."

The challenge is to make constructive use of both the positive and negative aspects of our historical and practical legacy and to supplement it with meticulous analysis of educing information data using a variety of scientific disciplines and conceptual frameworks. As Dr. Lehner explains, "Information gleaned from field experience constitutes a critical source of knowledge, and without question many of the lessons learned from such experiences are valid. But, equally without question, many are invalid. Which is which? Only objective, scientific research can help to distinguish between them." Pursuing and discovering "truth" is the central message of *Educing Information: Interrogation: Science and Art*. It is obvious from the hugely damaging, worldwide impact of the images from Abu Ghraib, and widespread allegations about abuses elsewhere, that U.S. educing information practices are ripe for review. Failure to act now risks not just the lives of prisoners and detainees, the success of coalition operations in Iraq and Afghanistan and the war on terror, or even our country's broader national security interests. Hanging in the balance is our very identity as a nation – the heart and soul of the United States and the values of life, liberty, and justice that American service members are daily fighting and dying to preserve. Clearly, we must persevere in this endeavor to find the truth.

About the Authors

Robert Fein is a forensic psychologist who specializes in threat assessment and the prevention of targeted violence. Since 2001, he has worked with various entities in the Intelligence Community on questions concerning risk assessment, roles of psychologists in the IC, and educing information. He is a member of the Intelligence Science Board, where he chairs the ISB Study on Educing Information. He is a director of the National Violence Prevention and Study Center and a consultant to the Directorate for Behavioral Sciences of the Department of Defense Counterintelligence Field Activity (CIFA). He also holds appointments at the Harvard Medical School and the University of Massachusetts Medical School.

Dr. Fein has spent the last thirty years working to understand and prevent targeted violence. He has conducted forensic mental health evaluations of several thousand violent offenders, has testified in state and federal courts on over 1,000 occasions on questions of "dangerousness," and has consulted on many hundreds of cases of potential workplace violence. He worked with the U.S. Secret Service for more than twenty years, and co-directed two major Secret Service operational studies of targeted violence: one on assassination; the other on school attacks. Dr. Fein received his Ph.D. from Harvard University in 1974 in Clinical Psychology and Public Practice. He received the American Academy of Forensic Psychology's Award for Distinguished Career Contributions to Forensic Psychology for 2003. *rfeinm@yahoo.com*

Robert F. Coulam, Ph.D., J.D., is Research Professor at the Simmons School for Health Studies in Boston. He is a policy analyst and lawyer who has been an academic and researcher for almost 30 years. His recent work focuses on interrogation and terrorism, with particular concern for legal and administrative oversight of interrogation, and how the U.S. and other countries select, organize, train, and manage interrogators. He also performs research using complex data and econometric methods to evaluate policy and operational problems in Medicare, Medicaid, and other health programs. In an earlier area of work, he wrote books and articles on problems of weapons acquisition and military command and control. He received his Ph.D. from Harvard University's John F. Kennedy School of Government and his law degree from Harvard Law School. *coulam@simmons. edu.*

Dr. **Randy Borum** is a Behavioral Science Consultant on counterintelligence and national security issues. He regularly teaches and consults with law enforcement agencies, the Intelligence Community, and the Department of Defense (DOD). As an Associate Professor at the University of South Florida, he has taught courses on Terrorism, Custodial Interrogation, Intelligence Analysis, and Criminal Psychology and is author/ co-author of more than 100 publications. In addition to having served as a sworn police officer for municipal departments in Maryland and Florida for more than five years, he has been an instructor with the U.S. Department of Justice's State and Local Anti-Terrorism Training

(SLATT) Program. Dr. Borum is a Board-Certified Forensic Psychologist who has worked for with the U.S. Secret Service for more than a decade helping to develop, refine and study behavior-based protocols for threat assessment and protective intelligence, and he also serves on the Forensic Psychology Advisory Board for the FBI's Behavioral Science Unit. He recently served as the Principal Investigator on the "Psychology of Terrorism" initiative for an agency in the U.S. Intelligence Community, and now serves on the United Nations' Roster of Experts in Terrorism. *borum@fmhi.usf.edu.*

Dr. **Gary Hazlett** has over 15 years of experience working as a psychologist with U.S. Army elements, primarily with Special Forces and Special Operations command units. He has conducted assessment and selection of personnel, leadership development, intelligence acquisition, and human performance research services for other government and DOD agencies to include the U.S. Army John F. Kennedy Special Warfare Center and School. Dr. Hazlett has conducted psychological assessments for the Special Forces candidacy program, components of the Adaptive Thinking/Leadership Development Program, and other SF leadership development programs. He has served and continues to serve on several national level panels on special applications of psychology in governmental organizations and the detection of deception. During the last eight years, Dr. Hazlett has been a principal investigator in research on the impact of stress on human performance and cognition, the impact of stress on biological systems, stress resilience, and enhanced methodologies for source validation in interrogation. Dr. Hazlett's military experience includes tours of duty in the first Persian Gulf War and in Afghanistan, where he worked directly as a consultant to intelligence operations. *woodardcodyconsulting@yahoo.com.*

Dr. **Mark Happel** is the Neuroscience Thrust Lead in The MITRE Corporation's Emerging Technology Office. Currently, he is studying the neural basis of deception using functional magnetic resonance imaging (fMRI) and Transcranial Magnetic Stimulation (TMS) in collaboration with the Center for Functional and Molecular Imaging at the Georgetown University Medical Center. He also holds an appointment as an Associate Professorial Lecturer at the George Washington University, where he teaches courses in machine learning. *mhappel@mitre.org.*

Dr. **Kristin E. Heckman** received her D.Sc. in computer science with a concentration in machine intelligence and cognition, and minors in neuropsychology and developmental psychology, from The George Washington University in 2004. She is currently a Lead Artificial Intelligence Engineer at The MITRE Corporation, working in support of the Intelligence Community to develop a science of deception. Dr. Heckman also holds an appointment as an Assistant Professorial Lecturer at The George Washington University, where she teaches courses in computer science and artificial intelligence. *kheckman@mitre.org.*

Colonel **Steven M. Kleinman,** USAFR, serves as the Reserve Senior Intelligence Officer and Mobilization Augmentee to the Director, Intelligence,

Surveillance, and Reconnaissance, HQ Air Force Special Operations Command. Col Kleinman formerly served as Director, Air Force Combat Interrogation Course and as DOD Senior Intelligence Officer for Special Survival Training. A graduate of the Joint Military Intelligence College, he received a Master of Science of Strategic Intelligence in August 2002. He is an independent contractor for the MITRE Corporation, where he has worked in support of the Intelligence Science Board's Study on Educing Information. *compass1@att.net.*

Ariel Neuman currently works as an attorney in Los Angeles. He graduated from Columbia University in 2001, where he majored in political science and served as president of the student body. In 2005, he graduated magna cum laude from Harvard Law School. He is looking forward to a career in public service. *ariel.neuman@post.harvard.edu.*

A native of San Juan, Puerto Rico, **Daniel Salinas-Serrano** is an attorney admitted to practice in the State of Florida and the Commonwealth of Puerto Rico. He graduated magna cum laude from Georgetown University in 2001, where he majored in international relations. In 2005, he obtained a Juris Doctor degree from Harvard Law School. An avid boater, Daniel looks forward to a long career in the law and public service. *dsalinasserrano@gmail.com.*

Daniel L. Shapiro, Ph.D., Associate Director of the Harvard Negotiation Project, is on the faculty at Harvard Law School and in the psychiatry department at Harvard Medical School/McLean Hospital. He founded and directs the Harvard International Negotiation Initiative (INI), which focuses on the psychology of human security. He has been on the faculty at the Sloan School of Management, Massachusetts Institute of Technology, and teaches negotiation to corporate executives and senior government officials. He has extensive international experience, including training Serbian members of Parliament, Middle East negotiators, Macedonian politicians, and U.S. officials. During the Bosnian War, he conducted conflict management training in Croatia and Serbia. Through funding from the Soros Foundation, he developed a conflict management program that now reaches one million people across twenty-five countries. Along with Roger Fisher (co-author of *Getting to YES*) Shapiro wrote *Beyond Reason: Using Emotions as You Negotiate*, which has appeared on numerous bestseller lists. *d_shap@yahoo.com.*

M.P. Rowe, Ph.D., has for two decades been Adjunct Professor of Negotiation and Conflict Management at the Sloan School of Management. Her teaching and research have emphasized "intangible" aspects of negotiation as well as the traditional "tangibles." She has elaborated on sources of power for people in negotiations who are traditionally seen "not to have any power." Rowe has been particularly interested in negotiations between individuals where an overt or covert interest of one party is to injure or seek revenge against another party, as distinguished from the more common case of individuals' negotiating over goods and services. Her recent articles deal with the importance of a systems approach to conflict management as distinguished from handling individual disputes and encounters. Her academic work has derived in part from nearly 35 years as an organizational ombudsman, where in dealing with hundreds of conflicts a year, she has had occasion to interview some thousands of people. *mr.negot@yahoo.com.*

Dr. **Paul Lehner** is currently a Consulting Scientist at the Center for Integrated Intelligence Systems in The MITRE Corporation. His research and work are focused on supporting judgment and decisionmaking across a broad spectrum of intelligence problems; including bio-surveillance, all-source analysis, technical data analysis and counter-deception analysis. Previously within MITRE, Dr. Lehner was the Chief Engineer of the Center for Enterprise Modernization (1999-2001) and the Chief Scientist of the Information Systems and Technology Division (1996 – 1999). Prior to joining MITRE, Dr. Lehner was an Associate Professor of Systems Engineering at George Mason University (1987 – 1996) and the Technical Director of the Decision Systems group at PAR Technology Corporation (1982 – 1986). Dr. Lehner has a Ph.D. in Mathematical Psychology and Masters in both Mathematics and Psychology from the University of Michigan. *plehner@mitre.org.*

An expert in online searching, MITRE Senior Information Analyst **Theresa M. Dillon** provides research and analytic support to engineers working for Defense Department and Intelligence Community sponsors. Ms. Dillon's work focuses on research in the domains of systems engineering, information technology, electronics, business, and intelligence. She also provides internal classroom training on Web-enabled literature databases and Internet searching. Ms. Dillon received her master of science degree in library science at the University of North Carolina at Chapel Hill and her undergraduate degree from Tufts University. *tdillon@mitre.org.*

INTRODUCTION

Intelligence Science Board Study on Educing Information

Phase 1 Report

Robert A. Fein, Ph.D.
June 2006

Study Background

Concerns about recent U.S. interrogation activities, subsequent investigations, and the efficacy of contemporary tactics, techniques, and procedures have led the Intelligence Science Board (ISB) to explore the current state of scientific knowledge regarding interrogation and related forms of human intelligence gathering. In September 2004 the ISB initiated a study on Educing Information (EI) to address these questions and to take the first steps toward developing the next generation of EI. The study is sponsored by the Defense Intelligence Agency (DIA), the Intelligence Technology Innovation Center (ITIC), and the Defense Department's Counterintelligence Field Activity (CIFA).

The study on Educing Information began with several premises:

1. For the foreseeable future, the U.S. government will need to obtain information from sources under U.S. control who are thought to possess information critical to national security and who present varying degrees of cooperativeness;

2. U.S. efforts to procure information from uncooperative sources will be most effective if they are based on sound knowledge of social and behavioral science; and

3. There are major overt and hidden costs to getting EI efforts "wrong" and tangible benefits to national security to getting them "right."

Terminology

The study deliberately chose to use the term "educing information," rather than "interrogation," to describe the focus of its activities. The term "educe," which means "to draw out or bring out," seems more accurate and useful in this context than "interrogate," which increasingly means different things to different people and has highly negative connotations for the general public.[1]

From a technical perspective, the study team's definition of EI encompasses "elicitation" (engaging with a source in such a manner that he or she reveals information without being aware of giving away anything of value), "strategic debriefing" (systematically covering topics and areas with a voluntary source who consents to a formal interview), and "interrogation" (interaction and conversation with a source who appears initially unwilling to provide information). EI implies a "system" of gathering information about and from a source and a spectrum of approaches, tools, activities, and techniques. This may involve investigative efforts, development of scenarios, and involvement of others (teams of interviewers and analysts, willing sources, and collaborators). Effective practice of EI usually extends beyond one-to-one interactions with a source.

While the term "eduction" describes the scope of the study team's investigations and recommendations, it has not yet come into widespread use. From a practical perspective, therefore, many of the team's research efforts have focused on functions and activities that are described as "interrogation," primarily because the source documents or the persons interviewed used that terminology. Moreover, the processes described often had the adversarial character that the term calls to mind. "Educing information," by contrast, encompasses the full range of approaches that, in the opinion of the study team, the Intelligence Community should explore as it seeks to obtain useful information from sources in the future.

Activities

Literature Review

Since September 2004 the EI study team has conducted extensive reviews of the behavioral and social science literature that deals directly or indirectly with interrogation, interviewing, and other EI-related activities. We have also examined military, intelligence, law enforcement, and investigative accounts pertaining to interviewing, interrogation, and other areas related to EI. The historical accounts spanned interrogations conducted by the United States and its allies and those conducted by adversaries. The Prologue above summarizes some of the more important programs and indicates why the United States abandoned this area of research. As a result of our reviews, we have compiled a collection of open source information on EI and a lengthy bibliography — the first of their kind. We have also studied Intelligence Community (IC) training manuals and learned from the experience of those involved with the military's SERE (Survival, Evasion, Resistance, and Escape) programs.

In parallel, the study team has followed public discussions about interrogation programs and practices that have received attention in the past several years,

---

[1] One public image of the word "interrogation" is illustrated in a quote profiling *Newsweek* investigative reporter Michael Isikoff: "Mike will pull your fingernails out over coffee discussing lawn care. He is just a born interrogator." (New York Times, 17 May 2005).

especially those used at Bagram Air Force Base in Afghanistan, Guantanamo Bay in Cuba, and various sites in Iraq. We have read media reports of "extraordinary renditions": transfers of persons under U.S. control to other countries in order to facilitate their interrogation. We have also taken note of legislative and judicial discourse and debate about the most appropriate interrogation "techniques" to use in particular settings for detainees deemed to fit into a given category, for example, those in the custody of the U.S. military.

Interviews and Consultations

We have consulted with U.S. experts, both within and outside of government, who possess considerable knowledge about EI. Study team members visited law enforcement and military training sites, attended training sessions, and talked with instructors and students. In the course of these visits, we interviewed persons with a wide range of experience in interviewing and interrogation, including practitioners, trainers, supervisors, and senior managers. We also sought guidance and advice from a group of government experts from IC, military, and law enforcement organizations. We have collaborated with staff of the National Defense Intelligence College (NDIC) on educational activities related to EI. We have obtained continuing counsel from senior members of the ISB, including experts in military intelligence, engineering, history, intelligence analysis, law and public policy, medicine, and the workings of the Intelligence Community.

Specifically, the study team has:

- Examined some of the costs of getting EI "wrong" and the benefits of getting EI "right";

- Reviewed behavioral science studies to glean what has been learned during the past fifty years about interviewing, interrogation, and other areas related to EI;

- Reviewed studies concerning both the "mechanical" and "non-mechanical" detection of deception. This task has included examination of fledgling research efforts to use neuroimaging technologies to determine if a person is being deceptive;

- Studied the development and operation of the World War II MIS-Y program;

- Reviewed the *KUBARK Counterintelligence Interrogation Manual* to ascertain how approaches to interrogation have and have not changed since the manual was written in 1963;

- Analyzed studies of law enforcement interviewing and interrogation practices as well as law enforcement teaching and training materials in these areas;

- Identified the primary "barriers to success" that must be addressed in the course of organizing, managing, and employing an effective U.S. EI capability in the context of current and anticipated future conflict scenarios;

- Begun to map the relevance of negotiation theory and practice to educing information and to further research in this area;
- Started to construct an EI research agenda that identifies promising areas for study that may improve EI practices;
- Gathered and organized a working bibliography and a computerized library of scientific and analytic articles related to EI; and
- Worked with the NDIC to make EI a subject of professional intelligence education.

Products of the Study

Attached to this report are ten papers commissioned by the Study on EI and an annotated bibliography of key work in English on EI from World War II to the present. Because they report on current or historical research and practice, most of them of necessity address aspects of "interrogation": the standard term used to date in intelligence, military, and law enforcement contexts to describe methods of obtaining information from sources.

To our knowledge, none of these papers duplicates the existing literature, classified or unclassified. However, the papers do not cover the full spectrum of EI or of the study's investigations, nor do they collectively constitute the justification for the study team's recommendations. Instead, they report on selected aspects of current research and practice that the U.S. government may wish to take into account as it moves toward a new model of EI for the twenty-first century. The study team offers these papers to stimulate better thinking, practice, research, teaching, and training. They are intended as the "first word" in next-generation discussions of EI, rather than as definitive statements.

The papers are:

1. **"Approaches to Interrogation in the Struggle against Terrorism: Considerations of Cost and Benefit"**

This paper explores areas of cost and benefit when interrogation choices are made. The discussion points out the complexity of our choices and the need for additional research to inform and *to discipline* how we think about these choices.

2. **"Approaching Truth: Behavioral Science Lessons on Educing Information from Human Sources"**

This paper reviews a wide range of material from the social and behavioral sciences on educing information. Few empirical studies directly address the effectiveness of interrogation in general, or of specific techniques, in generating accurate and useful information. The paper concludes that virtually none of the interrogation techniques used by U.S. personnel over the past half-century have been subjected to scientific or systematic inquiry or evaluation, and that the accuracy of educed information can be compromised by the way it is obtained. By contrast, a promising body of social science research on persuasion and interpersonal influence could provide a foundation for a more effective approach to educing information in intelligence-gathering contexts.

3. "Research on Detection of Deception: What We Know vs. What We Think We Know"

This review examines the scientific literature regarding our current capacity to detect deception by observing behavioral indicators and identifies additional research that might improve that capacity. The findings indicate that common beliefs about reliable cues to deception are frequently incorrect, and that the research in this area to date may be largely irrelevant to national security needs.

4. "Mechanical Detection of Deception: A Short Review"

This paper briefly reviews the mechanical methods created over the past century to detect deception. The development of a more effective means for detecting deception is predicated on research to build a sound theoretical basis for such a system. The study concludes that, despite the polygraph's shortcomings, there is currently no viable technical alternative. While some neuroscience-based alternatives have been proposed, these techniques pose significant problems and far more research is needed if they are to become sufficiently reliable for use in operational settings.

5. "KUBARK Counterintelligence Interrogation Review: Observations of an Interrogator. Lessons Learned and Avenues for Further Research"

This paper examines the *KUBARK Counterintelligence Interrogation Manual*, produced by the Central Intelligence Agency in 1963 (and declassified in 1997). The writer, an experienced interrogator, considers how current approaches to interrogation compare to approaches put forward forty years ago.

6. "Custodial Interrogations: What We Know, What We Do, and What We Can Learn from Law Enforcement Experiences"

This report explores both the literature and practice related to interrogation of criminal suspects in custody, focusing almost exclusively — as the literature and practice do — on eliciting confessions to crimes. The theoretical literature lays the groundwork for interrogation practice by identifying the reasons why suspects do or do not confess to crimes, while empirical findings pinpoint factors associated with admissions and denials. A comparison of theory and technique reveals that the interrogation techniques advocated in the literature take little account of the factors that the empirical research shows might affect a suspect's willingness to confess, and provide little or no guidance to varying approaches for different types of suspects.

The effectiveness of standard interrogation techniques has never been validated by empirical research. Moreover, techniques designed to obtain confessions to crimes may have only limited relevance to preventive investigations of terrorist-related activities.

7. **"Barriers to Success: Critical Challenges in Developing a New Educing Information Paradigm"**

This paper analyzes three fundamental barriers to successfully educing information from uncooperative sources: (1) linguistic/cultural barriers; (2) scientific/technical/subject matter barriers; and (3) interpersonal/intrapersonal barriers.

8. **"Negotiation Theory and Practice: Exploring Ideas to Aid Information Eduction"**

Information eduction can be viewed as a complex set of negotiations. Government officials have information needs, and sources have information they can disclose. The challenge is to determine how the government can negotiate most effectively for that information. This report therefore seeks to describe negotiation concepts that might assist the information educer.

9. **"Negotiation Theory and Educing Information: Practical Concepts and Tools"**

This paper offers basic tools from negotiation theory for possible discussion by those concerned with EI. The paper presents brief discussions of different possible *strategies* for EI, a brief discussion of the *sources of power* available to educers and sources, and then suggestions about *preparation for EI*.

10. **"Options for Scientific Research on Eduction Practices"**

Surprisingly, the last forty years have seen almost no scientific research examining eduction practices. The "interrogation approaches" taught in standard interrogation training (e.g., Army Field Manual 34-52) have remained largely unchanged since World War II, yet no scientific research substantiates the effectiveness of these approaches. Our current knowledge about eduction practices is based on feedback and lessons learned from field experience.

This paper argues two points: first, that scientific investigation of eduction practices is needed to supplement lessons learned from field experience, and second, that various research venues are available to examine these practices. Research approaches could include both retrospective analyses of data about past interrogations (including those that used harsh methods) and new studies that relate different eduction practices to the value of the information obtained.

11. **Educing Information Bibliography**

This selected, annotated bibliography includes the most useful items in English covering the theory, research, and pragmatics of interrogation over the past fifty years.

1
Approaches to Interrogation in the Struggle against Terrorism: Considerations of Cost and Benefit

Robert Coulam, Ph.D., J.D.
Simmons College School for Health Studies
June 2006

Abstract

The interrogation of suspects, witnesses, and others is an essential source of information in the struggle against terrorism. It is accordingly important for the United States to perform this function well. This paper considers how we might think about the costs and benefits of different approaches to interrogation and how we might balance costs and benefits to support decisions affecting U.S. interrogation efforts. As will become clear, any weighing of costs and benefits faces key uncertainties and areas of ignorance – most important, little rigorous information exists about the relative effectiveness of different techniques for educing information, and difficulties appear in identifying and weighing many qualitative benefits and costs. This discussion underscores the need for a stronger empirical foundation to support the choices of all kinds that we must make to perform this function well.

Introduction

Interrogation is a promising source of information to support the United States' struggle against terrorists. But there are difficult, competing values at stake in interrogation, and the tradeoffs among these values are at times discounted. One way to improve the choices that we make on interrogation is to understand the values at stake; that is, to be careful to identify all of the areas of cost and benefit that matter to us when interrogation choices are made. The discussion that follows explores areas of cost and benefit that have been the focus of contemporary decisions and debates. As a rule, for each of these objectives, "benefits" come from more effective performance in areas we care about, while "costs" generally reflect lesser performance.

The discussion is admittedly general in order to cover a relatively complete array of costs and benefits in a brief paper. These generalities necessarily mask many critical subtleties. Yet even this rudimentary summary suggests the complexity of our choices and the need for additional research to inform and to discipline how we think about these choices.

National Security

Obviously, the principal benefit of interrogation is to obtain information from suspects and others that will increase our understanding of terrorist adversaries,[2] thereby helping to protect our own population, support our allies, maintain civic order and stability, and preserve important institutions.

Given the character of terrorist operations and the capacities of the United States, human intelligence — information gained from people rather than from technical means, documents, and other non-human sources — is especially important in the struggle against terrorism. The U.S. government needs detailed information about its adversaries, as well as strategic and cultural understanding of how the information fits together. This information can help to forestall further attacks and weaken terrorist organizations. But U.S. intelligence networks are weak precisely in the regions where Al Qaeda and other terrorist cells play significant roles. Interrogation thus becomes an especially important way to find and elicit information.

The benefits of interrogation can be enormous (e.g., the prevention of a nuclear explosion), quite small (e.g., filling in a minor part of a much larger picture of terrorist activity, or merely showing that a suspect knows nothing of value), or somewhere in between those extremes. Poor performance in the interrogation function results in the loss of these benefits (a cost that with poor performance, we may not always recognize — we typically will be unaware of the information we fail to collect). Poor performance can also impose other costs, as described later in this paper.

Interrogation efforts might yield greater benefits if the United States used different ways to select, train, and organize interrogators, established different rules and leadership to govern interrogations, or used other approaches that might improve individual and organizational performance. The problem in understanding the benefits of effective interrogations is that — unless the U.S. government has rigorous information we do not know about — there is little systematic knowledge available to tell us "what works" in interrogation. *We do not know what systems, methods, or processes of interrogation best protect the nation's security.* For example, we lack systematic information to guide us as to *who* should perform interrogations. We do not know what benefits would result if we changed the way we recruit, train, and manage our interrogators.

---

[2] We focus on the process of obtaining information from suspects, but it should be understood that "interrogation" includes issues of how others — e.g., reluctant witnesses and intelligence sources — are treated. We also leave aside large questions of how information might be analyzed or synthesized to produce useful intelligence.

Coercion and Knowledge

Of particular concern, we do not fully understand a complex of issues surrounding the use of coercion. Coercion is an important issue in all types of interrogations — from local police precincts and petty crimes to distant centers of detention and serious terrorist threats. The costs of coercion in human, ethical, political, and other terms vary, but can be enormous. Even when these costs are acknowledged, contemporary discussions often assume that torture, physical coercion, and psychological coercion are effective ways to obtain information, especially in emergencies (e.g., when there is little time, as with "ticking bombs"). Torture and many forms of physical and psychological coercion have been used for centuries. Whether we like it or not, coercion might be more "effective" than other methods in some circumstances. Unfortunately, much of the current debate in this area proceeds as if we actually knew what those circumstances were. In fact, we do not, beyond anecdotal evidence adduced ad hoc.

This lack of understanding presents a troubling difficulty. Coercion may be the "lesser evil"[3] when it can prevent imminent assaults on national security that are substantially out of proportion to the costs of using coercion. But if other interrogation approaches are available that would more effectively obtain needed information — e.g., more informed or skillful methods — then we are descending into an ethical and security abyss if we use coercion in ignorance of all its implications. While our understanding will never be so complete as to make any of these choices easy or simple, we face a compelling security imperative to expand our knowledge about interrogation approaches. We should not simply assume that greater use of coercion will make interrogations more effective.

We can imagine at least four sources of information that might give us firmer empirical guidance:

- History – To inform current choices, we might look to the benefits and costs of interrogation methods used in past conflicts. As of 11 September 2001, the United States had not mounted "strategic" interrogation efforts in decades, so the relevant U.S. history is old — arguably going back to World War II.[4]

- Comparative practices – We also might look to the experience of other democratic countries that have a much longer history of conducting interrogations in the context of substantial and often imminent threats to their internal security. This source of knowledge includes the

---

[3] For a careful consideration of coercion in these terms, see Michael Ignatieff, The Lesser Evil: Political Ethics in an Age of Terror (Princeton: Princeton University Press, 2004).

[4] "Strategic interrogation" is commonly distinguished from "tactical interrogation." The latter is the kind of real-time interrogation that occurs in the midst of a conflict or battlefield. U.S. forces have long been familiar with tactical interrogation. Strategic interrogation concerns broader knowledge about enemy forces — in the present context, knowledge about the membership, organization, communication, finances, and plans of terrorist organizations. For an excellent study of strategic interrogation methods in World War II, see Steven M. Kleinman, "The History of MIS-Y: U.S. Strategic Interrogation During World War II," unpublished master's thesis, Joint Military Intelligence College, August 2002.

contemporary experience of other countries as well as their historical experience.

- Social science – The tools of social science have not been applied to the problems of interrogation in any substantial way,[5] yet such an effort could obviously be undertaken and might produce substantial benefits. This is especially true as the United States accumulates experience in interrogating suspected terrorists, and producing data that could be systematically analyzed. It is also clear that ongoing interrogation efforts present opportunities to evaluate methods with unprecedented rigor.[6] For example, what kinds of interrogation systems, approaches, or methods might yield accurate and useful information with which sources in which contexts?

- Casual empiricism and experience – Fourth, we might inform current policy choices on interrogation by drawing upon casual empiricism and the kind of expertise gained diffusely from experience. This type of information often guides policy choices in areas where there is little rigorous information — a situation that has long characterized the debate over methods and processes of interrogation.

The fourth source of instruction has been our primary guide to date (again, allowing for the possibility that more rigorous classified information exists, but has not been revealed to the public). That is an unnecessarily weak foundation to support the choices that we must make. In essence, we do not know enough to be able to calibrate the costs and benefits of different methods or processes.

The best we can do now is to recognize categories of benefits and costs at relatively general levels and subjectively weigh the results. We might also undertake some kind of effort to verify empirical relationships that are being casually inferred.

Intimidation of Terrorists and Their Supporters

To judge from the ways governments have used interrogation, there is a pervasive belief that coercive interrogation can intimidate terrorists and their supporters in ways that enhance the effectiveness of interrogations and perhaps even reduce the underlying terrorist threat. For example, a country that insists it will observe no limits on interrogation methods — that it will "take the gloves off"— may believe that this communicates resolve and will deter potential adversaries.

---

[5] For a review, see Randy Borum, "Approaching Truth: Behavioral Science Lessons on Educing Information from Human Sources," in Intelligence Science Board Study Phase 1 Report, *Educing Information* (Washington, DC: NDIC Press, 2006).

[6] The point here is not that ethically improper experiments should be performed, but rather that social science could help us to learn from data we already have or could reasonably and ethically collect. Note the discussion of research opportunities in Paul Lehner, *Options for Scientific Research on Eduction Practices* in *Phase 1 Report* (Intelligence Science Board Study Phase 1 Report, *Educing Information* (Washington, DC: NDIC Press, 2006).

It is difficult to evaluate whether and how much coercive interrogation actually affects terrorists and their support. Moreover, decisionmakers must be careful about assuming that tough interrogation techniques impress our adversaries. For example, would terrorists respect coercive interrogation more than they would respect less coercive, but more effective, interrogation? Or would they respect any other approach that *more substantially* undermined terrorist networks? While it may well be useful to intimidate terrorists, "intimidation" can mean far more than "being tough" and simply asserting physical dominance in interrogations. Indeed, some of the most critical actions that might truly intimidate terrorists are "boringly bureaucratic, achingly administrative"[7] and have nothing to do with coercion. A skilled interrogation — which encompasses far more than an exchange of questions and answers — might well elicit more information by using other methods.

Nevertheless, many believe that at a strictly operational level a general reputation for ruthlessness might make suspects more responsive in an interrogation setting, even if brutality in fact is never used. To our knowledge this belief rests on casual empiricism and has never been rigorously tested. The absence of such tests is one reason for the continuing debate over whether suspects (a) give *useful* information when they fear coercion, (b) to avoid coercion, simply tell interrogators what they think the interrogators want to hear, or (c) exhibit a mix of responses, depending on a variety of factors (e.g., personality, context, training, skill of the interrogator, and others). Examination of historical data might provide some indications of how suspects actually behave.

Ethical Concerns and the Rule of Law

Given the compelling need to protect the nation's security, governments experience considerable pressure to place the interrogation of suspected terrorists in "the twilight shadows of the law"[8] — especially given terrorists' propensities, much demonstrated, to exploit the laws and sensitivities of others but to observe few limits on their own behavior. The United States must consider the nuances of the Geneva Conventions as applied to suspected terrorists; terrorists demonstrate few such concerns.

In a democracy the legitimacy of government action is important to maintain support for what the government does in this struggle. Ethical concerns and the rule of law are cornerstones of that legitimacy, and the primary reason for conducting interrogations according to a high standard of ethics may be simply

---

[7] The phrase comes from Richard Cohen, discussing a very different problem, in "Deterring Common Sense," *Washington Post*, 24 January 2006, A17.

[8] H.C. 5100/94, *Public Committee against Torture in Israel v. The State of Israel*, 53 (4) P.D. 817 (1999), paragraph 40.

that it is widely believed to be the right thing to do.[9] These are important benefits to address in making choices about interrogation policy. As summarized by Israel's High Court of Justice in its ruling against the interrogation practices of that country's internal security service:

> This is the destiny of a democracy—it does not see all means as acceptable, and the ways of its enemies are not always open before it. A democracy must sometimes fight with one hand tied behind its back. Even so, a democracy has the upper hand. The rule of law and the liberty of an individual constitute important components in its understanding of security. At the end of the day, they strengthen its spirit and this strength allows it to overcome its difficulties.[10]

Thus, it is not enough to know whether "coercion works" in interrogation. Interrogation practices that offend ethical concerns and skirt the rule of law may indeed have narrow utilitarian value: It is *possible* that methods that "shock the conscience" and/or violate international or domestic law are effective in educing information in some situations.[11] But costs must be recognized: such practices may undermine the legitimacy of government action, weaken domestic support for the long struggle against terrorism, and eventually limit the government's ability to act. Of course, decisionmakers may believe that they can avoid this cost by keeping coercive interrogation practices secret. However, at least in the U.S. context, that strategy is questionable: Much of the secret effort (although we cannot know how much) will in due course become publicly known. More indirectly, such practices run the risk of undermining the democratic institutions that the struggle against terrorism is meant to defend. It is therefore costly if interrogation practices appear to violate our treaty obligations and domestic laws or offend ethical concerns, and instead follow selective policy imperatives or beliefs.

It is again difficult to evaluate *how costly* such behavior is. If interrogation practices undermine legitimacy, the effects will influence the behavior and beliefs of the populace in diffuse, and often indirect, ways. Obviously, behavior and beliefs are subject to many influences, not only the effects of our interrogation methods. But beliefs about ethical behavior and the rule of law are powerful. For example, overwhelming majorities of both parties in Congress supported the

---

[9] By discussing ethics and law together, we do not mean to imply that they are the same. Among other things, interrogation practices that offend ethical beliefs may not violate the law, and practices that are believed to be ethical may not be legal. Moreover, violations of law and ethics likely will have different impacts or consequences in particular circumstances. Notwithstanding these differences and others, law and ethics are treated together here for convenience — at the level of generality of this discussion, the effects of undermining the rule of law are similar to the effects of offending widely held ethical concerns. A more extensive discussion would recognize these similarities, but would address these two categories separately.

[10] H.C. 5100/94, *Public Committee against Torture in Israel v. The State of Israel*, paragraph 39.

[11] Note that ethics and law are linked in this context, because a "shock the conscience" standard is one test of the constitutionality of U.S. government action involving coercion. For example, see Seth F. Kreimer's discussion in "Too Close to the Rack and the Screw: Constitutional Constraints on Torture in the War on Terror," 6 *U. Pa. J. Const. L.* 278, 288-294 (November 2003).

McCain Amendment. This vote demonstrated the firm belief that U.S. interrogation methods should respect the law, avoid gross abuses, and adhere to a general sense of decency. It represents a collective resolve to assert the standard of law and humane behavior against pressures to use coercion and abuse.

International Support to Wage the Struggle against Terrorism

Domestic concerns about ethics and upholding the rule of law have an important international corollary. Interrogation methods that preserve the country's position as a moral leader in the struggle against terrorism enhance the ability of the United States to enlist international cooperation. This is not a unilateral struggle. The United States requires allied support for much of what needs to be done, including:

- Intelligence.– The vital role of strategic intelligence in combating terrorism demands unprecedented levels of cooperation between the intelligence agencies of the United States and other countries. We must encourage other countries to intensify their efforts to obtain intelligence that prevents attacks, share intelligence data that in the past might have been closely held, gather and share more comprehensive information on the movement of suspect funds and people, and act together against the common enemy.

- Diplomacy.– All of these added intelligence requirements — along with law enforcement, military, and other needs — translate into a much larger agenda for diplomacy, including expanded diplomatic cooperation in law enforcement, telecommunications, commerce (e.g., banking and financial information), and other areas.

It is more difficult to make progress in needed areas of diplomacy and intelligence if U.S. interrogation methods provoke strong international reactions.

Danger to Troops and Others at Risk of Capture

One key benefit that interrogation policy must address is the protection of our troops (and others, such as aid workers and contractors). This benefit derives from notions of reciprocity: specifically, the expectation that if our troops are captured they will receive more humane treatment if the United States treats its captives humanely. This concern over reciprocity has long been an important factor in international agreements on the treatment of detainees.[12]

Concern about reciprocity is based on the empirical assumption that terrorists will observe fewer rules if we observe fewer rules. This assumption may not be true. In a world where terrorist (and insurgent) adversaries behead captives, it is at least arguable that terrorists assume they will receive harsh treatment no matter what we do, within some range at least.[13] But it is also arguable that more humane

---

[12] See Michael Walzer, *Just and Unjust Wars: A Moral Argument with Historical Illustrations* (New York: Basic Books, 1977), Part Three.
[13] See Sabrina Tavernise, "Iraqis Found in Torture House Tell of Brutality of Insurgents," *New York Times*, 19 June 2005.

treatment would have some positive effect on our adversaries. This is another area where it would be useful, where possible, to test widely held assumptions against available evidence.

In the absence of real evidence, we can say only that a cost of more coercive interrogations *might* be the harsher treatment of our troops and others. Also, to the degree that international law on the treatment of detainees rests on widespread reciprocity over time, we undermine that fabric for this and future conflicts if we fail to observe certain limits in how we interrogate others.

Legal Problems for U.S. Troops and Officials

If other countries suspect the United States of using unacceptably coercive methods in interrogations, the U.S. may encounter legal problems in efforts to capture or extradite terrorists. For example, given obligations under the 1987 Convention Against Torture, allied countries might be unwilling to extradite suspected terrorists — even Bin Laden himself — if they believe there is a substantial likelihood that these suspects will be tortured in U.S. hands.[14] More ominously, foreign prosecutors could bring charges against U.S. officials and troops before international tribunals (e.g., charges of war crimes for U.S. conduct in third countries) or before their domestic tribunals (for U.S. behavior within those countries — for example, if U.S. agents break local laws by seizing or detaining terrorist suspects on foreign soil and subject them to abuse or maltreatment[15]). Conversely, if the United States has a record of treating captives — even suspected terrorists — humanely, other nations might be more willing to accede to U.S. requests for extradition, and U.S. troops might run less risk of being prosecuted for practices that, to their knowledge, are acceptable.

U.S. Leadership on Human Rights

The proper place of human rights among overall foreign policy objectives is a matter of debate. But there is little debate that the United States has been a leader in the human rights movement internationally for decades, and that this leadership has had some effect on the behavior of other countries. Upholding high standards even in its interrogation practices would further strengthen the U.S. reputation for respecting human dignity. By contrast, if the United States is seen as a country that tortures prisoners, it loses the moral standing that would allow it to press others to observe a higher standard of behavior. For example, when a recent State Department annual report on human rights criticized China and other countries for human rights violations, China peremptorily dismissed

---

[14] A foretaste of this difficulty occurred shortly after 11 September 2001, a time when allies were giving the United States enormous latitude to respond to the attacks. At this time, Britain was closely allied to the United States in all of the U.S. responses. But Britain put the United States on notice that— if British soldiers captured bin Laden — Britain would not extradite him to the United States unless the United States waived the death penalty. Germany declined to turn over an alleged top aide to bin Laden until the United States waived the death penalty.

[15] For example, see "Italy Prosecutor Seeks Arrest Warrants," Associated Press, 20 July 2005; "U.S. Faces Questions over 'Kidnappings' in Europe," Reuters, 20 May 2005; and Craig Whitlock, "Europeans Investigate CIA Role in Abductions," *Washington Post*, 13 March 2005, A1.

the criticisms, taking the United States to task for using a "double standard" in judging other countries' behavior.[16]

Creation of More Enemies

We do not fully understand the social, political, religious, and other dynamics that give rise to terrorist activities. We also do not know the extent to which specific actions by the United States and its allies actually change perceptions of the United States in Muslim and other countries. It is possible, for example, that America's culture, economy, and foreign policy (e.g., enduring support of Israel) already place the country beyond the pale for much of the radical Muslim audience. But an accumulation of specific actions that appear to show contempt for Muslim people might well affect how we are viewed,[17] especially among moderate Muslims whose opinion we seek to influence as part of our longer term struggle against terrorism.

Integrity of the Military

The U.S. military has a long tradition of adhering to the laws of war, including observance of conventions about the treatment of detainees. Part of this stems from self-interest (based on beliefs about how our troops will be treated in turn, as described earlier). Quite apart from concerns for reciprocity are questions about the integrity of military units and the values of military ethics. Interrogation that treats fighters from other countries in the same way U.S. troops hope to be treated might strengthen a sense of pride in the military profession. By contrast, interrogation that is unbounded by rules or becomes a form of sadism, for example, can erode military discipline and undermine the integrity and higher purposes of military units.

Resources

The last area of concern to note is perhaps the most conspicuous and quantifiable: financial and other resources. We will not discuss this aspect of costs and benefits at length, but it should at least be noted that different approaches to interrogation have different implications for scarce resources (money, skilled personnel, language capacity) and will not fit the existing capacities of all organizations equally well. In some contexts, those differences are important.

Conclusion

Given a continuing terrorist threat, the United States must obtain information through interrogations, but it must do so without undermining the purposes of the very effort that interrogations are supposed to serve. The country thus needs to understand the relative costs and benefits of alternative interrogation strategies and programs. While it is relatively easy to imagine the costs and benefits of alternative

---

[16] Edward Cody, "China, Others Criticize U.S. Report on Rights: Double Standard at State Dept. Alleged," *Washington Post*, 4 March 2005, A14.

[17] For example, see Somini Sengupta and Salman Masood, "Guantánamo Comes to Define U.S. to Muslims," *The New York Times*, 21 May 2005.

programs and strategies in the most general terms, it is not easy to estimate the magnitude of these costs and benefits or to weigh them carefully against each other, primarily because we have little *systematic empirical knowledge* about the most important relationships at stake.

Moreover, there is a trap in thinking in isolation about benefits and costs of any interrogation approach. The critical issue is always: "compared to what?" Decisions might be improved simply by paying explicit attention to the full range of costs and benefits at stake in decisions on interrogation and attempting to weigh them against each other, however imperfectly. Better results will require improved understanding, so that we can have greater confidence in making the difficult tradeoffs that are, in any event, certain to be required.

2
Approaching Truth:
Behavioral Science Lessons on Educing Information from Human Sources

Randy Borum, Psy.D.
University of South Florida
November 2005

[W]e insist, and have insisted for generations, that truth is to be approached, if not attained, through research guided by a systematic method. In the social sciences ... there is such a method.

— Sherman Kent (1949), *Strategic Intelligence for American World Policy*

Abstract

Few empirical studies in the social and behavioral sciences directly address the effectiveness of interrogation in general, or of specific techniques, in producing accurate and useful information. This paper summarizes existing theoretical and empirical findings and analyzes them in the framework of five topics: models for educing information, strategies to increase the willingness to provide information, strategies to overcome resistance, factors affecting the accuracy of educed information, and the effect of "stress and duress" techniques on obtaining information. Essentially none of the interrogation techniques used by U.S. personnel over the past half-century has been subjected to scientific or systematic inquiry or evaluation, and the accuracy of educed information can be compromised by the way it is obtained. By contrast, a promising body of social science research on persuasion and interpersonal influence could provide a foundation for a more effective approach to educing information in intelligence-gathering contexts. Research on persuasion, influence, compliance, and resistance has focused primarily on persons from Western cultures, and the results and insights may not apply equally or evenly across all cultures.

Introduction

In most cases, and for most types of threats to U.S. national security, one or more people — human sources — possess the most complete and timely information on our adversaries' preparations, planning, and intentions. Particularly in the contemporary threat environment, where the likelihood of local terrorist attacks greatly exceeds that of invasion by a foreign state, it would be difficult to overstate the importance of human source intelligence. Both policymakers and practitioners therefore need reliable information about effective and appropriate strategies and techniques to educe accurate information from human sources who may possess information vital to our national security and who appear unwilling to provide it.

The need to understand what approaches, techniques, and strategies are likely to produce accurate, useful information from an uncooperative human source seems self-evident. Surprisingly, however, these questions have received scant scientific attention in the last 50 years. *Almost no empirical studies in the social and behavioral sciences directly address the effectiveness of interrogation in general practice, or of specific techniques in generating accurate and useful information from otherwise uncooperative persons.*

Policies that govern how U.S. personnel obtain information must take into consideration issues of legality, ethics, morality, and national values. Yet, effectiveness remains the paramount issue. This paper and the larger study from which it is drawn seek to address these issues as part of an ongoing effort to improve human intelligence collection, and thereby protect U.S. national security.

Background

Most of the scientific articles dealing with interrogation-related topics apply to, and are derived from, a law enforcement (LE) context. However, the nature and objectives of police interrogations differ significantly from those in military or intelligence contexts. In essence, most LE interrogations seek to obtain a confession from a suspect, rather than to gather accurate, useful information from a possibly — but not necessarily — cognizant source. These are very different tasks. Moreover, there are remarkably few studies of actual interrogations in either criminal or intelligence contexts. Training manuals, materials, and anecdotes contain information about common and recommended practices and the behavioral assumptions on which they are based, but virtually none of those documents cites or relies upon any original research. It even appears that some of the conventional wisdom that has guided training and policy for half a century is at odds with existing scientific knowledge.

Without a scientific literature or systematic analysis — at least one available in open-source information — practitioners (i.e., "boots-on-the-ground" assets) and policymakers must make decisions on the basis of other sources and considerations. Primary among them are the iconic 17 techniques described in *U.S. Army Field Manual 34-52, Intelligence Interrogation*, which serves as the model or guide to intelligence interrogations for all the armed forces. These exact techniques have been included in successive editions for more than 50 years, yet even people intimately familiar with 34-52 are unaware of any studies or systematic analyses that support their effectiveness, or of any clear historical record about how the techniques were initially selected for inclusion. Instead, they continue to be used because they have "always" (as long as memory serves) been used.

The effort to re-evaluate, and perhaps even improve, policies and practices in this area would benefit greatly from systematic, scientific knowledge regarding the effectiveness of various techniques for educing information. To establish a baseline for greater understanding, this review examines theoretical and empirical findings in the social and behavioral sciences that might help policymakers and practitioners to understand the process of deriving accurate, useful information from human sources. The review draws from multiple areas within psychology, sociology, criminology, criminal justice, cognitive science, medicine, anthropology, cultic studies, communications theory, marketing, public health, and psycho- and socio-linguistics. While the study reviewed materials from many countries, analysis was limited to those published in English.

The findings are presented and analyzed within the functional framework of five guiding questions:

1. What models exist for educing information from uncooperative sources?

2. What strategies might increase or decrease a source's willingness to provide information?

3. What is resistance and what strategies exist for getting past it?

4. What key factors affect the accuracy of educed information?

5. What is known about the effect of "stress and duress" techniques for educing accurate, useful information?

Educing Information from Uncooperative Sources

Educing information is most productively envisioned as a process, rather than as an applied set of techniques. Moreover, the context of that process should be viewed broadly, not solely (or even primarily) as an across-the-table interaction between an educer and a source.

Many broad fields of study — including psychology, anthropology, linguistics, and communications — offer theories, concepts, methods, and research findings that may inform and further our understanding of the *process* of educing information from uncooperative sources. A model for understanding and studying the process of educing information could provide a platform and language for identifying actors, elements, actions, dynamics, and effects.[18] Major conceptual models from at least four areas of social science literature fulfill these functions:

---

[18] According to the *American Heritage Dictionary*, a model is "a schematic description of a system, theory, or phenomenon that accounts for its known or inferred properties and may be used for further study of its characteristics." As the term is used here, a model is distinguished from specific techniques or general themes, such as power, coercion, fear, or pain, which are discussed later.

communications, discourse analysis, persuasive message production/analysis, and negotiation theory.

Communications Models

Educing and providing information, at the most basic level, involve a process of communication. Since the 1940s researchers have been working to develop a comprehensive model of the communication process. While communications models cannot fully capture all key elements of information eduction, they offer some useful concepts and frameworks. First, they both identify and label the key components in a communication encounter (e.g., sender, message, medium, receiver). Second, they array these components in the framework of a dynamic process in which they interact with one another. Third, the transactive model in particular emphasizes the centrality of "fields of experience" that both source and receiver bring to the encounter and that surround the overarching process. In educing information, cultural factors and differences in experiences are critical to understanding how to bridge the gap between the intended and received message.

Discourse Analysis

Discourse analysis, a subdiscipline of linguistics, offers a narrower analytic framework. Its focus is strictly on discourse; that is, patterns of verbal or textual exchange. Stubbs (1983), one of the early and leading scholars of discourse analysis, defines the discipline as:

> the linguistic analysis of naturally occurring connected speech or written discourse. Roughly speaking, it refers to attempts to study the organisation of language above the sentence or above the clause, and therefore to study larger linguistic units, such as conversational exchanges or written texts. It follows that discourse analysis is also concerned with language use in social contexts, and in particular with interaction or dialogue between speakers. (Stubbs, 1983, 1; for this and other references, see bibliography at the end of this essay)

Persuasive Message Production/Analysis

Stephen Wilson coined the term "persuasive message production" to describe a subdiscipline of study that integrates research on gaining compliance with theories of message production. He poses as its central question: "When we want to convince another person to do something, why do we say what we do?"

Negotiation Theory

Theories and models of negotiation offer some useful concepts and terminology to describe the process by which people with apparently divergent "positions" interact. Two of its most important aspects are the explicit emphasis on understanding strategy rather than just tactics, and the distinction between negotiation or influence interactions based on "positions" versus those based on "interests." In the parlance of modern negotiation theory, a position is what negotiators say they want, while an interest is what they really want.

Negotiation theory centers on how people arrive at a solution rather than which solution they choose. It identifies three overarching stances or strategies. The first is a distributive strategy in which the negotiator's objective is to get all he/she can, regardless of equity or the perceptions of the other party(ies). Using the common "pie" metaphor, the goal is to get the whole pie or at least most of it. A second approach uses an integrative strategy, where the goal is to identify and implement solutions that meet the needs of all parties in the negotiation, often by not quibbling over the distribution of a particular limited resource but instead finding ways beyond that resource to meet each party's needs. This is referred to as "creating value," or, metaphorically, "expanding the pie." The third is a mixed-motive strategy. As its name implies, it blends the objectives of the other two approaches: It seeks solutions that serve the needs of as many parties to the negotiation as possible, but places equally high priority on getting one's own "fair share."

In a position-based negotiation, each party stakes out its objective (or position) and tries not to retreat from it. The negotiation operates within a distributive strategy, creating a competitive or adversarial dynamic, with the guiding ethos of seeking justice. By contrast, interest-based negotiations operate in an integrative or mixed-motive strategy, creating a collaborative dynamic, with the guiding ethos of problem solving.

Implications

Among these four theories, persuasive message production seems to provide unique methodological insights for studying the element of educing information that involves transactive exchanges of communication between an educer and source. Negotiation theory, however, seems better suited to identifying principles and overarching strategies — particularly interest-based stances — that might frame the overall information gathering process, and to providing language and perspectives that are not overtly adversarial.

Strategies Affecting Willingness to Provide Information

Educers of information must be skilled in understanding and applying a broad range of strategies, approaches, and techniques of persuasion and influence to gather information from people determined not to give it. Considerable social science literature on persuasion and influence may be relevant to the development of processes for educing information. Literally hundreds of researchers have contributed to the thousands of studies that comprise this body of work. For example, in the PsycINFO database of psychology publications (which is neither comprehensive nor exhaustive) between 1967 and mid-2005, the subject heading for "Persuasive Communication" contains 3,258 entries, the heading for "Attitude Change" contains 5,559, and the heading for "Interpersonal Influences" contains

4,405 published entries. Not surprisingly, however, virtually none of these studies replicate the context of an intelligence interrogation or use samples similar to the populations of interest. Nevertheless, these findings and concepts may help point the way toward a more specialized body of scientific or systematic inquiry.

Influence Strategies

Knowles and Linn (2004) drew one of the most fundamental distinctions among types of influence strategies, and one of the most useful for thinking about applications to educing information. They assume that most attitudes and judgments emerge from an "approach-avoidance" model of conflict (Knowles, Butler and Linn, 2001). Basically, this model rests on the premise that whenever we contemplate an act or objective, our decisions result from an internal struggle between forces that push or draw us toward the action (called approach motives) and those that inhibit or pull us away from it (called avoidance motives) (Dollard and Miller, 1950, Lewin, 1958, Miller, 1959). Knowles and Linn suggest that one major implication of this model is that:

> there are two fundamentally different ways to create change, two different strategies for promoting movement toward some goal. Alpha strategies promote change by activating the approach forces, thereby increasing the motivation to move toward the goal. By contrast, Omega strategies promote change by minimizing the avoidance forces, thereby reducing the motivation to move away from the goal (Knowles and Linn, 2004, 119, emphasis added).

Increasing a Source's Motivation to Share Information

Rapport

Most training materials and guides on law enforcement interrogation emphasize the need for one or more interrogators to develop a rapport with the subject. Indeed, rapport is widely regarded as an essential foundation for most successful LE interrogations. For example, a survey of 100 British detectives (Walkley, 1987) found that nearly half (42%) believed that a previous interviewer's failure to establish satisfactory rapport with a suspect had contributed to the suspect's denial. Once good rapport had been established with another detective the suspects typically confessed.

Rapport usually begins to develop during conversation — maybe even "small talk" — and serves at least two functions. First, research studies say, it helps to "induce" or facilitate compliance with subsequent requests — and gets the source talking. Second, it allows the educer to identify and assess potential motivations, interests, and vulnerabilities. The way the target perceives the agent (and their relationship) — and this may be important for educing information — becomes especially critical under conditions in which the target is unmotivated or unable to devote mental energy to thinking about the agent's arguments and analyzing them.

Persuasion

Since the early 1980s, Robert Cialdini (2001), a professor of psychology at Arizona State University, has attempted to distill, explain, and apply the plethora of existing research studies on interpersonal influence to make the general population more discerning about, and aware of, the persuasive attempts that constantly (and sometimes subtly) bombard them. Cialdini has concisely classified the six major strategies of persuasion that have been studied. All of them have proven remarkably effective over time with a range of tasks and different kinds of people.

Even though the research on these factors is voluminous and robust, none has been systematically studied in conditions similar to those of an interrogation. Thus, it is unknown how their effects might change in that context or how those effects might differ for persons from non-Western cultures. Nevertheless, they offer some promising guidance. The following summary does not do justice to the breadth and depth of the scholarly contributions made by Cialdini and other researchers, but it does identify the major "tried and true" strategies of interpersonal influence described in the social science literature.

Likeability

One significant factor (again, stronger in some situations than others) is how much we like the other person. Social scientists have examined what factors affect one's "likeability," and some of them are within an individual's control. Specifically, research — conducted primarily on Westerners — shows that we tend to like others who:

- Are physically attractive;
- Appear to like us (directly and indirectly communicated);
- Behave in a friendly and positive manner;
- Are similar to us;
- Are familiar to us;
- Cooperate with us or generally behave consistently with our own interests; and
- Appear to possess positive traits such as intelligence, competence, kindness, honesty, etc.

Authority

An agent's perceived authority is another major relationship-based determinant of influence. Social science research suggests that people are more likely to be influenced by the arguments of a person whom they perceive as an authority or an expert, especially on the topic of the discussion. Similarly, they are more likely to comply with requests made by someone who has status or authority or even someone with relevant expertise.

Reciprocity

There is a powerful — often unspoken — social norm of reciprocity, variously known as "give and take," a "two-way street," and "you scratch my back and I'll scratch yours." People are more likely to give to those from whom they have already received or expect to receive something. This applies not only to material goods, but also to social commodities such as favors and information. Research suggests that people are more likely to respond positively (affirmatively) to suggestions or requests for compliance from someone who has first provided a benefit to them than from someone who has not. Perhaps sources would be more willing to "give" to an educer if the educer has first given something (e.g., special rations, reading material) to them.

Commitment/Consistency

People want to see themselves — and be seen by others — as fulfilling their promises and commitments, possessing a coherent set of beliefs and values, and always acting in consonance with those beliefs. The implication is that people are more likely to cooperate or be influenced in a particular direction if a request is consistent with a previously declared commitment or statement of principle, or at least is not inconsistent with it. If an educer can persuade a source to commit to doing something, he or she can use that as leverage to get the source to follow through. Conversely, an educer could use the language of prior commitments— such as the Code of Conduct and argue that a particular request does not violate its provisions and that, perhaps, responding to the request would serve a "greater good" related to some other personality trait that the source valued highly.

Social Validation

One force that inclines people to action is whether others have performed the action before, and how many have done so. This works most powerfully when the "others" are similar in various ways (e.g., age, race, interests, socioeconomic status, etc.) to the target of the influence. For example, an intelligence source might be more likely to provide information if he believes others in his captured cohort have already done so.

Scarcity

Something that is abundant or easily attainable is not nearly as desirable as something scarce or rare. Studies have shown that people are more drawn to particular choices if their option to exercise them is limited. In an educing information context, an educer might offer an incentive for information that is only available to the source if he decides immediately (or within one hour), after which "all deals are off." The diminishing availability of the incentive will probably increase its potency.

Fear and Coercion

Fear

Some traditional notions of interrogation suggest that fear can be a powerful motivator, and that fear of an aversive consequence often affects behavior even more than actually delivering the consequence. Research — not conducted in interrogation contexts — seems to suggest that under certain conditions fear can facilitate compliance; however, it does not adequately address whether fear leads to more accurate and useful information (in, for example, an intelligence interrogation situation). That is, fear may motivate an enemy source to "talk," but not necessarily to provide accurate intelligence.

Research in social science, particularly in marketing and health education, suggests that the effectiveness of a threat appears to be determined largely by the perceived magnitude of the threat, the recipient's perceived vulnerability, and the perceived effectiveness of the proposed alternative to the feared outcome. Compliance seems most likely when the appeal to fear is high and the recommended behavior is perceived to be highly effective (Witte and Allen, 2000). This means the source must consider the threat credible and must believe that the educer will withdraw it if the source complies. For example, some experienced interrogators have suggested that threatening a source with death is not particularly effective because the source may believe that an educer who is willing to kill him might be willing — even likely — to kill him whether he complies or not. The source's motivation to comply therefore diminishes.

Coercion

Little social science literature speaks directly to the effectiveness of coercive tactics in educing accurate, useful information, but there is literature on how coercive influence strategies, such as inducing fear, affects relationships. The induction of fear or pain appears to be a critical element. If a source views the educer as the cause of his aversive situation, he may react against it by increasing his resistance and determination not to comply (see the next section). Research has shown consistently that recipients of punishment or aversive stimuli do distinguish between unpleasant sensations that are self-inflicted or naturally occurring and those intentionally caused by another person. One implication for educing information seems to be that the source should not view the primary educer as the cause of any negative consequences; someone else should wear the black hat if necessary. Ideally, the source should perceive that he alone is responsible for his situation.

More generally, social science research indicates that a perception of coercion can negatively affect the tenor of the relationship between the educer and the source and decrease the likelihood that the source will comply or cooperate. Research both in North America and in Asia (China) has shown that using coercive influence strategies causes targets (or sources, in the context of educing information) to feel disrespected, whereas persuasion strategies communicate respect. Thus, importantly, coercion creates a competitive dynamic that facilitates rejection of the other party's position where persuasion creates a cooperative dynamic that facilitates greater openness to the other party's position and productive conflict resolution (Tjosvold and Sun, 2001). A similar line of research has shown that rational persuasion — and avoidance of "pressure" — increases the likelihood of target commitment in influence interactions (Yukl et al., 1996). Interestingly, using coercive strategies also has an effect on agents — typically instilling in them a more negative evaluation of the target, including his or her ability to think. This effect is not found among agents who use strategies of rational persuasion (O'Neal et al, 1994).

Under conditions that simulate an intelligence interrogation, indirect strategies for eliciting information (i.e., acquiring information through interaction by means other than asking for it directly) may be more effective than direct, high-pressure techniques. In one of the few open-source studies on the effectiveness of military "resistance training," 58 cadets at the Royal Norwegian Naval Academy were subjected to a simulated prisoner-of-war exercise. Some had received a pre-training experiential exercise in resisting interrogation, others were given only a pre-training lecture. Perhaps of greatest interest is that the use of indirect interrogation techniques significantly reduced the amount of "prisoner" communication confined to name, rank, military number, and date of birth (from 24% to 0% in the lecture group and from 61% to 5% in the experiential pre-training group). More importantly, the indirect strategy (as opposed to a direct one) also increased the percentage of compromising statements revealed by the "prisoners" from 22% to 37% in the lecture group and from 0% to 15% in the experiential pre-training group (Laberg, Eid, Johnsen, Eriksen, and Zachariassen, 2000).

New-Age Technologies

Although the social sciences provide a rich menu of proven or promising influence strategies, researchers always look for ways to achieve results more quickly, more efficiently, or more covertly. Two influence strategies in the genre of "new-age technologies" have attracted the interest of some persons involved in interrogation training: neurolinguistic programming (NLP) and subliminal persuasion.

NLP

A blend of linguistics and psychology, NLP is more of a system of communication than a psychological theory. NLP has many facets, but the claims that have garnered the most attention from interrogators are the claimed ability to unconsciously develop a powerful rapport with another person that would virtually bring that person under a hypnotic spell, and the ability to understand and read people's internal mental processes by listening to the sensory words they use and by observing their eye movements.

Since NLP was first introduced in the 1970s, many research studies in the United States and Europe have sought to prove or disprove some of NLP's claims.[19] Almost none of the studies examining the effects of unconscious (covert) NLP rapport-building techniques such as pacing and mirroring have found that NLP techniques carry significant advantages. In studies where NLP strategies had a

---

[19]   A large database of abstracts from NLP articles and studies can be retrieved at: http://www.nlp.de/cgi-bin/research/nlp-rdb.cgi?action=res_entries.

positive effect on rapport, they tended to be no more effective than traditional listening skills taught to beginning counselors. In essence, research has failed to substantiate claims that NLP creates nearly magical powers of influence.

Other work has examined NLP's theory that people possess mental capabilities and perform mental operations according to a "primary representational system" (i.e., visual, auditory, or kinesthetic) that is reflected in their language and eye movements. NLP posits that observations of a person's eye movements can reveal how the person is mentally accessing or representing the experience of their response. Some interrogation trainers have applied these principles as though they might also be useful indicators of deception. The preponderance of empirical research, however (even by "believers" in NLP) has failed to produce strong evidence for the existence of primary representational systems or for the claimed associations between eye movement patterns and internal mental processing. A 1987 National Research Council panel concluded that: "The committee finds no scientific evidence to support the claim that neurolinguistic programming is an effective strategy for exerting influence."[20] No credible scientific studies since that time would substantially modify that conclusion.

Subliminal Persuasion

Subliminal persuasion has also been of interest to those concerned with strategies for interpersonal influence. Subliminal messages are defined as those delivered "beneath the threshold of conscious awareness." Particularly since the Korean War, theories have emerged that people may be receptive to messages that they barely notice (or do not notice) and that these messages can shape behavior. If, in fact, persuasive messages can be perceived and can affect behavior without the subject's awareness, this approach could have application to managing uncooperative sources without coercion (albeit, with its own set of ethical dilemmas).

For more than 30 years marketing researchers have studied the ability of various subliminal advertising (persuasive) stimuli to affect the behavior of potential consumers. However, Nick Epley of Cornell University, a leading researcher in the area of subliminal persuasion, concludes simply that "the resulting body of work...has produced far from impressive results...." Similarly, research evaluations of audio material with subliminally embedded messages (such as those promoting self-esteem or weight loss) have shown that they produce no effects beyond what people expect to experience (Greenwald, Spangenberg, Pratkanis, and Eskenazi, 1991; Pratkanis, 1992). Eight years later, another review (Moore and Pratkanis, 2000) reported that "recent scientific evidence continues to support our original appraisal that actions, motives, and beliefs are NOT susceptible to manipulation through the use of briefly (i.e., subliminally) presented messages or

---

[20] *Enhancing Human Performance: Issues, Theories and Techniques*, Report of the Commission on Behavioral and Social Sciences and Education (Washington, DC: The National Academies Press, 1988), 21.

directives. If anything the case against subliminal manipulation is stronger now than ever…" (2nd paragraph).

Overcoming Resistance

One of the central features of educing information in intelligence-gathering contexts is that the human source, at least initially, may be uncooperative or unwilling to provide what is requested. That unwillingness is generally regarded as "resistance," although the term has a variety of specific meanings.

The previous section noted that resistance may actually increase if a source feels coerced. Research (Brehm 1966; Brehm and Brehm, 1981) suggests that two factors determine the strength of resistance: (1) the number and importance of the freedoms that are threatened and (2) the nature of that threat. Threats that are perceived to lack legitimacy (arbitrary), and are more blatant (rather than subtle), direct (rather than indirect), and demanding (rather than delicate) tend to evoke *more* resistance. For example, anecdotal case analyses of actual police interrogations have shown psychologic reactance-like effects where subjects respond to pressure and negative feedback by becoming *less* suggestible and *less* compliant (Gudjonsson, 1995).

Most persuasion researchers focus on inducements and Alpha strategies for interpersonal influence (see the discussion under "Influence Strategies"). Knowles and Linn have produced some of the most relevant results and potentially important road markers for the next generation of knowledge on how to manage resistance to social influence. Their findings (Knowles and Linn, 2004) suggest that it is possible to minimize a person's motivation to resist being influenced. These findings have direct implications for persons involved in educing information from uncooperative sources. They recently proposed seven categories of Omega Persuasion Strategies, noting that the list is likely neither inclusive nor exhaustive.

I. Sidestep Resistance

The best way to handle resistance is not to raise it. To accomplish that in an interrogation context, however, is almost impossible. Nevertheless, there may be ways to minimize or reduce its intensity or natural escalation. One possible strategy is to redefine the relationship between agent and target. For example, salespeople have reframed their roles as consultants engaged in a long-term (beyond the sale), collaborative relationship with the buyer (client). People may feel less need to be wary of a consultant than a salesman (Knowles, Butler, and Linn, 2001; Knowles and Linn, 2004).

A second approach is to depersonalize the interaction. Rather than offering directives, suggestions, or persuasive arguments, an agent might talk about a parallel situation or may even develop a metaphor. Other suggested strategies to sidestep resistance are to minimize the request (Freedman and Fraser, 1966) by beginning with small and less-threatening requests; propose a less desirable alternative (which accounts for the dynamic underlying the good cop/bad cop technique; Rafaeli and Sutton, 1991); or push the choice into the future, because distant prospects are more optimistic and less driven by "avoidance" forces (Knowles and Linn, 2004).

II. Address Resistance Directly

Another category of approaches seeks to reduce resistance by addressing or assuaging its causes directly. This might be done either by offering some guarantee that the most feared outcome will not occur or by arguing against the reasons for the target's resistance.

III. Address Resistance Indirectly

Alternatively, one could choose to address resistance in a more indirect way by removing the "need" for resistance. One strategy is to bolster the target's sense of competence and self-esteem (Jacks and O'Brien, 2004); another is to focus the resistance by casting the target in a different social role, such as that of the expert.

IV. Distract Resistance

Distraction can also reduce resistance. Resistance requires some attention to be optimally effective. Petty and Cacioppo (1986) have proposed a model of attitude change called the Elaboration Likelihood Model (ELM). The basic premise is that when people have both motivation and ability, they prefer to process a persuasive message through a "central route" in which the response derives from a careful analysis of the message quality. A mild distraction can occupy the target's attention, thereby diminishing his/her resources available to counter-argue or otherwise critically analyze the quality of the message (Haaland and Venkatesan, 1968; Petty and Brock, 1981; Knowles and Linn, 2004).

V. Disrupt Resistance

One of the most fascinating — and potentially promising — categories of counter-resistance strategies involves disruption. As with the distraction strategies, the goal of disruption is to occupy the resistance process so that the persuasive message is delivered without hindrance. Disruption — as the term is used here — differs from an external distraction such as a loud noise. Instead, the disruption is delivered as part of the message, but is designed to create mild and momentary confusion (for example, by transposing "Code of Conduct" into "Conduct of Code"). According to the research, confusion reduces resistance, and can be a particularly effective tool of influence when combined with a follow-up persuasive message (reframe). Some studies have determined that the disruption must be mild and must occur before the reframing to get the desired effect. Obviously, it could be nearly impossible to implement such a subtle strategy when communicating through a translator, but the effects of the technique shown to date mark it as worthy of further consideration.

VI. Consume Resistance

A longstanding maxim of interrogation training is that "every man has his breaking point." In the social science literature, the concept that comes closest to that of breaking is regulatory depletion, which postulates that the human capacity to control one's own responses (self-regulation) draws on a finite and limited resource. Regulation requires effort and that effort uses up some of a person's regulatory energy, so that less is available for subsequent responses (Muraven, Tice and Baumeister, 1998, 775).

Existing research suggests that one common and modestly sized store of energy fuels any and all forms of regulatory activity. Theoretically, then, one's regulatory capacity could be entirely depleted. However, repeated cycles of exertion and restoration may serve to strengthen regulatory capacity and perhaps make subjects more resilient (Baumeister, Muraven, and Tice, 2000; Strayhorn, 2002); thus, overwhelming or depleting a person's resistance in the short term may be theoretically possible, but may impose a cost in the longer term.

VII. Use Resistance to Promote Change

Never try to teach a pig to sing. It wastes your time, and it annoys the pig.

One of the most intriguing approaches to getting past resistance is to use it. The theory and concepts behind the idea of using resistance draw from several sources, including the work of psychotherapists Victor Frankl and Milton Erickson, who used unconventional strategies (for example, telling an insomniac to try to stay awake) to bypass their patients' resistance and effect therapeutic change (Weeks and L'Abate, 1982). Examples include what is popularly called "reverse psychology"; the professional term commonly ascribed to this technique is "paradoxical intention." Other studies suggest that acknowledging (or preempting) resistance can help to reduce it, for example, by preceding a persuasive message by saying something like: "I know you're determined not to listen to anything I say, but…" When this works, it appears that the target resists the acknowledgement or suggestion of resistance (Linn and Knowles, 2002).

Although Hans Gerz (Frankl, 1967) is said to have claimed that paradoxical intention is successful in 80–90% of cases, many of the documented successes are anecdotal and are ascribed to a small cadre of "master" therapists. Findings garnered over the last 15 years suggest that these techniques may only work for people who are inclined to resist direct suggestions.

Implications

Research findings support the idea that different strategies may be required for different sources (and maybe even under different conditions). In a context in which information is being educed, different sources will have different degrees of, and strategies for, resisting. An educer must constantly assess and monitor the source to develop insight that can inform plans and strategies for educing information.

Factors Affecting Accuracy

Educing information from a human source requires some understanding of how people in general acquire, process, store, and retrieve information. Without this knowledge, it is possible to misinterpret or even contaminate stored information so that not even the source can any longer discern the "real truth."

There is a common misconception that the human mind acts like a video recorder, capturing all experiences exactly as they occur and storing them in a cortical archive until they need to be retrieved. To put it charitably, such a model over-estimates and mischaracterizes both the nature and capacity of human information processing. Perceiving, storing, and retrieving information are active mental processes. A multitude of factors at any of these three levels can affect a person's ability to acquire information, and to retrieve and represent it accurately (e.g., Neisser and Winograd, 1988; Roediger, 1996; Schacter, 1995).

Perception

Humans do not passively record events as they occur in the environment. Rather, they are active gatherers and processors of sensory information. They selectively attend to certain elements while filtering out others, all the while actively interpreting their possible meanings and interrelationships.

Perceptions become the assumed reality on which people operate. This has a number of important implications for educing information. First, the educer can control many facets of the source's detention and confinement in a way that "constructs" the source's perception and construal of his situation. These constructions can facilitate or inhibit the source's motivation to provide information. Second, however, the educer must recognize that the desired information, as stored in the source's mind, is a product of his or her construction of it, not necessarily of how it existed in its original form.

Memory

The "modal model" of memory is one of the most widely used contemporary frameworks for understanding the elements of human memory processing. The model posits three stages of memory. The first is sensory memory, in which stimuli are only momentarily registered to facilitate perception. The second is short-term memory (STM) or what some call "working memory." The function of STM is simply to hold information while it is being processed (to be eliminated or transferred to long-term memory). The third stage is long-term memory (LTM). Scholars debate whether information in LTM is permanent or not.

Just as human perceptions are constructed, rather than recorded, memories themselves are "reconstructions" (Bartlett, 1932). A substantial body of research shows that event memories can be altered by information inserted or suggested in attempts to retrieve them (Loftus, Miller, Burns, 1978; Loftus, 1979; Loftus and

Ketcham, 1994; Roediger and McDermott 1995). One proposed cause of these errors is difficulty in distinguishing the "source" of a given unit of information; an inconsistent distinction separates information acquired internally (in one's head) from externally (actual experience). Moreover, stress, even at moderate levels, has been found to impair memory recall (de Quervain et al., 2000; Henson, Shallice, and Dolan, 1999; Lupien et al., 1998; Nadel and Jacobs, 1998; Payne, Nadel, Allen, Thomas, and Jacobs, 2002).

Accuracy of Educed Information

A variety of factors such as stress, fatigue, distraction, and intoxication can impair the capacity to retrieve and perceive memories accurately. At the extreme, for example, there is a significant social science literature addressing the apparently rare, but disturbing, issue of people confessing to crimes they did not commit. The most critical implications for intelligence are that interrogation tactics can lead the source to provide information that is inaccurate (intentionally or unintentionally) even though the information may seem to conform to the interrogator's expectations, and also that the process of interrogation itself can affect a source's ability to recall known information accurately.

One distinction between interrogations conducted in LE and intelligence contexts is that the primary objective in most U.S. law enforcement interrogations is to obtain a confession rather than to educe information. The presumption or expectation of guilt at the outset of an interrogation has been shown to influence interrogators' questioning strategy and cause them to exert more pressure to confess. It also affects the interrogator's inferences and judgments about the suspect's guilt.

This body of research underscores the importance of obtaining not merely *information* through education, but specifically *accurate* and *useful* information. It also provides a sobering reminder that some eduction methods — such as inducing stress, fatigue, distraction, and intoxication — have the potential to affect not only a source's motivation to provide accurate, useful information, but also his capacity to do so.

"Stress and Duress"

Determining what constitutes a "stress and duress" technique is a matter of some debate. Social science research, however, has studied the effects of certain techniques that have been used in the past (some quite widely), particularly those commonly alleged by various groups to produce undue stress and duress in detainees. True interrogative confession has been modeled as "a complicated and demanding decision-making process" (Gudjonsson, 1992, 64). Of particular interest, then, is how those effects might alter an uncooperative individual's motivation or capacity to provide accurate, useful information.

Research describes the psychological and emotional effects of strategies sometimes used to diminish resistance, specifically physical discomfort, sleep deprivation, and sensory deprivation. None of the studies, however, addresses definitively whether these tactics indeed diminish resistance to persuasion and influence or promote compliance in populations relevant to this inquiry. One notable research program (MKULTRA), which ultimately was shut down by the U.S. government because of ethical concerns, suggested that these techniques led to changes in behavior, making at least some persons more passive and pliable. However, although it was designed to inform interrogations, most of the research was not conducted in the context of interrogation. The 1963 "KUBARK Counterintelligence Interrogation" Manual reflects some of the perceived implications of this line of research. Strikingly, since that time very little empirical research has been conducted on these techniques and the ways in which they may or may not affect relevant interrogation outcomes.

Torture

Much of the social science research on the issue of torture may not apply to the process of educing information. The term "torture" is used with very little consistency in the literature. One basic distinction is between torture used for punishment and torture used for leverage (to facilitate compliance or to elicit information). The tactics, effects, and resistance strategies may be quite different from one type to the next. Research does exist on the social and psychological consequences of torture (e.g., Somnier et al, 1992) but not on the applicability of those effects to educing information.

Evidence from social science suggests that there are similarities in the psychological effects of torture and of internment as a Prisoner of War. Among the common features are enforced captivity, fear and terror, pain and suffering, and shame and humiliation. A feeling of powerlessness has been posited as the central component of humiliation. It is possible that future research about the experiences of POWs who have been tortured while in captivity in past wars may help to inform some questions about torture that relate to educing information.

Pain and Physical Discomfort

Although pain is commonly regarded as a facilitator of compliance or diminisher of resistance, there appears to have been little or no empirical research addressing these questions. The PsycINFO database contains embedded topic headings for terms such as "Resistance," "Aversive Stimuli," "Pain," "Attitude Change," and Compliance," yet, there are virtually no "hits" and definitely no relevant hits for any given pair of these predictor and outcome terms. For example, among thousands of articles on each topic individually, there are no articles at the intersection of "aversive stimuli" and "resistance."

Reports about the treatment of POWs and foreign prisoners in China documented the use of physical abuse, but studies of the role of assault in promoting attitude change and in eliciting false confessions (even from U.S. servicemen) revealed that it was ineffective. Belief change and compliance was more likely when physical abuse was minimal or absent (Biderman 1960).

Sleep Loss/Deprivation

Sleep loss/deprivation is associated with:

- General cognitive slowing (Dinges and Kribbs, 1991)
- Impaired attention (Hockey, 1970; Norton, 1970)
- Diminished concentration (Williams, Lubin, and Goodnow, 1959)
- Impairment in cognitive functions associated with right anterior hemisphere or subcortical areas such as motor, rhythm, receptive and expressive speech, memory, and complex verbal arithmetic functions (Kim et al., 2001)
- Impaired decisionmaking involving the unexpected, innovation, revising plans, competing distractions, and effective communication (Harrison and Horne, 2000)
- Reduced capacity for logical and sequential thought (Blagrove, Alexander, and Horne, 1995; Horne, 1988b; Williams and Lubin, 1967)
- Decreased accuracy in time estimation, and both immediate and delayed recall (Taylor and McFatter, 2003)
- Negative effects on mood (Lieberman et al., 2002)
- Alteration of the body's immune system (Everson, 1997)
- Increased perception of physical pain (hyperalgesia) (Kundermann et al., 2004)
- Decreased motivation (Wilkinson, 1961, 1964; Horne and Pettitt, 1985; Meddis, 1977)
- Increased suggestibility (Blagrove, Cole-Morgan, and Lambe, 1994; Blagrove, 1996).

On this last point it is worth noting that suggestibility increases specifically under conditions simulating an interrogation. At least one study has found that "the effect on suggestibility of one or two night's sleep loss is comparable to the difference in suggestibility between true and false confessors." (Blagrove, 1996, p. 57)

Sensory Deprivation

Sensory deprivation is associated with:

- Impairment in higher mental functions and complex intellectual tasks (Myers, Murphy, Smith, and Goffard, 1966; Kitamura, 1967)
- Increased susceptibility to influence (under some conditions) (Myers et al., 1966)
- Heightened hypnotic susceptibility (Sanders and Reyher, 1969)
- Diminished EEG activity correlated with apathetic, lethargic behavior, and a reduction in stimulation seeking behavior (Scott and Gendreau, 1969)
- Behaving in a way that is more boring and unlikable (Zuckerman et al., 1970)

- Increased anxiety and depression (Zuckerman et al., 1970)
- Greater instability of beliefs and of both peripheral and central attitudes (Tetlock and Seudfeld, 1976; Seudfeld and Borrie, 1978)
- Cognitive disorganization (Seudfeld and Borrie, 1978)
- Increased persuadability (Seudfeld and Borrie, 1978)
- Increased compliance behavior (beyond usual social influence conditions) (Moscovici and Doms, 1982)

Key Findings

The review presented above is mainly descriptive. This section highlights some of the more important findings and their potential implications.

- From the perspectives of both research and practice, educing information is most productively viewed as a dynamic and reciprocal process rather than as a discrete event, task, or series of face-to-face encounters.

- U.S. personnel have used a limited number of interrogation techniques over the past half-century, but virtually none of them — or their underlying assumptions — are based on scientific research or have even been subjected to scientific or systematic inquiry or evaluation.

- The potential mechanisms and effects of using coercive techniques or torture for gaining accurate, useful information from an uncooperative source are much more complex than is commonly assumed. There is little or no research to indicate whether such techniques succeed in the manner and contexts in which they are applied. Anecdotal accounts and opinions based on personal experiences are mixed, but the preponderance of reports seems to weigh against their effectiveness.

- The accuracy of educed information can be compromised by the manner in which it is obtained. The effects of many common stress and duress techniques are known to impair various aspects of a person's cognitive functioning, including those functions necessary to retrieve and produce accurate, useful information.

- Psychological theory and some (indirectly) related research suggest that coercion or pressure can actually *increase* a source's resistance and determination not to comply. Although pain is commonly assumed to facilitate compliance, there is no available scientific or systematic research to suggest that coercion can, will, or has provided accurate useful information from otherwise uncooperative sources.

- Research studies on important related issues such as persuasion, influence, compliance, and resistance have mainly (although not exclusively) focused on persons from Western cultures. Findings from the fields of intercultural psychology and anthropology suggest that patterns, meanings and modes of interpersonal interaction may be different in non-Western cultures, so there is not yet a clear scientific basis to anticipate that results and insights will apply equally or evenly across cultures. Moreover, many encounters involving information eduction in intelligence-gathering contexts occur through translators. While there is good reason to suspect that the effects and/or implementation of interpersonal strategies may be different when using a translator as a conduit for communication, the exact nature and extent of that impact on educing information has not been scientifically determined.

- A moderately strong body of social science research provides a potential road map to a new generation of strategies and approaches for overcoming resistance without the use of high-pressure, coercive techniques.

- Social science research on persuasion and interpersonal influence could provide a foundation for creating an elegant, elaborate, and powerful U.S. approach for educing information in intelligence-gathering contexts.

Summary Highlights

What models exist for educing information from uncooperative sources?

Constructing a conceptual model of "U.S." information eduction could provide a platform to label and identify actors, elements, actions, dynamics, and effects to describe and conceptualize the process. The field of persuasive message production offers some relevant research methods, while negotiation theory offers principles and provides a language and interest-based perspective that are not overtly adversarial.

What strategies might increase or decrease a source's willingness to provide information?

Considerable social science literature on persuasion and influence may be relevant to the development of processes for educing information. The six most consistent factors affecting interpersonal influence are reciprocity, scarcity, liking, authority, commitment/consistency, and social validation. Fear can sometimes be a motivator when apprehension is high and the recommended behavior is believed to be highly effective. People who believe they are being coerced are likely to feel disrespected and become less likely to comply or cooperate. Neither neurolinguistic programming nor subliminal suggestion appears to be an effective or promising agent of influence.

What is resistance and what strategies exist for getting past it?

Resistance is a common reaction to influence or compliance attempts. The social science literature identifies numerous strategies to help overcome it. They include sidestepping it, addressing it directly, addressing it indirectly, distracting it, disrupting it, consuming it, or using it.

What key factors affect the accuracy of educed information?

The mind does not operate like a video camera. Perceiving, storing, and retrieving information are active mental processes. A multitude of factors at any of these three levels — including questioning strategies — can affect a person's ability (not just willingness) to acquire information and to retrieve and represent it accurately.

What is known about the effect of "stress and duress" techniques for educing accurate, useful information?

Social science research describes the psychological and emotional effects of strategies sometimes used to diminish resistance, specifically physical discomfort, sleep deprivation, and sensory deprivation. Generally speaking, the stress and fatigue produced under these conditions can impair the capacity to accurately retrieve and perceive memories. None of the studies, however, addresses definitively the issue of whether these tactics do indeed diminish resistance to persuasion or influence, or promote compliance in relevant populations. Although pain is commonly expected to facilitate compliance or diminish resistance, little or no empirical research has addressed this topic.

References

Bartlett, F.C. (1932). *Remembering: An Experimental and Social Study.* Cambridge: Cambridge University Press.

Baumeister, R. F., Muraven, M., and Tice, D. M. (2000). "Ego Depletion: A Resource Model of Volition, Self-Regulation, and Controlled Processing." *Social Cognition* 18, 130-150.

Biderman, A. (1960). "Social-Psychological Needs and Involuntary Behavior As Illustrated by Compliance in Interrogation." *Sociometry* 23, 120-147.

Blagrove, M. (1996). "Effects of Length of Sleep Deprivation on Interrogative Suggestibility." *Journal of Experimental Psychology: Applied* 2, 48-59.

Blagrove, M., Alexander, C. A., and Home, J. A. (1995). "The Effects of Chronic Sleep Reduction on The Performance of Cognitive Tasks Sensitive to Sleep Deprivation." *Applied Cognitive Psychology* 9, 21-40.

Blagrove, M., Cole-Morgan, D., and Lambe, H. (1994). "Interrogative Suggestibility: The Effects of Sleep Deprivation and Relationship with Field-Dependence." *Applied Cognitive Psychology* 8, 169-179.

Brehm, J. (1966). *A Theory of Psychological Reactance.* New York: Academic Press.

Brehm, S. and Brehm, J. (1981). *Psychological Reactance: A Theory of Freedom and Control.* New York: Academic Press.

Cialdini, R. B. (2001). *Influence: Science and Practice (4th ed.).* Boston: Allyn and Bacon.

de Quervain, D. J., Roozendaal, B., Nitsch, R. M., McGaugh, J. L., and Hock, C. (2000). "Acute Cortisone Administration Impairs Retrieval of Long-Term Declarative Memory in Humans." *Nature Neuroscience* 3, 313-314."

Dinges, D.F., Kribbes, N.B (1991). *"Performing While Sleepy: Effects of experimentally-induced Sleepiness."* In T. H. Monk (ed), *Sleep, Sleepiness and Performance,* Chichester, England: Wiley, 97-128.

Dollard, J., and Miller, N. E. (1950). *Personality and Psychotherapy.* New York: McGraw-Hill.

Epley, N. (Undated). *Investigating the Possibility (and Plausibility) of Subliminal Persuasion. Laboratory Manual.* Available online at: http://www.csic.cornell.edu/201/subliminal/

Everson, C. (1997). "Sleep Deprivation and the Immune System." In M. Pressman and W. Orr (Eds.) *Understanding Sleep: Evaluation and Treatment of Sleep Disorders.* Washington, D.C.: American Psychological Association, 401-424.

Frankl, V. (1967) *Psychotherapy and Existentialism.* New York: Washington Square Press.

Freedman, J. L., and Fraser, S. C. (1966). "Compliance without Pressure: The Foot-in-the-Door Technique." *Journal of Personality and Social Psychology* 4, 195-202.

Greenwald, A.G., Spangenberg, E.R., Pratkanis, A.R., and Eskenazi, J. (1991). "Double-Blind Tests of Subliminal Self-Help Audio Tapes." *Psychological Science* 2, 119-122.

Gudjonsson, G. (1992). *The Psychology of Interrogation, Confessions and Testimony.* New York: Wiley.

Gudjonsson, G. (1995). "I'll Help You Boys As Much As I Can" – How Eagerness to Please Can Result in a False Confession." *Journal of Forensic Psychiatry* 6, 333-342.

Haaland, G., and Venkatesan, M. (1968). "Resistance of Persuasive Communications: An Examination of the Distraction Hypotheses." *Journal of Personality and Social Psychology* 9, 167-170.

Harrison, Y. and Horne, J. (2000). "The Impact of Sleep Deprivation on Decision Making: A Review." *Journal of Experimental Psychology-Applied* 6, 236-249

Henson, R. N. A., Shallice, T., and Dolan, R. J. (1999). "Right Prefrontal Cortex and Episodic Memory Retrieval: A Functional MRI Test of the Monitoring Hypothesis." *Brain* 122 (Pt 7), 1367-1381.

Hockey, G. R. J. (1970). "Changes in Attention Allocation an a Multicomponent Task Under Loss of Sleep." *British Journal of Psychology* 61, 473-480.

Horne, J. A. (1988b). *Why We Sleep.* Oxford, England: Oxford University Press.

Horne, J. A., and Pettitt, A. (1985). "High Incentive Effects on Vigilance Performance during 72 Hours of Total Sleep Deprivation." *Acta Psychologica* 58, 123-139.

Jacks, J. Z., and O'Brien, M. E. (2004). "Decreasing Resistance by Affirming the Self." In E. Knowles and J. Linn (eds.), *Resistance and Persuasion.* Mahwah, NJ: Lawrence Erlbaum Associates, 235-257.

Kim, D., Lee, H., Kim, M., Park, Y., Go, H., Kim, K., Lee, S., Chae, J., and Lee, C. (2001). "The Effect of Total Sleep Deprivation on Cognitive Functions in Normal Adult Male Subjects." *International Journal of Neuroscience* 109, 127-137.

Kitamura, S. (1967). "Psychological Studies on Sensory Deprivation." *Japanese Journal of Aerospace Medicine and Psychology* 4, 44-50.

Knowles, E. S., Butler, S., and Linn, J. A. (2001). "Increasing Compliance by Reducing Resistance." In J. Forgas and K. Williams (eds.), *Social influence: Direct and Indirect Processes.* New York: Psychology Press.

Knowles, E. S., and Linn, J. A. (eds.). (2004). *Resistance and Persuasion.* Mahwah, N.J.: Lawrence Erlbaum Associates.

Kundermann, B., Krieg, J., Schreiber, W., and Lautenbacher, S. (2004). "The Effect of Sleep Deprivation on Pain." *Pain Research and Management* 9, 25-32.

Laberg, JC, Eid, J., Johnsen, BH, Eriksen, BS, and Zachariassen, KK (2000). "Coping with Interrogations." In C. McCann and R. Pigeau (eds.), *The Human in Command: Exploring the Modern Military Experience.* New York: Kluwer Academic/Plenum Publishers.

Lewin, K. (1958). Group Decision and Social Change. In G. E. Swanson, T. M. Newcomb, and E. L. Hartley (Eds.), *Readings in Social Psychology,* rev. ed. New York: Holt, 459-473.

Lieberman H., Tharion W., Shukitt-Hale B., Speckman K., and Tulley R. (2002). "Effects of Caffeine, Sleep Loss and Stress on Cognitive Performance and Mood during U.S. Navy SEAL Training." *Psychopharmacology* 164, 250-261.

Loftus, E.F. (1979). The Malleability of Human Memory. *American Scientist* 67, 312-320.

Loftus, E.F. and Ketcham, K. (1994) *The Myth of Repressed Memory.* NY: St. Martin's Press.

Loftus, E.F., Miller, D.G., and Burns, H.J. (1978). Semantic Integration of Verbal Information into a Visual Memory. *Journal of Experimental Psychology: Human Learning and Memory* 4, 19-31.

Lupien, S.J., DeLeon, M, DeSanti S, Convit A, Tarshish, C., Nair, NPV, McEwen, B.S., Hauger, R.L., and Meaney, M. (1998). Longitudinal Increase in Cortisol during Human Aging Predicts Hippocampal Atrophy and Memory Deficits. *Nature Neuroscience* 1, 69-73.

Meddis, R. (1977). *The Sleep Instinct.* London: Routledge.

Miller, N. E. (1959). "Liberalization of Basic S-R Concepts: Extensions of Conflict Behavior, Motivation, and Social Learning." In S. Koch (ed), *Psychology: A Study of a Science*, Vol. 2. New York: McGraw-Hill, 196-292.

Moore, T. and Pratkanis, A. (2000). *An Update on Subliminal Influence.* Available online at: http://www.srmhp.org/archives/subliminal-influence.html.

Moscovici, S. and Doms, M. (1982). "Compliance and Conversion in a Situation of Sensory Deprivation." *Basic and Applied Social Psychology* 3, 81-94.

Muraven, M., Tice, D. M., and Baumeister, R. F. (1998). "Self-Control As Limited Resource: Regulatory Depletion Patterns." *Journal of Personality and Social Psychology* 74, 774-789.

Myers, T., Murphy, D., Smith, S. and Goffard, S. (1966). *Experimental Studies of Sensory Deprivation and Social Isolation.* HumRRO Technical Report. No. 66-8, x-70.

Nadel, L., and Jacobs, W. J. (1998). "Traumatic Memory Is Special." *Current Directions in Psychological Science* 7, 154-157.

Neisser, U. and Winograd, E. (1988). *Remembering Reconsidered: Ecological and Traditional Approaches to the Study of Memory.* New York, NY: Cambridge University Press

Norton, R. (1970). "The Effects of Acute Sleep Deprivation on Selective Attention." *British Journal of Psychology* 61, 157-161.

O'Neal, E., Kipnis, D., and Craig, K. (1994). "Effects on the Persuader of Employing a Coercive Influence Technique." *Basic and Applied Social Psychology* 15, 225-238.

Payne, J.D., Nadel, L., Allen, J.J.B., Thomas, K.G.F. and Jacobs, W.J. (2002). "Stress Increases False Memories." *Memory* 10, 1-6.

Petty, R. E., and Brock, T. C. (1981). "Thought Disruption and Persuasion: Assessing the Validity of Attitude Change Experiments." In R. E. Petty, T. M. Ostrom, and T. C. Brock (eds.), *Cognitive Responses in Persuasion.* Hillsdale, NJ: Erlbaum, 55-79.

Petty, R. E., and Cacioppo, J. T. (1986). *Communication and Persuasion: Central and Peripheral Routes to Attitude Change.* New York: Springer-Verlag.

Pratkanis, A. (1992). "The Cargo Cult Science of Subliminal Persuasion." *Skeptical Inquirer* 16, 260-272.

Rafaeli, A., and Sutton, R. I. (1991). "Emotional Contrast Strategies as Means of Social Influence: Lessons from Criminal Interrogators and Bill Collectors." *Academy of Management Journal* 34, 749-775.

Roediger, H. (1996). "Memory Illusions." *Journal of Memory and Language* 35, 76-100.

Roediger, H.L. and McDermott, K.B. (1995). "Creating False Memories: Remembering Words Not Presented in Lists." *Journal of Experimental Psychology: Learning, Memory,& Cognition* 21, 803-814.

Sanders, R. and Reyher, J. (1969). "Sensory Deprivation and the Enhancement of Hypnotic Susceptibility." *Journal of Abnormal Psychology* 74, 375-381.

Schacter, D. (ed.) (1995). *Memory Distortion: How Minds, Brains, and Societies Reconstruct the Past.* Cambridge, MA: Harvard University Press.

Scott, G., and Gendreau, P. (1969). "Psychiatric Implications of Sensory Deprivation A Maximum Security Prison." *Canadian Psychiatric Association Journal* 14, 337-340.

Suedfeld, P., and Borrie, RA (1978). "Sensory Deprivation, Attitude Change and Defence Against Persuasion." *Canadian Journal of Behavioral Science* 10, 16-27.

Somnier, E., Vesti, P., Kastrup, M., and Genefke, I. K. (1992). "Psychosocial Consequences of Torture: Current Knowledge and Evidence." In M. Basuglu (ed.), *Torture and Its Consequences: Current Treatments Approaches.* Cambridge University Press, Cambridge, UK.

Strayhorn, J. M. (2002). "Self-Control: Toward Systematic Training Programs." *Journal of the American Academy of Child and Adolescent Psychiatry* 41, 17-27.

Stubbs, M. (1983). *Discourse Analysis: The Sociolinguistic Analysis of Natural Language.* Oxford: Basil Blackwell.

Taylor, D.J. and McFatter, R.M. (2003). "Cognitive Performance after Sleep Deprivation: Does Personality Make a Difference?" *Personality and Individual Differences* 33, 1179-1193.

Tetlock, P. E., and Suedfeld, P. (1976). "Inducing Belief Instability without a Persuasive Message: The Roles of Attitude Centrality, Individual Cognitive Differences, and Sensory Deprivation." *Canadian Journal of Behavioral Science* 8, 324-333.

Tjosvold, D. and Sun, H. (2002) "Understanding Conflict Avoidance: Relationship, Motivations, Actions, and Consequences." *International Journal of Conflict Management* 13, 42–164.

Walkley, J. (1987). *Police interrogation: A Handbook for Investigators.* Cambridge,. Great Britain: Black Bear Press Limited.

Witte, K., and Allen, M. (2000). "A Meta-Analysis of Fear Appeals: Implication for Effective Public Health Campaigns." *Health Education and Behavior* 27, 591-615.

Weeks, G. and L'Abate, L. (1982). *Paradoxical Psychotherapy: Theory and Practice with Individuals, Couples and Families.* New York: Brunner/ Mazel Publishers.

Wilkinson, R. (1961). "Interaction of Lack of Sleep with Knowledge of Results, Repeated Testing, and Individual Differences." *Journal of Experimental Psychology* 62, 263-271.

Wilkinson, R. (1964). "Effects of Up To 60 Hours' Sleep Deprivation on Different Types of Work." *Ergonomics* 7, 175-186.

Williams, H. L., and Lubin, A. (1967). "Speeded Addition and Sleep Loss." *Journal of Experimental Psychology* 73, 313-317.

Williams, H. L., Lubin, A., and Goodnow, J. J. (1959). "Impaired Performance with Acute Sleep Loss." *Psychological Monographs: General and Applied* 73, 1-26.

Wilson, S. R. (2002). *Seeking and Resisting Compliance. Why People Say What They Do When Trying to Influence Others.* Thousand Oaks, Calif.: Sage Publications.

Yukl, G., Kim, H., and Falbe, C. M. (1996). "Antecedents of Influence Outcomes." *Journal of Applied Psychology* 81, 309-317.

Zuckerman, M., Persky, H., Miller, L. and Levine, B. (1970). "Sensory Deprivation Versus Sensory Variation." *Journal of Abnormal Psychology* 76, 76-82.

3
Research on Detection of Deception
What We Know vs. What We Think We Know

Gary Hazlett, Psy.D.
November 2005

Abstract

This review examines the scientific literature regarding our current capacity to detect deception by observing behavioral indicators and identifies additional research that might improve that capacity. It focuses on methods that can be used in person-to-person communication without extensive technological support. The findings indicate that common beliefs about reliable cues to deception are frequently incorrect, and that research in this area to date may be largely irrelevant to national security needs. The study recommends that the United States adopt an aggressive, focused plan to support research and development of enhanced capabilities to validate information and the veracity of sources. Such a plan should concentrate on understanding actual behavior and should prioritize projects on the basis of operational needs, operational realities, cost, and potential return on investment.

Introduction

The capacity of the United States to engage in effective intelligence collection and counterterrorism operations has historically been handicapped by the relatively low quantity and quality of human source intelligence available to inform planning and decision-making.

In response, the U.S. government has decided to increase significantly the number of human intelligence collectors operating in the field. However, more collectors will not by themselves produce real improvements in performance. New, more effective tactics, techniques, and procedures, along with better training, are also necessary. Specifically, the Intelligence Community must improve its abilities to develop information from human sources through debriefing, elicitation, and interrogation efforts. Despite the best efforts of dedicated human intelligence collectors, the Intelligence Community has become highly dependent upon technical means for breakthroughs in intelligence collection.

Background

Our adversaries are often more sophisticated now than in the past and the U.S. advantage in high-tech surveillance capabilities has diminished over the years. Both practical and political considerations account for past trends away from development and use of human sources for intelligence collection and toward substantial reliance upon imagery and communications interception technology. First and foremost, this approach worked; in fact, for many years, it worked extremely well. It leveraged the huge technological and financial advantages of the United States over most of the rest of the world, providing data collection capabilities that allowed the Intelligence Community access almost anywhere it cared to look. Unfortunately (in this context), the technological disparity between countries has grown narrower. As a result, our competitors and adversaries better understand our capabilities, which allows them to develop countermeasures that have diminished the return on our technology-based collection methods.

Our adversaries are different than in the past. While it still remains almost impossible for another nation to move an armored division without being seen, high-tech surveillance systems offer relatively little capacity to track the movements of individuals belonging to a terrorist organization.

Given the dispersed nature and small size of terrorist organizations, direct interaction with people is required to develop the kinds of information needed to inform and direct intelligence operations. The challenge is to identify when information and sources developed through human contact are valid.

Determining Veracity

Methods of detecting when an individual is attempting to deceive a listener constitute a primary basis for assessing the potential utility and validity of information obtained from human sources. A significant amount of scientific study has focused on this topic. Overall, data to this point suggest that for all groups, novice to professional, accuracy in determining when someone is being deceptive is only marginally better than chance.[1-22]

The two primary approaches to detecting deception rely on psychophysiological and behavioral indicators. Psychophysiological methods involve monitoring and assessing physiological reactions to events; for instance, through use of heart rate and function monitors[23-26], skin conductance sensors,[27,28] thermal photography, voice frequency analysis[29], and brain activation patterns measured via electronic wave patterns [30-33] or via magnetic resonance imaging, etc. Detailed examinations of these and other methods appear elsewhere in the literature[16,34,35] or within papers sponsored through the current study on educing information, such as the study by Heckman and Happel in this document.

The present review covers scientific findings regarding our current capacity to detect deception by using behavioral indicators: all actions, statements, or responses that another person can reasonably monitor through observation. It focuses only on those methods that can be used in person-to-person communication, without the aid of extensive technological support. While technologically based methods are potentially valuable tools in some settings, the human collector remains the most deployable and adaptable tool that can be put in the field. Moreover, pragmatic considerations frequently make application of more complex or elaborate technologies impractical or impossible. The review also suggests additional research to enhance the ability to detect deception.

Cues to Deception

Beliefs vs. Reality

People who adopt the belief that there are reliable cues to deception are frequently incorrect. Significant research has studied people's beliefs about indicators that someone is being deceptive and their own attitudes and confidence about their personal ability to be deceptive. A summary of 57 studies examining beliefs about nonverbal cues to deception indicated that many people do not actually know what they think they know: in other words, their beliefs are just as often wrong as they are right.[36] These patterns of erroneous beliefs are widespread and are found equally among professional interrogators/investigators and novices.[7,37-40]

Research into beliefs and attitudes about deception may have value for predicting how people might try to conceal deception on the basis of their own beliefs about cues to deception. This research may also facilitate the identification of erroneous beliefs that intelligence collectors may hold and that should be corrected in training. However, the study of attitudes and beliefs does not in itself provide information on which cues to deception actually work. Therefore, this line of research may at best provide indirect support to the development of effective and reliable methods for detecting deception.

Most behavioral research discusses indicators of deception in terms of nonverbal, paralinguistic, and verbal behaviors. The literature also contains global judgments of behavior that may potentially have some utility.

Nonverbal Behavioral Cues

Most nonverbal cues to deception do not appear useful. To succeed at deception, individuals must control the information that they provide. People can generally exercise control over what they say; therefore, verbal output is subject to considerable crafting on the part of the individual attempting to be deceptive. The literature assumes that nonverbal behavior is more likely to fall outside a subject's full awareness and thus may provide a better source of cues for detecting deception. (Yet, as noted below, verbal cues may actually offer some insight.) For the purposes of this review, nonverbal behaviors encompass all those observable behaviors that may or may not accompany language, such as body movements, gestures, posture, eye gaze, etc.

A recent extensive review of the literature compiled the results from 116 research reports involving 120 independent subject samples.[41] This analysis identified 158 cues to deception, but indicated that most of the nonverbal behaviors studied proved ineffective and unreliable as indicators. Popularly held beliefs as to what might be effective cues to deception included behaviors such as gaze aversion or level of eye contact; movements of the legs, feet, head and trunk; shifting body positions; and "covering gestures" such as placing a hand over the mouth while talking, ear tugging, etc. None of these was rigorously substantiated by the research, although a small subset demonstrated reasonable power. They included fewer hand and finger movements while talking, fewer illustrating gestures accompanying speech, dilation of the pupils,[42] and some elements of a system developed by Ekman and associates [43,44] for evaluating subtle, small, and short-lived shifts in facial expression. However, analysis of microfacial expressions and pupillary dilation generally requires the use of recording equipment and represents methods that may not be practicable for field operatives.

Verbal Cues

We should listen closely to what people say. Verbal cues to deception involve what people actually say, i.e., the content of their communication. Researchers have attempted to develop methods for evaluating verbal behaviors more systematically.[45] Two approaches frequently cited are Statement Validity Assessment and Reality Monitoring, both of which have been extensively reviewed by Vrij.[36] Overall, these methods seek to validate statements on the assumption that true statements differ from fabricated ones in a variety of significant dimensions.[41,46]

Statement Validity Assessment involves the use of criteria-based content analysis,[47,48] which attempts to provide some common methodology for evaluating the content of verbal communications. These criteria include analyses of the logic and structure of verbal reports along with the presence or absence of various types of details, context, and spontaneous, qualitative evaluations by the speaker of his or her own recall. Reality Monitoring attempts to determine the validity of statements by assessing the clarity and realism of a story, along with contextual information that indicates the presence or absence of details that link elements of time, space, and sensory perceptions with the primary content of a subject's story.[49] These techniques were originally developed to gauge whether allegations by children represented true statements, but laboratory studies using college students indicated that they could also be used with adults. Over time they were used to assess the likely truthfulness of statements made by criminal defendants vs. victims. The most recent analysis of their effectiveness, conducted by Vrij, [46] was restricted to field studies involving real-world criminal cases.

The results of studies on verbal behavioral cues appear rather positive. Generally, they indicate that deceptive narratives contained less content (e.g., fewer overall details, fewer unusual details, less contextual and sensory information, fewer quotations or descriptions of interactions), more logic problems (e.g., unstructured reproductions, less logical structure, less plausible relations), and differences in the subjects' expressed evaluations of their own stories (e.g., less expressed self-doubt, fewer tentatively phrased statements, more absolutely negative statements or complaints, fewer spontaneous corrections to the story, and lower frequencies of admitting to lack of clear recall). [36,41,46]

The same set of reviews, involving analysis of over 150 studies, suggested that several criteria used in both the Statement Validity Assessment and Reality Monitoring failed to differentiate true from false statements. These criteria included the degree of apparent complexity in statements, the presence of unexpected complications, self references, reports of subjective mental states, superfluous details, and descriptions of verbal and nonverbal interactions. Taken as a whole, neither the criteria set from the Statement Validity Assessment nor the Reality Monitoring approach appears sufficiently reliable and valid to serve as a unitary technique for evaluating the veracity of subject statements.[36,46-48,50-53] However, some of the component elements show promise.

Paralinguistic Cues

Most paralinguistic cues do not appear to be effective; however, voice stress analysis may merit further investigation. Paralinguistic cues encompass all those behaviors associated with the production of speech but separate from the actual content. As with nonverbal cues, the results appear rather disappointing. The rate at which subjects speak, the presence of various disturbances suggesting uncertainty (e.g., "ums" and "ahs"), the length of verbal response, various kinds of pauses, response latency, and loudness do not appear to be reasonable cues to deception.[41] However, the amount of time spent talking in a response, higher voice pitch, or other indications of voice tension appear to be potentially useful cues. Again, the changes in pitch or indications of voice tension have generally been sufficiently small that the unaided ear cannot discriminate them reliably. Previous reviews of voice stress technologies soundly criticized their reliability and validity.[29] Despite this, recurrent positive findings in this area[36,41,54,56] may suggest that voice stress analysis may have been dismissed prematurely.

Global Judgments

Focusing on specific cues to deception may actually narrow an observer's focus to the point of neglecting data that could be important for validating the source or the information itself. Instead of relying on the presence or absence of a specific cue to deception, some research has recorded global judgments of observers who are asked to synthesize their observations and assess subject behavior. These synthesized assessments show some promise in differentiating true vs. fabricated statements.[41,57] Specifically, people who were accurately identified as being deceptive were more likely to have been assessed by observers as less cooperative, more uncertain, more nervous, more ambivalent, more inconsistent in content presentation, less friendly or pleasant, and more expressive facially.

Moderator Variables

Many other variables may have an impact on our capacity to detect deception effectively. Examples of relevant research include studies on the impact of interviewer and interviewee personality characteristics,[58,59,60,61,62,63] expectancy effects,[13,64] social biases,[65-67] and interviewer and interviewee confidence,[68,69] to name a few. These studies highlight the very complex nature of this problem and the need for substantially more research on these moderator variables.

Promising Avenues

Alternative methods are emerging and merit study. Some research efforts have started to explore new methods for validating information. They include the use of probability theory to assess choice patterns, covert physiological sensor systems to assist observers in real time, challenges to story construction based on memory research,[41,70] and intentional distortion methodology to assess report stability vs. malleability.

Limitations of Current Research Findings

To this point, this review might suggest that some practical means are available to assist intelligence personnel in validating sources and information. Unfortunately, shortcomings in the research designs that tested these indicators dictate caution in relying upon these means at this point.

Motivational/Stress Problem

Most research subjects are relatively calm and undermotivated and do not represent the populations of interest. In real life, any interrogation situation is likely to cause high levels of physiological arousal and distress in innocent and guilty parties alike. Individuals who attempt to conceal information in real situations probably have a high level of motivation to deceive successfully. It is almost impossible to obtain the same levels of motivation and arousal in volunteer subjects. With the exception of field studies developed from real-world situations, most of the research conducted to date entails little or no stress or true incentive to deceive effectively: of 120 samples in the DePaulo analysis,[41] 68 samples were classified as using subjects who were under no stress. Researchers are acutely aware of this problem and have sought to develop laboratory situations that entail some degree of distress or arousal in subjects, but for the most part they have been unable to sample behavior involving moderate to higher ranges of motivation and arousal. It is not known whether these higher levels would result in different patterns of response, although that assumption seems logical.[71]

In most studies, individuals serving as observers/judges are asked to make assessments that have little personal significance. This situation is unlike that facing an intelligence collector, who would generally be highly motivated to obtain information.

Sampling Problems

Subject Sampling

Research has not looked at enough of the right kind of people. Most studies (over 80 percent) have used college students, while those in applied settings generally involve incarcerated criminals. The resultant problem is obvious. College students tend to be drawn from the upper end of the intellectual range, are more likely to come from relatively affluent socioeconomic backgrounds, and are much younger and more limited in life experience than the populations of interest in the national security context. While criminal populations may make generalization of findings more reasonable for law enforcement personnel, they present limitations for the intelligence collector. The population of criminals in the United States consists disproportionately of individuals in the low average range of intelligence or worse. In addition, criminals as a group are likely to have substantially more experience in interrogation/questioning situations than the rest of the population. Law enforcement may be at the point of developing real capabilities to work with below-average intelligence criminals and academic researchers may have a good understanding of above-average intelligence college students, but these results may have only limited relevance to intelligence collection.

Most studies also used a relatively small sample size, with an average of 40 subjects per study.[41] Such small samples may allow validation of only the most powerful cues and may discount many moderately effective ones.

Behavior Sampling

Most studies typically use very short snippets of data — commonly less than 1 minute — whereas in a real-world situation an interviewer may observe a subject over a much longer time frame, with the option of repeated contacts. Therefore, results to date may only reflect those variables that have efficacy in that short time frame.

Most studies involve people in an observer role who watch a tape of someone being questioned. In real-world applications, the people responsible for detecting deception are likely to be participating in the exchange and to be working by themselves. Research suggests that in the participant mode detection success is likely to be below 50%, or at the level of chance.[72,73]

Finally, much of the research uses a 50/50 paradigm, wherein the base rate of true vs. false reports is equal. The likelihood that this reflects reality seems small. Our results to date may thus represent a skewed construction of the real-world problem.

Cross-Cultural Representation

We know almost nothing about how our current methods work with various Asian, Middle Eastern, Central and South American, or African populations. Research to date has focused primarily on samples drawn from modern, Western countries (primarily the United States and Europe), with a few studies involving Jordanian,[74,75] Saudi,[58] Chinese,[76,77] and Japanese[78,79] subjects. Of all the limitations in the existing body of research literature, this is the most troubling. In the DePaulo review of studies involving 120 samples, 101 were drawn from the United States or the United Kingdom and only 4 came from non-Western cultural groups.[41] Thus, from the standpoint of intelligence gathering, they do not address the populations of interest and utility. Although Ekman and his associates hold that microfacial expression changes represent a fairly universal phenomenon.[80,81,82] there is little evidence to suggest the existence of universals in nonverbal and paralinguistic behaviors across cultures. This absence of universals may also hold true even for speech content analysis.[77] Until a technique can be reasonably evaluated with a specific cultural group, it would be unwise to assume that technique has utility with that group.

Summary of Findings

We do not really know what we think we know. Overall, knowledge of behavioral indicators that might assist in the detection of deception is very limited and provides little reliable information that could assist intelligence collectors operating anywhere outside the United States or Europe. Despite some progress in the ability to assess common criminals, results gleaned from the domestic population of criminals and college undergraduates may help us little in dealing with uncooperative detained soldiers or committed and possibly resistance-trained followers of radical movements.

Very little is actually known about current populations of interest. In addition, this review failed to locate a single study examining the impact on deception detection of using interpreters/translators in questioning subjects. There is little reason to assume that data generalize across cultures, particularly Third World populations.

The severe methodological shortcomings in research to date should lead us to question whether what we think works really does, or what we think doesn't work indeed does not. Existing research results, drawn from non-stressful situations, may have prompted the premature abandonment of potentially useful methods.

Suggested Approaches

The U.S. government needs to implement an aggressive, focused strategic plan for supporting behavioral research and developing enhanced capabilities to validate information and sources. Such a plan should focus on understanding actual behavior and prioritize projects on the basis of operational needs, operational realities, cost, and potential return on investment.

Operational Needs

The Intelligence Community should work with field operatives to identify and prioritize their most important and urgent operational needs and associated research goals. Examples might include screening public transportation passengers, improving interrogation techniques and results, validating embassy walk-ins as legitimate sources, or improving field operatives' capacity to elicit and validate information from sources in the field and rebuild a viable human intelligence capability. The length of time needed to develop and field a method should be one consideration.

Operational Realities

The primary tool in human intelligence collection is the operative on the ground. This role necessitates moving within the society of potential sources and talking to individuals who may or may not be motivated to assist the United States in obtaining information. The practical reality is that this individual cannot carry around a polygraph machine, an electroencephalogram, or any other elaborate, bulky equipment. High technology-assisted methods may be appropriate at ports of entry, where it is possible to control movement and contact with subjects within a fixed facility, but such technology would be of limited use for most collection tasks. Moreover, electroencephalograms and magnetic resonance imaging are often relatively easy to defeat.[2,33,83-85] The Intelligence Community needs to provide operatives the necessary tools and training to work effectively with contacts on the ground. It is in this environment that behavioral techniques may have the most potential value.

Cost

High-technology programs naturally cost more to research and field than behavioral methods.

Return on Investment

The Intelligence Community should consider the research and development costs, the time it takes to push the results of the investment into the field, and the potential impact on mission accomplishment. In this light, development of behavioral methods may have an advantage, given that the near-term cost is low, the payoffs can be high, and the techniques can be rapidly moved into the field.

Recommendations

The Intelligence Community should follow certain guidelines when considering how to proceed:

1. Study actual behavior that may indicate deception, rather than cultural myths about such indicators. The two are not the same.

2. Avoid simple replication of the research already conducted. At this point, we may know as much as we can and need to know about college students in the United States and Europe. New research should overcome at least some of the limitations of previous studies outlined earlier.

3. Insist on targeted populations of interest. The absence of research using subjects who represent the cultural groups of interest to the Intelligence Community is the most significant problem with research to date.

4. Focus on techniques that can be readily taught to the current generation of field operatives. Even more important, focus on developing techniques that are practical in terms of the real-world parameters where they will be applied.

5. Emphasize field testing to allow rapid assessment, revision, and adaptation of methods.

6. Integrate field operations personnel in prioritizing, developing, and refining new tools. This will ensure a reality check before time, money,

and personnel are wasted on concepts that sound good in the laboratory but often are impractical in the field.

7. Stay ahead of the competition. The center of mass for research in this area should not be China,[76] Japan[2,5,31,78,85,86] or even Israel.[2,23] Every technique has its limitations, and aggressive discovery will also allow the United States to stay ahead of competitors and provide training and countermeasures to ensure U.S. personnel retain a field advantage.

8. Make and maintain a commitment. When the next major terrorist attack occurs, the government should honestly be able to say, "We did the best we could."

References

1. Akehurst, L., R. Bull et al. (2004). "The Effects of Training Professional Groups and Lay Persons to Use Criteria-Based Content Analysis to Detect Deception." *Applied Cognitive Psychology* 18, 877-891.

2. Ben-Shakar, G., and Dolev, K. (1996). "Psychophysiological Detection through the Guilty Knowledge Technique: Effect of Mental Countermeasures." *Journal of Applied Psychology* 81(3), 273-281.

3. Burgoon, J.K., Buller, D.B., Ebesu, A.S., and Rockwell, P. (1994). "Interpersonal Deception: V. Accuracy in Deception Detection." *Communication Monographs* 61 (4), 303-325.

4. Chahal, K., and Cassiday, T. (1995). "Deception And Its Detection In Children: A Study Of Adult Accuracy." *Psychology, Crime and Law* 1 (3), 237-245.

5. Colwell, K., C. K. Hiscock et al. (2002). "Interviewing Techniques and the Assessment of Statement Credibility." *Applied Cognitive Psychology* 16, 287-300.

6. DePaulo, B. M., and Pfeifer, R. L. (1986). "On-The-Job Experience and Skill at Detecting Deception." *Journal of Applied Social Psychology*, 16, 249-267.

7. DePaulo, P.J., and DePaulo, B.M. (1989). "Can Deception by Salespersons and Customers Be Detected Through Nonverbal Behavioral Cues?" *Journal of Applied Social Psychology* 19 (18, part 2), 1552-1577.

8. Ekman, P. (1996). "Why Don't We Catch Liars?" *Social Research* 63 (3), 801-817.

9. Ekman, P., O'Sullivan, M. and Frank, M.G. (1999). "A Few Can Catch a Liar." *Psychological Science* 10 (3), 83-86.

10. Ekman, P., and O'Sullivan, M. (1991). "Who Can Catch a Liar?" *American Psychologist* 46 (9), 913-920.

11. Frank, M.G., Paolantonio, N., Feeley, T.H., and Servoss, T.J. (2004). "Individual and Small Group Accuracy in Judging Truthful and Deceptive Communication." *Group Decision and Negotiation* 13 (1), 45-49.

12. Garrido, E., and Masip, J. (1999). "How Good Are Police Officers at Spotting Lies?" *Forensic Update* 58, 14-21.

13. Granhag, P.A., and Stromwall, L.A. (2000). "Effects of Preconception on Deception Detection and New Answers to Why Lie-Catchers Often Fail." *Psychology, Crime and Law* 6 (3), 197-218.

14. Kraut, R. E., and Poe, D. (1980). "Behavioral Roots of Person Perception: The Deception Judgments of Customs Inspectors and Laymen." *Journal of Personality and Social Psychology* 39, 784-798.

15. Levine, T. R., Park, H. S., and McCornack, S. A. (1999). "Accuracy in Detecting Truths and Lies: Documenting the 'Veracity Effect'." *Communication Monographs* 66 125-144.

16. MacLaren , V. V. (2001). "A Quantitative Review of the Guilty Knowledge Test." *Journal of Applied Psychology* 86 (4), 674-683.

17. Mann, S., Vrij, A., and Bull, R. (2004). "Detecting True Lies: Police Officers' Ability to Detect Suspects' Lies." *Journal of Applied Psychology* 89 (1), 137-149.

18. Porter, S., Woodworth, M., and Birt, A.R. (2000). "Truth, Lies, and Videotape: An Investigation of the Ability of Federal Parole Officers to Detect Deception." *Law and Human Behavior* 24 (6), 643-658.

19. Vrij, A., Edward, K., Roberts, K.P., and Bull, R. (2000). "Detecting Deceit Via Analysis of Verbal and Nonverbal Behavior." *Journal of Nonverbal Behavior* 24 (4), 239-263.

20. Vrij, A., Edward, K., and Bull, R. (2001). "Police Officers' Ability to Detect Deceit: The Benefit of Indirect Deception Detection Measures." *Legal and Criminological Psychology* 6 (2), 185-196.

21. Vrij, A., and Mann, S. (2001). "Who Killed My Relative? Police Officers' Ability to Detect Real-Life High-Stake Lies." *Psychology, Crime, and Law* 7, 119-132.

22. Wang, G., Chen, H., and Atabakhsh, H. (2004). "Criminal Identity Deception and Deception Detection in Law Enforcement." *Group Decision and Negotiation* 13 (2), 111-127.

23. Elaad, E. (1998). "The Challenge of the Concealed Knowledge Polygraph Test." *Expert Evidence* 6, 161-187.

24. Engelhard, I.M., Merckelback, H. and van den Hout, M.A. (2003). "The Guilty Knowledge Test and the Modified Stroop Task in Detection of Deception: An exploratory study." *Psychological Reports* 92 (2), 683-691.

25. Hirota, A, Sawada, Y., Tanaka, G, Nagano, Y., Matsuda, I., Takasawa, N. (2004). "A New Index for Psychophysiological Detection of Deception: Applicability of Normalized Pulse Volume." *Journal of Physiological Psychology and Psychophysiology* 21 (3), 217-230.

26. Podlesny, J. A., and Raskin, D. (1977). "Physiological Measures and the Detection of Deception." *Psychological Bulletin* 84, 782-799.

27. Amato-Henderson, S.L. (1997). "Effects of Misinformation As Revealed Through the Concealed Knowledge Test." *Dissertation Abstracts International: Sciences and Engineering.* 57 (8-B), 5370.

28. Raskin, D. C., Kircher, J. C., Horowitz, S. W., and Honts, C. R. (1988). "Recent Laboratory and Field Research on Polygraph Techniques." In J. C. Yuille (ed.), *Credibility Assessment*. Dordrecht, Netherlands: Kluver Academic Publishers.

29. Haddad, D., Walter, S., Ratley, R., and Smith, M. (2002). "Investigation and evaluation of voice stress analysis technology." U.S. Department of Justice, unpublished final report.

30. Farwell, L. A., and Donchin, E. (1991). "The Truth Will Come Out: Interrogative Polygraphy ("Lie Detection") With Event-Related Brain Potentials." *Psychophysiology* 28(5), 531-547.

31. Hira, S., and Matsuda, T. (1998). "Contingent Negative Variation (CNV) in the Detection of a Deception Task Using a Serial Presentation of Pictures." *Japanese Journal of Psychology* 69 (2), 149-155.

32. Rosenfeld, J.P., Rao, A., Soskins, M., Reinhart-Miller, A. (2003). "Scaled P300 Scalp Distribution Correlates of Verbal Deception in an Autobiographical Oddball Paradigm: Control for Task Demand." *Journal of Psychophysiology* 17 (1), 14-22.

33. Soskins, M.R. (2002). "Profile Measures in and Countermeasures to Brainwave Based Deception Detection." *Dissertation Abstracts International: The Sciences and Engineering* 63 (4-B), 2102.

34. Fiedler, K, Schmid, J., and Stahl, T. (2002). "What is the Current Truth about Polygraph Lie Detection?" *Basic and Applied Psychology* 24 (4), 313-324.

35. Patrick, C. J., and Iacono, W. G. (1991). "Validity of the Control Question Polygraph Test: The Problem of Sampling Bias." *Journal of Applied Psychology* 76 (2), 229-238.

36. Vrij, A. (2000). *Detecting Lies and Deceit: The Psychology of Lying and the Implications for Professional Practice*. Chichester, UK: Wiley.

37. Anderson, D. E., DePaulo, B. M., Ansfield, M. E., Tickle, J. J., and Green, E. (1998). "Beliefs about cues to deception: Mindless Stereotypes or Untapped Wisdom?" *Journal of Nonverbal Behavior* 23, 67-89.

38. Bond, C. F., Kahler, K. N., and Paolicelli, L. M. (1985). "The Miscommunication of Deception: An Adaptive Perspective." *Journal of Experimental Social Psychology* 21, 331-345.

39. Stromwall, L.A., and Granhag, P.A. (2003). "How to Detect Deception? Arresting the Beliefs of Police Officers, Prosecutors and Judges." *Psychology, Crime and Law* 9(1), 19-36.

40. Vrij, A., Semin, G. R., and Foppes, J.H. (1996). "Lie Expert's Beliefs about Nonverbal Indicators of Deception." *Gedrag en Organisatie* 9 (1), 15-28.

41. DePaulo, B. M., Lindsay, J. J., Malone, B. E., Muhlenbruck, L., Charlton, K., and Cooper, H. (2003). "Cues to Deception." *Psychological Bulletin* 129 (1), 74-118.

42. Lubow, R.E., and Fein, O. (1996). "Pupillary Size in Response to a Visual Guilty Knowledge Test: New Technique for the Detection of Deception." *Journal of Experimental Psychology: Applied* 2 (2), 164-177.

43. Ekman, P. (1993). "Facial Expression and Emotion." *American Psychologist* 48 (4), 384-392.

44. Ekman, P., and Friesen, W. V. (1978). *Facial Action Coding System.* Palo Alto, CA: Consulting Psychologists Press.

45. Newman, M.L., Pennebaker, J.W., Berry, D.S., and Richards, J.M. (2003). "Lying Words: Predicting Deception from Linguistic Styles." *Personality and Social Psychology Bulletin* 29 (5), 665-675.

46. Vrij, A. (2005). "Criteria-Based Content Analysis: A Qualitative Review of the First 37 Studies." *Psychology, Public Policy, and Law* 11 (1), 3-41.

47. Rassin, E. (2000). "Criteria-Based Content Analysis: The Less Scientific Road to Truth." *Expert Evidence* 7 (4), 265-278.

48. Ruby, C.L., Brigham, J.C. (1997). "The Usefulness of the Criteria-Based Content Analysis Technique in Distinguishing Between True and Fabricated Allegations: A Critical Review." *Psychology, Public Policy, and Law* 3 (4), 705-737.

49. McCornack, S. A., and Parks, M. (1986). "Deception Detection and the Other Side of Trust." In M. L. McLaughlin (ed), *Communication Yearbook* 9 (377-389). Beverly Hills, CA: Sage.

50. Doris, J. (1994). "Commentary on Criteria-Based Content Analysis." *Journal of Applied Developmental Psychology* 15 (2), 281-285.

51. Gumpert, C.H., and Linblad, F. (2000). "Expert Testimony on Child Sexual Abuse: A Qualitative Study of the Swedish Approach to Statement Validity Analysis." *Expert Evidence* 7 (4), 279-314.

52. Masip, J., Sporer, S.L., Garrido, E., and Herrero, C. (2005). "The Detection of Deception with the Reality Monitoring Approach: A Review of the Empirical Evidence." *Psychology, Crime and Law* 11 (1), 99-122.

53. Parker, A.D., and Brown, J. (2000). "Detection of Deception: Statement Validity Analysis as a Means of Determining Truthfulness or Falsity of Rape Allegations." *Legal and Criminological Psychology* 5 (2), 237-259.

54. Druckman, D., Rozelle, R. M., and Baxter, J. C. (1982). *Nonverbal Communication.* Beverly Hills: Sage.

55. Dulaney, E. F. (1982). "Changes in Language Behavior as a Function of Veracity." *Human Communication Research* 9, 75-82.

56. Zuckerman, M, DeFrank, R. S., Hall, J. A., Larrance, D. T., and Rosenthal, R. (1979). "Facial and Vocal Cues of Deception and Honesty." *Journal of Experimental Social Psychology* 15, 378-396.

57. Feeley, T. H., and deTurck, M. A. (1995). "Global Cue Usage in Behavioral Lie Detection." *Communication Quarterly* 43, 420-430.

58. Alanazi, F. M., and Rodriguez, A. (2003). "Power Bases and Attribution in Three Cultures." *The Journal of Social Psychology* 143 (3), 375-395.

59. Burgoon, J.K., Buller, D.B., and Guerrero, L.K. (1995). "Interpersonal Deception: IX. Effects of Social Skill and Nonverbal Communication on Deception Success and Detection Accuracy." *Journal of Language and Social Psychology* 14 (3), 289-311.

60. Feeley, T. H., and Young, M. J. (2000). "Self-Reported Cues about Deceptive and Truthful Communication: The Effects of Cognitive Capacity and Communicator Veracity." *Communication Quarterly* 48, 101-119.

61. Millar, M.G., and Millar, K. (1995). "Detection of Deception in Familiar and Unfamiliar Persons: The Effects of Information Restriction." *Journal of Nonverbal Behavior* 19 (2), 69-84.

62. Porter, S., Campbell, M.A., Stapleton, J. (2002). "The Influence of Judge, Target, and Stimulus Characteristics on the Accuracy of Detecting Deception." *Canadian Journal of Behavioural Science* 34 (3), 172-185.

63. Vrij, A., and Graham, S. (1997). "Individual Differences between Liars and the Ability to Detect Lies." *Expert Evidence: The International Digest of Human Behaviour Science and Law* 5, 144-148.

64. Kassin, S.M., Goldstein, C.C., and Savitsky, K. (2003). "Behavioral Confirmation in the Interrogation Room: On The Dangers of Presuming Guilt." *Law and Human Behavior* 27 (2), 187-203.

65. Hartwig, M., Granhag, P.A., Stromwall, L.A., and Anderson, L.O. (2004). "Suspicious Minds: Criminals' Ability to Detect Deception." *Psychology, Crime and Law* 10 (1), 83-95.

66. Meissner, C.A., and Kassin, S.M. (2002). "'He's Guilty!': Investigator Bias in Judgments of Truth and Deception." *Law and Human Behavior* 26 (5), 469-480.

67. O'Sullivan, M. (2003). "The Fundamental Attribution Error in Detecting Deception: The Boy-Who-Cried-Wolf Effect." *Personality and Social Psychology Bulletin* 29 (10), 1316-1327.

68. Cole, T. (2005). "Deception Confidence in Romantic Relationships: Confidently Lying to the One You Love." In Shohov, S.P. (ed), *Advances in Psychology Research* 34, 127-139.

69. DePaulo, B.M., Charlton, K., Cooper, H., Lindsey, J.J., and Muhlenbruck, L. (1997). "The Accuracy-Confidence Correlation in the Detection of Deception." *Personality and Social Psychology Review* 1 (4), 346-357.

70. Fisher, R. P., and Geiselman, R. E. (1992). *Memory-Enhancing Techniques for Investigative Interviewing: The Cognitive Interview.* Springfield, IL: Charles C. Thomas.

71. Frank, M.G., and Feeley, T.H. (2003). To Catch A Liar: Challenges for Research in Lie Detection Training. *Journal of Applied Communication Research* 31 (1), 1-15.

72. Buller, D.B., Strzyzewski, K.D., and Hunsaker, F.G. (1991). "Interpersonal Deception: II. The Inferiority of Conversational Participants as Deception Detectors." *Communications Monographs* 58 (1), 25-40.

73. Granhag, P.A. and Stromwall, L.A. (2001). "Deception Detection: Interrogators' and Observers' Decoding of Consecutive Statements." *The Journal of Psychology* 135 (6), 603-620.

74. Al-Simadi, F.A. (2000). "Detection of Deceptive Behavior: A Cross-Cultural Test." *Social Behavior and Personality* 28 (5), 455-461.

75. Bond, C.F., Jr., and Atoum, A.O. (2000). "International Deception." *Personality and Social Psychology Bulletin* 26 (3), 385-395.

76. Le, J., Wu, X, and Cao, N. (2002). "An Assessment of Decision-Making in Deception Detection: A Trial of Bayesian Theory." *Psychological Science* (China) 25 (6), 656-659.

77. Wong, J. (2000). "The Token 'Yeah' in Nonnative Speaker English Conversation." *Research on Language and Social Interaction* 33 (1), 39-67.

78. Fukoda, K. (2001). "Eye Blinks: New Indices for the Detection of Deception." *International Journal of Psychophysiology* 40 (3), 239-245.

79. Kam, K.Y. (2004). "A Cultural Model of Nonverbal Deception Communications: The Independent and Interdependent Self-Construals as Predictors of Deceptive Communication Motivation and Nonverbal Behavior under Deception." *Dissertation Abstracts International: Humanities and Social Sciences* 65 (1-A), 22.

80. Ekman, P., Friesen, W.V., O'Sullivan, M., Chan, A., Diacoyanni-Tarlatzis, I., Heider, K., Krause, R., LeCompte, W.A., Pitcairn, T., Ricci-Bitti, P.E., Scherer, K., Tomita, M., and Tzavaras, A. (1987). "Universal and Cultural Differences in Judgments of Facial Expressions of Emotion." *Journal of Personality and Social Psychology* 53 (4), 712-717.

81. Ekman, P. (1994). "Strong Evidence for Universals in Facial Expression: A Reply to Russell's Mistaken Critique." *Psychological Bulletin* 115, 268-287.

82. Izard, C. E. (1994). "Innate and Universal Facial Expressions: Evidence from Developmental and Cross-Cultural Research." *Psychological Bulletin* 115, 288-299.

83. Honts, C. R., Raskin, D. C., and Kircher, J. C. (1994). "Mental and Physical Countermeasures Reduce the Accuracy of Polygraph Tests." *Journal of Applied Psychology* 79 (2), 252-259.

84. Rosenfeld, J.P., Soskins, M., Bosh, G., and Ryan, A. (2004). "Simple, Effective Countermeasures to P300-Based Tests of Detection of Concealed Information." *Psychophysiology* 41(2), 205-219.

85. Sasaki, M., Hira, S., and Matsuda, T. (2001). "Effects of a Mental Countermeasure on the Physiological Detection of Deception Using the Even-Related Brain Potentials." *Japanese Journal of Psychology* 72 (4), 323-328.

86. Yamamura, T., and Sasaki N. (1990). "Heart Rate as an Index of Psychophysiological Detection of Deception in the Guilty Person Paradigm Using the Paired Control Question Technique." *Japanese Journal of Physiological Psychology and Psychophysiology* 8 (2), 61-69.

4
Mechanical Detection of Deception: A Short Review

Kristin E. Heckman, D.Sc.
Mark D. Happel, D.Sc.
with the assistance of
Janice R. Ballo, Research Librarian
The MITRE Corporation
November 2005

Abstract

This paper presents a short review of the mechanical methods developed to detect deception over the past century. The paper is divided into two main sections, psychophysiological mechanisms and neurological mechanisms, based on the two primary means of mechanically acquiring the metrics used to detect deception. Within these two sections, each mechanism and its potential for deployment is described.

The development of a more effective means for detecting deception is predicated on research to build a sound theoretical basis on which to design such a system. The study finds that, despite the polygraph's shortcomings, there is currently no viable technical alternative to polygraphy. While some neuroscience-based alternatives have been proposed, there are significant problems with these techniques and far more research is needed if they are to become sufficiently reliable for use in operational settings.

Introduction

Society has long wished to combat corruption, crime, and dishonesty by using scientific techniques and technologies. The notion that honesty can be found and identified scientifically has led to the development of a variety of deception detection mechanisms throughout the last century. The value of some of these mechanisms is limited, either because the mechanism's validity has drawn recurrent rejection (e.g., truth serums) or for policy reasons (e.g., the polygraph).

The need for accurate and reliable means of detecting attempts by individuals to deceive others, particularly intelligence and law enforcement professionals, is compelling. Yet it is all too readily apparent that the current technical and methodological means for detecting intentional deception by individuals are inadequate.

Given this need and a century of effort, why has no effective solution been found to the problem of detecting deception? Myriad opinions have been put forth to answer this question, but it is clear that this is an exceedingly difficult problem, in part because of the difficulty of defining the general concept of deception (Happel, 2005).

Psychophysiological Mechanisms

Psychophysiology is a branch of science that studies subtle physiological changes (such as respiration and skin surface temperature) that are not readily evident to either an outside observer or the individual. Researchers study these changes in autonomic (involuntary) and somatic (somewhat more controllable) responses to understand the psychological processes of the organism as a whole. These physiological changes are then used to indicate and differentiate among these psychological processes.

Needless to say, there is much debate in the scientific community as to the validity of the assumption that autonomic and somatic responses reflect cognitive and/or emotional processing. Some evidence supports the link between specific emotional states and certain physiological responses, such as startle/surprise and increased periorbital temperature (Pavlidis and Levine, 2002). However, there is no evidence supporting the assumption that autonomic and somatic responses reflect intentional deception. Although some of these measurements have been correlated, to varying degrees, with intentional deception (or, at least, with the emotional response that generally accompanies such deceptive strategies), there is no widely accepted scientific theory that demonstrates a causal link between the cognitive processes involved in deception and the autonomic and somatic responses measured by mechanisms such as the polygraph. Unanswered questions remain with regard to individual differences in deception that result from the impact of individual life experiences on underlying emotional, cognitive, and social processes. These unanswered questions extend to differences in cultural and ethnic-based beliefs, attitudes, and practices regarding truth and deception. These questions must be addressed before significant progress can be made in using psychophysiological means to detect deception by individuals.

This section discusses several technologies that measure autonomic and somatic responses to detect deception. These include the polygraph, electrogastrogram, radar vital signs monitor, facial expressions, eye blinks, saccades, and fixations, voice stress analysis, thermal imaging, and truth serums/narcoanalysis. It should be noted that the Department of Defense Polygraph Institute (DoDPI) is researching several emerging technologies, including laser Doppler vibrometry (LDV) and Eye Movement Memory Assessment (EMMA). LDV is a method of remotely measuring and assessing individual physiological responses to emotional stress. Changes in respiration, cardiovascular activity, muscle contraction, and body tremor can be measured from a distance of hundreds of feet when there is a direct line of sight. EMMA is an eye tracking system that follows the pattern of a subject's visual attention to a scene, specifically how the subject's eye scans a familiar object versus an unfamiliar object. The DoDPI has published no review studies to date. These methods may hold promise, but are not currently ready for deployment.

Polygraph

Subtle bodily changes such as heart rate, blood pressure, and skin resistance are amplified and recorded onto a multichannel writing instrument known as the polygraph. The polygraph is typically used in conjunction with one or more of a set of related tests: the Guilty Knowledge Test (GKT), also known as the Concealed Information Test (CIT) (Ben-Shakhar and Elaad, 2002); the Comparison Question Test or Control Question Test (CQT) (Raskin and Honts, 2002); or the Relevant/ Irrelevant Test (RIT) (Iacono, 2000). It should be noted that although the CQT is the most widely used test in North America, its scientific validity has been criticized (Gronau et al., 2005; Ben-Shakhar et al., 2002). In contrast, the GKT/ CIT, widely used only in Japan, has been supported as an objective test (Gronau et al., 2005; Ben-Shakhar et al., 2002).

The typical method of scoring the physiological records is for the polygrapher to look globally at the charts for a "lie response": an assumed specific response pattern uniquely associated with lying. Another, more objective, method of scoring the charts is to measure the relative magnitude of the responses (Backster, 1962); that is, when the difference between the relevant and control question response levels reaches a certain quantitative point, the decision is made to classify the examinee as deceptive.

The polygraph is the most widely employed technical means for detecting deception. It is also perhaps the most controversial. Almost since its introduction, polygraphy and its direct technological ancestors have been the subjects of legal proceedings and Supreme Court decisions, including the Frye case (*Frye v. United States*, 54 App. D.C. 46, 293 F. 1013 [1923, D.C. Cir.], in which the testimony of polygraph pioneer William Marsten was excluded) and the more recent Scheffer case (*United States v. Scheffer*, 523 U.S. 303 [1998]). Ironically, the federal government relies extensively on the polygraph for forensic investigations and personnel security, yet the results of polygraph tests are generally inadmissible in federal courts (Greeley, 2004).

Potential

The accuracy of the polygraph is a matter of controversy. Some researchers believe that the current system with the CQT is no better than chance (c.f. Ben-Shakhar, 1991; Furedy, 1996; Saxe, 1991). Other researchers estimate the accuracy at 75% to 80% (i.e., one error, on average, in four to five trials): Elaad and others (1992) with the GKT/CIT, MacLaren (2001) with the GKT/CIT, and Patrick and Iacono (1991) with the CQT. Supreme Court Justice John P. Stevens found "a host of studies that place the reliability of polygraph tests at 85 to 90 percent" (*United States v. Scheffer*, 523 U.S. 303, 333, quoted in Greeley, 2004, p. 129).

The use of the polygraph for security screening or prescreening has been particularly controversial. There is little research into the screening application compared to polygraphy focused on single-issue criminal cases (Iacono, 2000; Krapohl, 2002). In 1983, the U.S. Congress's Office of Technology Assessment concluded that "the available research evidence does not establish the scientific validity of the polygraph test for personnel security screening" (Office of Technology Assessment, 1983). Recently, the National Academy of Sciences published a critical review of the state of the art in polygraphy, in which it concluded that:

> Polygraph testing yields an unacceptable choice for [Department of Energy] DOE employee security screening between too many loyal employees falsely judged deceptive and too many major security threats left undetected. Its accuracy in distinguishing actual or potential security violators from innocent test takers is insufficient to justify reliance on its use in employee security screening in federal agencies (Committee to Review the Scientific Evidence on the Polygraph, 2002, 6-8).

These findings, particularly those related to error rates (especially the rate of false positives for innocent subjects) and the lack of basic theoretical support, lead to the conclusion that polygraphy, as currently implemented in the United States, is insufficient for meeting the needs of national security via employee/individual screening. The process and application of polygraph testing can be further improved, although it cannot currently be determined whether these improvements will meet national security requirements. However, the use of the GKT/CIT in conjunction with other psychophysiological measures (such as skin conductance response, respiration line length, eye blink rate, and finger-pulse volume) has shown promise in distinguishing between informed and uninformed subjects (Ben-Shakhar and Dolev, 1996; Ben-Shakhar et al., 1999; Elaad and Ben-Shakhar, 1997; Timm, 1982; Cutrow et al., 1972). Use of the GKT/CIT for employee/individual screening would require pre-examination work to acquire known factual data for the development of relevant item sets to test the subject's veracity.

Electrogastrogram

The electrogastrogram (EGG) is a device used to diagnose the improper functioning of stomach muscles or of the nerves controlling those muscles. Electrodes placed on the stomach surface measure the electrical waves, or pulses, as they progress downward from the top of the stomach. The stomach typically pulses three times per minute.

Two researchers (Hutson, 2005) conducted an experiment to test their hypothesis that the gastrointestinal tract is uniquely sensitive to mental stress because of the communication between the central nervous system and the enteric nervous system. Sixteen subjects were given a set of playing cards and told not to reveal them. Simultaneous EGG and electrocardiogram (EKG) recordings were taken as the subjects viewed pictures of playing cards on a computer, and responded to questions as to whether the viewed cards matched any of those in their set of cards. Subjects were instructed to lie only if one of the viewed cards matched one of the cards in their hand. Subjects were offered $20 for lying successfully. The result showed that both lying and truth-telling affected cardiac symptoms; however, only lying was associated with gastric symptoms. The EGG showed a significant decrease in the percentage of normal gastric slow waves when the subject was lying that corresponded to a significant increase in the average heart rate.

Potential

EGG is a non-invasive procedure that usually takes approximately three hours in a clinical, diagnostic setting. As with the polygraph, EGG recordings would be subject to artifacts from anxiety and stress that may not result from intentional deception. EGG measurements are also subject to motion artifacts (such as respiration, cardiac signals, and possible myoelectrical activity from other organs) that can spoil the results (Liang et al., 1997). These artifacts can be removed manually with much subjectivity, or via commercially available signal processing software run on a personal computer.

The results of the EGG are analyzed by waveform and spectral analysis methods, thereby requiring a powerful personal computer. It is likely that this technique would have to be combined with another to increase its accuracy and reliability in detecting deception. Given that only one study has been conducted to date using this technique in a deception detection task, more research is needed to determine the accuracy and reliability of this method.

Radar Vital Signs Monitor

The radar vital signs monitor (RVSM) remotely measures psychophysiological motion processes such as heartbeat, respiration, and eye blinks using electromagnetic waves in the gigahertz frequency range. For example, the RSVM does not sense the actual heartbeat but the motion of the chest and body during cardiac and respiration cycles (Geisheimer and Greneker, 2000; Geisheimer and Greneker, 2001).

This technology is the product of several research projects conducted over the past ten years at the Georgia Tech Research Institute (GTRI). Experiments conducted at GTRI have shown that respiration and heartbeat data can be sensed from nearly any portion or orientation of the thorax. The RVSM had to be slightly modified to detect eye blinks. Although the researchers believe other eye motions may be present in the signals, they produce smaller amplitudes than the eye blinks (Geisheimer and Greneker, 2000; Geisheimer and Greneker, 2001).

Potential

RVSM technology is non-invasive, portable, and remote. RVSM can be placed out of the subject's sight; such covert use of this technology could diminish the use of countermeasures. However, because of RVSM's sensitivity in detecting motion, any stray motions within the sensor's beam will be measured and potentially could interfere with the desired signal. Body movements such as rocking or swaying could be potential countermeasures to this technology. Sophisticated signal processing is required to extract the desired signal from the noise. Potential solutions to these movement countermeasures are being researched (Geisheimer and Greneker, 2000; Geisheimer and Greneker, 2001).

RVSM transmits at a frequency of 24.1 GHz, where skin reflects approximately 73% of the wave; the rest of the energy is quickly dissipated in the first several millimeters of the body. Given radiation safety concerns, the Federal Communications Commission (FCC) radio frequency exposure regulations have set a maximum permissible exposure level of 1 mW/cm^2 averaged over thirty minutes for a transmission frequency of 24.1 GHz. These exposure limits can be met at a distance of 12.85 cm from the RVSM transmitter (Geisheimer and Greneker, 2000; Geisheimer and Greneker, 2001).

Because RVSM technology measures some of the same psychophysiological responses as the polygraph, it is subject to the same criticisms (see Section 2.1). Due to the lack of published results in the literature, it appears that researchers have not yet explored this technology in the context of detecting deception. Given this lack of scientific validation, RVSM is probably not ready to be deployed.

Facial Expressions

Human emotional responses can be recognized through facial expressions (Ekman, 1994; Izard, 1994). According to Ekman (1972), a specific set of facial expressions appears to be generated by the emotions of anger, disgust, fear, happiness, sadness, surprise, and to a lesser degree contempt, embarrassment, interest, pain, and shame. Ekman (1972) further states that these emotions are universally generated and recognized across all cultures. Ekman and Friesen (1978) developed the Facial Action Coding System (FACS) to measure all visible facial muscle movements, not just those presumed to be related to emotion, as well as head and eye movements. In approximately 100 to 300 hours, an individual can learn to code facial expressions based on the characteristic pattern of bulges, wrinkles, and movements for each facial Action Unit (AU), as well as to code the intensity of each AU. Ekman and Friesen (1978) identified forty-four AUs that can occur singly or in complex combinations.

A review of the literature shows that research into automatic recognition of FACS AUs is limited (Tian et al., 2003). Deception detection experiments have only coded FACS AUs manually (Ekman, 1985; Ekman et al., 1991; Frank and Ekman, 1997). Despite this, the current state of the art is briefly reviewed here. In 2001, two teams (Carnegie Mellon University and the University of Pittsburgh — referred to as CMU/Pitt, and the University of California, San Diego, and the Salk Institute — referred to as UCSD/Salk) were tasked to quantitatively analyze spontaneous facial expressions to estimate AUs (Cohen et al., 2001; Bartlett et al., 2001). Both teams independently developed a non-intrusive automatic facial expression recognition system capable of handling non-frontal pose, moderate out-of-plane head motion, and moderate occlusion from head motion, eyeglasses, gestures, talking, subtle facial actions, and rapid facial motion. It should be noted that neither system was fully automated; each involved some degree of manual preprocessing. The CMU/Pitt team (Cohen et al., 2001) required less manual preprocessing than the UCSD/Salk team (Bartlett et al., 2001). Both systems were tested with spontaneous facial behavior video recorded from a prior study of deception (Frank and Ekman, 1997). However, no analysis was made of AUs based on deception/truth-telling conditions. Only two AU categories were recognized: eye blinks (see the section on "Eye Blinks, Saccades and Fixations" below) and brow region movement. The CMU/Pitt team recognized AUs in the brow region with 57% accuracy, and the UCSD/Salk team recognized brow raises with 91% accuracy and discriminated between brow raises and brow lowering with 94% accuracy. All of these accuracies were based on agreement with human coders.

Since these first efforts in 2001, two real-time, fully automated systems have been developed to recognize facial expressions (Tian et al., 2003; Littlewort et al., 2004). Both systems classify facial expressions according to the following emotion categories: happiness, sadness, surprise, disgust, fear, anger, and neutral. One significant difference in the testing of these two systems is that Littlewort et al. (2004) tested their system on a group of subjects instructed to generate a specific series of facial expressions, whereas Tian et al. (2003) tested their system on subjects looking at other subjects who displayed spontaneous facial expressions. This difference is relevant for real-world applications because it has been shown that spontaneous facial expressions differ from posed expressions in several ways (Ekman, 1991).

Potential

Spontaneous facial expression measures can be recorded non-intrusively, and without the subject's awareness, provided there is direct line of sight. The measures can be made in real time via portable technology (a video camera and computer system capable of high-speed image processing). However, to date there has been no research into an automated means of measuring deception on the basis of facial expressions. Measurements of facial expressions and deception have been limited to manual coding by trained humans, which is labor intensive, human-observer dependent, and difficult to standardize. Significant research efforts are required to determine whether FACS measurements are sufficient for an automated system to distinguish between truth and deception; that is, whether measures of additional factors, such as body posture and tone of voice, might be necessary.

Eye Blinks, Saccades, and Fixations

An eye blink occurs when one or both eyes are closed and opened rapidly. Ocular movements are typically divided into fixations and saccades. A saccade is a rapid, intermittent eye movement that occurs when the eyes look quickly from one thing to another. The human eye saccades because only the central part of the retina has a high concentration of color-sensitive nerve endings that are capable of formulating a high-resolution mental map of the scene being viewed. The eye fixates when it pauses in a particular position. The resulting series of fixations and saccades is called a scanpath.

The literature has explored eye blinks and their relationship to cognitive processes, particularly attention and vigilance; however, only one study of their relationship to deception has been found. Fukuda (2001) measured subject eye blinks while performing a guilty knowledge card test using an automatic eye blink analysis system developed by Matsuo and Fukuda (1996). With this head-mounted video recording system, it is possible to identify blinks and their timing with respect to stimuli, and to analyze the eye blink waveform. Ten subjects were presented with eight sets of five playing cards, and instructed to select one of the five cards in each of the eight sets to be the "lie" card. Subjects were then serially presented with the five cards on a computer display, and pressed a "no" key to indicate that none of the five cards presented was the card they had selected. The results showed that subject blink rate pattern discriminated between relevant and irrelevant stimuli.

The CMU/Pitt team (Cohn et al., 2001; Moriyama et al., 2002) measured and classified eye blinks with their automated facial expression analysis system. Their system achieved an overall accuracy of 98%, with 100% accuracy between blinks and non-blinks, in an analysis of 335 single and multiple blinks and non-blinks. These accuracies were based on agreement with human coders. The UCSD/Salk team (see the previous section, "Facial Expressions") also achieved an overall accuracy of 98% for detecting blinks (Bartlett et al., 2001). Both of these studies used spontaneous facial behavior video recorded from a prior study of deception (Frank and Ekman, 1997) for testing. However, no analysis was made of eye blinks based on deception/truth-telling conditions.

The literature on saccadic eye movement is similar to the eye blink literature in that much attention is paid to inferences about cognitive activity, but only one study of saccadic eye movement and deception has been found. Baker et al. (1992) studied the horizontal eye movements of ten subjects responding to autobiographical questions presented via a computer display. The subjects initially answered all questions truthfully, then were told to lie in response to a subset of the questions. The authors partitioned subject reaction time into three components. The first was the time spent reading the questions. This component did not distinguish between the deception and truth conditions. The second was the time spent thinking of an answer (i.e., think time). This component identified lying in five of the ten subjects. The third was the time spent fixating during think time. The measure of this component was significantly longer for nine subjects in the deception condition. These results suggest that saccadic eye movements during response generation are irrelevant to deception. Instead, the amount of fixation time during think time, when it is assumed that subjects are generating responses, is more indicative of deception.

Baker and others (Baker et al., 1992) also studied saccadic and fixation activity during the five-second inter-trial interval (ITI); that is, during the period of time after which one question has been removed from the computer screen and the subject has indicated readiness for the next question, and before the next question appears on screen. The authors hypothesized that during the ITI, subjects may be reviewing their answers. Based on their results, the authors rejected this hypothesis and concluded that the effects of a trial ended with the subject's indication of readiness for the next trial.

Potential

Eye blink measurements can be recorded non-intrusively and without the subject's awareness, provided there is direct line of sight. The measurements can then be automatically post-processed, with some minimal amount of manual preprocessing required. Although this processing (both pre and post) cannot be conducted in real time, the technology (a video camera and computer system capable of high-speed image processing) is portable. To date, no research results suggest any characteristic pattern(s) of eye blinks, saccades, or fixations that correlate with deceptive behavior. Much more research must be conducted to determine, first, whether eye behavior is indicative of underlying deception, and second, the accuracy of systems measuring this behavior in real-world situations with ethnically diverse individuals.

Voice Stress Analysis

Voice stress analysis (VSA), sometimes called psychological stress evaluation (PSE), is based on the use of a machine developed in 1964 by Charles R. McQuiston. Presumably, this machine detects laryngeal micro-tremors in the voice. When people speak, air is pushed upward from the lungs to the vocal cords. This causes the vocal cords to vibrate as the air continues to flow upward to the mouth, through the tongue, teeth, and lips to form speech. According to McQuiston, the amount of blood in the vocal cords drops as a result of stress and the micro-tremors disappear. The voice stress analyzer searches for the disappearance of this normal tremor when the individual speaks (Van Damme, 2001).

VSA was developed because the U.S. Army wanted "a remote lie detector" as an alternative to the polygraph (i.e., one that did not require physical contact with the subject's body). Given that the transmission of these micro-tremors and the stress occur simultaneously, VSA could be used to analyze a narrative conversation, not just "yes" or "no" responses (this was considered an additional advantage over the polygraph). The first VSAs appeared on the market in 1970, a product of Dektor Counterintelligence and Security, Inc. (McQuiston was one of its founders). Approximately twelve years later, the Verimetrics system (also invented by McQuiston) appeared. This system allowed personal computers to produce charts. The Computer Voice Stress Analyzer (CVSA) appeared on the market shortly thereafter. The CVSA allowed real-time analysis by eliminating the need to record on magnetic tape. There have been additional adaptations of the VSA, such as the Diogenes Voice Stress Analysis System in 1996, Truster in 1997, and Truster Pro/Vericator in 1998.

Potential

Research has not yet established a consistent relationship between micro-tremors and deception. Scientific evidence has shown that VSAs are not effective in detecting deception, and that none of the VSAs has yielded detection rates above chance levels in controlled situations (Horvath, 1982; Hollien et al., 1987). A 2002 final report on the investigation and evaluation of VSA technology, funded by the U.S. Department of Justice, concluded that

> It is clearly unlikely that a single measure such as that based on the CVSA, could be universally successful in assessing stress (such as that which might be experienced during the act of deception). However, it is not inconceivable that under extreme levels of stress, that muscle control throughout the speaker will be affected, including muscles associated with speech production. The level and degree to which this change in muscle control imparts less/more fluctuations in the speech signal cannot be conclusively determined, since even if these tremors exist, their influence will most certainly be speaker dependent (Haddad et al., 2002).

The preliminary results from a comparative analysis of the CVSA, the Vericator, and the polygraph showed that the CVSA and the Vericator performed no better than the polygraph in correctly classifying subjects as deceptive. The Vericator, however, was more accurate than the polygraph in correctly identifying truthful subjects (Palmatier, 1996). Although VSAs are field deployable, the results to date suggest that the reliability of VSA technology does not exceed that of the polygraph.

Thermal Imaging

Microcirculation and changes in underlying muscle activity have an impact on skin surface temperature (SST). A variety of additional factors, such as embarrassment and sweating, also effect changes in facial SST. Radiant energy or natural heat (infrared) emissions from the human body can be measured via a technique known as thermography. Infrared radiometry can be used to measure body surface heat non-invasively, that is, via a camera, with no skin contact. The camera is typically connected to and controlled by a personal computer running software designed for thermal imaging. This technology allows for real-time, highly automated data analysis.

Two studies have been published on the use of thermal imaging to measure facial SST during deception detection tasks. One of these studies was conducted by the DoDPI in conjunction with a group from Honeywell Laboratories led by Ioannis Pavlidis. These two groups have produced a series of publications (Ryan and Pollina, 2002; Pavlidis and Levine, 2001; Pavlidis et al., 2002; Pavlidis, 2004), all of which appear to be based on the same study originally conducted at DoDPI. The study used a mock crime scenario in which participants stabbed a mannequin and stole its money. The papers report different results in regard to the percentage of correctly identified guilty subjects (subjects who lied about their innocence):

DoDPI reports 70% (Ryan and Pollina, 2002), Pavlidis (2004) and Pavlidis and Levine (2001) report 78%, and Pavlidis et al. (2002) report 75% (this is probably because the papers report a variety of cohort sizes).

This thermal imaging study was conducted in conjunction with a polygraph examination. According to the DoDPI report, thermal imaging of the eye and nose facial region, combined with the polygraph, resulted in the highest accuracy rates: 83% for polygraph and SST of the eye and nose regions, compared to 67% for the polygraph alone. It should be noted that DARPA has funded research conducted by Pavlidis and others (Murthy et al., 2004; Murthy and Pavlidis, 2005) to measure breathing function remotely via thermal imaging.

The second study was conducted by Barron Associates, Inc. (BAI) and researchers from the University of Virginia (Burkholder and Parker, 2005). However, the results of this study are proprietary, and distribution is limited to U.S. government agencies only.

Potential

Thermal imaging allows rapid, automated analysis of changes in regional facial blood flow. It can be conducted non-invasively, covertly, and in real time. A thorough review of the literature revealed that only two investigations of thermal imaging and deception have been conducted to date. This suggests that thermal imaging is an emerging technology requiring more investigation and more peer review from the scientific community before it is ready for deployment.

Truth Serums/Narcoanalysis

A variety of drugs have been referred to as truth serums: scopolamine, sodium amytal, and sodium pentothal. All of these drugs inhibit control of the nervous system and reduce inhibitions. Currently, sodium amytal and sodium pentothal are used most commonly as anesthetics, and less commonly to recover repressed memories (Odesho, 2004). However, the three substances are best known as a result of being administered as "truth drugs" during police interrogations. Their use in all of these settings is sometimes referred to as narcoanalysis. When these serums are used, it is assumed that the subject will respond to questions by providing truthful answers, or at least what the subject believes to be truthful answers, because the drug makes it difficult for the subject to provide false information.

Dr. Robert House initiated the use of "truth serum" in the 1920s when he interrogated two suspected criminals injected with scopolamine (Winter, 2005). During the 1930s the Scientific Crime Detection Laboratory (SCDL) at Northwestern University conducted experiments with scopolamine, both in the laboratory and in criminal investigations. This highly visible work lent support for scopolamine and other drugs in extracting truthful information (Winter, 2005). Although a number of studies were conducted in the 1940s and 1950s to assess both the accuracy and veracity of truth serum-derived information, their results varied significantly (Odesho, 2004). In the decades to follow, truth serums were used by the U.S. military and intelligence agencies during the Cold War and the Korean War to release repressed memories, detect soldier malingering, and conduct prisoner of war (POW) interrogations (Odesho, 2004). During the 1950s and 1960s, a U.S. intelligence agency had active programs of developing and testing drugs with truth serum properties, such as LSD (Select Committee on Intelligence, 1977).

Potential

Truth serums do not force the subject to tell the truth. Instead, they typically cause the subject to become more talkative. Thus, although a subject's inhibitions have been lowered, there is no guarantee that any of the information elicited will be accurate. Given that none of these substances has been shown to be 100% effective in obtaining truthful information, there has been much dispute regarding the legality and ethical implications of their use. *State v. Pitts* was a precedent-setting case on the admissibility of sodium amytal interview evidence. The New Jersey Supreme Court concluded in 1989 that:

> This evidence [sodium amytal] was excluded by the trial court. The Court now predicates its approval of the trial court's exclusion of this evidence on two factors: the use of the sodium amytal interview as a means to ascertain the "truth" of defendant's belief or motive for killing the victim...

> The experts further concurred that the results of a sodium amytal interview are not considered scientifically reliable for the purpose of ascertaining truth as such. Nevertheless, the results of sodium amytal are useful (Supreme Court of New Jersey, 1989).

Although other jurisdictions reject the admissibility of truth serum interview evidence for the purpose of establishing truth in a legal setting, the use of these drugs for interrogation purposes has been reconsidered in the wake of recent terrorist activities (Odesho, 2004; Keller, 2005). The Department of Justice's Office of Legal Counsel sent a memorandum to the President in 2002, suggesting that such use might be permissible (Bybee, 2002).

Throughout history, truth serums have been correlated with abusive interrogations and involuntary confessions (Winter, 2005). Article 17 of the 1949 Geneva Convention Relative to the Treatment of Prisoners of War places restrictions on the detainment powers that may be used to interrogate POWs; however, the language does not outlaw the use of truth serums (Geneva Convention, 1949). Given that this international law applies only to prisoners of war, the interpretation of POW status will likely further cloud the legal and ethical debate surrounding the resurgence of truth serums.

Neurological Mechanisms

Dissatisfaction with the lack of a clear causal chain from the psychological decision to deceive, to the autonomic functions (e.g., skin conductance, respiration) currently measured by the polygraph, has led some researchers to seek measurements that are closer to the biophysical seat of decision making. The field of neuroscience has long sought to "understand the biological basis of consciousness and the mental processes by which we perceive, act, learn, and remember" (Kandel, 2000, p. 5). Revolutionary improvements in neuroscientific techniques, combined with the sophisticated signal processing techniques made practical by advances in information processing technology over the past few decades, have made it possible to observe the neurophysiological processes of the brain itself with increasingly greater resolution in time and space.

This section reviews these advanced techniques for studying the relationship between cognitive and neural processes. These include electroencephalography, magnetoencephalography, positron emission tomography, functional magnetic resonance imaging, near infrared spectroscopy, and transcranial magnetic stimulation. Empowered by these techniques, some neuroscience researchers have chosen to forgo the measurement of autonomic responses and seek instead to correlate deception and brain neurophysiology.

Electroencephalography (EEG)

EEG measures the changes in the electrical field potentials produced by the sum of the neural postsynaptic potentials in the brain by means of electrodes placed on the surface of the skin covering the head and face. The changes directly related to specific perceptual or cognitive events are called event-related potentials (ERPs). EEG/ERP studies require sophisticated signal processing to separate the ERP components from the ongoing baseline electrical waves and consequently require substantial computing power. EEG laboratories in the early 1980s typically relied upon cumbersome, room-sized computers, while advances in information processing technology have made EEG using desktop computers a practical reality.

Investigations of EEG/ERP as a means for detecting deception date back to the late 1980s. Rosenfeld et al. (1987) and Donchin and Farwell (1991) reported success using EEG techniques to identify specific ERPs that were correlated to the recognition of guilty knowledge. In 1991 the Central Intelligence Agency (CIA) funded Farwell to further develop his technique, but chose not to continue the funding after an independent panel reported in 1993 that the developer was unwilling to release details of his approach, viewing them as proprietary. Further, the CIA, Secret Service, and FBI considered the technique to be of limited value because it was based on a guilty knowledge paradigm and was therefore useless for screening applications (United States Government Accounting Office, 2001). EEG-based deception detection research is ongoing (e.g., Rosenfeld et al., 2004; Vendemia et al., 2003).

Potential

EEG-based approaches have the advantages of good temporal resolution, equipment that is relatively portable (at least in comparison to some of the other alternative technologies), and present few safety concerns. On the negative side, the higher density electrode arrays used in some approaches are tricky and time-consuming to emplace properly, and the experience of wearing the electrode array while being questioned may be onerous for some (although children undergoing EEG examinations in clinical situations seem to tolerate the experience reasonably well). Rosenfeld et al. (2004) have found these techniques to be vulnerable to certain kinds of countermeasures by the subject. Simple countermeasures such as facial movement may create artifacts. In addition, because the P300 component of the ERP represents cognitive activity occurring within 300–500 milliseconds after stimulus onset, stimulus presentations must be repeated for the data to be based on summation waveforms (Donchin and Farwell, 1991).

Magnetoencephalography (MEG)

Neuronal activation results in a flow of electrical currents, which produces a weak magnetic field. The magnetic field can be measured by a magnetometer placed outside the skull. This method of recording brain activity is called magnetoencephalography (MEG). The area in the brain that has been activated by a stimulus can be localized by detecting the magnetic fields measured by a series of MEG recordings.

A thorough review of the literature revealed no studies dealing with MEG and deception, though there is active research on a closely related topic: MEG and memory. Temporal resolution is one reason MEG is used in studies of memory as opposed to other neuroimaging technologies. That is, MEG allows a detailed analysis of the timing of changes in activation associated with recognition. Gonsalves et al. (2005) conducted a prototypical study using MEG and the "remember" versus "know" recognition memory paradigm. This paradigm can be generally described as follows. Subjects are presented with previously viewed stimuli and novel stimuli. The subjects are instructed to respond based on the type of memory they have for the stimulus: that is, if they can recollect the exact episode in which they saw the stimulus, they would give a "remember" response; if they have a "feeling of knowing" the stimulus, they would give a "know" response. Finally, if the subjects believe they have never seen the stimulus before, they would give a "new" response.

The results of the Gonsalves study suggest that the medial temporal cortex rapidly signals memory strength by way of reduced activations. The authors conclude that this may provide a basis for the subjective perception of whether a stimulus is familiar ("remember" or "know") or novel ("new"). The ability to establish "ground truth" relevant to an individual's memory would clearly assist the process of detecting deception. It should be noted that this method is comparable to the GKT/CIT when it is used in conjunction with skin conductance, heart period variability, and respiratory sinus arrhythmia.

Potential

MEG is a noninvasive technique. However, it is typically performed with a large, expensive piece of instrumentation that must be contained in an expensive, magnetically shielded room to reduce external magnetic disturbances. MEG is therefore not portable. MEG recordings are subject to artifacts from eye blinks, eye movements, and mechanical movements of the body that occur in conjunction with heartbeat and breathing. Subjects must remove all magnetic material, such as watches, jewelry, and eyeglasses, to prevent these types of movement artifacts.

The results of the study discussed in this section suggest that further MEG studies may assist in understanding the role of memory within the evolving set of candidate neural subsystems (discussed elsewhere in the Neurological Mechanisms subsections) involved in the generation of deception. However, given the apparent lack of published studies on MEG and deception, it is clear that MEG is not yet ready for deployment.

Positron Emission Tomography (PET)

Positron emission tomography (PET) is a nuclear medicine medical imaging technique. The first human PET scanner was developed in 1973. A PET scanner produces a three-dimensional image of functional brain activity. First, a radiolabeled positron emitting tracer is injected into a subject's bloodstream. This tracer stays in the bloodstream and moves via circulation. Blood flows at different rates in the brain depending on the level and location of neural activity. Areas of higher blood flow will contain a larger amount of radioactive tracer, and will therefore emit a stronger signal. This signal is measured by the PET scanner, which scans slices of the brain. The images of these slices are then used to compare the distribution of radioactivity, thus allowing a nuclear medicine physician or radiologist to map the changes in regional cerebral blood flow (rCBF) that accompany changes in neuronal activity.

To date, only one study has been conducted using PET to measure brain activity during deception (Abe et al., 2005). In this study, subjects viewed photographs related to experienced and unexperienced events. In one deception condition, subjects were instructed to lie in response to the photos of experienced events: that is, they were to pretend not to know the experienced event. In the other deception condition, subjects were instructed to lie in response to the photos of unexperienced events: that is, they were to pretend to know the unexperienced event. During both types of deception, the dorsolateral, ventrolateral, and medial prefrontal cortices were active. The anterior cingulate cortex was active only during the deception condition in which subjects were pretending not to know.

Activation of the dorsolateral and ventrolateral cortices and the anterior cingulate cortex support the findings of several functional magnetic resonance imaging (fMRI—see section below) studies of deception (Langleben et al., 2002; Ganis et al., 2003; Kozel et al., 2004a,b). However, there is some conflict between this PET study and previous fMRI studies in regard to the laterality of dorsolateral prefrontal cortex activation. The PET study showed significant activation in the left hemisphere, whereas Kozel et al. (2004a) reported activation in the right hemisphere, Lee et al. (2002) in the bilateral hemisphere, Kozel et al. (2004b) in the more anterior part of the prefrontal cortex with right dominance, and Ganis et al. (2003) reported bilateral activation. It is possible that this conflict is due to the different experimental designs used in these studies; however, these conflicts clearly indicate the need for more neuroimaging studies of deception.

The differences in experimental design may also explain the activation of the anterior cingulate cortex only during the pretending not to know condition, versus the consistent anterior cingulate activation reported by Langleben et al. (2002), Ganis et al. (2003), and Kozel et al. (2004a,b).

Potential

PET scanning is invasive and non-portable. Scientific PET investigations require clearance by an ethics committee because of the injection of radioactive material, and because multiple scans of a subject should be limited. Only a few hospitals and universities can perform PET scans because of the high costs of producing the radioisotopes used in the process. Given these limitations, and that the laboratory results of one PET study conflicted with the results of several fMRI studies of deception, this technology is not ready to be deployed.

Functional Magnetic Resonance Imaging (fMRI)

fMRI is a relatively recent technique (circa early 1990s) that uses a powerful static magnetic field, usually 1.5 to 5 tesla (T) or more, to align the nuclear spins of protons in the sample under study (e.g., the subject's brain). If the equilibrium spin alignment is perturbed with a transmitted radiofrequency pulse, the sample will emit a corresponding transmission as it returns to equilibrium. Because the magnetic properties of oxygenated hemoglobin differ from those of deoxygenated hemoglobin, the emitted signal is differentiable. Consequently, the fMRI system can form a sequence of images of the brain indicating those areas in which the oxidative brain metabolism — and, by inference, the neural activity — is higher during the performance of one task than in another (e.g., lying compared to telling the truth). fMRI relies on large superconducting magnets, cooled with cryogens to within a few degrees of absolute zero, to produce the intense static magnetic field required.

The last five years have seen the publication of several research papers describing the use of fMRI as a means of detecting deception.

- Spence et al. (2001) investigated subjects who saw or heard statements about their own activities that day and signaled whether they concurred with the statement by pressing the appropriate button (yes or no). However, if the display used a particular color, the subject was to "lie" by pressing the incorrect button.
- Langleben et al. (2002) used images of playing cards to implement a modified version of the polygraph GKT/CIT paradigm. Participants were given a playing card and instructed to attempt to fool a computer that was evaluating their responses by denying that they had that particular card when queried, but to respond truthfully otherwise. The subjects were promised a modest reward ($20) if they succeeded.
- Lee et al. (2002) investigated a malingering paradigm in which subjects pretended to have a memory impairment by making intentional errors, at their own discretion, during a forced-choice memory task using numbers and autobiographical information.

- Ganis et al. (2003) examined the differences between truthful responses and memorized lies that fit into a plausible but fictitious autobiographical story, and spontaneous lies that were not part of a coherent story. Subjects responded to visually presented questions using button presses or verbal responses, received auditory cues instructing them whether or not to lie, and were told that a human judge would review their responses to try to tell if they were lying.
- Kozel et al. (2004a) had the subjects visit a room that contained six objects, of which two were resting on $50 bills. During the subsequent testing, the subjects were instructed to report accurately the association of one of the objects with the bill (subject's choice), and to report that the remaining bill had been located under a different object than in fact was the case. The subjects were promised they could keep the bills if they were able to fool a human research assistant as to the actual location of the bills.

While each of the above studies reported the ability to distinguish deceptive and truthful responses on the basis of the fMRI spatial images, there were also significant differences among the results. This is hardly surprising, given the differences between the study designs. Some of the key differences include whether the subject can choose to lie or is told to do so, the stimulus and response modalities, the subjects' motivation and emotional involvement, the specific kind of lie being probed, and the subject's degree of involvement with a human judge of deceit (the deceived or target individual described above).

Potential

As a device for detecting deception, fMRI has some significant disadvantages. It is not portable; the typical fMRI facility usually consists of the fMRI device itself (including a superconducting magnet weighing 20,000 lbs or so) located in a magnetically shielded room, a separate control room, and an equipment room filled with amplifiers, power supplies, computers, and data storage devices. These facilities require a significant capital investment. The noise level during scanning is uncomfortably high (necessitating protective ear coverings), and even relatively minor head motion during the scan can spoil the results. Such movements could be effective countermeasures for resistant subjects. There are also some safety hazards associated with MRI. Some injuries, including at least one fatality, have occurred when metallic objects were brought into the scanning room (against established safety policies) and were hurled by the intense magnetic field into the magnet's bore (where the unfortunate subject was located). Because the magnetic field can also dislodge surgically implanted ferromagnetic materials, such as pins or aneurysm clips, not everyone can be safely scanned by MRI. In addition, pregnant women and people with claustrophobia are generally not scanned for research purposes (Huettel, Song, and McCarthy, 2004).

Some researchers are attempting to commercialize the results of early neuroscience-based research efforts. Farwell formed the firm Brain Fingerprinting Laboratories to promote his EEG-based technique following the termination of his government funding. Langleben has applied for a patent for an fMRI-based approach, and No Lie MRI, Inc. (www.noliemri.com) is working to commercialize it. Likewise, Kozel and George have applied for a patent for another fMRI-based approach and are, in conjunction with Cephos Corp., working to develop and market it. Despite these start-up efforts, and the attention fMRI has attracted from the press, its use in detecting deception is clearly still in its infancy. No current brain imaging test has been shown to diagnose common psychiatric disorders such as schizophrenia (Williamson, 2002). It therefore is unlikely that a behavior as complex as deception can currently be "diagnosed" with any of the existing brain imaging techniques.

Functional Near-Infrared-Spectroscopy (fNIRS)

Functional near-infrared spectroscopy (fNIRS) is a functional optical imaging modality that measures changes in the concentration of deoxygenated and oxygenated hemoglobin during functional brain activation. Brain activation increases rCBF, which, in turn, increases regional cerebral blood oxygenation. Oxygenated and deoxygenated hemoglobin exhibit characteristic optical properties in the visible and near-infrared light range. Because of this, concentration changes in regional oxygenated and deoxygenated hemoglobin during brain activation (e.g., while a subject is engaged in a task such as lying) can be measured optically. This is done by introducing specific wavelengths of light at the scalp. The depth at which this light can be accurately measured is approximately two centimeters below the scalp (Villringer and Chance, 1997). The ability to monitor brain function with fNIRS was demonstrated in 1993 (Hoshi and Tamura, 1993; Kato et al., 1993).

Two studies have been conducted to date using fNIRS with the GKT/CIT (Bunce et al., 2005; Izzetoglu et al., 2002). Izzetoglu et al. (2002) found that the level of hemoglobin oxygenation during the "lie" task was higher than the level during the "truth" task. Bunce et al. (2005) found that inferior and middle prefrontal cortical areas were associated with some forms of deliberate deception. These results corroborate the findings of several fMRI studies of deception (Ganis et al., 2003; Lee et al., 2002; Loughead et al., 2004; Spence et al., 2001). It should be noted that there were several limitations to the Bunce et al. fNIRS study. First, only a small area of the cortex was imaged; thus, the potential activity of other brain areas is unknown. Second, some precision in measuring rCBF was lost due to the placement of the optodes.

Potential

fNIRS is a minimally intrusive, portable, affordable system. However, it can only image cortex, and this is a limitation because fMRI studies have indicated that areas of the brain below two centimeters from the scalp (such as anterior cingulate cortex and superior frontal cortex) are active during deception (Ganis et al., 2003; Lee et al., 2002; Loughead et al., 2004; Spence et al., 2001). Whole-head fNIRS systems that would allow a greater area of the cortical surface to be imaged are being developed; however, they are not portable. Given these limitations and the few laboratory studies of fNIRS and deception conducted to date, this technology is not ready to be deployed.

Transcranial Magnetic Stimulation (TMS)

Transcranial magnetic stimulation (TMS) was introduced in 1985. It involves placing an electromagnetic coil on the scalp. A high-intensity current is then rapidly turned on and off in the coil. This produces a powerful magnetic field, with a strength of about 2T, that lasts for about 100 to 200 microseconds. The magnetic field passes through the skin, soft tissue, and skull, and induces an electrical current in neurons. This, in turn, causes a neuronal depolarization that can have observable behavioral effects, such as body movement and speech production difficulties, as well as unobservable effects, such as producing temporary scotomas (blind spots) and phosphenes (perceptual flashes of light). The area of depolarization is limited to a depth of about two centimeters below the brain's surface, because the magnetic field declines logarithmically with distance from the electromagnetic coil.

TMS has primarily been studied in conjunction with mood disorders, neurological disorders, and a variety of cognitive processes (such as language, memory, and emotion). To date there appears to have been only one study using TMS in a deception paradigm (Lo et al., 2003). In this study, subjects were to respond in their imagination (i.e., not verbally) to four sets of questions during TMS. These four sets of questions were divided into two types of response conditions: "Yes" or "No" (to questions such as "Are you a man?") and short, free-form responses (to questions such as "How old are you?"). The subjects were asked to respond truthfully to two sets of questions and untruthfully to the other two sets. Motor-evoked potentials (i.e., contractions of contralateral muscles) were also recorded. The results showed increased cortical excitability when subjects were generating deceptive responses. This was found in both types of response conditions (i.e., Yes/No and free-form). These results support the results of previous fMRI studies on deception (Spence et al., 2001; Lee et al., 2002; Langleben et al., 2002), which showed increased cortical activity, commonly in the premotor areas.

Potential

TMS is a non-invasive, portable technique. There are usually no adverse effects from TMS, though some subjects have reported mild headaches and discomfort at the site of the stimulation. This pain is most likely due to the repetitive stimulation of peripheral facial and scalp muscles, and responds well to treatment with aspirin or acetaminophen. Another known adverse effect is a high-frequency noise artifact that can cause short-term changes in hearing threshold. This can be avoided with the use of ear plugs. The most serious adverse effect has been seizure. Although the number of individuals who have received TMS is unknown, it is likely in the thousands. Seizures during TMS are known to have occurred in seven individuals, including six normal subjects (Wasserman et al., 1996a; Pascual-Leone et al., 1993; Wasserman et al., 1996b). The risk of seizure is related to the parameters of stimulation (magnetic intensity, pulse frequency, training duration, and inter-training intervals). No seizures have been reported with single-pulse TMS or repetitive TMS (rTMS, that is, repeated, rhythmic TMS) delivered at a slow frequency ($\leq$ 1 Hz, that is, once per second). Although there is a growing understanding of the rTMS parameter combinations that result in a spreading, excitatory neural response signaling an impending seizure, this risk may limit loosely supervised use of rTMS.

TMS will most likely be a valuable technique to the neuroscience community because it provides the capacity to excite or inhibit focal cortical areas, thereby elucidating causal relationships between neural structures and behavior. However, its effectiveness in detecting or inhibiting deceptive responses or thoughts has not been sufficiently explored. Additional studies and an established record of proper safety precautions are needed before TMS is ready for deployment.

Discussion

The review presented above clearly shows that every mechanical device that has been used to detect deception has both positive and negative aspects. VSAs, thermal imaging, and facial expression analysis are the only techniques that allow rapid, real-time analysis that is highly automated. However, the performance of VSAs in detecting deception has not been shown to exceed that of the polygraph; it does not even approach the accuracy of the polygraph used in conjunction with the GKT/CIT. The performance of thermal imaging has been demonstrated in only one peer-reviewed study. Systems for automatic analysis of facial expressions have not yet been tested in a deception detection experiment.

In terms of the invasiveness of the techniques, RVSM, facial expression analysis, eye blinks, saccades, and fixations, voice stress analysis, and TMS are non-invasive; the polygraph, EGG, EEG, MEG, fMRI, and fNIRS are invasive because they require physical contact; and truth serums/narcoanalysis and PET are the most invasive. In terms of portability, RVSM, facial expression analysis, eye blinks, saccades, and fixations, VSAs, truth serums/narcoanalysis, and TMS are the most portable; the polygraph, EGG, thermal imaging, EEG, and fNIRS are portable, but require more equipment; MEG, PET, and fMRI are not portable. To some extent, portability is highly correlated with cost because of the equipment required. However, the cost of technical expertise (such as that associated with the highly portable TMS) must also be considered.

Some of these mechanisms have proven useful for diagnostic purposes (e.g., EGG, EEG, MEG, PET, fNIRS, and fMRI) or treatment purposes (e.g., truth serums/narcoanalysis and TMS) in a clinical setting. However, these techniques are not devoid of potential physical side effects (e.g., TMS headaches). It should be noted that there may be accompanying psychological side effects as a result of undergoing a medical procedure (such as in individuals with "white coat syndrome"), or receiving medical treatment via truth serums/narcoanalysis (such as in individuals who recover unpleasant, repressed memories). The costs and benefits of using truth serums/narcoanalysis must especially be weighed given that there is currently no drug that produces "truth." In conjunction with these issues, ethical and legal issues must be taken into consideration before employing these types of techniques for non-clinical purposes such as detecting deception.

Conflicting Approaches

The most significant problem is that none of these mechanical devices has been scientifically shown to be capable of accurately and reliably detecting deception. Of the tests used in conjunction with these mechanical devices, only the GKT/CIT has been shown to be reliable and based on objective methods.

There are two schools of thought on the approach to solving this problem. One, referred to as "theory first," states that there must first be a sound theoretical basis on which to design such a system. The second, referred to as "system first," asserts that such a system can be developed in the absence of a theory.

Those who subscribe to the "theory first" school of thought believe that additional research is needed to assert and test hypotheses that explain why lying causes measurable changes (somatic, autonomic, or neurological), and not simply to establish a correlation between the act of lying and particular values of, or changes in, the observed features. They state that observation of a correlation, without knowledge of an underlying causal theory, requires several key assumptions before the results of the research can be used for operational purposes.

- According to the "accuracy assumption," the pattern of features correlated with deception will be present *if* deception is taking place. It also assumes that the test will in fact detect any of the possible types of deception the subject may choose to use and that the test is designed to detect (e.g., memorized scenarios).
- According to the "specificity assumption," the pattern of features correlated with deception will be observed *only if* deception is actually taking place. In other words, it will not be affected by one or more of the many other psychological or physiological processes that may also have been occurring during the research study (e.g., indigestion), but that may be mistaken for deception. Note that the use of a correlation with a theory provides no guidance as to what impact, if any, a countermeasure might have on the accuracy or specificity of the test.
- According to the "sample generalization assumption," the results of a research study based on the specific sample of subjects tested can be applied to any other sample drawn from the larger population of those requiring a polygraph test. The operational sample may include individuals who are significantly different in some respect from the sample used to determine the original correlation (e.g., subjects with psychopathological syndromes, subjects from other cultures, etc.).

Bashore and Rapp (1993) and Iacono (2000) recommended that research efforts directed toward the further development of polygraphy be abandoned in favor of basic research aimed toward the development of "a *science* of deception detection [emphasis in original]" (Iacono, 2000). Cacioppo and his colleagues have stated that:

> Little is gained, for instance, by simply generating an increasingly lengthy list of correlates between specific psychological variables and additional psychophysiological measures. A scientific theory is a description of causal interrelations. Psychophysiological correlations are not causal. Thus, in scientific theories, psychophysiological correlations are monstrosities. (Cacioppo, Tassinary, and Berntson, 2000, p. 20)

Unfortunately, without an underlying theory on which to base logical inferences, observation of a pattern correlated with deception for a given sample of the population gives little guidance as to when the above assumptions are valid. The only recourse is exhaustive testing of all of the possible combinations of factors, which is clearly an impractical undertaking.

Those who subscribe to the "system first" school of thought believe that it is possible to develop a functional and useful system without waiting for the development of an underlying theory that is universally accepted by the scientific community. They reason it is not likely that such a theory will be developed in the short term or that it will receive rapid peer review and acceptance by the scientific community. Rather than wait for this to come to fruition, the deception detection community would be better served by continuing to attempt to develop a device that works, and then later determining why the device works.

The logic behind this school of thought comes from the process of scientific understanding, that is, the cyclic process of developing hypotheses, making observations, testing the hypotheses, drawing conclusions, and modifying the hypotheses accordingly when they no longer support the dominant paradigm. Methods that work have been developed throughout history in medicine and other sciences in the absence of a correct theory, or with only a marginal understanding of how and why they work. For example, when aspirin was first used a century ago it was believed to have no effect on the heart, but it is now known that aspirin benefits the heart, and why (Nordenberg, 1999).

Current Status

In its study of polygraphy, the National Research Council concluded that:

> One cannot have strong confidence in polygraph testing or any other technique for the physiological detection of deception without an adequate theoretical and scientific base. A solid theoretical and scientific base can give confidence about the robustness of a test across examinees and settings and against the threat of countermeasures and can lead to its improvement over time. (Committee to Review the Scientific Evidence on the Polygraph, 2002, p. 3–27)

It is apparent that the "adequate theoretical and scientific base" must include a causal explanation of how the psychological processes involved in deception can result in the physiological or neurological processes observed during deception. Unfortunately, such an explanation will not be easy to develop and is unlikely to be available in the short term. The psychology of deception is not a mature field, and the neural mechanisms that underlie the ability to intentionally suppress, distort, or fabricate information are not yet well understood. Consequently, if the National Research Council is correct in stating that confidence in a given technique will require a solid theoretical base, then a significant research investment into the underlying neuropsychological mechanisms of deception must be made before any practical system for detecting deception can be developed and employed.

Even if the National Research Council is wrong, and the "system first" school of thought is correct, other problems may need to be solved before any practical system for deception detection can be developed, tested, and operationally deployed in the field. These problems are characteristic of experimentation in an artificial laboratory setting. Such research does not typically result in subjects' experiencing the same level of threat, motivation, stress, or fear that is likely to be experienced by a subject in a real-world situation involving detection of deception. The demographics of the cohorts used in these, usually university, experiments are likely to differ greatly from those of individuals of interest in the field. These problems make it difficult to use the findings of laboratory research as a basis on which to develop a practical deception detection system.

Thus, despite the polygraph's shortcomings, there is currently no viable technical alternative to polygraphy. After reviewing the EEG and fMRI deception detection efforts, as well as some other psychophysiological candidate techniques (e.g., VSA), the National Research Council concluded that "some of the potential alternatives show promise, but none has yet been shown to outperform the polygraph. None shows any promise of supplanting the polygraph for screening purposes in the near term" (Committee to Review the Scientific Evidence on the Polygraph, 2002, p. 6–15). This does not imply that these efforts have no value. On the contrary, the results to date show that these approaches have promise, and may even be viable in some situations where their level of accuracy is acceptable. However, much more research is needed if these techniques are to become operationally useful and reliable in situations that require a higher level of accuracy.

References

Abe, Nobuhito, Suzuki, Maki, Tsukiura, Takashi, More, Etsuro, Yamaguchi, Keiichiro, Itoh, Masatoshi, and Fujii, Toshikatsu. (2005). "Dissociable Roles of Prefrontal and Anterior Cingulate Cortices in Deception." *Cerebral Cortex*, DOI 10.1093/cercor/bhi097, 2 May.

Baker, L., Goldstein, R., and Stem, J. A. (1992). *Saccadic Eye Movements in Deception*. Report No. DoDPI92-R-0003, December. Department of Defense Polygraph Institute, Fort McClellan, Alabama.

Backster, C. (1962). "Method of Strengthening Our Polygraph Technique." *Police* 6, 61–68.

Bartlett, Marian S., Braathen, Bjorn, Littlewort-Ford, Gwen, Hershy, John, Fasel, Ian, Marks, Tim, Smith, Evan, Sejnowski, Terrence J., and Movellan, Javier R. (2001). *Automatic Analysis of Spontaneous Facial Behavior: A Final Project Report*. UCSD MPLab TR 2001.08, 31 October. University of California, San Diego and the Salk Institute, San Diego, California.

Bashore, T. R. and Rapp, P. E. (1993). "Are There Alternatives to Traditional Polygraph Procedures?" *Psychological Bulletin* 113, 3–22.

Ben-Shakhar, G. (1991). "Clinical Judgment and Decision-Making in CQT-Polygraphy: A Comparison with Other Pseudoscientific Applications in Psychology." *Integrative Physiological and Behavioral Science* 26 (3), 232–240.

Ben-Shakhar, G., and Elaad, E. (2002). "The Guilty Knowledge Test (GKT) as an Application of Psychophysiology: Future Prospects and Obstacles." In Kleiner, M. (ed), *Handbook of Polygraph Testing* (87–102). San Diego: Academic Press.

Ben-Shakhar, G., Bar-Hillel, Maya, and Kremnitzer, Mordechai. (2002). "Trial by Polygraph: Reconsidering the Use of the Guilty Knowledge Technique in Court." *Law and Human Behavior* 26 (5), October, 527–541.

Ben-Shakhar, G., and Dolev, K. (1996). "Psychophysiological Detection Through the Guilty Knowledge Technique: The Effects of Mental Countermeasures." *Journal of Applied Psychology* 81, 273–281.

Ben-Shakhar, G., Gronau, N., and Elaad, E. (1999). "Leakage of Relevant Information to Innocent Examinees in the GKT: An Attempt to Reduce False-Positive Outcomes by Introducing Target Stimuli." *Journal of Applied Psychology* 84, 651–660.

Bunce, Scott C., Devaraj, Ajit, Izzetoglu, Meltem, Onaral, Banu, and Pourrezaei, Kambiz. (2005). "Detecting Deception in The Brain: A Functional Near-Infrared Spectroscopy Study of Neural Correlates of Intentional Deception." *Proceedings of SPIE*, 5769, 24–32.

Burkholder, Jason O. and Parker, B. Eugene Jr. (2005). *Remote Thermal Imaging for Reliable Deception Detection*. Office of Naval Research, Report No. FTR_303, 14 March [Requires a Form 55].

Bybee, Jay S. (2002). Memorandum from Bybee, Assistant Attorney General, Office of Legal Counsel, to Alberto R. Gonzales, Counsel to the President, 1 August: http://news.findlaw.com/nytimes/docs/doj/bybee80102mem.pdf.

Cacioppo, J. T., Tassinary, L. G., and Berntson, G. G. (2000). "Psychophysiological Science." In Cacioppo, J. T., Tassinary, L. G., and Berntson G. G. (eds.), *Handbook of Psychophysiology* (2d ed.) (3–23). Cambridge, UK: Cambridge University Press.

Cohen, Jeffrey F., Kanade, Takeo, Moriyama, Tsuyoshi, Ambadar, Zara, Xiao, Jing, Gao, Jiang, and Imamura, Hiroki. (2001). *Final Report: A Comparative Study of Alternative FACS Coding Algorithms*, CIA Contract # 2000-A128400-000, 9 November. Carnegie Mellon University and University of Pittsburgh, Pittsburgh, Pennsylvania.

Committee to Review the Scientific Evidence on the Polygraph, Division of Behavioral and Social Sciences and Education, National Research Council (2002). *The Polygraph and Lie Detection*. Washington, DC: The National Academies Press.

Cutrow, R. J., Parks, A., Lucas, N., and Thomas, K. (1972). "The Objective Use of Multiple Physiological Indices in the Detection of Deception." *Psychophysiology* 9, 578–588.

Donchin, E. and Farwell, L. A. (1991). "The Truth Will Out: Interrogative Polygraphy ("Lie Detection") with Event-Related Brain Potentials." *Psychophysiology* 28 (5), September, 531–547.

Ekman, P. (1972). "Universal and Cultural Differences in Facial Expressions of Emotion." In Cole, J. K. (ed), *Nebraska Symposium on Motivation 1971* (207–283). Lincoln, NE: University of Nebraska Press.

Ekman, P. (1985). *Telling Lies: Clues To Deceit in the Marketplace, Politics, and Marriage*. New York, NY: Norton.

Ekman, P. (1994). "Strong Evidence for Universals in Facial Expression: A Reply to Russell's Mistaken Critique." *Psychological Bulletin* 115, 268–287.

Ekman, P. and Friesen, W. V. (1978). *The Facial Action Coding System*. Palo Alto, CA: Consulting Psychologists Press.

Ekman, P., O'Sullivan, M, Friesen, W. V., and Scherer, K. (1991). "Invited Article: Face, Voice, and Body in Detecting Deceit." *Journal of Nonverbal Behavior* 15, 125–135.

Elaad, E., Ginton, A, and Jungman, N. (1992, October). "Detection Measures in Real-Life Criminal Guilty Knowledge Tests." *Journal of Applied Psychology* 77 (5), 757–767.

Elaad, E., and Ben-Shakhar, G. (1997). "Effects of Item Repetitions and Variations on the Efficiency of the Guilty Knowledge Test." *Psychophysiology* 34, 587–596.

Frank, M. and Ekman, P. (1997). "The Ability to Detect Deceit Generalizes across Different Types of High-Stake Lies." *Journal of Personality and Social Psychology* 72, 1429–1439.

Fukada, Kyosuke. (2001). "Eye Blinks: New Indices for the Detection of Deception." *International Journal of Psychophysiology* 40, 239–245.

Furedy, J. J. (1996). "Some Elementary Distinctions among, and Comments Concerning, the 'Control' Question 'Test' (CQT) Polygrapher's Many Problems: A Reply to Honts, Kircher, and Raskin." *International Journal of Psychophysiology* 22 (1–2), April-May, 53–59.

Ganis, G., Kosslyn, S. M., Stose, S., Thompson, W. I., and Yurgelun-Todd, D. A. (2003). "Neural Correlates of Different Types of Deception: An fMRI Investigation." *Cerebral Cortex* 13, 830–836.

Geisheimer, J. and Greneker, E. F. III. (2000). "Remote Detection of Deception Using Radar Vital Signs Monitor (RVSM) Technology." *Proceedings, IEEE 34th Annual 2000 International Carnahan Conference on Security Technology*, Ottawa, Ontario, Canada, 170–173.

Geisheimer, J. and Greneker, E. F. III. (2001). "A Non-Contact Lie Detector Using Radar Vital Signs Monitor (RVSM) Technology." *IEEE Aerospace and Electronic Systems Magazine* 16 (8), August, 10–14.

Geneva Convention Relative to the Treatment of Prisoners of War. (1949). art 17, 6, UST. 3316, 12 August (consented to by the U.S. Senate on July 6, 1955, with reservations).

Gonsalves, Brian D., Kahn, Itamar, Curran, Tim, Norman, Kenneth A., and Wagner, Anthony D. (2005). "Memory Strength and Repetition Suppression: Multimodal Imaging of Medial Temporal Cortical Contributions to Recognition." *Neuron* 47, 1 September, 751–761.

Greely, H. (2004). "Prediction, Litigation, Privacy, and Property: Some Possible Legal and Social Implications of Advances in Neuroscience." In Garland, G. (ed), *Neuroscience and the Law: Brain, Mind, and the Scales of Justice* (114–156). New York: Dana Press.

Gronau, Nurit, Ben-Shakhar, Gershon, and Cohen, Asher. (2005). "Behavioral and Physiological Measures in the Detection of Concealed Information." *Journal of Applied Psychology* 90 (1), 147–158.

Haddad, Darren, Walter, Sharon, Ratley, Roy, and Smith, Meagan. (2002). "Investigation and evaluation of voice stress analysis technology." Document No 193832, 20 March, Award No. 98-LB-VX-A013.

Happel, M. D. (2005). "Neuroscience and the Detection of Deception." *Review of Policy Research* 22 (5), 667–685.

Hollien, H, Geison, L, and Hicks, J. W. Jr. (1987). "Voice Stress Evaluators and Lie Detection." *Journal of Forensic Science* 32 (2), March, 405–418.

Horvath, F. (1982). "Detecting Deception: The Promise and the Reality of Voice Stress Analysis." *Journal of Forensic Science* 27 (2), April, 340–351.

Hoshi, Y. and Tamura, M. (1993). "Detection of Dynamic Changes in Cerebral Oxygenation Coupled to Neuronal Function during Mental Work in Man." *Neuroscience Letters* 150, 5–8.

Huettel, S. A., Song, A.W., and McCarthy, G. (2004). *Functional Magnetic Resonance Imaging.* Sunderland, MA: Sinauer Associates.

Hutson, Stu. (2005). "Gut Reactions May Rumble a Liar." NewScientist.com Breaking News, October 31. Available at http://www.newscientist.com/article.ns?id=dn8238 as of 8 November, 2005.

Iacono, W. G. (2000). "The Detection of Deception." In Cacioppo, J. T., Tassinary, L. G., and Berntson G. G. (Eds.), *Handbook of Psychophysiology (2d ed.)* (772–793). Cambridge, UK: Cambridge University Press.

Izard, C. E. (1994). "Innate and Universal Facial Expressions: Evidence from Developmental Cross-Cultural Research." *Psychological Bulletin* 115, 288–299.

Izzetoglu, Kurtulus, Yurtsever, Gunay, Bozkurt, Alper, Yazici, Birsen, Bunce, Scott, Pourrezaei, Kambiz, and Oraral, Banu. (2002). NIR spectroscopy measurements of cognitive load elicited by GKT and target categorization. *Proceedings of the 36th Hawaii International Conference of System Sciences (HICSS'03)*, Hawaii.

Kandel, E. (2000). "The Brain and Behavior." In Kandel, E. R., Schwartz, J. H., and Jessell, T. M. (Eds.), *Principles of Neural Science (4th ed.)* (5-18). New York: McGraw-Hill.

Kato, T, Kamie, A, Takashima, S, and Ozaki, T. (1993). "Human Visual Cortical Function during Photic Stimulation Monitoring by Means of Near-Infrared Spectroscopy." *Journal of Cerebral Blood Flow Metabolism* 13, 516–520.

Keller, Linda M.. (2005). "Is Truth Serum Torture?" *American University International Law Review* 20 (3), 521–612.

Kozel, F. A., Padgett, T. M., and George, M. S. (2004a). "A Replication Study of the Neural Correlates of Deception." *Behavioral Neuroscience* 118, 852–856.

Kozel, F. A., Revell, L. J., Lorberbaum, J. P., Shastri, A., Elhai, J. D., Horner, M. D., Smith, A., Nohas, Z., Bohning, D. E., and George, M. S. (2004b). "A Pilot Study of Functional Magnetic Resonance Imaging Brain Correlates of Deception in Healthy Young Men." *Journal of Neuropsychiatry and Clinical Neuroscience* 16 (3), 295–305.

Krapohl, D. J. (2002). "The Polygraph in Personnel Screening." In Kleiner, M. (ed), *Handbook of Polygraph Testing* (217–236). San Diego: Academic Press.

Langleben, D. D., Schroeder, L., Maldjian, J. A., Gur, R. C., McDonald, S., Ragland, J. D., O'Brien, C. P., and Childress, A. R. (2002). "Brain Activity during Simulated Deception: An Event-Related Functional Magnetic Resonance Study." *Neuroimage* 15, 727–732.

Lee, T. M. C., Liu, H. I., Tan, L. H., Chan, C. C. H., Mahankali, S., Feng, C. M., Hou, J., Fox, P. T., and Gao, J. H. (2002). "Lie Detection by Functional Magnetic Resonance Imaging." *Human Brain Mapping* 15, 157–164.

Liang, J, Cheung, J. Y., and Chen, J. D. (1997). "Detection and Deletion of Motion Artifacts in Electrogastrogram Using Feature Analysis and Neural Networks." *Annals of Biomedical Engineering* 25 (5), September-October, 850–857.

Littlewort, Gwen, Bartlett, Marian Stewart, Fasel, Ian, Susskind, Joshua, and Morvellan, Javier. (2004). "Dynamics of facial expression extracted automatically from video." *Proceedings of the 2004 IEEE Computer Society Conference on Computer Vision and Pattern Recognition Workshops (CVPRW'04)* 5, 80–88.

Lo, Y. L., Fook-Chong, S., and Tan, E. K. (2003). "Increased Cortical Excitability in Human Deception." *NeuroReport* 14 (7), May, 1021–1024.

Loughead, J., Busch, S., Nick, P., Childress, A. R., Gur, R., and Langleben, D. (2004). "Brain Activity During Deception: An Event-Related Functional MRI Study." *10th Annual Meeting of the Organization for Human Brain Mapping*, Budapest, Hungary, 13-17 June.

MacLaren, V. V. (2001). "A Quantitative Review of the Guilty Knowledge Test." *Journal of Applied Psychology* 86 (4), August, 674–683.

Matsuo, T. and Fukuda, K. (1996). "A Development of Automatic Analyzing System of Eyeblinks Recorded in the Video Image." *Japanese Journal of Physiology, Psychology, and Psychophysiology* 14, 17–21. (In Japanese with English abstract)

Murthy, Ramya, Pavlidis, Ioannis, and Tsiamyrtzis, Panagiotis. (2004, September 1–5). "Touchless Monitoring of Breathing Function." *Proceedings of the 26th Annual International Conference of the IEEE EMBS*, San Francisco, CA.

Murthy, Ramya and Pavlidis, Ioannis. (2005). *Non-Contact Monitoring of Breathing Function Using Infrared Imaging*. Technical Report Number UH-CS-05-09, 9 April. Department of Computer Science, University of Houston, Houston, TX.

Nordenberg, T. (1999). "An Aspirin A Day – Just Another Cliché?" *FDA Consumer Magazine*. Publication No. (FDA) 99-1287, March-April.

Odesho, Jason, R. (2004). "Truth or Dare?: Terrorism and 'Truth Serum' in the Post-9/11 World." *Stanford Law Review* 57, October, 209–255

Office of Technology Assessment, U.S. Congress (1983). *Scientific Validity of Polygraph Testing: A Research Review and Evaluation - A Technical Memorandum*. Washington, D.C.: OTA-TM-H-15.

Palmatier, J. J. (1996). *The Validity and Comparative Accuracy of Voice Stress Analysis As Measured by the CVSA: A Field Study Conducted In A Psychophysiological Context*. Appeared as incomplete Report No. DoDPI97-P-0003 (published in 1996), under the same title. Note: Also unfinished draft title assigned Report No. DoDPI97-P-0002. U.S. Department of Defense Polygraph Institute, Ft. Jackson, SC.

Pascual-Leone, A., House, C. M., Reese, K., Shotland, L. I., Grafman, J., Sato, S., Valls-Sole, J., Brasil-Neto, J. P., Wasserman, E. M., Cohen, L. G., and Hallet, M. (1993). Safety of rapid-rate transcranial magnetic stimulation in normal volunteers. *Electroencephalography in Clinical Neurology* 89, 120–130.

Patrick, C. J. and Iacono, W. G. (1991). A comparison of field and laboratory polygraphs in the detection of deception. *Psychophysiology* 28 (6), November, 632–638.

Pavlidis, Ioannis T. and Levine, James A. (2001). "Monitoring of Periorbital Blood Flow Rate through Thermal Image Analysis and Its Application to Polygraph Testing." *Proceedings of the 23rd Annual International Conference of the IEEE Engineering in Medicine and Biology Society (EMBS'01)*, Istanbul, Turkey, 25-28 October.

Pavlidis, Ioannis T., Eberhardt, Normal L., and Levine, James A. (2002). "Seeing through the Face of Deception." *Nature* 415 (6867), 3 January, 35–36.

Pavlidis, Ioannis T. (2004). "Lie Detection Using Thermal Imaging." *Proceedings of SPIE* 5405, 270–279.

Pollina, Dean A. and Ryan, Andrew H. (2002). *The Relationship between Facial Skin Surface Temperature Reactivity and Traditional Polygraph Measures Used in the Psychophysiological Detection of Deception: A Preliminary Investigation*. Report No. DoDPI02-R-0007, March. Department of Defense Polygraph Institute, Fort Jackson, SC.

Raskin, D. C., and Honts, C. R. (2002). "The Comparison Question Test." In Kleiner, M. (ed), *Handbook of Polygraph Testing* (1–47). San Diego: Academic Press.

Rosenfeld, J. P., Nasman, V. T., Whalen, R., Cantwell, B., and Mazzeri, L. (1987). Late vertex positivity as a guilty knowledge indicator: a new method of lie detection. *International Journal of Neuroscience* 34 (1–2), 125–129.

Rosenfeld, J. P., Soskins, M., Bosh, G., Ryan, A. (2004). "Simple, Effective Countermeasures to P300-Based Tests of Detection of Concealed Information." *Psychophysiology* 41 (2), 205–219.

Saxe, Leonard. (1991). "Science and the CQT Polygraph: A Theoretical Critique." *Integrative Physiological and Behavioral-Science* 26 (3), July-September, 223–231.

Select Committee on Intelligence. (1977). Project MKULTRA, the CIA's program of research in behavioral modification. Joint Hearing before the Select Committee on Intelligence, and the Subcommittee on Health and Scientific Research of the Senate Committee on Human Resources, 95th Congress, 1st Session.

Spence, S. A., Farrow, T. F., Herford, A. E., Wilkinson, I. D., Zheng, Y., and Woodruff, P. W. (2001). "Behavioural and Functional Anatomical Correlates of Deception In Humans." *NeuroReport* 12, 2849–2853.

Supreme Court of New Jersey. (1989). 116 N.J. 580; 562 A.2d 1320; 1989 N.J. LEXIS 73.

Tian, Ying-li, Brown, Lisa, Hampapur, Arun, Pankanti, Sharat, Senior, Andrew, and Bolle, Ruud. (2003). "Real World Real-Time Automatic Recognition of Facial Expressions." *Fourth IEEE International Workshop of Performance Evaluation of Tracking and Surveillance (PETS-ICVS'03)*, Graz, Austria, 31 March.

Timm, H. W. (1982). "Effects of Altered Outcome Expectancies Stemming from Placebo and Feedback Treatments on the Validity of the Guilty Knowledge Technique." *Journal of Applied Psychology* 67, 391–400.

Moriyama, Tsuyoshi, Kanade, Takeo, Cohn, Jeffrey F., Xiao, Jing, Ambadar, Zara, Gao, Jiang, and Imamura, Hiroki (2002). "Automatic Recognition of Eye Blinking in Spontaneously Occurring Behavior." *16th International Conference on Pattern Recognition (ICPR'02)* 4, 40078.

United States Government Accounting Office (2001). *Federal Agency Views on the Potential Application of "Brain Fingerprinting."* Washington, DC: GAO-02-22.

Van Damme, Guy. (2001, April). "Forensic Criminology and Psychophysiology: Truth Verification Tools, With a Special Study of Truster Pro." *Crime Research in South Africa* 2 (2).

Vendemia, J. M. C. (2003). *Neural Mechanisms of Deception and Response Congruity to General Knowledge Information and Autobiographical Information in Visual Two-Stimulus Paradigms with Motor Response* (in press). Department of Defense Polygraph Institute (DoDPI99-P-0010).

Villringer, A. and Chance, B. (1997). "Non-Invasive Optical Spectroscopy and Imaging of Human Brain Function." *Trends In Neuroscience* 20, 435–442.

Wasserman, E. M., Grafman, J., Berry, C., Hollnagel, C., Wild, K., Clark, K., and Hallett, M. (1996a). "Use and Safety of a New Repetitive Transcranial Magnetic Stimulation." *Electroencephalography in Clinical Neurology* 101, 412–417.

Wasserman, E. M., Cohen, L. F., Flitman, S. S., Chen, R., and Hallett, M. (1996b). "Seizures in Healthy People with Repeated Safe Trains of Transcranial Magnetic Stimuli." *Lancet* 347, 825–826.

Williamson, Peter C. (2002). "Imaging Brain Chemistry and Function in Neuropsychiatric Disorders." *The Canadian Journal of Psychiatry* 47 (4), May, 313–314.

Winter, Alison. (2005). "The Making of 'Truth Serum'." *Bulletin of History in Medicine* 79, 500–533.

5
KUBARK Counterintelligence Interrogation Review: Observations of an Interrogator

Lessons Learned and Avenues for Further Research

Steven M. Kleinman, M.S.
February 2006

Abstract

A careful reading of the KUBARK manual is essential for anyone involved in interrogation, if perhaps for no other reason than to uncover a definition of interrogation that accurately captures the fundamental nature of interrogation while also concretely establishing what it is not (i.e., a game between two people to be won or lost). A major stumbling block to the study of interrogation, and especially to the conduct of interrogation in field operations, has been the all-too-common misunderstanding of the nature and scope of the discipline. Most observers, even those within professional circles, have unfortunately been influenced by the media's colorful (and artificial) view of interrogation as almost always involving hostility and the employment of force – be it physical or psychological – by the interrogator against the hapless, often slow-witted subject. This false assumption is belied by historic trends that show the majority of sources (some estimates range as high as 90 percent) have provided meaningful answers to pertinent questions in response to direct questioning (i.e., questions posed in an essentially administrative manner rather than in concert with an orchestrated approach designed to weaken the source's resistance).

Introduction

The KUBARK[21] Counterintelligence Interrogation Manual, produced by the Central Intelligence Agency in 1963 (and declassified in 1997), has become an icon of Cold War subterfuge and a lightning rod for those who allege that the United States continues to employ similar coercive interrogation techniques in the new conflict of the 21st century: the Global War on Terror. In an emphatic article, Alfred W. McCoy provides a sweeping review of the development of the KUBARK manual and its disturbing legacy throughout the remaining course of Cold War history.[22] McCoy makes a compelling argument that coercive interrogation methods, such as those set forth in the KUBARK manual, carry a far-reaching negative impact on U.S. foreign policy: a premise with critical implications for current counterinsurgency operations in Iraq.

Rather than address these geopolitical concerns, this review will concern itself exclusively with the potential for lessons learned that could be derived from a highly controversial document. Just as important ideas for enhancing security practices can be elicited from a felon convicted of armed robbery, in looking past the ignominy of KUBARK's intended use, one can find useful insights into the dynamics of intensive intelligence interrogation that can lead to principles applicable to current challenges.

Observations

Interrogation: A Definition

> *There is nothing mysterious about interrogation. It consists of no more than obtaining needed information through responses to questions.*[23]

> *An interrogation is not a game played by two people, one to become the winner and the other the loser. It is simply a method of obtaining correct and useful information.*[24]

Some might argue that these definitions fail to distinguish interrogation from a debriefing. While there are far more similarities than differences between the two activities, what ultimately separates an interrogation from a debriefing

---

[21] The term "KUBARK" is the Central Intelligence Agency cryptonym for a counterintelligence collection operation conducted in the early 1960s. In the cryptonym system employed by the CIA, the first two letters (the "digraph") may refer to a country or a specific clandestine or covert activity, while the remaining word (in this instance, "BARK") may refer to a specific operation or recruited source.

[22] Alfred W. McCoy, "Cruel Science: CIA Torture and U.S. Foreign Policy," *The New England Journal of Public Policy* (Winter 2005): 209-262.

[23] Central Intelligence Agency, KUBARK Counterintelligence Interrogation, Washington, DC, 1963, 1; available at http://www.parascope.com/articles/0397/kubark06.htm. Hereafter cited as KUBARK.

[24] KUBARK, 85.

rests in the nature of two fundamental elements: psychological set and physical setting.

- Psychological Set. In the context of a *debriefing*, the debriefer and the source have essentially committed to the primary, shared purpose of producing actionable intelligence, even though each may be motivated by dramatically different personal objectives. The debriefer seeks the fulfillment of tasked intelligence collection objectives, while the source may act out of a sense of patriotism (e.g., a legal traveler[25] reporting information learned while traveling abroad) or may be seeking preferential treatment from government authorities (e.g., a defector). In the course of an *interrogation*, both parties approach the interaction with different — and at times widely conflicting — sets of expectations and objectives. While the interrogator may share the debriefer's objective of obtaining actionable intelligence, he or she may expect to encounter a source who seeks to resist, withhold, distort, and deceive.

- Physical Setting. A legal traveler, in essence, submits voluntarily to the questioning of the debriefer, and reserves the right (in most instances) to end the session and depart at any time. It is therefore in the debriefer's best interest to make the experience a positive one for the source. By contrast, an interrogator enjoys a significant degree of control over the movement of the source, the duration of the encounter, and often the degree of liberty available to the source (at that moment and for the immediate future). The interrogator has the option of leveraging his/her control over these factors — in the form of the "threat" of continued detention or the "reward" of early release or expanded privileges — as a means of influencing the source's responsiveness to questioning.

Focus on Communist Methods of Interrogation

The intelligence service which is able to bring pertinent, modern knowledge to bear upon its problems enjoys huge advantages over a service which conducts its clandestine business in eighteenth century fashion. It is true that American psychologists have devoted somewhat more attention to Communist interrogation techniques, particularly "brainwashing," than to U.S. practices. Yet they have conducted scientific inquiries into many subjects that are closely related to interrogation: the effects of debility and isolation, the polygraph, reactions to pain and fear, hypnosis, and heightened suggestibility.[26]

---

[25] Legal travelers are individuals who may lawfully travel to a foreign country for commercial, personal, or government purposes who may be debriefed upon their return by a representative of the Intelligence Community for information of intelligence interest obtained in the normal course of their official duties or personal activities. Legal travelers are not tasked (officially requested or directed) to collect information.

[26] KUBARK, 2.

The study of hostile interrogation methods has been an essential undertaking in the noble effort to better prepare U.S. personnel to endure and withstand the challenges they might face if taken prisoner. However, no similar effort has ever been undertaken to better prepare U.S. intelligence personnel for their important role in gleaning critical intelligence data from enemy prisoners and detainees. The reasons for this omission remain unknown.

Operating with a dearth of research in support of offensive interrogation methodology, the writers of the KUBARK manual appear to have found themselves in a situation not unlike that experienced by interrogation personnel today. In essence, KUBARK's coercive methods reflected concepts derived from research into hostile methods — government research carried out specifically to help identify effective countermeasures — and then "reverse engineered" selected principles to meet operational requirements. It is interesting to note that the KUBARK manual (and the methods it proposes) was substantially informed by studies conducted by Albert Biderman, a sociologist and principal investigator for an Air Force Office of Scientific Research contract to review literature on the stresses associated with captivity.[27]

In large measure, the abuses — alleged or actual — perpetrated by U.S. interrogation personnel since the advent of the war on terror can be explained (albeit not defended) by the very same dynamic. With interrogation doctrine reflecting little change from the 1960s and producing few substantial successes in the current battlespace, commanders, operators, and intelligence officers have sought an alternative. In considering options, it became readily apparent that the experts in Survival, Evasion, Resistance, and Escape (SERE) were the "only other game in town."

While offensive and defensive interrogation operations have much in common, there are intractable differences. Defensive interrogation training is designed to help U.S. personnel withstand the unique stresses of all manner of exploitation — including the employment of coercive methods — to protect information and avoid becoming pawns in an adversary's attempt to generate useful propaganda. To prepare personnel for this substantial challenge, resistance training seeks to create a systematic threat environment to achieve "stress inoculation." This includes exposing trainees to intensive role-played interrogation scenarios. In the course of many years of experience in such practical exercises, many of the resistance instructors have become accomplished role-play interrogators.

However, there are three fundamental reasons why experience as a resistance instructor does not necessarily prepare someone for service as an intelligence interrogator. First, resistance instructors — portraying interrogators from potential adversarial nations that have shown disregard for international convention on the treatment of prisoners — routinely employ a wide range of coercive methods that often fall well outside Geneva Convention guidelines. Second, although questioning is an important element of the role-play exercise, this activity does

---

[27] KUBARK, 110–111.

not reach the depth required in an intelligence interrogation. Third, resistance instructors, though talented professionals, lack the training, linguistic skills, and subject matter expertise required of interrogation personnel. In sum, the employment of resistance instructors in interrogation — whether as consultants or as practitioners — is an example of the proverbial attempt to place the square peg in the round hole. (NOTE: In the months after 11 September 2001, special operations personnel, many of whom have received resistance training, were quick to request interrogation support from the SERE community based on well-entrenched memories of the skill and polish of resistance instructors during intense role-play scenarios.)[28]

The Objective of an Interrogation: Information or Confession?

> *[U]nlike a police interrogation, the [intelligence] interrogation is not aimed at causing the interrogatee to incriminate himself as a means of bringing him to trial. Admissions of complicity are not...ends in themselves but merely preludes to the acquisition of more information.*[29]

While interrogations conducted to support law enforcement objectives have many similarities to those designed strictly to satisfy intelligence requirements, there are several subtle yet important differences. The methods employed within each context are essentially interchangeable, with discernible differences identifiable only in nuance. At the same time, the fundamental objectives can be strikingly different. From a process perspective, the ultimate objective of the interrogation will inform — and significantly influence — the methodology employed.

The confession that can be such a monumental achievement in the law enforcement world is often of little interest to the Intelligence Community. Conversely, the exhaustive detail necessary to support subsequent intelligence analysis and production often ranges far beyond that needed to support a conviction. While law enforcement seeks to establish responsibility, the Intelligence Community seeks to exploit knowledgeability. In sum, law enforcement attempts to understand the past; intelligence attempts to probe the future.

Other key differences must be clearly understood. Law enforcement officials must adhere to federal and state laws pertaining to rights of the accused (including legal representation and the right to remain silent), standards of evidence, investigative parameters established by the prosecution, and limits on the duration of custody. In contrast, the activities of intelligence officials are governed by international and federal guidelines pertaining to the treatment of prisoners, priority intelligence requirements, the need to manage a potentially

---

[28] During his recall to active duty from June 2003 to January 2005, the author served as the Department of Defense Senior Intelligence Officer for Special Survival Training.
[29] KUBARK, 4–5.

long-term exploitation process, and the pursuit of actionable information and/or information that corroborates or contributes to intelligence data gathered from other sources.

As noted previously, what ultimately informs the methodology employed to collect data from a source is, in large measure, the nature of the information sought. It is critical, then, to understand the vital differences between gathering information to support a criminal case and gathering information to support foreign intelligence production.

	Criminal Case	Foreign Intelligence
Objective:	Conviction	Understanding
Standard:	Legal Code	Analytical Methodology
Limits:	Rules of Evidence	None[30]
Protections:	Fifth Amendment	None[31]
Confession:	Considerable Value	Relative Value[32]

An analysis of these critical factors would suggest that interrogators operating in support of foreign intelligence requirements be afforded a considerably greater degree of flexibility than law enforcement personnel. While the two interrogation contexts have numerous areas of commonality, it is imperative that the strategies, tactics, and techniques developed for each reflect the differences between them. Without this understanding, the potential exists for significant error in application and practice.

One explanation for this can be found in the *specificity principle*. Arising from studies in the field of kinesiology (the science of human movement), the specificity principle suggests that the closer two activities are to one another — without becoming the same activity — the more practice in one will degrade skills in the other. To borrow an example from sports, the individual who plays softball and also participates in a bowling league (activities that require vastly different skill sets) would not find his or her skill in one sport impaired by participation in the other. Conversely, the individual who plays both racquetball and squash would likely encounter difficulties in transitioning from one activity to the other, especially in areas such as strategy, timing, and focus. It is precisely in the areas of *strategy, timing, and focus* that law enforcement and intelligence interrogation are critically different.

---

[30] Any and all information collected by the U.S. Intelligence Community outside the United States from non-U.S. Persons may be used for intelligence analytical purposes.

[31] While the Constitution of the United States specifically protects individuals from unreasonable searches and self-incrimination, the non-U.S. Person intelligence source does not enjoy these same protections.

[32] A "confession" obtained from an intelligence source only has value to the extent that it establishes direct access to the information reported. For intelligence purposes, the other interrogatives (e.g., why, how, how many, when again) are more important than confirmation of an individual "who."

Qualities of an Effective Interrogator

A number of studies of interrogation discuss the qualities said to be desirable in an interrogator...perhaps the four qualifications of chief importance to the interrogator are 1) enough operational training and experience to permit quick recognition of leads; 2) real familiarity with the language to be used; 3) extensive background knowledge about the interrogatee's native country; and 4) a genuine understanding of the source as a person...of the four traits listed, a genuine insight into the source's character and motives is perhaps most important but least common.[33]

The human intelligence (HUMINT) career field has long employed various psychological testing protocols (e.g., Minnesota Multiphasic Personality Inventory, California Psychological Inventory, etc.), in conjunction with exhaustive background investigations, in an effort to both identify those candidates with the inherent aptitude and/or personality profile for a given operational activity and to screen out those who would likely prove ill-suited and/or ill-equipped for the profession. A similar psychological screening protocol (without the background investigation) has been employed in the SERE career field in an effort to eliminate those candidates with the highest apparent probability for acting out violently or abusively while interacting with students during intensive practical exercises. For application to the interrogation discipline, a critical underpinning of such screening efforts is the availability of a "model" of a successful interrogator...and it is unlikely that a properly vetted model exists.

While identifying effective methods and processes is a key element of the Intelligence Science Board's EI project mandate, designing a means for selecting candidates with the highest potential for success in implementing these methods and processes is of equal importance. Research in this regard should be acutely informed by the following three considerations:

- Those in hierarchical authoritarian structures have a documented tendency to engage in what appears to be "acceptable" inhumane behavior toward others, as demonstrated in the famous "Stanford University Experiment" (Haney, Banks, and Zimbardo, 1973).

- Dr. Howard Gardner's seminal work on multiple intelligences suggests that certain people might be naturally gifted with uncommon abilities and aptitudes in various areas, including (for EI purposes) **interpersonal intelligence** (the capacity to understand the intentions, motivations and desires of other people) and **intrapersonal intelligence** (the capacity to understand oneself, to appreciate one's feelings, fears and motivations).[34]

---

[33] KUBARK, 1011.
[34] See, for example Howard Gardner, Ph.D., *Frames of Mind: The Theory of Multiple Intelligences* (New York: BasicBooks, 1983).

- Perhaps the most important single trait of individuals who have demonstrated long-term success in HUMINT operations is an *exceptional aptitude for dealing with ambiguity*. Whether this characteristic can be reliably measured remains to be seen.

The "Magic" of Rapport:[35] The Emotional Component of Interrogation

> *One general observation is introduced now, however, because it is considered basic to the establishment of rapport, upon which the success of non-coercive interrogation depends…The skilled interrogator can save a great deal of time by understanding the emotional needs of the interrogatee. Most people confronted by an official — and dimly powerful — representative of a foreign power will get down to cases much faster if made to feel, from the start, that they are being treated as individuals.[36]*

Despite the impressive success achieved by interrogators who have mastered the skill of effectively establishing rapport with a source — the celebrated Luftwaffe interrogator Hanns Scharff[37] providing but one well-known example — methods for rapport-building continue to receive relatively little attention in current interrogation training programs. There seems to be an unfounded yet widespread presumption that all persons inherently possess the skills necessary for building rapport and therefore do not require any supplemental training to hone this ability. While the KUBARK manual has gained a degree of infamy through its association with coercive means, it also, in an interesting stroke of irony, consistently emphasizes the value of rapport-building as an essential tool for the interrogator.

The devaluation of rapport — that is, building an *operational accord* with a source — as an effective means of gaining compliance from a resistant source is in large measure the product of the misguided public debate over the role of interrogation in the Global War on Terror, one that seems invariably to focus on the "ticking bomb" scenario. The point can be safely made that for every instance where a source *might* have information about an imminent, catastrophic terrorist event, there are hundreds (possibly thousands) of interrogations where the information requirements are far less urgent and the opportunity exists for a

---

[35] Rapport is one of the interrogator's most powerful tools in gaining a source's cooperation. It must be made clear that, in the context of an interrogation, the term "rapport" is not limited to the idea of friendship that builds between two individuals (although this may actually occur over the course of an extended interrogation). For the purposes of this paper, the term will be used to imply a state in which a degree of accord, conformity, and or/affinity is present within a relationship. Source: Jerry Richardson, *The Magic of Rapport* (Capitola, CA: Meta Publications, 1987), 13.

[36] KUBARK, 11.

[37] Raymond F. Toliver, *The Interrogator: The Story of Hanns Joachim Scharff, Master Interrogator of the Luftwaffe* (Atglen, PA: Schiffer Publishing, Ltd., 1997).

thoughtful, systematic approach. In the case of the latter, the interrogator might be well served in designing an effective approach regime by asking himself/herself, as recommended in the KUBARK manual, "'How can I make him *want* to tell me what he knows?'[38] rather than 'How can I trap him into disclosing what he knows?'" [39] Operational accord seeks to effectively, albeit subtly, gain the source's cooperation and maintain that productive relationship for as long as possible without betraying indicators of manipulation or exploitation on the part of the interrogator.

One constructive paradigm for interrogation, yet one that is rarely considered, views it in terms of a recruitment (or even, perhaps, a seduction). Returning to the basic definition of interrogation noted at the beginning of this paper, *it consists of no more than obtaining needed information through responses to questions.* To achieve that objective, one can "pull" (i.e., elicit compliance) or "push" (i.e., coerce capitulation). While the former is likely to obtain information that can often exceed the interrogator's expressed scope of interest — as the source often possesses both greater depth and breadth of knowledgeability than the interrogator might assume — the latter will, in the best of circumstances, only obtain information responding to questions directly asked. Even then the information will often be limited to the minimum necessary to satisfy the interrogator.

Effectively establishing an operational accord with a source — especially in a cross-cultural setting — must become a major component of interrogator training and included in that problem set of necessary yet *difficult to define, measure and train* skills needed by all HUMINT operators. A review of studies in interpersonal conflict resolution and relationship-building under competitive circumstances (e.g., sales, counseling, negotiation, etc.) can provide a meaningful starting point from which to launch original research for specific application in the interrogation context.

Reliability of Casual Observation

> *Great attention has been given to the degree to which persons are able to make judgments from casual observations regarding the personality characteristics of another...the level of reliability in judgments is so low that research encounters difficulties, when it seeks to determine who makes better judgments...the interrogator is likely to overestimate his ability to judge others than to underestimate it, especially if he has had little or no training in modern psychology.*[40]

The reliability of casual observations made by interrogators has too often gone unchallenged. Unfortunately, the fact that someone is a "trained" interrogator is

---

[38] The term "want" in this context refers to creating conditions that make cooperation appear to be an attractive, even self-serving alternative for the source rather than a characterization of the source's efforts to escape physical or psychological force.

[39] KUBARK, 12.

[40] KUBARK, 12–13.

too frequently construed as evidence that the individual possesses an uncommon ability to make rapid and *valid* assessments of a source with little background information or direct exposure to support that judgment.

While extensive and consistent experience in interrogation can offer a person the opportunity to develop above-average assessment skills, this ability is contingent upon several important factors. First, each assessment must be subsequently evaluated to determine validity (once additional corroborating or contradicting information is available) and the method(s) used explicitly described, deconstructed, and recorded to definitively capture that cause and effect for future study and possible employment. Second, the key processes used in a given assessment should be examined, evaluated, and corroborated or discredited by trained behavioral science professionals. Finally, the individual interrogator must be sufficiently disciplined to avoid drawing unsupported, possibly self-serving conclusions as to his or her assessment skills. In this regard, it would be helpful to keep in mind the caveat set forth in the KUBARK manual: *An interrogation is not a game played by two people, one to become the winner and the other the loser.*

Assessment, in the context of interrogation, is a multi-dimensional concept. The interrogator must be able to effectively — and accurately — assess a source's emotional state, psychological set, veracity, and knowledgeability. Individuals cannot attain the ability to meet such a broad-based challenge successfully in a single, even months-long training course. Training in assessment must begin early in an interrogator's professional preparation and be followed by continuous study, research, and practice. Although a considerable body of knowledge already exists in this area and could be profitably mined for supporting techniques and procedures, new and original studies of assessment in the unique context of interrogation are needed.

Analytical Support to Interrogation

> *The interrogator should be supported whenever possible by qualified analysts' review of his daily "take;" experience has shown that such a review will raise questions to be put and points to be clarified and lead to a thorough coverage of the subject in hand.*[41]

In prosecuting the Global War on Terror, the targets of primary interest from both an operational and intelligence perspective are terrorism's critical centers of gravity: financing, transportation, logistics, communications, and safe havens. Just as it would not be reasonable to expect any single analyst to be an accomplished subject matter expert in more than one (or possibly two) of these areas, it should not be assumed that any single interrogator can be prepared to explore the full knowledgeability of sources who have information pertaining to these key target areas. It is therefore important for interrogators to have on-scene analytical support for precisely the purposes identified in the above quotation.

---

[41] KUBARK, 13.

While the Joint Interrogation Facilities established during the 1990-91 Gulf War were equipped with on-site intelligence support centers, the level of expertise of the personnel assigned and the real-time access to intelligence information systems fell short of what would be required of a world-class effort. In contrast, the World War II Joint Interrogation Center at Fort Hunt, VA, included a robust analytical support annex that was shaped by, and expanded in response to, the specific needs of the interrogation cadre. As a result, interrogators were able to design highly productive lines of questioning, effectively detect attempts at deception, and often obtain compliance from prisoners as a result of the semblance of dominant knowledge (a graphic example of Cialdini's *authority principle* in persuasion[42]).

Interrogation centers would be well-served by the support of an on-site analytical cell staffed with bona fide subject matter experts and configured to exploit secure information systems that would facilitate real-time access to larger intelligence centers. This would have a considerable positive impact on the ultimate value of the intelligence products generated at the field level. Given the historical precedent, this is clearly an eminently achievable goal.

Psychological Assessment: Categorizing Sources by Personality Type

> *The number of systems devised for categorizing human beings is large, and most of them are of dubious validity.*[43]

> *Every interrogator knows that a real understanding of the individual is worth far more than a thorough knowledge of this or that pigeon-hole to which he has been consigned. And for interrogation purposes, the ways in which he differs from the abstract type may be more significant than the ways in which he conforms.*[44]

The pursuit of a valid means of quickly and accurately assessing a source's psychological set — presumably with the objective of identifying an avenue for expeditiously obtaining compliance in the form of meaningful answers to pertinent questions — has been something of a search for the Holy Grail in the world of interrogation. This quest raises three fundamental questions:

- Is it possible to conduct a meaningful psychological assessment of a resistant source?

- Would such an assessment provide substantial assistance in the interrogation of that source?

- Would the administration of such testing violate governing professional standards of ethics?

---

[42] Robert B. Cialdini, Ph.D., *Influence: The Psychology of Persuasion* (New York: William Morrow, 1993), 208-236.

[43] KUBARK, 19.

[44] KUBARK, 20.

Certainly, the last question must be satisfactorily answered before a sanctioned effort can be launched to study the feasibility suggested by the first two. Ethical considerations aside, the use of some manner of personality assessment presents intriguing possibilities. As the quotations above indicate, the KUBARK manual appears to dismiss the potential of in-depth assessment, noting that an interrogator "does not dispose of the time or personnel to probe the depths of each source's individuality."[45] Instead, it suggests some form of categorizing sources based on observations made in early rounds of interrogation. Even then, the manual is quick to emphasize that this method, "like other interrogation aids, [is] a scheme of categories [that] is useful only if recognized for what it is — a set of labels that facilitate communication but are not the same as the persons thus labeled."[46]

In contrast, at least one account would appear to support the concept of a formal program for assessing sources. According to Orrin DeForest, a CIA intelligence officer and interrogator during the Vietnam War, psychological testing was employed with significant success. The test, based on work conducted by Dr. John Gittinger, sought to measure IQ in addition to three other components of personality reflected in demonstrated propensities toward Externalizing or Internalizing, Regulation or Flexibility, and Role Adaptivity or Role Uniformity.[47] This test was administered to the interrogator and interpreter staff (and used to design tailored training programs and subsequent assignments) as well as to the Vietcong undergoing interrogation. According to DeForest's account, this tool proved consistently effective and a valuable supplemental tool used in conjunction with other creative systems for interrogation.[48]

Perhaps the most important role psychological testing can play in interrogation is as a means for enhancing communication and accord between two people; anything beyond this would be an unexpected windfall. If a current or emerging testing protocol would prove valid in accurately measuring a relevant component of the source's personality — and thereby assisting the interrogator to design an effective means of approach — it would offer an important alternative that could help stem the trend of default to coercion that has occurred too often in the course of dealing with a resistant high-value source.

Screening: Overlooking a Critical Phase of the Exploitation Process

The purpose of screening is to provide the interrogator, in advance, with a reading on the type and characteristics of the interrogatee...even a preliminary estimate, if valid, can be a boon to the interrogator because it will permit him to start with

---

[45] KUBARK, 20.

[46] KUBARK, 20.

[47] Orrin DeForest, *Slow Burn: The Rise and Bitter Fall of American Intelligence in Vietnam* (New York: Simon and Schuster, 1990), 62-65.

[48] Some observers might find it curious that a source would voluntarily submit to psychological testing, yet this is precisely what occurred. This seemingly inexplicable compliance may be a result of a "conditioned reflex" to completing the ubiquitous paperwork intractably associated with military/paramilitary service.

generally sound tactics from the beginning. [T]he second and related purpose of screening is to permit an educated guess about the source's probable attitude toward the interrogation. An estimate of whether the interrogatee will be cooperative or recalcitrant is essential to planning because very different methods are used in dealing with these two types. It is recommended that screening be conducted whenever personnel and facilities permit.[49]

In strategic and operational settings, where depth and accuracy of information take precedence over timeliness, screening is a critical component of the overall interrogation process. Every effort must be made not only to assess the knowledgeability and cooperation of the source, but — of supreme importance — to vet the individual in a manner that provides the interrogator with a high degree of confidence in the source's identity.

This point, while seemingly obvious, has proven anything but in the course of current interrogation operations. From the detention center in Guantanamo Bay, Cuba, to Bagram Air Base, Afghanistan, to various interrogation facilities in Iraq, reports abound of prisoners held in detention and interrogated at length because of mistaken identification. Several factors contribute to this unfortunate situation, including difficulties in transcribing names from Arabic, Pashto, and Urdu into English; classic cross-cultural misunderstandings; and a high-threat operating environment that leads many to err on the side of capture rather than release.

Whatever the causative factor, properly conducted screening operations can make a significant contribution on two important fronts. First, from a counterinsurgency perspective, false identification and internment can inflame an already tenuous relationship between an occupying power and the indigenous population. The false imprisonment of even a single individual can cause a profound shift in the insurgent/counterinsurgent dynamic as evidenced by the French experience in Indochina and Algeria and the U.S. experience in Vietnam and Iraq. Each instance of mistaken imprisonment, especially if it involves some form of mistreatment, shifts those who previously supported the foreign presence toward a more neutral position, those who formerly were neutral may begin to support the insurgents, and the insurgents may adopt a more militant campaign, one made all the more robust by a sudden influx of new supporters and combatants. This untoward cascading effect can be relatively simple to prevent through the establishment of a vigorous screening program that systematically filters out the innocent while identifying those of genuine intelligence interest.

Second, from an interrogation perspective, a proper screening effort helps to ensure the efficient allocation of available assets — interrogators, interpreters, and analysts — to those sources with the greatest potential knowledgeability. As one historical example, the U.S. strategic interrogation program in place during World War II (MIS-Y) employed a multi-tiered screening process that required

---

[49] KUBARK, 30–33.

an enemy prisoner of war (EPW) of potential major intelligence interest to be progressively screened for knowledgeability, expertise, and access at the scene of capture, at subsequent points of detention, upon embarkation from the European Theater, and upon disembarkation in the United States. Only those prisoners who had been assessed as being of the highest value were ultimately interrogated at the Fort Hunt Joint Interrogation Center. Ahead of its time in managerial acumen, MIS-Y effectively used the "80/20" principle to better focus its considerable resources on that small segment of the EPW population able to meet the most pressing intelligence information requirements of the war effort.

The later stages of the screening process were informed by guidelines and methods taught by MIS-Y personnel. The last stage almost always included direct examination by MIS-Y interrogators before final determination of the EPW's status. In this regard, it is important to note that the MIS-Y personnel involved in the screening process were experienced interrogators. In contrast, the KUBARK manual recommends that "screening should be conducted by interviewers, not interrogators."[50]

Chess in the Real World

> *No two interrogations are the same. Every interrogation is shaped definitively by the personality of the source — and of the interrogator, because interrogation is an intensely interpersonal process. The whole purpose of screening and a major purpose of the first stage of interrogation are to probe the strengths and weaknesses of the subject. Only when these have been established and understood does it become possible to plan realistically.*[51]

Building upon the fundamental definition of interrogation noted previously, the KUBARK manual provides a conceptual perspective on interrogation— that of an "intensely interpersonal process" — that offers invaluable clues in the search for relevant supporting research and methodologies. Social scientists have rigorously studied other *intensely interpersonal processes* — counseling and therapy, negotiation, sales, conflict mediation, and even formal debate, to name but a few. Within the myriad studies investigating the dynamics involved in these activities, one is likely to uncover concepts with direct application to interrogation and/or useful protocols for designing studies on the interrogation process.

The KUBARK manual also challenges interrogators to view each source as unique, therefore requiring judicious planning and a flexible approach tailored to that individual's specific strengths and weaknesses. This is especially important for those interrogators who run default programs comprising a limited array of approaches that have worked well in the past on a dramatically different

---

[50] KUBARK, 30.
[51] KUBARK, 38.

source pool. The disciplined interrogator must constantly battle the tendency to expect, and subsequently to look for, commonalities from one source to another. This is especially true when dealing with sources from a foreign and possibly little-understood culture and linguistic background. While a studied awareness of culture is important in planning for the exploitation of a given source, that newfound understanding can also cause the interrogator to catch only the cultural overtones and miss the individual nuances that would prove critical to gaining compliance.

The effort to build a useful model of the interrogation process must begin with a conceptual framework. Important components of that framework are flexibility, individuality, and constant adaptability. Inherent in the underlying philosophy is the requirement to search for general trends and individual nuance, commonalities and unique differences.

Ultimately, the successful model must generate an effective strategy for successful performance in keeping with the Law of Requisite Variety, a principle drawn from the study of cybernetics with remarkable application to the context of interrogation.[52] Cybernetic theory suggests that in the competition between two processes within a closed system, the one with greater variety of options will be successful. Applying the Law of Requisite Variety to the context of an interrogation, the individual with the larger number of available options (e.g., strategies, behaviors, etc.) should prevail. It is therefore of great importance that the interrogator always have at least one more method of leveraging compliance than the source has for resisting.[53]

Saving Face: Helping the Source to Concede

Another key to the successful interrogation of the resisting source is the provision of an acceptable rationalization for yielding. As regression proceeds, almost all resisters feel the growing internal stress that results from wanting simultaneously to conceal and divulge...To escape the mounting tension, the source may grasp at any face-saving reason for compliance— any explanation which will placate both his own conscience and the possible wrath of former superiors and associates if he is returned to [his place of origin]. It is the business of the interrogator to provide the right rationalization at the right time. Here too the importance of understanding the interrogatee is evident; the right rationalization must be an excuse or reason that is tailored to the source's personality.[54]

---

[52] Essentially, the Law of Requisite Variety states that the greater the variety of actions available to a control system, the larger the variety of perturbations (i.e., challenges to its control) for which it is able to compensate. (Source: Principia Cybernetic Web, URL: http://pespmc1.vub.ac.be/REQVAR.html)

[53] Richardson, *The Magic of Rapport*, 15-17.

[54] KUBARK, 41.

This point highlights a central, two-dimensional element of the interrogation process. At a fundamental level, the challenge for the interrogator is to make it as difficult (and unattractive) as possible for the source to resist and/or make it as easy (and attractive) as possible for the source to cooperate. Choice of the component upon which to focus is driven by both individual and contextual factors. With regard to the former, the interrogator must judiciously select the strategy that presents the greatest promise of success given a specific source — a decision based on extended observation and assessment. At the same time, the choice of strategy should enable the interrogator to most effectively leverage his or her personal strengths, professional experience, skills in the range of interrogation tradecraft, and language ability. Concurrently, a number of circumstantial variables must be assiduously considered, to include the time available for the interrogation (or series of interrogations), the nature of the existing information requirements, the physical setting, and the operational/intelligence information available about the source, his organization, and activities. The calculus involved represents a subset of the KUBARK concept noted above.

From a social science perspective, this dynamic suggests the possibility of several behavioral theories at work, including *approach/avoidance* (Lewin, 1935)[55] and *bind-strain* (Milgram, 1974).[56] Exploration of these two theories (and perhaps others) might explain, at least in part, the compliance-resistance dilemma facing the source, and uncover methods for shaping the source's behavior.

The *Alternative Question*[57] methodology frequently employed in law enforcement interrogations specifically seeks to present the source with what the KUBARK manual describes as an "acceptable rationalization for yielding." Offering an attractive option other than outright confession to a heinous crime, the alternative question allows the source to "save face" by agreeing with the interrogator's characterization of the criminal behavior as inherently positive in intent or objective.[58]

While often effective in eliciting a confession, the alternative question method may be problematic when it comes to collecting intelligence information. In presenting a source with two possible "alternatives" (e.g., "Did you plan to use C4 or Semtex as the explosive in that device?"), the interrogator runs the risk of

---

[55] As first described by Dr. Kurt Lewin, approach-avoidance conflict results from the stress of simultaneous attraction to and repulsion by the same goal.

[56] In Dr. Stanley Milgram's *Model of Obedience*, individuals may *bind* to an authority figure through reinforcing acts of obedience (and thereby externalize responsibility for specific acts), yet also encounter *role strain* when that obedient behavior becomes uncomfortable (e.g., when the acts violate the individual's personal moral values or when bringing harm to another contradicts the individual's self-image).

[57] An alternative question is a question that presents two or more possible answers and presupposes that only one is true.

[58] An example of an alternative question might be, "Did you start the fire at your company because you wanted to hurt people or as a way of calling attention to the fact that your contributions to the company have been consistently ignored for many years and you felt you had no other options available to you?" Regardless of how an individual responds, there is an admission of guilt.

undermining the objectivity and accuracy of the information obtained. In contrast, an open-ended question (e.g., "What type of explosive did you plan to use in that device?") requires the source to answer on the basis of his personal experience/ knowledge, without the benefit of clues or restrictions contained in the question.

A Systematic Approach to Interrogation: More Than the Sum of Its Parts

Therefore, it is wrong to open [an] interrogation experimentally, intending to abandon unfruitful approaches one by one until a sound method is discovered by chance. The failures of the interrogator, his painful retreats from blind alleys, bolster the confidence of the source and increase his ability to resist. While the interrogator is struggling to learn from the subject the facts that should have been established before the interrogation started, the subject is learning more and more about the interrogator.[59]

This passage contains an exceptionally important warning, one that an interrogator must always keep in mind: while the interrogator is watching (and listening to) the source, the source is watching (and listening to) the interrogator.

The interrogator often enters the interrogation with two distinct advantages. First, sources may be suffering from the shock of capture that undermines their psychological and emotional stability (often causing them to say and do things against their own interests). Second, while a long-serving intelligence officer may have the experience of dozens of interrogations behind him or her, it is often the source's maiden voyage into this uncertain territory. The interrogator can quickly surrender these advantages, however, by approaching the source in a hesitant, indecisive manner. This false start can be largely avoided through careful planning.

The MIS-Y interrogators of the Joint Interrogation Center routinely invested six hours in preparation for every hour spent in the actual interrogation of a prisoner. Their approaches, including alternatives, were carefully designed on the basis of extensive observation and assessment of the source. Intensive study of pertinent military, technical, economic, and/or political materials enabled the interrogators to demonstrate a solid understanding of the topics raised during the interrogation (contributing to the development of Cialdini's *authority* effect). They were similarly prepared to question the source systematically, including the ability to consistently and logically follow up on new avenues of inquiry as they unfolded. Not only did this disciplined operating procedure enhance the depth and breadth of the information collected, but it also facilitated a strong degree of control over the source. Opportunities for the prisoner to gain confidence from the miscues of an ill-prepared interrogator were rare.

---

[59] KUBARK, 42.

Anticipating Resistance: The Importance of Being Shrewd

> *It is useful to recognize in advance whether the information desired would be threatening or damaging in any way to the interests of the interrogatee.*[60]

Resistance to questioning is the primary barrier to entry in the context of interrogation. The challenge to the interrogator is to manage resistance effectively while systematically working to overcome it.

As an interrogator explores a given source's range of knowledgeability, he or she must be judicious in framing questions while concomitantly concealing the true focus of intelligence interest. One productive approach is to concentrate initially on areas that do not appear to provoke concern, and therefore resistance, on the part of the source. This requires *shrewd* questioning by the interrogator. In essence, shrewd questioning demands that the interrogator carefully consider the possible range of answers and responses (emotional and/or psychological) a question may elicit *before* it is asked, and selectively postpone asking the most provocative questions until later in the process.

Posing potentially provocative questions in the course of developing rapport/ accord with a source (or doing so too quickly after such an operational relationship has been established) can seriously — and at times irreversibly — undermine that cooperative relationship. In addition, drawing upon Cialdini's concept of the *consistency* principle,[61] it is important to avoid creating a situation where the source has the opportunity to formally assume a resistance posture either by word or deed. If allowed to do so, Cialdini's research would suggest that the source might be under additional self-induced pressure to remain consistent in his or her defiance.[62]

Capturing the Advantages of Technology: Monitoring Interrogations

> *Arrangements are usually made to record the interrogation, transmit it to another room, or do both. Most experienced interrogators do not like to take notes. Not being saddled with this chore leaves them free to concentrate on what sources say, how they say it, and what else they do while talking or listening. Another reason for avoiding note-taking is that it distracts and sometimes worries the interrogatee. In the course of several sessions conducted without note-taking, the subject is likely to fall into the comfortable illusion that he is not talking for the record.*[63]

---

[60] KUBARK, 44.

[61] The consistency principle suggests that if individuals make an expressed commitment — by word or by action — toward a goal or idea, they are more likely to honor that commitment.

[62] Cialdini, 57–113.

[63] KUBARK, 46.

The fundamental objective of an interrogation is to collect useful information, and that information must be recorded in a manner that will ensure it can be faithfully incorporated in formal reporting. In a bygone era, taking notes was the only realistic option. The information age, however, which makes an astonishing array of technical devices available to surreptitiously capture the sounds and images of an interrogation, presents the interrogator with a host of attractive options that yield significant operational benefits.

As noted above, the simple act of taking notes provides the source with a graphic reminder of the interrogator's primary goal — the collection of actionable intelligence — despite the well-orchestrated approaches designed to disguise that intent. In addition, when the interrogator appears to make note only of exchanges pertaining to certain topics, this not only transmits to the source an indicator of what is important to the interrogator, but also strongly hints at what the interrogator does and does not know.

There are myriad reasons to employ monitoring, audiovisual recording, and transcription technology to relieve the interrogator of this counter-productive burden, from the ability to accurately capture the information provided by the source to the opportunity to carefully analyze the source's behavioral cues, to providing a visual record of events to guard against the mistreatment of prisoners (and unfounded allegations of prisoner abuse). In contrast, there is really no compelling reason for interrogators not to avail themselves of this advantage (where available). The promise of technology, in the form of field-deployable recording equipment and well-designed, well-equipped, long-term interrogation facilities, should be expeditiously embraced. The return on investment would likely be extraordinary.

The Dual Nature of Interrogation

> *Once questioning starts, the interrogator is called upon to function at two levels. He is trying to do two seemingly contradictory things at once: achieve rapport with the subject but remain an essentially detached observer. Or he may project himself to the resistant interrogatee as powerful and ominous (in order to eradicate resistance and create the necessary conditions for rapport) while remaining wholly uncommitted at the deeper level, noting the significance of the subject's reactions and the effectiveness of his own performance. Poor interrogators often confuse this bi-level functioning with role-playing, but there is a vital difference. The interrogator who merely pretends, in his surface performance, to feel a given emotion or to hold a given attitude toward the source is likely to be unconvincing; the source quickly senses the deception.*[64]

Once again, the KUBARK manual eloquently captures the essence of the internal dynamic of the accomplished interrogator. Reaching this state of almost unconscious competence requires a consistent regimen of training, experience, reflection, and peer review that can take years.

A likely factor driving the progressive "dumbing down" of interrogation and interrogation training in the United States has been the ubiquitous treatment of the craft in movies and Hollywood. Viewers are treated to endless examples of the calculating, quick-witted interrogator who can rapidly assess the vulnerabilities of the source/prisoner and instantaneously devise and orchestrate an approach that almost immediately leverages compliance. Of course, what the viewer does not see (or, therefore, remember) is that these five-minute long vignettes are carefully scripted and repeatedly rehearsed. The actors do not deal with a constant chain of unknowns, nor are they asked to remain joined in the intense interpersonal exchange for hours, perhaps days, on end. It is critical that this artificial and often unrealistic view of interrogation not be allowed to influence doctrine for the real world.

Pressures and the Non-Coercive Interrogation Model

> *The term non-coercive is used...to denote methods of interrogation that are not based upon the coercion of an unwilling subject through the employment of superior force originating outside himself. However, the non-coercive interrogation is not conducted without pressure. On the contrary, the goal is to generate maximum pressure, or at least as much as is needed to induce compliance. The difference is that the pressure is*

---

[64] KUBARK, 48.

generated inside the interrogatee. His resistance sapped, his urge to yield is fortified, until in the end he defeats himself.[65]

The concept of "pressure" is an elusive one to capture in a manner that wins universal acceptance. For this reason, the term itself has played a significant, if misunderstood role with respect to allegations of prisoner mistreatment. This can be illustrated in the following recurring scenario:

> A senior commander, whose forces have engaged a challenging insurgent adversary, rightfully seeks to gain every available advantage, including that possible through timely and tailored intelligence gathered from recently captured detainees. Interrogators, diligently employing the U.S. Army tactical interrogation model—one designed for a more conventional military paradigm—encounter difficulties in obtaining the desired intelligence information from suspected terrorists, captured insurgents, and other high-value detainees. In this highly charged environment, commanders direct interrogators to "increase the pressure" on the prisoners without additional guidance as to how that order might be acted upon. Operating without advanced training in the needed interrogation tradecraft and lacking guidance from doctrine tailored to the circumstances, some interrogators (the majority of whom are young and relatively inexperienced) interpret the order to "increase the pressure" as meaning anything from extending the length of interrogations to pushing (and at times exceeding) the envelope of accepted methods. In a small number of cases, it is interpreted as meaning increased physicality.

In the context of an interrogation, myriad environmental factors may generate pressure (i.e., stress) within an individual. At the same time, it is important — and the KUBARK manual suggests — not to overlook the influence of the source's self-induced pressures. For the purposes of this paper, self-induced pressures will be defined as those resulting from an individual's interpretation of, and chosen response to, events, both real and imagined. Understanding this dynamic, the challenge for the interrogator is to skillfully (and carefully) manage the level of pressure in a manner that moves the interrogation toward its established objectives.

Nonetheless, pressure is an exceedingly difficult quality to measure accurately, especially on the exclusive basis of external observation. Additional degrees of difficulty are introduced by the cultural and linguistic barriers that are almost always present in an interrogation setting, individual responses to pressure, current levels of physical and emotional health, and time held in detention. Given this complex matrix, interrogators find themselves walking a very fine line,

---

[65] KUBARK, 52.

seeking to induce sufficient pressure to obtain the desired level of cooperation and compliance, but not so much pressure as to violate international convention or cause a sudden and/or severe emotional or psychological breakdown on the part of the source.

If the application and management of pressure are inherent components of the interrogation process, interrogators require a far more sophisticated understanding of the dynamics involved and more useful methods for accurately identifying and measuring that pressure. Cross-cultural studies are of great interest in this regard as an interrogator must, at the very least, appreciate the culturally based pressures a given source will likely encounter as he or she decides whether to cooperate or resist.

Deconstructing Resistance

> *Most resistant interrogatees block off access to significant [intelligence] in their possession for one or more of four reasons. The first is a specific negative reaction to the interrogator…The second cause is that some sources are resistant "by nature"— i.e., by early conditioning — to any compliance with authority. The third is that the subject believes that the information sought will be damaging or incriminating for him personally, that cooperation with the interrogator will have consequences more painful for him than the results of non-cooperation. The fourth is ideological resistance. The source has identified himself with a cause, a political movement or organization…Regardless of his attitude toward the interrogator, his own personality, and his fears for the future, the person who is deeply devoted to a hostile cause will ordinarily prove strongly resistant under interrogation.*[66]

"If you know your enemy and know yourself, you need not fear the result of a hundred battles. But, if you know yourself but not the enemy, for every victory gained you will also suffer a defeat." This timeless observation from the renowned strategist Sun Tzu is as true in the interrogation room as it is on the battlefield. An interrogator acting upon this counsel would be reasonably expected to spend considerable time in identifying and deconstructing the source's resistant posture and strategies. Unfortunately, current interrogation training — and thus the subsequent interrogation processes employed in the field — fail to invest sufficient time and energy in this important area.

Sales professionals and clandestine case officers are well-schooled in identifying areas of resistance and quickly designing a strategy for overcoming that resistance. The interrogator must be similarly skilled. And while resistance

---

[66] KUBARK, 53–54.

may be driven by intra- and/or interpersonal factors (one of the challenges of assessment addressed previously), there are two other key areas to consider.

The KUBARK manual correctly notes the substantial role ideological affiliation and commitment can play in a source's resistance posture. In some instances (e.g., Al Qaeda), the source may be a product of years of fundamentalist religious schooling (e.g., the madrassas), where intense, rote learning has filled students' minds with selected passages from spiritual texts. In the course of this training, they have embraced the "belief" that their cause is divinely inspired (which can place the interrogator on the side of "evil"). The inability to deconstruct this resistance posture remains a major hurdle in the current war on terrorism. The development of a useful counterstrategy will need to be informed by a solid understanding of the target cultures, ideologies, and languages to be relevant and effective.[67]

While much of the resistance posed by sources is ad hoc in nature, one cannot overlook the role of formalized resistance training. As the so-called *Al Qaeda Manual* attests, that organization has compiled a systematic resistance strategy for employment by operatives taken into custody.[68] The impact of this training is revealed in certain consistencies in the behaviors of detainees at Guantanamo Bay that suggest the use of resistance strategies (e.g., claims of abuse, repetitive recitations of religious passages, etc.). Even then, the challenge for interrogators is not inconsequential. First, interrogators must confirm that a source is actually employing a systematic resistance strategy. Second, they must identify the components of that strategy. Finally, they must devise an effective counterstrategy.

To address the concept of resistance meaningfully requires a broad array of subject matter experts. Behavioral scientists can assist in developing methods for identifying personality-driven factors. Cultural, political, and theological experts are needed to better understand the significant environmental components in play. Accomplished linguists might assist in clarifying where apparent resistance might actually be the result of misunderstood questions (or answers). SERE specialists — experts in designing and teaching resistance strategies — would be an invaluable resource in helping to recognize, confirm, and deconstruct the resistance strategies encountered by interrogators. Finally, it might require this wealth of resources to correctly assess if a source's failure to answer a pertinent question is the result of defiance or poor knowledgeability.

---

[67] In the author's recent discussion of this challenging scenario with a SERE psychologist, there emerged the novel idea of applying deprogramming methods used in the U.S. and abroad to help "rescue" individuals from the destructive influence of religious cults.

[68] A document described as an Al Qaeda training manual was discovered by the Manchester (England) Metropolitan Police Department in the course of a raid on the home of a suspected Al Qaeda operative. The manual was located on a computer hard drive found at the site, in a file labeled "the military series" relating to the "Declaration of Jihad." (Source: http://www.usdoj.gov/ag/manualpart1_1.pdf)

Nonverbal Communication

Human beings communicate a great deal by non-verbal means. Skilled interrogators, for example, listen closely to voices and learn a great deal from them. An interrogation is not merely a verbal performance; it is a vocal performance, and the voice projects tension, fear, a dislike of certain topics, and other useful pieces of information. It is also helpful to watch the subject's mouth, which is as a rule much more revealing than his eyes. Gestures and postures tell a story. If a subject normally gesticulates broadly at times and is at other times physically relaxed but at some point sits stiffly motionless, his posture is likely to be the physical image of his mental tension. The interrogator should make a mental note of the topic that caused such a reaction.[69]

The role of nonverbal cues in the communication process is almost universally recognized. Some researchers (Mehrabian, 1971) have suggested that as much as 90% of communication is transmitted via nonverbal channels (i.e., gestures, vocal modalities, etc.). At the same time, the underlying meaning of specific physical gestures and vocal qualities seems subject to passionate debate. *Crossing his arms means he is closed and defiant! Her posture of leaning forward indicates she is listening and engaged in the idea being presented to her.* While the social science literature is filled with numerous — and often conflicting — studies on nonverbal communication, professionals who work in the interpersonal context (e.g., counselors, salespersons, interrogators, etc.) often rely heavily upon their understanding of nonverbal behavior to complete their work.

At a fundamental level, the process of "reading" body language is not unlike that used in a polygraph examination. The critical first step is to establish a baseline for the person being examined. Just as people show individual variation in blood pressure and heart rate, people similarly exhibit dramatically different gestures and voice inflections to supplement their verbal communications. Familial, regional, and cultural background can have a significant influence on an individual's repertoire of nonverbal behaviors. At the same time, some researchers, most notably Desmond Morris, suggest there are a number of gestures that consistently communicate the same message across cultural and linguistic boundaries.[70]

Parallel Worlds: Inside and Outside the Interrogation Room

The history of interrogation is full of confessions and other self-incriminations that were in essence the result of a substitution of the interrogation world for the world outside. In other words,

---

[69]   KUBARK, 54–55.

[70]   See, for example, Desmond Morris, *Manwatching: A Field Guide to Human Behavior* (1979) or *Bodytalk: The Meaning of Human Gestures* (1995).

as the sights and sounds of an outside world fade away, its
significance for the interrogatee tends to do likewise. That world
is replaced by the interrogation room, its two occupants, and
the dynamic relationship between them. As [the] interrogation
goes on, the subject tends increasingly to divulge or withhold
in accordance with the values of the interrogation world rather
than those of the outside world.[71]

Inside the interrogation room, the principals (interrogator and source) maneuver through two primary, interdependent spheres: the physical setting and the psychological set. While the source can only realistically influence the latter, the skillful interrogator can actively manipulate both of these elements in a manner designed to achieve the overarching goal of obtaining source compliance. In the effort to induce the source to respond meaningfully to pertinent questions, the underlying strategy set forth in the KUBARK manual is systematically to separate the source from anchors of the "outside world" and reset the operative value system to those of the "interrogation world."

Perhaps the most important understanding for the interrogator to draw from this concept is that forecasting events within the interrogation world is problematic if the prediction is based on trends in the outside world. One excellent example of this conundrum is provided by Orrin DeForest's experience during the Vietnam War. Common sense would deem it unlikely that a prisoner would willingly complete a written psychological examination (especially one that would subsequently be used in formulating an effective means of exploiting that prisoner). Yet that is precisely what repeatedly occurred.

This opens up tremendous possibilities for creativity on the part of the interrogator. Employing Cialdini's principle of *social proof*, for example, the interrogator could convince the source that every one of his co-detainees has cooperated fully with the interrogator (who, operating under the rules of the *interrogation world*, can assume the persona of the helpful interviewer). Even though experience in the outside world tells the source that his colleagues were disciplined soldiers committed to the cause, as the outside world "fades away" so does his confidence in the assumptions made there.

The most important point to be made in this observation is that the *truth* of the interrogation room can range widely from that of the outside world. Those involved in the quest for new and better strategies for educing information must remain ever cognizant of this unique phenomenon.

Reconnaissance: Maintaining an Outcome-Orientation

Two dangers are especially likely to appear during the
reconnaissance. Up to this point, the interrogator has
not continued a line of questioning when resistance was

---

[71] KUBARK, 57–58.

encountered. Now, however, he does so, and rapport may be strained. Some interrogatees will take this change personally and tend to personalize the conflict. The interrogator should resist this tendency. If he succumbs to it, and becomes engaged in a battle of wits, he may not be able to accomplish the task at hand. The second temptation to avoid is the natural inclination to resort prematurely to ruses and coercive techniques in order to settle the matter then and there. The basic purpose of the reconnaissance is to determine the kind and degree of pressure that will be needed in the third stage. The interrogator should reserve his fire-power until he knows what he is up against.[72]

This passage suggests two very important guidelines for the interrogator. First, the approach to any source must be measured, systematic, and always *outcome-oriented*. What this means is that the interrogator should understand the phased nature of interrogation, that "victories" sought early can result in later "failures," and that — and this is of critical importance — one's ego should be checked at the door. The outcome-oriented approach facilitates a more reasoned, objective interrogation process, with the goal of obtaining actionable intelligence being primary. In contrast, how the source ultimately views the interrogator (e.g., as omnipotent, incompetent, clever, a genius, a dunce, etc.) is of little long-term importance.

The second point refers back to the observations on the *dual nature of interrogation*. The interrogator must constantly manage the internal-external reference dynamic in a manner that best supports the approach(es) being employed. The interrogator is present, interacting with the source, and appears to respond (believably so) in appropriate ways to the unfolding events. At the same time, the interrogator checks his or her natural emotional responses (e.g., sympathetic feelings for the source's plight, anger at the source's insults, etc.) and replaces them with fabricated responses — accompanied by nonverbal cues consistent with the response — that move the interrogation process toward the desired outcome.

As noted earlier, SERE instructors are required to complete a psychological examination and interview prior to working directly with students in resistance role-play exercises. The objective is to screen out those who appear to present a significant potential for abusing their authority. Psychological screening for interrogators might incorporate a similar filtering mechanism that would, for example, attempt to screen out candidates who demonstrate low levels of self-control. Although the now-famous Zimbardo experiment has shown that even apparently healthy, stable individuals can succumb to the authoritarian influence of power, this should not stand in the way of further research to identify personality traits, belief systems, and/or values that might enable an organization

---

[72] KUBARK, 60.

to reliably filter out those individuals with the highest probability of acting out inappropriately (i.e., abusively, violently, etc.) in the interrogation room.

In sum, the interrogation process can be an emotionally charged, high-intensity activity that requires a considerable degree of self-control — accompanied by strategic thought and action — on the part of the interrogator. The unique challenges set before the interrogator strongly underscore the importance of 1) a systematic screening and selection process, 2) comprehensive initial and ongoing training, and 3) continuous assessment of the interrogator (including a self-assessment) as well as that of the team.

Question Design: Tools of the Trade

> *Debriefing questions should usually be couched to provoke a positive answer and should be specific. The questioner should not accept a blanket negative without probing. For example, the question "Do you know anything about Plant X?"is likelier to draw a negative answer than, "Do you have any friends who work at Plant X?"or "Can you describe its interior?"*[73]

Planning, preparation, approaches, rapport-building, detection of deception, and subject matter expertise are all key elements of the overall interrogation process. In a real sense, however, each of these is but a supporting player to the art of effective questioning. Going back to the fundamental definition of interrogation set forth previously ("it consists of no more than obtaining needed information through responses to questions"), it becomes readily apparent that the entire effort hinges upon the ability of the interrogator to methodically ask meaningful questions of the source.

Of all the skills required of the accomplished interrogator, none is more important than mastery of interrogatives. Rudyard Kipling went straight to the heart of the matter when he observed, *"I kept six honest serving-men (they taught me all I knew); their names are what and why and when and how and where and who."*[74] These six questions provide the basic tools of the trade that can enable the skilled interrogator to expertly probe a source's knowledge with laser-like precision while adroitly disguising intent.

Research in the social sciences, communication theory, and linguistics has uncovered a number of useful understandings about the potential power of well-designed questions that could have immediate application in interrogation. Subtle changes in syntax, for example, have shown to greatly enhance the persuasive power of a given question (Davis and Knowles, 1999). Additional study is required to assess the effect of such questioning techniques through the cross-cultural filter.

---

[73] KUBARK, 62.
[74] From Rudyard Kipling's *Just So Stories.*

Veracity vs. Knowledgeability

It is important to determine whether the subject's knowledge of any topic was acquired first hand, learned indirectly, or represents merely an assumption. If the information was obtained indirectly, the identities of sub-sources and related information about the channel are needed. If statements rest on assumptions, the facts upon which the conclusions are based are necessary to the evaluation.[75]

One of the weaknesses attributed specifically to human intelligence (and especially to interrogation) is the questionable reliability of the information provided by a source. "Prisoners often lie!" is the oft-repeated mantra chanted by those who have ardently embraced the technical side of intelligence gathering (while overlooking the numerous examples of how camouflage, concealment, and deception or spoofing have successfully fooled imagery and signals intelligence analysts, respectively). Nonetheless, reliability is a critical factor in the human intelligence equation.

Simply stated, source reliability can be broken down into two categories: veracity and knowledgeability. Veracity refers to the truthfulness of the source, while knowledgeability refers to the scope of first-hand information a source possesses. Although two fundamentally different concepts, they can, at times, become interwoven.

- A source may tell the interrogator the truth about the topics raised in the course of the interrogation. The source may, however, have a wider range of knowledgeability than he or she has allowed to become known. Essentially, the source has told the truth…just not the whole truth.

- Conversely, a source may tell the interrogator more than he or she really knows. In an effort to secure some real or imagined form of reciprocity from the interrogator, the source speaks truthfully about all he or she knows…and then some. This "extra" may be the product of speculation, imagination, and/or fabrication.

- The end game of deception, then, occurs in two primary ways: 1) the source might purposefully falsify information and/or 2) the source might withhold known information on specific topics. While there are unique dangers inherent in each of these scenarios, both could lead to corrupted data being reported as intelligence information.

In addition to systematic questioning techniques and subject-matter expertise, assessing the veracity and knowledgeability of the source requires that the interrogator have a third critical skill: detecting deception. Scientific (and popular) literature abounds with studies of how, why, and when people deceive. Searching for reliable indicators, researchers have focused on body movements (e.g., micro-

---

[75] KUBARK, 62.

expressions), vocal cues (e.g., changes in pitch), verbal errors (e.g., so-called Freudian slips), language patterns (e.g., repeating the question), and measurable changes in physiological processes (e.g., polygraph examination and voice stress analysis). While many individuals — including interrogators — are convinced of their ability to effectively and consistently detect deception, most are unable to clearly describe the set of behaviors that provided that insight. Further, most studies indicate that these individuals' confidence in their lie-catching ability is not substantiated by performance in controlled conditions.

Although numerous studies have investigated the ability of one individual to reliably identify another's efforts to deceive, these studies have been conducted almost exclusively in the safe environment of laboratory conditions. For the "deceiver," there really are no significant consequences involved if he or she is "caught." As a result, there is minimal stress involved, yet most theorists suggest that it is stress that causes the psycho-physical changes that, in turn, are manifested by external cues (e.g., stereotypical grooming behaviors).

The Strategy of Non-Coercive Interrogation

> *If source resistance is encountered during screening or during the opening or reconnaissance phases of the interrogation, non-coercive methods of sapping opposition and strengthening the tendency to yield and to cooperate may be applied. Although these methods appear here in an approximate order of increasing pressure, it should not be inferred that each is to be tried until the key fits the lock. On the contrary, a large part of the skill and the success of the experienced interrogator lies in his ability to match method to source. The use of unsuccessful techniques will of itself increase the interrogatee's will and ability to resist.*[76]

> *The effectiveness of most of the non-coercive techniques depends upon their unsettling effect. The interrogation situation is in itself disturbing to most people encountering it for the first time. The aim is to enhance this effect, to disrupt radically the familiar emotional and psychological associations of the subject. When this aim is achieved, resistance is seriously impaired.*[77]

The KUBARK manual offers a broad array of useful insights into the interrogation process — insights gleaned from extensive real-world experience. While the coercive approaches are rightfully rejected, it is clear the intelligence officers and behavioral scientists who contributed to this manual spent considerable time studying and reflecting upon their craft. It is up to the current generation of practitioners to sort through this treatise to uncover the invaluable take-aways.

---

[76] KUBARK, 65.
[77] KUBARK, 65-66.

One of those can be found in the above passage. Interrogators must consistently guard against taking actions that will prove counterproductive as the process unfolds. Rather, interrogation must be approached in a **systematic** fashion, thinking, as a chess master must, several steps ahead of the interrogatee. This is where the aforementioned *Law of Requisite Variety* comes into play, as the interrogator always maintains at least one more method of obtaining compliance — be it a new line of questioning, an alternative approach, or a well-crafted ruse (see below) — than the source has means of resisting. But, as the manual states, employing those options in a confused, ill-conceived manner will only "increase the interrogatee's will and ability to resist."

The KUBARK manual offers specific techniques (i.e., approaches) for use in a non-coercive interrogation setting. Several of these have potential for application in current intelligence collection operations.

Going Next Door

> *Occasionally the information needed from a recalcitrant interrogatee is obtainable from a willing source...[t]he labor of extracting the truth from an unwilling interrogatee should be undertaken only if the same information is not more easily obtainable elsewhere....*[78]

One of the fallacies of interrogation — and one that continues to be a significant factor in driving the use of coercive techniques — is the concept that *every* detainee is a unique, invaluable, and irreplaceable source of intelligence information and therefore must be leveraged into compliance. As with the "ticking nuclear bomb" scenario so often cited in the debate over just how far U.S. interrogators should go to force a source to cooperate, such instances are extremely rare. Nonetheless, there is almost a default pattern wherein the path of *greatest resistance* is taken with a recalcitrant source rather than taking the more strategic route of seeking the same information from a more accessible and compliant source.

This common miscue is based on two fundamental errors in judgment. The first is an ego-based error. While persistence is a critical characteristic of many successful interrogators, the most accomplished among them focus their finite resources (e.g., time and energy) on the challenges that present the most attractive risk/gain ratio. After spending sufficient time to establish that the source's resistance posture will be a significant hurdle, the wise interrogator quickly asks himself/herself, in keeping with the KUBARK manual guidance quoted above, "Where else can I obtain the information I need?" Such prudent interrogators are not driven by the need to demonstrate their skill in overcoming a particular source's line of resistance; rather, they are driven by the intractable need to obtain the desired information from whatever source is liable to offer it up.

---

[78]   KUBARK, 66.

Second, there is the tactical error of assuming that a source's level of resistance is directly correlated with his level of knowledgeability. While common sense might suggest a logic inherent in this assumption, reality will quickly correct it. Resistance is the direct product of several key factors: training, life experience, personality, commitment to a cause, deep-seated feelings about the interrogator and/or his country of origin, and even anger at the manner in which the source has been treated since capture. Any one of these can lead the truck driver to protect the already compromised route he was to drive during an operation more fiercely than a less-motivated nuclear engineer will protect the key to disabling a radioactive dispersal device.[79]

Nobody Loves You

> *An interrogatee who is withholding items of no grave consequence to himself may sometimes be persuaded to talk by the simple tactic of pointing out that to date all of the information about his case has come from persons other than himself. The interrogator wants to be fair. He recognizes that some of the denouncers may have been biased or malicious...the source owes it to himself to be sure that the interrogator hears both sides of the story.*[80]

(See observations under next heading.)

Joint Suspects

> *If two or more interrogation sources are suspected of joint complicity in acts directed against U.S. security, they should be separated immediately. If time permits, it may be a good idea (depending upon the psychological assessment of both) to postpone interrogation for about a week. Any anxious inquiries from either can be met with a knowing grin and some such reply as, "We'll get to you in due time. There's no hurry now."*[81]

The primary difference between these two approaches is that in the first the source is presented with evidence — largely implicit — that other, unnamed, unknown (to the source), and as yet unseen detainees have provided information that reflects negatively upon him, while in the second scenario the interrogator refers directly to damaging information gathered from other detainees known to the source.

Leveraging one source against another is a common police tactic (the central idea of the classic "prisoner's dilemma") and is especially useful when dealing

---

[79] A radioactive dispersal device is often referred to in the media and in popular literature as a "dirty bomb."

[80] KUBARK, 67.

[81] KUBARK, 70.

with sources who have limited or no training in resistance strategies. With sufficient validated intelligence supporting him, the interrogator can effectively present information to source A that was allegedly (and plausibly) provided by source B. The wedge thus placed, in conjunction with time and careful orchestration, can be effective in eliciting progressively more information independently from each source.

The All-Seeing Eye

> *The interrogator who already knows part of the story explains to the source that the purpose of the questioning is not to gain information; the interrogator knows everything already. His real purpose is to test the sincerity (reliability, honor, etc.) of the source. The interrogator then asks a few questions to which he knows the answers. If the subject lies, he is informed firmly and dispassionately that he has lied. By skilled manipulation of the known, the questioner can convince a naïve subject that all his secrets are out and that further resistance would be not only pointless but dangerous.*[82]

Similar to the *We Know All* approach outlined in U.S. Army Field Manual 34-52, the All-Seeing Eye has proven consistently effective with a broad array of sources.[83] While simple in concept, as with other effective approaches, the underlying dynamic can be far more complex. In this instance, two fundamental activities occur to render it effective in obtaining compliance from a resistant source.

First, Cialdini's *authority* principle plays an important part in this approach. The source, convinced that the interrogator knows as much as (perhaps more than) he does, sees little to be gained from protecting information of such apparently little value, especially if he anticipates that the consequences of withholding such information are undesirable. Second, recalling the premise that two of the interrogator's primary objectives are to increase the stress the source internalizes about the consequences of resistance while simultaneously reducing the internalized stress over the prospect of cooperating, this approach systematically targets the latter. By maintaining this approach over time, the interrogator is able to introduce a new and perhaps unexpected factor in the source's resistance/cooperation calculus.

Ivan Is a Dope

> *It may be useful to point out to a hostile [source] that the cover story was ill-contrived, that the other service botched the job,*

---

[82] KUBARK, 67.

[83] The author refers to this approach as "The Exquisite Ruse," and has used it with great effect in interrogation operations conducted during Operations JUST CAUSE, DESERT STORM, and IRAQI FREEDOM.

that it is typical of the other service to ignore the welfare of its agents. The interrogator may personalize this pitch by explaining that he has been impressed by the [source's] courage and intelligence.[84]

This approach also leverages the psychological and emotional partition between aforementioned values outside the interrogation room and those inside the interrogation room. By using this approach effectively, the interrogator continues to separate the source from his or her external anchors. In this instance, that anchor is a belief in the parent service's skill in managing cover to properly protect the source operationally. This has direct application to the interrogation of suspected terrorists, not only as it relates to cover support, but also to the threat briefings, operational planning, and equipment provided to the source by his or her sponsoring organization.

A key element of *systematic interrogation* is systematic innovation. Rather than assume that the approaches outlined in U.S. Army Field Manual 34-52 are the limit of their repertoire of tactics, interrogators should view those approaches as only the very beginning. The drafters of the KUBARK manual demonstrated the value to be found in the ability to adapt to new challenges, design innovative strategies, identify through practical experience what appears to consistently work well, *and* share these novel concepts with other interrogators. If a central clearinghouse for new interrogation tactics, techniques, and procedures existed — a means of capturing and widely disseminating the experience and insights of operators in the field — it is quite probable that the art of interrogation would currently be taught and practiced in a significantly different and far more effective fashion.

The Need to Communicate

...continued questioning about lofty topics that the source knows nothing about may pave the way for the extraction of information at lower levels...complaints that he knows nothing of such matters are met by flat insistence that he does know, he would have to know, that even the most stupid men in his position know...after the process has continued long enough, the source was asked a question to which he did know the answer. Numbers of [former] American [POWs] have mentioned "the tremendous feeling of relief you get when [the interrogator] finally asks you something you can answer...I know it seems strange now, but I was positively grateful to them when they switched to a topic I knew something about."[85]

---

[84] KUBARK, 72.
[85] KUBARK, 75.

In yet another example of the many conundrums of the interrogation room, common sense would suggest that sources would find an advantage in being asked questions concerning topics about which they knew little or nothing. Such circumstances do not place them in a position where they felt pressure to deceive ("falsify") or purposely withhold ("conceal") information. As reported by U.S. POWs who were subjected to this manner of questioning during the Korean War, however, it often proved true that the inability to answer questions created tremendous pressure and, as the quotation above illustrates, the opportunity finally to address questions within the scope of their experience and knowledgeability proved a welcome relief. The need to communicate is surprisingly powerful, and more powerful still under traumatic circumstances.

Cialdini provides another perspective that may be a relevant factor at play in this approach. In his *rejection-then-retreat* scenario, when one asks for something difficult (a request that might often be denied) and then asks for something less demanding, the compliance rate for the lesser demand is higher when the demand is preceded by the more difficult demand than when the questions are asked in isolation.[86] In the context of interrogation, a source may be reluctant to answer sweeping questions about organizational plans and intentions, but, in contrast, may be less guarded about lower-level details. Although declining to answer questions about strategic-level topics, the source may feel less pressure to keep from answering questions about tactical-level topics.

Taking into account Cialdini's *consistency principle* (i.e., people tend to act in a manner consistent with formal, public statements made or positions taken previously),[87] this strategy would probably work more effectively when the interrogator asks the strategic-level question, but, sensing hesitation on the part of the source, withdraws it *before* the source has the chance to resist. If allowed to formally assume a resistance posture, the pressure to remain consistent with that decision may have a greater influence than the relief gained from being able to respond to a question with which the source is more comfortable.

What internal dialogue takes place within a source in response to various approaches? Can Cialdini's principles of persuasion explain, at least in part, why a given approach elicits compliance from a source? Do certain trends in behavior in the interrogation room prove valid in a sufficient number of cases that they can be routinely employed with a high degree of probability of ultimately proving effective? The review of available literature strongly suggests that these critical questions, and others, have not been satisfactorily addressed with regard to the traditional approaches and other tactics, techniques, and procedures still being employed. The move to the next generation of strategies for educing information depends on research that can uncover the answer to these questions. Once this has been accomplished, ineffective methods can be eliminated from the training curricula and replaced by innovative strategies complete with a valid description of the underlying factors that are essential to success.

---

[86] Cialdini, 36–51.
[87] Cialdini, 57–113.

> *The aim of the* Alice in Wonderland *or confusion technique is to confound the expectations and conditioned reactions of the interrogatee. He is accustomed to a world that makes sense, at least to him: a world of continuity and logic, a predictable world. He clings to this world to reinforce his identity and powers of resistance. The confusion technique is designed not only to obliterate the familiar, but to replace it with the weird...as the process continues, day after day as necessary, the subject begins to try to make sense of the situation, which becomes mentally intolerable...he is likely to make significant admissions, or even to pour out his story.*[88]

SERE psychologists have identified the inability to effectively forecast near-term events as a major stressor in the detention environment. Adults grow accustomed to having a reasonable degree of control over their lives, which enables them to make accurate predictions about basic events such as when they go to sleep, when they wake up, when they eat, and when they use the toilet. In addition, if they find themselves encountering unpleasant circumstances (e.g., an annoying neighbor, a time-wasting work associate, etc.), it is normally within their power to escape those stressful situations at will (or least minimize the time spent engaged with the unattractive individual). In detention, avoidance may not be an option.

The KUBARK principle described in the passage above suggests that an interrogator is able to generate a significant degree of pressure on a source through the purposeful creation of confusing circumstances that effectively remove the source's ability to make predictions. In effect, the source struggles to find a familiar logic to the chain of events, the nature of the interactions, and purpose of the exchanges with the interrogator. As the struggle proves unsuccessful, the level of stress can dramatically rise to an exceptionally uncomfortable level. According to the KUBARK manual, sources may offer up information to the interrogator in an effort to overtly introduce "sense" to their chaotic circumstances. In discussing that information, the source has recaptured a degree of comforting predictability.

From the source's perspective, the experience of being detained and interrogated would seem to have inherent elements of disorder and ambiguity. The effect this has on a given source (negative or positive) would appear, then, to be directly correlated with each source's need for order and level of comfort/ discomfort with ambiguity. While the literature on Communist methods of interrogation frequently references the value of confusion in obtaining compliance, it is less clear as it applies to obtaining relevant, accurate information. Perhaps additional study is warranted on the effects of confusion as well as a means for rapidly assessing a source's tolerance for disorder and ambiguity.

---

[88]   KUBARK, 76.

The Regression Factor: The Fundamental Objective of Coercive Methodology

All coercive techniques are designed to induce regression...the result of external pressures of sufficient intensity is the loss of those defenses most recently acquired by civilized man: "the capacity to carry out the highest creative activities, to meet new, challenging, and complex situations, to deal with trying interpersonal relations, and to cope with repeated frustrations. Relatively small degrees of homeostatic derangements, fatigue, pain, sleep loss, or anxiety may impair these functions." As a result, "most people who are exposed to coercive procedures will talk and usually reveal some information that they might not have revealed otherwise."[89]

The deprivation of stimuli induces regression by depriving the subject's mind of contact with an outer world and thus forcing it in upon itself. At the same time, the calculated provision of stimuli during interrogation tends to make the regressed subject view the interrogator as a father-figure. The result, normally, is a strengthening of the subject's tendencies toward compliance.[90]

Listening to the post-9/11 debate over guidelines for the interrogation of terrorist suspects, one could easily conclude that coercive methods are not only effective, but also substantially *more* effective than non-coercive methods in obtaining actionable intelligence from resistant sources. Even those opposed to the use of coercive methods fail to challenge this premise, exclusively focusing their arguments instead on the legal and moral issues at stake.

Those issues aside, from a geopolitical perspective alone, a judicious risk/gain assessment of this course of action is of critical importance, as the consequences are considerable. This was dramatically illustrated by the anti-American demonstrations throughout the Muslim world in response to revelations of the abuses at the Abu Ghraib prison in Iraq. Ironically, while those risks are not exceptionally difficult to ascertain, the potential for gain is arguably problematic since the scientific community has never established that coercive interrogation methods are an effective means of obtaining reliable intelligence information. In essence, there seems to be an unsubstantiated assumption that "compliance" carries the same connotation as "meaningful cooperation" (i.e., a source induced to provide accurate, relevant information of potential intelligence value).[91]

---

[89] KUBARK, 83.

[90] KUBARK, 90.

[91] Claims from some members of the operational community as to the alleged effectiveness of coercive methods in educing meaningful information from resistant sources are, at best, anecdotal in nature and would be, in the author's view, unlikely to withstand the rigors of sound scientific inquiry.

The concept of regression appears to be a consistent theme in much of the research conducted on long-term detention and interrogation, a considerable portion of which involved the experiences of U.S. military personnel held prisoner during the Korean conflict. The psychologist Martin Orne, writing in 1961, noted that:

> [C]onditions of interrogation are sometimes conducive to
> a regression on the part of the source. The interrogator can
> exercise complete control of the source's physical being
> — his primitive needs such as elimination, eating, and
> sleeping, and even bodily postures. He is also in a position
> to reward or punish any predetermined activity on the part
> of the captive. This tends to create a situation where the
> individual feels unable to observe any control over himself.
> This extreme loss of control is handled in a variety of ways,
> one of which is regression to a childlike state of dependence
> on and identification with the aggressor...some prisoners
> adopt a cooperative role because of the need to reassure
> themselves that they retain some control over their behavior
> in the coercive situation. Complying "voluntarily" for such
> cases is less threatening, and may be regarded by them as less
> shameful, than losing control completely over their actions.[92]

Assuming for a moment that this regression dynamic accurately describes the underlying process that leads a once-resistant source toward compliance,[93] the use of interrogation techniques to bring about regression still raises a number of key questions:

1. What precise means are required to obtain this end?

2. What are the overarching management and operational requirements for orchestrating such a process?

3. Is the length of time required for the regression to occur reasonable enough to render it a useful method of obtaining time-sensitive intelligence?

4. What are the long-term effects of the regression experience?

5. Are individuals subjected to this condition profoundly changed?

6. Is their emotional and psychological stability significantly harmed such that treatment is required to address — and reverse — the condition?

7. What are the legal and moral issues involved?

---

[92] Martin T. Orne, "The Potential Uses of Hypnosis in Interrogation," in *The Manipulation of Human Behavior*, ed. Albert D. Biderman and Herbert Zimmer (New York: John Wiley and Sons, Inc., 1961), 206. Hereafter referred to as *The Manipulation of Human Behavior*.

[93] Two additional important points with respect to regression warrant further comment. First, a given individual's response to circumstances designed specifically to cause regression cannot be reliably predicted in advance. Second, regression in general receives far less professional acceptance as a psychological concept today than was true in the 1950–1960 timeframe.

8. How would the revelation of this form of interrogation be received by various audiences, domestic and foreign?

9. Would the use of coercive methods — real or alleged — have an impact on the treatment of U.S. personnel held captive in adversarial hands?

10. Would the use of forced regression as a sanctioned method of exploitation be viewed as being consistent with long-standing U.S. values and military traditions?

11. The above considerations notwithstanding, *does the use of regression consistently produce reliable, actionable intelligence information?*

In *The Manipulation of Human Behavior*, Biderman decried the fact that, in 1961, the "dearth of sober information on interrogation has had the unfortunate consequence of facilitating the exploitation of United States prisoners of war by Communist captors."[94] While he was specifically addressing a research shortfall that undermined training in the resistance to interrogation for U.S. military personnel, the same observation remains essentially true over 40 years later with regard to the paucity of relevant information on effective tactics, techniques, and procedures for the interrogation of adversarial detainees under U.S. control.

Obstacles to Meaningful Intelligence: The Negative Effects of Coercion

> *[T]he response to coercion typically contains "at least three important elements: debility, dependency, and dread."*[95]

> *"[A]mong the American POWs pressured by the Chinese Communists, the DDD syndrome in its full-blown form constituted a state of discomfort that was well-nigh intolerable."*
> *If the debility-dependency-dread state is unduly prolonged, however, the [source] may sink into a defensive apathy from which it is hard to arouse him.*[96]

> *Psychologists and others who write about physical or psychological duress frequently object that under sufficient pressure subjects usually yield but that their ability to recall and communicate information accurately is as impaired as the will to resist.*[97]

> *...a strong fear of anything vague or unknown induces regression, whereas the materialization of the fear, the infliction of some form of punishment, is likely to come as a relief. The subject finds that he can hold out, and his resistances are strengthened.*

[94] Albert Biderman, "Introduction – Manipulations of Human Behavior," in *The Manipulation of Human Behavior*, 4.
[95] KUBARK, 83.
[96] KUBARK, 84.
[97] KUBARK, 84.

*In general, direct physical brutality creates only resentment,
hostility, and further defiance.*[98]

As these passages from the KUBARK manual suggest, the very means by
which coercive methods undermine the source's resistance posture may also
concomitantly degrade his ability to report the intelligence information they
possess in a valid, comprehensive fashion. There would, then, appear to be a
very fine line that the interrogator would need to walk deftly as he uses sufficient
force to cause the source to yield to questioning, but not so much as to impede the
source's ability to answer those questions meaningfully.

In examining this complex issue, it is important to keep clearly in mind that
interrogations take place in real-world settings, without the controls available
in the safety of the institutional research environment. Managing levels of
internalized pressure experienced by a source subjected to coercive means is
most definitely neither a science nor a precise art. The pressure interrogators and
overseers would seek to measure is an elusive entity, one that can only be gauged
by highly subjective standards. Levels of pressure introduced by coercive methods,
as with torture in general, are often in the eye of the beholder as illustrated in the
following passage from *Phoenix and the Birds of Prey*, an account of Operation
Phoenix, conducted during the Vietnam War:

> Some people define torture as the infliction of *severe* physical pain
> on a defenseless person. I define torture as the infliction of *any* pain
> on a defenseless individual because deciding which activities inflict
> severe pain is an excessively complicated and imprecise business.
> (Original italics)[99]

The KUBARK manual offers unique and exceptional insights into the
complex challenges of educing information from a resistant source through non-
coercive means. While it addresses the use of coercive methods, it also describes
how those methods may prove ultimately counterproductive. Although criticized
for its discussion of coercion, the KUBARK manual does not portray coercive
methods as a necessary — or even viable — means of effectively educing
information.

Shock of Capture: A Strategic Inflection Point in an Interrogation

*The manner and timing of arrest can contribute
substantially to the interrogator's purposes. "What we
aim to do is to ensure that the manner of arrest achieves,
if possible, surprise, and the maximum amount of mental
discomfort in order to catch the suspect off balance and
to deprive him of the initiative."*[100]

---

[98] KUBARK, 90–91.
[99] Mark Moyer, *Phoenix and the Birds of Prey* (Annapolis, MD: Naval Institute Press, 1997), 90.
[100] KUBARK, 85.

According to the tactical interrogation model, a source should be questioned as soon as possible after capture to obtain time-perishable intelligence information. In the strategic interrogation model, the importance of the time component has less to do with the nature of the intelligence sought than with exploiting a unique window of vulnerability in the detention experience.

Only a small percentage of military personnel, and a much smaller percentage of terrorists and insurgents, have been exposed to resistance training that includes the stress-inoculation of intensive practical exercises. As a result, the trauma and the perceived chaos of capture — the so-called "shock of capture" — and initial detention will likely prove profoundly unsettling and cause detainees to do and say things against their interest that, upon reflection under more stable circumstances, they would not do or say. In most instances, newly captured detainees expect the worst in terms of treatment at the hands of the enemy and only later draw strength from the realization that they will not be killed or brutally tortured. By exploiting this initial period of overwhelming confusion, the well-trained and prepared interrogator may be able to obtain useful information through the immediate questioning of a source.

The shock of capture phenomenon is not necessarily limited to the initial point of detention. Every time the detainee is transferred to new surroundings — a new cell, a different wing of the current holding facility, or an entirely new facility — a measure of shock of capture will likely occur. The detainee can be presented with a strange setting, a different routine, new guards, and a fresh interrogator. The rules of engagement in effect at the previous place of confinement may no longer apply in the new facility. The trauma born of confusion, ambiguity, and negative expectations can produce a new period of capture shock that an interrogator can strategically exploit.

A creative and often effective strategy for profiting from the shock of capture phenomenon is to use a *dislocation of expectations* approach. For example, anticipating mistreatment in the hands of the "infidels," the detainee may steel himself for the worst, preparing mentally to respond to harsh approaches, abusive language, and a blatant disregard for personal and cultural preferences. With such hardened expectations, the detainee may be ill prepared to encounter someone who affords him better treatment and demonstrates an impressive understanding of his culture and language. Without a clear strategy at the ready for resisting this unexpected turn of events, the source may find himself — similar to the situation described above — responding to questions that he might choose to ignore or outright refuse to answer later on.

Interrogation is both an art and a science, with the proportion attributed to each difficult to determine precisely. In many instances, a "principle" of interrogation (i.e., a concept or method that has proven consistently applicable in a variety of circumstances) may have an equally true obverse. The KUBARK manual emphasizes the importance of conducting early "reconnaissance" of a source: screening and initial interrogation sessions designed exclusively to assess personality, to identify strengths, and to probe for weaknesses. Only after this has been accomplished would the interrogator begin the formal examination process. Such an approach has often proven effective.

The shock of capture phenomenon, by contrast, suggests that there are instances where a brief window of opportunity presents itself for the interrogator to question the source with little or no preliminary assessment. This approach has also proven effective.

Which method is better? If research were able to provide a valid answer, or to point to a protocol that could assist an interrogator in making the correct call on a consistent basis, this would then become an element of the overall interrogation process that could be moved from the category of "art" to "science." Until then, the selection of an approach for dealing with newly detained sources remains not unlike the artist's selection of paint from a palette filled with an array of attractive hues…the appropriateness of the selection largely reflects the talent of the artist.

The Challenge of Apathy

> Little is gained if confinement merely replaces one routine with another. Prisoners who lead monotonously unvaried lives "cease to care about their utterances, dress, and cleanliness. They become dulled, apathetic, and depressed." And apathy can be a very effective defense against interrogation.[101]

> Little is known about the duration of confinement calculated to make a subject shift from anxiety, coupled with a desire for sensory stimuli and human companionship, to a passive, apathetic acceptance of isolation and ultimate pleasure in the negative state. Undoubtedly, the rate of change is determined almost entirely by the psychological characteristics of the individual.[102]

Once again, this observation demonstrates the unique challenge of source management: a challenge made even more complex by the introduction of coercive measures. Perhaps the principle to be drawn here is that the interrogator may use the advantage of physical setting (i.e., confinement, routine, movement) to his advantage…but only to a point. The prolonged effort to influence psychological set by controlling the physical setting can quickly and unexpectedly become counterproductive when, as in the scenario cited above, the source's routine existence and distant hope of release cause him to view his circumstances — and his life, his future, and the prospects for change — with apathy.

This brings up a larger point about the fundamental nature of interrogation as either a "push" or "pull" ("control" or "rapport") phenomenon. In the former, the

---

[101] KUBARK, 86.
[102] KUBARK, 87.

interrogator seeks to use his control advantages to introduce external, "moving away" pressure on the source to comply. For example, the interrogator can place the source in isolation; establish mind-numbing routine or constant, unsettling change in the source's daily activities; or introduce physicality into the interaction. The myriad forms of coercive methods essentially attempt to obtain capitulation in this manner.

By contrast, the "pull" approach views interrogation as not unlike a recruitment. The interrogator, having invested sufficient time in assessing the source's personality and — most important — that which the source values, seeks to introduce internal, "moving toward" pressure. When this is deftly accomplished, the interrogator presents the source with an attractive goal (i.e., freedom, better treatment, communication with family) that appears to be within the source's sphere of influence through cooperative behavior. In essence, the source comes to recognize — through implicit or explicit communication from the interrogator — that the source's actions can achieve these goals. For the interrogator, the challenge is to ensure that the path to the source's objectives will lead directly through the accomplishment of the interrogator's own objectives. In a recruitment, this might mean that to achieve the source's goal (e.g., removing the autocratic regime currently ruling his country, sending his children to college in the United States, etc.), the source would need to help the case officer by agreeing to serve as an agent reporting on specific targets of intelligence interest. In an interrogation, the line between the source and his or her goal (e.g., early release) runs directly through the interrogator's objective (i.e., actionable intelligence on priority information requirements).

While a dearth of evidence exists regarding the efficacy of either the "push" or "pull" model of interrogation, there are two important considerations, one relating to time intensity and the other to the scope of information. Both approaches are likely to be time-intensive (despite the seemingly popular belief that coercive measures are more likely to produce the desired intelligence in time to resolve the "ticking time-bomb" scenario). But in the best of circumstances, it is anticipated that the control model would obtain information only in direct response to the specific questions posed. In contrast, the "rapport" model is more likely to obtain not only similar kinds of information, but also additional information within the scope of the source's knowledgeability that was not necessarily addressed by the interrogator. In the former, the source seeks minimal fulfillment of requirements to move away from the pressure of control; in the latter, the source is more prone to provide satisfaction of requirements and additional self-initiated reporting to enhance rapport…and expedite movement toward objectives.

The Effects of Isolation

> *"The symptoms most commonly produced by isolation are superstition, intense love of any other living thing, perceiving inanimate objects as alive, hallucinations, and delusions."*
> *The apparent reason for these effects is that a person cut off from external stimuli turns his awareness inward, upon*

himself, and then projects the contents of his own unconscious outwards....[103]

The stated objective of using isolation in the context of an interrogation is not to inflict punishment, but to leverage the source into compliance, a state in which the source is willing to answer pertinent questions on areas within the scope of the source's knowledgeability and direct access. Given the following description of interrogation, drawn from U.S. Army Field Manual 34-52, *Intelligence Interrogation*, obtaining source compliance would appear to be a critical step in the overall process.

> *Interrogation is the process of questioning a source to* obtain the maximum amount of usable information. *The goal of any interrogation is to* obtain reliable information in a lawful manner, in a minimum of time, and to satisfy intelligence requirements *of any echelon of command.*[104] *(Emphasis added)*

Since holding detainees under specific conditions of isolation for a sufficient period of time appears to produce compliance — the willingness to respond to questioning — and since compliance is a key step in the interrogation process, logic would therefore suggest that isolation would be an effective interrogation technique. The problem arises when one introduces an additional, indispensable element to the concept of compliance. Given that the objective of an interrogation, as set forth in FM 34-52, is to obtain *usable* and *reliable* information (and in a *lawful* manner), compliance means not just the *willingness* to answer questions, but also the *ability*.

Hinkle, whose medical studies serve as a major reference cited in the KUBARK manual, raises fundamental questions about the ability of a source subjected to extended isolation to provide meaningful, coherent answers in response to an interrogator's questions. He observed that "Any attempt to produce compliant behavior by procedures which produce...disturbances of homeostasis, fatigue, sleep deprivation, isolation, discomfort, or disturbing emotional states carries with it the *hazard of producing inaccuracy and unreliability.*"[105] (Emphasis added.)

Much of the Cold War-era research on Communist methods of interrogation sanctioned by the U.S. Government was conducted to obtain a better understanding of, and therefore an enhanced ability to withstand, coercive interrogation methods. Therefore, emphasis on the subject's vulnerability to compliance-inducing techniques overshadowed the concept of the source's ability to report information

---

[103] KUBARK, 88.

[104] Department of the Army, *U.S. Army Intelligence And Interrogation Handbook* (Guilford, CT: The Lyons Press, 2005), 8.

[105] Lawrence E. Hinkle, Jr., "The Physiological State of the Interrogation Subject as it Affects Brain Function," in *The Manipulation of Human Behavior*, 43.

reliably.[106] Perusing the literature on long-term isolation, one quickly draws the conclusion that the subject experiences profound emotional, psychological, and physical discomfort, and that such abuse would therefore fail to measure up to the standards for the treatment of prisoners as set forth in international accords and U.S. Federal statutes. In this alone, it fails one criterion of interrogation noted in FM 34-52: *lawfulness*.

From a purely operational perspective, the effects of isolation can truly be a double-edged sword. Isolation, especially in the initial stages of an interrogation, is a fundamental strategy designed to prevent a source from collaborating with other detainees (e.g., coordinating an overarching "story") as well as from drawing emotional and psychological strength from time spent in the company of associates. This notwithstanding, the literature also suggests that effects of isolation can significantly and negatively impact the ability of the source to recall information accurately. Given that source veracity and the reliability of HUMINT source reporting have long been viewed as problematic within the Intelligence Community, long-term isolation of sources appears unlikely to produce useful data.

The Interrogator's Checklist

The KUBARK manual sets forth an Interrogator's Checklist of 50 questions (although several have been deleted for security reasons) that would be exceptionally useful in guiding the interrogator through all phases of the interrogation process. With an uncommon degree of both depth and breadth, the questions are arranged sequentially, enabling the interrogator not only to carefully consider a broad range of complex factors involved in an extended interrogation, but also to evaluate the results of the interrogation objectively. This latter aspect would foster the type of reflection necessary to continually improve knowledge, skills and abilities.

The checklist includes several questions that are particularly noteworthy. It asks the interrogator, for instance, to consider whether the interrogation is even necessary or if the information requirements could be satisfied through other, overt sources (the *"Going Next Door"* approach cited previously). The checklist reminds the interrogator of the importance of rapport, asking if it has been established properly during the opening phase of the interrogation. If the interrogator anticipates that the source will be resistant, it directs the interrogator's focus to the source of that resistance (e.g., fear, political convictions, stubbornness, etc.).[107]

Intelligence analysts have described the changing tactics and strategies employed by terrorists and insurgents as indicative of a learning organization.

---

[106] This is an especially important observation to recall as individuals from the SERE community contribute to the study of educing information from resistant sources. As with the research studies that support them, SERE training and practical exercises focus on issues pertaining to compliance rather than information reporting reliability.

[107] KUBARK, 105–109.

The U.S. interrogation effort must similarly learn and adapt to the emerging challenges it faces in gathering information from detainees. This checklist can serve as a useful template for building a contemporary version tailored to meet the unique requirements of educing information in response to current and future challenges to the national security interests of the United States.

Bibliographic Reference

The KUBARK manual includes an extensive bibliography, including a number of references produced by the notable researchers Biderman and Hinkle. Also included are several military documents pertaining to interrogation developed at Fort Holabird, the former center for military HUMINT operational training. For security reasons, a number of references have been excised completely (evidenced only by the remaining entry number in the bibliography).

Findings

A careful examination of the KUBARK manual yields a wealth of potentially valuable concepts that either have the potential for immediate application in the development of a next generation of tactics, techniques, and procedures for educing information or that warrant further study by relevant professionals. While most of these have been identified previously, a few additional observations — some of which cross over two or more of the topics addressed earlier — merit specific comment.

- A theme that recurs in the KUBARK manual is that interrogation is defined both by its intensely interpersonal nature and intractably shaped by the unique personalities of both the interrogator and the source. This observation suggests both an important avenue of research as well as a notable caution. In describing interrogation as an "interpersonal" event, it offers social scientists an important sense of how to approach — at least initially — this complex activity. At the same time, it seems to offer a reminder that, in many important ways, each interrogation is unique and therefore one must be cautious in trying to apply a strategic template that would prove effective in each case.

- Because interrogation is a complex process, practitioners of the art of interrogation require extensive training and progressive, supervised experience to meet current and emerging operational requirements. From the moment of capture, the value of a given source's knowledgeability begins to degrade as the gap in direct access to the information of intelligence interest widens and memory for detail diminishes. The windows of opportunity to gather information in response to priority intelligence requirements are finite, especially those involving high-value targets. In the course of an interrogation, errors in strategy, approach planning, and actions are in many instances irreversible.

- In seeking to identify an effective protocol for selecting and training a cadre of interrogators who would ultimately be able to perform at this level, the Intelligence Community might derive value from reviewing selection and training models for activities involving similarly intense psycho-physical operations (e.g., sports, martial arts, surgery, psychotherapy, etc.). Consideration might be given to modeling this internal-external reference dynamic as executed by high-performing individuals with the objective of designing methods for developing and enhancing the necessary supporting skills and strategies.

- The study of nonverbal communication highlights a central theme in the Educing Information study: How do we know what we know? Given that the search for timely, accurate, and responsive intelligence information from a source can be easily corrupted by the misreading of a single gesture or voice inflection, the importance of this avenue of research cannot be overstated.

6
Custodial Interrogations: What We Know, What We Do, and What We Can Learn from Law Enforcement Experiences

Ariel Neuman
Daniel Salinas-Serrano

Harvard Law School
April 2005

Conducted under the supervision of Professor Philip Heymann[108]

[108] Completion of this paper would have been impossible without the invaluable assistance and support of many individuals. First, we thank Harvard Law School professor Philip Heymann, Dr. Robert Fein, and Secret Service Agent (Ret.) Bryan Vossekuil for their invaluable and unwavering support, counsel, and advice throughout. Our countless meetings and conversations helped direct our research and shape ideas without which our efforts would have come to a screeching halt. We are also indebted to Supervisory Special Agent Brian Boetig, of the Federal Bureau of Investigation's Law Enforcement Communication Unit, and the rest of the helpful staff at the FBI Academy in Quantico, Virginia, for making our visit there an informative one. Likewise, our research would have been significantly undermined without the incalculable assistance and hospitality of Mark Fallon, Deputy Assistant Director of the Naval Criminal Investigative Service Training Academy, and the rest of the staff at the Federal Law Enforcement Training Center in Glynco, Georgia. Finally, we would like to thank Daniel J. Coleman, Deputy Superintendent and Commander of the Homicide Unit of the Boston Police Department, Colin Sturgeon, Detective Superintendent of the Police Service of Northern Ireland, and Lieutenant Albert F. Pierce, Jr., MIT Police Department, for sharing their incomparable experience and perspectives on the topic of custodial interrogation. Any and all mistakes or omissions contained in this paper are the sole responsibility of its authors.

Abstract

This report explores both the literature and practice related to interrogation of suspects in custody, focusing almost exclusively – as the literature and practice do – on eliciting confessions to crimes. The theoretical literature lays the groundwork for interrogation practice by identifying the reasons why suspects do or do not confess to crimes, while empirical findings pinpoint factors associated with admissions and denials. Almost all manuals on interrogation techniques cover the same aspects of successful interrogation as the seminal Reid Technique: (1) characteristics/qualifications of the interrogator; (2) pre-interrogation fact gathering and analysis; (3) the interrogation setting; (4) pre-interrogation interview and rapport-building; (5) analysis of behavioral symptoms; (6) interrogation of the suspect; (7) detection of deceit; and (8) securing the confession. A comparison of theory and technique reveals that the interrogation techniques advocated in the literature take little account of the factors that the empirical research shows might affect a suspect's willingness to confess, and provide little or no guidance to varying approaches for different types of suspects.

Against this background, the report next reviews training and practice at the Federal Bureau of Investigation, the Federal Law Enforcement Training Center, and the Homicide Division of the Boston Police Department, as well as the personal experience of a senior detective in the MIT Police Department. Findings indicate that federal and local organizations provide little training specifically on interrogation; moreover, agencies do not collect data to establish whether their operatives actually apply the training they do receive, nor to evaluate the effectiveness of different interrogation approaches. Law enforcement officers report that innate personality traits and on-the-job learning, rather than formal instruction or guidelines, determine success as an interrogator.

The authors also interviewed senior officials in Northern Ireland to determine how practices in other countries differ from those in the United States. A detective superintendent of the Police Service of Northern Ireland noted that rules recently adopted in Great Britain almost preclude confessions by suspects; instead, interrogation is viewed as a part of an information-gathering process.

While few U.S. jurisdictions require that interrogations be videotaped, the law enforcement entities that use the practice report that it does not appear to reduce the effectiveness of interrogations. In fact, videotaping should benefit both the practice and outcome of interrogations by providing a record for the courts and allowing supervisors to review and if necessary correct the practices of their staffs.

The effectiveness of standard interrogation techniques has never been validated by empirical research. Moreover, techniques designed to obtain confessions to crimes may have only limited relevance to preventive investigations of terrorist-related activities. The authors recommend further research addressing both issues, and also suggest that the United States consider adopting the practice of providing intensive training to a select group of professionals who would then conduct all interrogations.

Introduction

This paper has three primary purposes. First, it reviews the literature available on the topic of interrogation to offer an organized and cohesive survey of the available knowledge on the topic. Second, it seeks to present an overview of how several domestic and foreign law enforcement agencies handle interrogations, both in training and practice. Finally, the paper attempts to frame questions for further study and to discern some potential lessons to be learned from law enforcement for current and future terrorism-related situations in which interrogations might be a relevant component.

This paper, like the project that sponsored it, does not attempt to offer novel approaches to custodial interrogation, or to present groundbreaking psychological insights into this investigative tool. The scope of the paper is further limited by the subject matter it covers. It is decidedly not a general study on all possible aspects and issues of police interviewing; instead, it focuses on situations that conform generally to Inbau, Reid, Buckley, and Jayne's definition of interrogation: "the accusatory questioning of a suspect involving active persuasion that occurs in a controlled environment when an investigator is reasonably certain of a suspect's guilt, for the purpose of learning the truth."[109] Thus, interviews of witnesses and victims are outside the purview of this project; the paper deals only with interrogations of suspects who are in custody or otherwise in an environment controlled by the interrogators. Similarly, although there is a vast body of law relevant to custodial interrogations, analysis of the relevant legal precedents and rules is beyond the scope of this project. Finally, even though Inbau et al., as well as many other authors, suggest that the goal of an interrogation may be something

---

[109] Fred Inbau et al., *Criminal Interrogations and Confessions*, 4th ed. (Sudbury, MA: Jones and Bartlett Publishers, 2004), 5–6.

other than obtaining a confession, the paper mainly focuses on literature, techniques, and practices aimed at eliciting confessions.[110]

To these ends, the paper is divided into three parts. Part I provides a survey and review of the literature on interrogations. Section 1 focuses on the theoretical and psychological literature about interrogations and confessions. Section 2 presents and analyzes the empirical data available to support the theoretical approaches and models. Section 3 surveys the practical literature on interrogations, covering the major techniques and practical manuals on the subject. Section 4 briefly describes how an interrogation can "go wrong," and Section 5 discusses the extent to which the practical literature takes the empirical data into account.

Part II presents a survey of law enforcement training and practice with respect to interrogation. Sections 6, 7, and 8 review the Federal Bureau of Investigation (FBI), the Federal Law Enforcement Training Center (FLETC), and the Boston Police Department Homicide Division, respectively. Section 9 presents a case study of the training and practices of one very experienced U.S. interrogator, while Section 10 examines practices in other countries, specifically Great Britain and Israel. Section 11 then presents a survey of the arguments, issues, and practices related to the video-recording of interrogations, and Section 12 attempts to tie all of the practices together and compare them to the empirical and practical literature presented in Part I.

Finally, in Part III, we offer some general conclusions and recommendations for further study and research. Most important, we present some thoughts about the relationship between, and applicability of, law enforcement interrogation techniques and practices to the current terrorism problem.

PART I. LITERATURE REVIEW

Section 1. Theoretical Approaches to Confessions

Incriminating statements and confession in the context of a criminal investigation usually entail serious consequences, ranging from reputational and financial penalties to deprivation of liberty or life.[111] Nonetheless, a substantial number of interrogations yield a confession or some sort of incriminating statement. This section explores the possible explanations for this phenomenon offered by the psychological literature on interrogation and confessions.

---

[110] Compare Inbau (noting that interrogation is best conceived as the psychological undoing of deception) with R. Leo, "Inside the Interrogation Room," *The Journal of Criminal Law and Criminology* 86, no. 2 (Winter 1996), 279 (assuming that an interrogation is successful when the suspect provides the detective with at least some incriminating information) and Gisli H. Gudjonsson, *The Psychology of Interrogation and Confessions: A Handbook* (New York: Wiley, 2003), 2 (stating that interrogations, like interviews, are a way of gathering information for use in further enquiries, but are normally associated with criminal suspects).

[111] Gudjonsson, p. 115.

Factors Inhibiting Confession

Gisli Gudjonsson identifies five factors that make it difficult for people to confess to crimes they have committed. The first is the *fear of legal sanctions*.[112] Generally, the severity of the potential sanction is directly proportional to the seriousness of the offense and, as mentioned above, may include financial sanctions, deprivation of liberty, and even the death penalty. Additionally, the mere possibility of having a criminal record may be a powerful inhibitory force for first-time offenders.[113] Second, Gudjonsson points to *reputational concerns* as a factor that may inhibit suspects from confessing.[114] He suggests that the higher the person's standing in the community, the greater his or her reluctance to confess.[115] Third, Gudjonsson notes that an *individual's resistance to admit to him or herself what he or she has done* may also hinder confessions.[116] Thus, the more reprehensible the offense, the more likely offenders are to exercise denial when interrogated.[117] Fourth and somewhat related, a *subject's desire to keep his or her family and friends ignorant about the crime* may also affect his or her willingness to confess.[118] Finally, *fear of retaliation*, whether real or perceived, may influence a subject's decision.[119] In this context, a suspect may implicate others by confessing to a crime and, fearing retaliation, may thus refuse to confess. Indeed, Gudjonsson notes that in some cases the fear of retaliation may be greater than the fear of legal sanctions.[120]

Theoretical Models of Confession

A review of the available literature on interrogations and confessions reveals various theoretical explanations of why suspects confess during custodial interrogations. The following models examine confessions from different perspectives and, taken together, provide important insights into the subject.[121]

The Reid Model

Drawing on the nine steps of interrogation devised by Inbau et al., Jayne provides a theoretical-psychological model for the so-called Reid Technique.[122] This model conceives of an interrogation as the psychological undoing of deception.[123] According to Jayne, in the context of criminal interrogation deception can be defined as "a selected behavior of distorting or denying the truth for the

---

[112] *Id.*
[113] *Id.*
[114] *Id.*, p. 116.
[115] *Id.*
[116] *Id.*
[117] *Id.*
[118] *Id.*, p. 116.
[119] *Id.*
[120] *Id.*
[121] *Id.*, p. 117.
[122] Brian C. Jayne, "The Psychological Principles of Criminal Interrogation," in Fred E. Inbau, et. al., Criminal Interrogation and Confessions, 3rd edition (Baltimore, MD: Williams and Wilkins, 1986), 327-347. For a full explanation of the practical aspects of the Reid Technique, see discussion below.
[123] Jayne, p. 327.

purpose of benefit to the individual."[124] Furthermore, in this context the common motivation for all deception is avoidance of the consequences associated with telling the truth.[125] The two types of consequences of being truthful are labeled "real" and "personal."[126] Real consequences generally involve financial penalties or the loss of freedom or life, while personal consequences involve lowered self-esteem and damaged integrity and reputation.[127] According to the model, successful deception is reinforced in accordance with operant conditioning principles whereby undetected lying is rewarding and increases the chances of further lying.[128]

However, successful socialization teaches individuals that it is wrong to lie, which in many people brings about internal conflicts comprising feelings of frustration and anxiety.[129] The model predicts that the increased levels of anxiety associated with lying induce a person to confess.[130] The level of anxiety is assumed to increase linearly from omission to evasion to blatant denial.[131] Jayne notes that subjects may try to reduce anxiety through body movements or physical activities, which work by displacement or distraction.[132] Additionally, the mind attempts to reduce anxiety through "a series of hypothetical constructs called defense mechanisms," which operate within the individual by distorting or denying reality.[133] The two main defense mechanisms relevant to interrogation are *rationalization* and *projection*.[134] Rationalization is the "act of redescribing what a person does in such a way as to avoid any responsibility for the consequences of his behavior."[135] Through the second defense mechanism, projection, a subject "shifts the blame for his own thoughts or actions onto another person, place, or thing" (e.g., the victim, alcohol use, etc.).[136] Although, as noted, the defense mechanisms of projection and rationalization function by distorting or denying reality, this "does not mean that the individual loses touch with reality; reality has merely been redefined."[137]

According to the Reid Model, a suspect confesses when the perceived consequences of a confession are more desirable than the anxiety generated by the deception.[138] The basic tenet of the model is that the interrogator can psychologically manipulate both the perceived consequences of confessing

---

[124] *Id.*
[125] *Id.*
[126] *Id.*
[127] *Id.*, p. 328.
[128] *Id.*
[129] *Id.*, p. 329.
[130] *Id.*
[131] *Id.*, p. 330.
[132] *Id.*
[133] *Id.*, 331.
[134] *Id.*
[135] *Id.*
[136] *Id.*
[137] *Id.*
[138] *Id.*, p. 332.

and the suspect's anxiety to obtain a confession.[139] Thus, according to the Reid Model, the goal of an interrogation is to "decrease the suspect's perception of the consequences of confessing, while at the same time increasing the suspect's internal anxiety associated with his deception."[140] Jayne identifies three basic concepts relevant to the interrogator's manipulation of the subject's perception of consequences and anxiety: *expectancy, persuasion,* and *belief.*[141] Expectancy refers to "a want or goal perceived as desirable or inevitable." At the outset of an interrogation deceptive subjects expect that, if they confess, the consequences (as they perceive them at that time) are inevitable, and that the most desirable goal would be not to confess.[142] Persuasion is "a form of communication wherein the listener's attitudes, beliefs, or perceptions are changed."[143] Persuasion can change expectancies, i.e., a suspect's view of what is desirable.[144] Belief, in turn, is "the vehicle of persuasion," in that a suspect's beliefs are not fact and are therefore subject to interpretation and external influence.[145] In this context, an interrogator must strive to "change the suspect's *perception* of the consequences of confessing or the suspect's *perception* of the anxiety associated with deception by influencing the subject's beliefs.[146]

According to the model, there are four essential criteria for changing the suspect's expectancies and beliefs in order to garner a confession.

- First, the subject must perceive the interrogator as a credible source of information.[147] According to Jayne, credibility is based on sincerity, knowledge, and demeanor.[148]

- Second, the interrogator must develop insight into the subject's attitudes and weaknesses.[149] It is particularly important that the interrogator assess the consequences that the suspect is trying to avoid by denial, and evaluate the suspect's ability to tolerate anxiety.[150]

- Third, the subject must internalize the interrogator's suggestion, because this will change expectancies if the individual can be led to internalize the interrogator's message.[151] This involves a three-stage process.[152]

- First, the suspect must comprehend the interrogator's ideas (relating).[153]

---

[139] *Id.*
[140] *Id.*
[141] *Id.,* p. 333.
[142] *Id.*
[143] *Id.*
[144] *Id.*
[145] *Id.*
[146] *Id.*
[147] *Id.,* p. 334.
[148] *Id.*
[149] *Id.,* p. 334-335.
[150] *Id.,* p. 335.
[151] *Id.*
[152] *Id.,* p. 336.
[153] *Id.*

- Second, the suspect must agree and concur with the message communicated by the interrogator (acceptance).[154]

- Third, the suspect must internalize or believe the interrogator's suggestions (believing).[155] This last point underscores the importance of suggestibility in the confession process: the more suggestible the suspect, the easier it is, theoretically, to obtain a confession.[156]

- Finally, the interrogator must constantly monitor the subject's feedback to determine whether or not the subject accepts the theme, whether the subject's anxiety should be intensified, or if the timing of the presentation of an alternative question is right.[157]

In this context, Jayne suggests several manipulative ploys that interrogators can use to reduce the perceived consequences of confessing and increase the perceived anxiety associated with deception. According to Jayne, perceived consequences are generally reduced through the development of themes that employ *rationalization* and/or *projection*.[158] As defense mechanisms, rationalization and projection reduce anxiety by altering the suspect's perceptions of the likely consequences of self-incriminating admissions.[159] Jayne notes that these two mechanisms are most effective in reducing the perceptions concerning "real" consequences, whereas using sympathy and compassion as ploys is relatively more effective in overcoming inhibitions about the perceptions of "personal" consequences.[160] Similarly, Jayne notes that anxiety must be independently increased without increasing perceived consequences.[161] Statements or actions intended to increase anxiety "must be directed at the suspect's perception of himself within the interrogation environment."[162] Ultimately, the success of the interrogation depends on the extent to which the interrogator is successful in identifying psychological vulnerabilities, exploiting them to alter the suspect's belief system and perceptions of the consequences of making self-incriminating admissions, and persuading him to accept the interrogator's version of the "truth."

As explained in detail in Section 3, Jayne's psychological model has been incorporated into a comprehensive interrogation technique, the Reid Technique, which has been described as the "most influential practical manual" on interrogation.[163] According to Gudjonsson, the Reid Technique rests on the following basic assumptions:[164]

---

[154] *Id.*

[155] *Id.*, p. 337.

[156] *See* interrogative suggestibility discussion below.

[157] Jayne, *see* note 122, p. 340.

[158] *Id.*

[159] *Id.*

[160] *Id.*, p. 341.

[161] *Id.*, p. 342.

[162] *Id.*, p. 343.

[163] Gudjonsson, *see* note 110, p. 11.

[164] *Id.*

- Many criminal investigations can only be solved by obtaining a confession.

- Unless offenders are caught in the commission of a crime they will ordinarily not give a confession unless they are interrogated over an extended period of time in private, using persuasive techniques comprising trickery, deceit and psychological manipulation.

- To break down resistance, interrogators will need to employ techniques that normally would be seen as unethical by the public.

Given these assumptions, Gudjonsson notes that the technique is broadly based on two processes:[165]

1. Breaking down denials and resistance, and

2. Increasing the suspect's desire to confess.

More specifically, the Reid Technique employs two main psychological strategies throughout its nine steps of interrogation: *maximization* and *minimization*.[166] Maximization involves frightening suspects into a confession by exaggerating the strength of evidence against them and the seriousness of the offense.[167] Minimization, in contrast, involves tricking suspects into a false sense of security and thus into confessing by offering sympathy, providing face-saving excuses, partly blaming the victim or circumstances for the alleged offense, and minimizing the seriousness of the charges.[168]

Gudjonsson argues that the techniques advocated by Inbau and his colleagues are practically and ethically problematic because they are inherently coercive insofar as they communicate implicit threats and promises to suspects.[169] Although it is outside the purview of this paper, we note that Gudjonsson's main criticism of the Reid Technique and its underlying psychological model is that their coercive nature yields a far greater proportion of false confessions than is tolerable. This criticism and concern over false confessions has been echoed by other psychologists and experts in interrogations and confessions.[170]

The authors of the Reid Technique counter that the criticisms are better aimed at actual law enforcement practice and misuse of the technique. According to the John E. Reid and Associates official website, "the goal of the interrogation process is to develop the truth. It is not a process designed to obtain a confession by any means from any suspect."[171] The authors assert that by following the

---

[165] *Id.*

[166] *Id.*, p. 21.

[167] *Id.*

[168] *Id.*

[169] *Id.*

[170] For further criticism of the Reid Technique, see R. Leo and R.J. Ofshe, "The Consequences of False Confessions: Deprivation of Liberty and Miscarriages of Justice in the Age of Psychological Interrogation," *Journal of Criminal Law and Criminology* 88, no. 2 (1998), 429-496.

[171] John E. Reid and Associates, *Defending the Reid Technique of Interrogation,* at http://www.reid.com/educational_info/critictechniquedefend.html, accessed 13 March 2005.

nine steps of their technique "[t]he interrogator [...] will be meeting all of the guidelines established by the courts in conducting proper interrogations to develop admissible confessions from guilty suspects."[172]

Decision-Making Model

Hilgendorf and Irving have suggested an alternative concept of interrogations and confessions.[173] Their model provides a framework for analyzing "the circumstances in which any particular confession was made in terms of the decision-making task of the suspect, the information with which he is provided, the social pressures which are brought to bear on him, and the physical character of the interrogation."[174] It conceptualizes interrogation as a complicated and demanding decision-making process.[175] The subject of an interrogation must make many choices, some of which include whether to speak or remain silent; whether to make self-incriminating admissions or a confession; whether to tell the truth, part of the truth, or lie; how to answer the questions asked by the interrogator; and what attitude to adopt toward the police.[176]

Hilgendorf and Irving's model predicts that subjects will seek to make the best possible choice among the courses of action available by choosing "that course for which the product of (1) the probability of occurrence and (2) the value to him (or utility) of the consequences, is largest."[177] The subject's action will have consequences for him or her: criminal charges may be filed; he or she may be detained; the police may check the information provided for accuracy and truthfulness.[178] Thus, he or she will attempt to evaluate the probabilities of each consequence's occurrence, and his or her decision about how to act will be a "result of some balancing of the likelihood of various consequences in relation to their utilities for him [or her]."[179] Consequently, an interrogation subject's decisions are determined by:

- Perceptions of the available courses of action.

- Perceptions concerning the probabilities of the likely occurrence of various consequences attached to these courses of action.

- The utility values or gains attached to these courses of action.

Hilgendorf and Irving make clear that the subject's decision making is governed not by the objective probabilities that given consequences may occur, but by the subjective probabilities of their occurrence.[180] In other words, decisions

---

[172] *Id.*

[173] E.L. Hilgendorf and B. Irving, "A Decision-Making Model of Confessions," in *Psychology in Legal Contexts: Applications and Limitations*, M.A. Lloyd-Bostock, ed. (London, UK: Macmillan, 1981), 67-84.

[174] *Id.*, p. 81.

[175] *Id.*, p. 69.

[176] *Id.*

[177] *Id.*

[178] *Id.*

[179] *Id.*, p. 70.

[180] *Id.*, p. 71.

are not based on what is objectively likely to happen, but on what the suspect believes at the time to be the likely consequences.

Hilgendorf and Irving argue that threats and inducements, even when slight and implicit, can markedly influence the suspect's decision to confess because of the perceived power the police have over the situation and the apparent credibility of their words. Similarly, they point to a number of social, psychological, and environmental factors that can affect or seriously impair the suspect's decision making during police interrogation. The most salient factors as listed by Gudjonsson are as follows:[181]

- The police can manipulate the social and self-approval utilities (like the suspect's feelings of competence and self-esteem) during interrogation in order to influence his decision-making.

- The interrogators can manipulate the suspect's perceptions of the likely outcome concerning a given course of action. For example, interrogators can minimize the seriousness of the offense.

- Interrogators can impair the suspect's ability to cope with information processing and decision-making through various means like social, psychological and environmental manipulation.

Hilgendorf and Irving conclude that, given the interrogator's considerable authority, the interrogation situation puts strong pressure on suspects to place excessive emphasis in their decision making on the approval or disapproval of the interrogator, and to be extremely sensitive to all communications, both verbal and non-verbal, that they receive from the interrogator.[182] Physical confinement supports and facilitates these pressures, and the effect becomes more pronounced the longer the detention lasts. The combined effect of these pressures and other forms of environmental and situational stress inherent in custodial interrogations can adversely affect "efficient performance on the complex decision-making task" confronting interrogation subjects.[183]

Psychoanalytic Model

Gudjonsson points out that this model rests upon the assumption that "the feeling of guilt is the fundamental cause of confessions."[184] Based on Freudian concepts of the id and ego, Reik's work attempts to show that the unconscious compulsion to confess plays a seminal role in crime.[185] According to Reik, a confession is "an attempt at reconciliation that the superego undertakes in order to settle the quarrel between the ego and the id."[186] Thus, a confession primarily serves the role of relieving people of the overwhelming feeling of guilt occasioned

---

[181] Gudjonsson, see note 110, p. 122.
[182] Hilgendorf and Irving, see note 173, p. 81.
[183] Id.
[184] Gudjonsson, see note 110, p. 122.
[185] Theodor Reik, *The Compulsion to Confess: On the Psychoanalysis of Crime and Punishment*, translated by Katherine Jones (New York: Farrar, Straus and Cudahy, 1959).
[186] Id., p. 216.

by their crime. Following Reik's lead, Berggren espoused a psychological model that seeks to explain the need of individuals to confess. In general, the model postulates that people's knowledge of their transgression produces a sense of guilt, which is experienced as oppressive and depressing.[187] The confession relieves the individual from the guilt, producing important cathartic effects. However, as Gudjonsson points out, the model remains controversial at best, as its foundational theses have limited acceptance in the scientific community.[188]

Interaction Process Model

This model proposes that, regardless of a suspect's actual involvement in a crime, the interaction among three main sets of factors determines the individual's initial response to an allegation and the eventual outcome of an interrogation.[189] These sets of factors are:[190]

- Background characteristics of the suspect and offense
- Contextual characteristics of the case
- Interrogator's questioning techniques

The first set of factors includes the suspect's age, sex, and criminal history, as well as the type and severity of the offense under investigation.[191] The second set encompasses the strength of the available evidence against the suspect and the suspect's access to legal advice.[192] According to the model, the interrogator's questioning techniques are influenced by his beliefs about and attitudes toward the characteristics of the suspect and the case, which in turn affect the suspect's initial response to an allegation.[193] The suspect's subsequent and final responses during questioning will be determined by his calculation of the relative advantages of response change (i.e., from an initial denial to an admission), brought about by the interrogator's reaction to the suspect's initial response.[194]

After analyzing 1,000 cases in which suspects were interviewed by police officers in England, Moston, Stephenson, and Williamson suggested that police interviewing techniques played a relatively minor role in influencing confessions for two main reasons.[195] First, most admissions were freely volunteered at the outset of interviews, and those suspects who denied an accusation at the outset typically maintained this denial throughout, even in the face of seemingly incontrovertible proof of guilt.[196] Second, the authors found that police interviewing skills were

---

[187] E. Berggren, *The Psychology of Confessions* (Leiden, The Netherlands: E.J. Brill, 1975).

[188] Gudjonsson, see note 110, p. 122.

[189] Stephen Moston, "From Denial to Admission in Police Questioning of Suspects," in *Psychology, Law and Criminal Justice*, Graham Davies et al. eds. (UK: Walter de Gruyter, 1996), 92.

[190] *Id.*

[191] *Id.*

[192] *Id.*

[193] *Id.*

[194] *Id.*

[195] S. Moston et al., "The Effects of Case Characteristics on Suspect Behaviour During Police Questioning, *British Journal of Criminology* 32 (1992), 23-40.

[196] Moston, see note 195, p. 92.

almost nonexistent and interrogators employed only a limited range of questioning techniques.[197] According to Gudjonsson, the main limitation of the model is that it does not focus on the mental state and cognitive processes of the suspect.[198]

Interrogation as Dialogue

An alternate and less traditional view conceives of interrogation as a dialogue between suspect and interrogator, "characterized by an adversarial element."[199] This model places great importance on understanding how the interrogation fits into the scheme of critical dialogues in which individuals engage every day so as to allow interrogators to overcome hurdles encountered in the interrogation process and to give them ideas of how to move the dialogue forward at stalled moments.

Although Walton suggests that the interrogation is a form of information-seeking dialogue, he recognizes that "to conduct an interrogation as if it were a persuasion dialogue, or a normal information-seeking dialogue, would result in argumentation that is inappropriate, and even useless for this purpose."[200] Moreover, unlike a traditional critical conversation, broken into stages where both participants decide when to move from one stage to the next, the stages of the interrogation (formative, preparatory, argumentation, and closing) "proceed not by the agreement of both parties, but by the unilateral choices of the interrogator."[201] Indeed, "interrogation is a type of asymmetrical dialogue in which one party tends to be very powerful and the other party tends to be very passive."[202] Because of this, Walton argues that "the questioner must use tricky techniques to get any results."[203] Walton's recommendations for the questioner include to 1) "appear friendly and cooperative, even sympathetic to the respondent;" 2) "be very patient, and give plenty of time for answers;" 3) "be methodical, and go by a list of questions that have been previously prepared;" 4) "repeat questions that have not yet been answered;" and 5) have the interrogation "go on for a long, indefinite period of time."[204]

Within the context of interrogation as dialogue, Walton then identifies a number of argumentation techniques that may be used in interrogations. The first suggested technique is "*the easiest way out*," whereby the interrogator seeks to "wear the respondent down, and then inform him that if [he] just confess[es], or give[s] [the interrogator] the desired information, then [his] problems will be over."[205] Similarly, the interrogator can use "*the only way out*" technique whereby he or she makes the conditions "unbearable for the respondent…such

---

[197] *Id.*
[198] Gudjonsson, see note 110, p. 124.
[199] Douglas Walton, "The Interrogation as a Type of Dialogue," *Journal of Pragmatics* 35, no. 12 (December 2003), 1771-1802.
[200] *Id.*, p. 1798.
[201] *Id.*
[202] *Id.*, p. 1799.
[203] *Id.*, p. 1778.
[204] *Id.*
[205] *Id.*, p. 1784.

that he [finds] it intolerable to continue."[206] Additionally, the interrogator can use his *authority* as a leverage mechanism, and Walton recommends that he or she interrogate "an uneducated or unintelligent criminal suspect as if [he or she] were questioning a child."[207] Walton also points to other techniques such as use of hypnosis, catching the subject off guard, fostering the belief that the suspect is not being interrogated, misrepresenting the law, distorting the seriousness of the offense, using threats, leading the suspect to believe that the interrogators already know everything, and sympathizing with the subject.[208]

According to Walton, understanding the rules of dialogue that interrogation participants follow, whether consciously or unconsciously, should, in theory, help the interrogator understand both his approaches and responses to the suspect, as well as the suspect's various approaches and responses during the course of the interview. This would allow the interrogator to adjust, take unexpected tacks, and generally conduct a more successful interrogation. Walton formulates ten rules for questioner ("proponent") and suspect ("respondent") in the interrogation dialogue, assuming "that the respondent does not want to give out the information, or at least all of it, but wants to appear compliant by taking part in the dialogue."[209] Taking Walton's assumptions, the "rules" of the interrogation dialogue for questioner and suspect are:[210]

1. The respondent needs to take care not to inadvertently say something that might give out the information he wants to conceal, or to allow the proponent to infer it;

2. The proponent may coerce the respondent to reveal the information through threats or sanctions, but only by the means allowed;

3. The proponent needs to pose questions to the respondent, and these questions can, and often should be, leading, loaded, and deceptive;

4. The respondent should answer in formulations that are vague, ambiguous, misleading, or confusing, if that will help serve his ends;

5. The proponent should probe critically into the respondent's prior replies, and try to use them to extract information;

6. The respondent should take care to try to be consistent in his replies and in the commitments that can be inferred from them;

7. If the proponent finds inconsistencies in the respondent's commitments, or implausible statements, or statements that are

---

[206] *Id.*, p. 1785.
[207] *Id.*
[208] *Id.*, p. 1785-86.
[209] *Id.*, p. 1780.
[210] *Id.*

inconsistent with information from other sources, she should ask questions that critically examine them;

8. If the proponent extracts the information she wants from the respondent, then she has achieved her goal and the dialogue concludes in her favor;

9. If the proponent terminates the interrogation without getting the information she wants, and the respondent preserves his interests, the dialogue concludes in the respondent's favor;

10. The two parties can use any arguments, even ones considered irrelevant or fallacious from the viewpoint of a critical discussion, to achieve their ends.

Walton also points out that "appeals to fear and threats have long been known to be powerfully effective arguments,"[211] and that the "logically fallacious" character of such threats does not diminish their effectiveness in the interrogation dialogue.[212] Of course, if the suspect/respondent is totally unresponsive, Walton's rules have little application, and one must turn to the Reid Technique or other techniques explored in this paper in order to obtain information from the suspect.

Cognitive-Behavioral Model

Mainly espoused by Gudjonsson, the cognitive-behavioral model views confessions as resulting from "the existence of a particular relationship between the suspect, the environment and significant others within that environment."[213] It suggests that it is helpful to look at the "antecedents" and "consequences" of confessing behavior within the framework of behavioral analysis.[214] Antecedents are the kinds of events occurring prior to interrogation that may trigger or facilitate the confession.[215] Consequences refer to the effects of a confession or admission upon the subject. There are two major types: *short term* and *long term*.[216] Short-term consequences occur within minutes or hours of the suspect's confession, while long-term consequences manifest themselves within days, weeks, months, or years of the confession.[217] The types of consequences depend on the nature and circumstances of the case and the psychological characteristics of the individual concerned.[218]

As explained below, antecedents and consequences are construed in terms of social, emotional, cognitive, situational and physiological events.[219] Though these are discussed in greater detail below, the following Table provides a

---

[211] *Id.*, p. 1788.
[212] *Id.*
[213] Gudjonsson, see note 110, p. 124.
[214] *Id.*
[215] *Id.*, p. 125.
[216] *Id.*
[217] *Id.*
[218] *Id.*
[219] *Id.*

useful yet non-exhaustive illustration of the typical antecedents and consequences associated with confessions.

Antecedents	Consequences	
	Short-Term	*Long-Term*

Social
    Isolation; police
    pressure
	Police approval/praise	Disapproval

Emotional Distress	Feelings of relief	Feelings of guilt, shame

Cognitive
    "The police know I
    did it."
 	
    "The truth will come
    out in the end."
 	
    "Perhaps I did do it
    but I can't
    remember it."
	"It's good to get it off my
	chest."
	
	"My solicitor will sort it
	out."
	
	"How could I have done
	such a dreadful thing?"
		"What is going to happen
		to me now?"
		
		"This is very
		    serious.'"
		
		"I'm now certain I had
		nothing to do with it."

Situational:
    Nature of the arrest:
    Confinement?
    Solicitor present?
    Caution understood?
    Familiarity with
    police procedures?
	Charged, allowed access
	to a solicitor
		Judicial proceedings

Physiological
    Aroused physical
    state, inhibitions
    reduced by alcohol
    or drugs; drug
    withdrawal
	Arousal reduction	Arousal returns to base
		level

The antecedents and consequences of confessions.[220]
Source: The authors.

---

[220]   *Id.*

Social Events

The first type of social influence that an interrogation exerts upon the subject is isolation from his or her family and friends.[221] Interrogation manuals commonly place great emphasis on isolating the suspect from any external influence that may reduce his or her willingness to confess.[222] The second kind of social influence, police pressure, relates to the nature of the interrogation itself.[223] As is illustrated by the Reid Model described above, the social process and interaction between interrogator and subject is an important factor in obtaining a confession. In this context, the immediate consequence of confessing is social reinforcement by the police interrogators, who might praise the subject for cooperation and for owning up to what he or she has done.[224] Additionally, the subject may be allowed access to visitors such as family members and, in some cases, may be allowed to go home.[225] The long-term consequences commonly involve the defendant's having to come to terms with social disapproval from the media and the general public.[226]

Emotional Events

Being arrested and brought to a police station is an undoubtedly stressful event. Generally, suspects can be expected to experience considerable levels of anxiety and distress, caused mainly by the uncertainty of the situation, the fear of what will happen at the station, the fear of being locked in a cell, and the fear of the consequences regarding the offense.[227] There are two distinct emotional experiences relevant to confessions: guilt and shame.[228] Shame is best viewed as a degrading, humiliating experience, and it often accompanies a sense of exposure.[229] In contrast, guilt is associated with some real or imagined past transgression that is inconsistent with the person's internalized values and standards.[230] Whereas a feeling of guilt motivates people to confess, a feeling of shame has the reverse effect.[231] After confessing, suspects may experience a sense of emotional relief as the immediate pressure is lifted and they have greater certainty about their immediate future.[232] However, at the prospect that the subject's role in or commission of the crime will become known, a feeling of shame sometimes sets in or becomes exacerbated.[233]

---

[221] *Id.*, p. 126.
[222] *Id.*
[223] *Id.*
[224] *Id.*
[225] *Id.*
[226] *Id.*
[227] *Id.*
[228] *Id.*
[229] *Id.*
[230] *Id.*
[231] *Id.*
[232] *Id.*
[233] *Id.*, p. 127.

Cognitive Events

Cognitive factors comprise the suspect's thoughts, interpretations, assumptions, and perceived strategies of responding to the interrogative situation.[234] According to Gudjonsson, it is important to remember that the suspect's behavior during the interrogation is likely to be more influenced by his or her perceptions, interpretations, and assumptions about what is happening than by the actual behavior of the police/interrogators.[235] One possible cognitive antecedent to a confession occurs when the suspect perceives the evidence against him as being strong; he is more likely to confess if he believes there is no point in denying the offense.[236] Another possible cognitive factor involves suspects' "talking themselves into confessing" if they believe the interrogator will not relent until he has obtained a confession, or if they believe that the police have sufficient evidence to prove that they committed the offense.[237] An innocent person's faith that the truth will eventually come out through the criminal justice system can also facilitate a (false) confession.[238] Finally, innocent suspects who begin to doubt their own recollection of events in the face of pressing interrogation may eventually yield to the suggestions of the interrogator and come to believe that they committed the crime.[239]

The immediate cognitive consequences of confessing may relate to thoughts associated with the easing of the pressure.[240] For some suspects, especially innocent ones, the belief that their legal representative will sort everything out may predominate.[241] On the other hand, suspects who mistakenly accept guilt because of confusion about their recollection and acceptance of the interrogator's suggestions may come to wonder how they could have committed such a deed and have no recollection of it.[242] Eventually, after their confusion subsides, they may again become fully convinced that they had nothing to do with the crime to which they previously confessed.[243]

Situational Events

These factors are potentially infinite. As Gudjonsson points out, "the circumstances of the suspect's arrest (e.g., being arrested suddenly in the early hours of the morning) may affect the suspect's ability to cope with the subsequent interrogation."[244] Similarly, the time and conditions of confinement prior to interrogation may affect the subject's performance: "being locked up in a police cell for several hours or days may 'soften up' subjects (i.e., weaken their resistance)

---

[234] Id.
[235] Id.
[236] Id.
[237] Id.
[238] Id.
[239] Id.
[240] Id.
[241] Id.
[242] Id.
[243] Id.
[244] Id.

and make them more responsive to interrogation."[245] Conversely, familiarity with police procedures and interrogation "is likely to provide suspects with knowledge and experience that make them more able to understand and assert their rights."[246] The immediate situational consequence commonly associated with a confession is that the suspect is charged with the offense.[247] The long-term consequence is possible prosecution and judicial proceedings.[248]

Physiological Events

The physiological antecedent to a confession is "heightened arousal, which includes increased heart rate, blood pressure, rate and irregularity of respiration, and perspiration."[249] These occur because "suspects are commonly apprehensive, worried and frightened."[250] Once the suspect has confessed, "there is likely to be a sharp reduction in his level of physiological and subjective arousal because of greater certainty about the immediate future."[251] Arousal may then return to its normal level, though Gudjonsson notes that uncertainty about the pending charge or prosecution "may lead to an increased subjective and physiological state of arousal."[252]

Interrogative Suggestibility

Some experts, led by Gudjonsson and Clark, have dedicated considerable research to the application of suggestibility in police interrogation.[253] Interrogative suggestibility is central to the social-psychological model described above. There are two main theoretical approaches to interrogative suggestibility: the *individual differences approach* and the *experimental approach*.[254] Although they offer different perspectives, the models complement each other.[255] The former approach is best illustrated by the work of Gudjonsson and Clark[256] and the latter by the work of Schooler and Loftus.[257] The experimental approach places emphasis on "understanding the conditions under which leading questions are likely to affect the verbal accounts of witnesses."[258] Thus, interrogative suggestibility is viewed as being "mediated by a central cognitive mechanism, referred to as discrepancy

---

[245] *Id.*, p. 127-128.
[246] *Id.*, p. 128.
[247] *Id.*
[248] *Id.*
[249] *Id.*
[250] *Id.*
[251] *Id.*
[252] *Id.*
[253] Gisli H. Gudjonsson, "The Application of Interrogative Suggestibility to Police Interviewing," in *Human Suggestibility*, John F. Schumaker, ed. (UK: Routledge, 1991), 279-288.
[254] *Id.*, p. 279.
[255] *Id.*, p. 279.
[256] Gisli H. Gudjonsson and N. Clark, "Suggestibility in Police Interrogation: A Social-Psychological Model," *Social Behaviour* 1 (1986), 83-104.
[257] J.W. Schooler and E.F. Loftus, "Individual Differences and Experimentation: Complementary Approaches to Interrogative Suggestibility," *Social Behaviour* 1 (1986), 105-12.
[258] Gudjonsson, see note 253, p. 279.

detection."[259] The implication drawn from the model is that people are suggestible "when the conditions are such that they are unable to discriminate satisfactorily between what they observed and what is suggested to them."[260]

On the other hand, the individual differences approach "has specific applicability to police interrogation and views suggestibility as being dependent upon the coping strategies that people can generate and implement when confronted with the uncertainty and expectations of the interrogative situation."[261] The model tries to "explain individual differences in suggestibility," and its main premise is that "people vary considerably in their reactions to police interrogation, even when the conditions of the situation are similar."[262] Gudjonsson and Clark define interrogative suggestibility as "the extent to which, within a closed social interaction, people come to accept the messages communicated during formal questioning, as the result of which their subsequent behavioral response is affected."[263] Thus, the definition implies the following five interrelated components:[264]

- A closed social interaction between interrogator and subject.
- A questioning procedure that involves two or more participants.
- A suggestive stimulus.
- Acceptance of the suggestive stimulus.
- A behavioral response to indicate whether or not the suggestion is accepted.

Given these characteristics, Gudjonsson argues that interrogative suggestibility differs from other types of suggestibility in four respects:[265]

- It involves questioning procedures within a closed social interaction.
- The questions asked deal mainly with past experiences and events, recollections, and remembered states of knowledge, as opposed to traditional types of suggestibility, which are primarily concerned with motor and sensory experiences of the immediate situation.
- It has a strong component of uncertainty related to the cognitive processing capacity of the individual.
- It typically involves a highly stressful situation with important consequences for the person being interviewed.

Thus understood, the Gudjonsson model is "essentially a social-psychological model, where interrogative suggestibility is construed as arising through a particular relationship between the person, the environment, and significant

---

[259] *Id.*
[260] *Id.*
[261] *Id.*
[262] *Id.*
[263] *Id.*, p. 280.
[264] *Id.*
[265] *Id.*, p. 280-281.

others within that environment."[266] The model recognizes and incorporates the importance of feedback to interrogative suggestibility, and conceptualizes it as "a signal communicated by an interrogator to a witness [or suspect], after he/she has responded to a question or a series of questions, intended to strengthen [(positive feedback)] or modify [(negative feedback)] subsequent responses of the witness [or suspect]."[267] The interrogator can communicate feedback both implicitly and explicitly.[268] Repeated questioning is one example of *implicit negative feedback*.[269] *Implicit positive feedback* may consist of providing refreshments, praise, or sympathy to the subject after he or she begins to give desired answers to the interrogator's questions.[270] *Explicit negative feedback*, on the other hand, consists of open statements by the interrogator to the effect that he or she thinks that the interviewee has made a mistake or is lying.[271] Similarly, an interrogator may offer *explicit positive feedback* by using responses like "good," "that's right," or "now we are getting somewhere" to reinforce wanted or accepted answers by the subject.[272] Gudjonsson argues that feedback, and especially negative feedback, may have "dramatic effects upon the subsequent behavior of an interviewee."[273] He suggests that negative feedback has two distinct effects: "it (a) makes interviewees change or *shift* their previous answers, and (b) heightens their responsiveness to further leading questions."[274]

As mentioned above, Gudjonsson's model states that interrogative suggestibility is "dependent upon the coping strategies that subjects can generate and implement when dealing with the *uncertainty* and *expectations* of interrogation."[275] According to Gudjonsson, the three necessary prerequisites for the process of suggestibility are *uncertainty*, *interpersonal trust*, and *expectation of success*.[276]

The *uncertainty* derives from the fact that the subject does not know for certain the right answer to a question and is therefore potentially open to suggestion.[277] This may occur, for example, when the subject's memory about the event is incomplete or nonexistent.[278] According to Gudjonsson, subjects can only be described as suggestible when they "privately accept the suggestion offered or at least believe it to be plausible."[279] Thus, suggestible subjects are different from compliant ones, who "accept a suggestion contained in a leading question,

---

[266] *Id.*, p. 281.
[267] *Id.*.
[268] *Id.*
[269] Gudjonsson, see note 110, p. 350.
[270] *Id.*
[271] *Id.*
[272] *Id.*
[273] *Id.*, p. 350-51.
[274] *Id.*, p. 351.
[275] Gudjonsson, see note 253, p. 281.
[276] *Id.*
[277] *Id.*
[278] Gudjonsson, see note 110, p. 348.
[279] *Id.*

knowing that it is wrong, because they are eager to please the interrogator or are reluctant to disagree with the suggestion openly."[280]

Interpersonal trust is important because, to yield to suggestion, the subject must believe "that the interrogator's intentions are genuine and that there is no trickery involved in the questioning."[281] According to Gudjonsson, interviewees who are suspicious of the interrogator's intentions "will be reluctant to accept suggestions offered, even under conditions of increased uncertainty."[282] Finally, Gudjonsson points out that although uncertainty and interpersonal trust are necessary to make people yield to suggestion they are not sufficient, because an uncertain subject can answer with "don't know," "not sure," or "can't recall."[283] Consequently, it is important that the interrogator communicate, either implicitly or explicitly, an expectation of success about the subject's performance: the goal is to make the subject feel that he or she should be able, and indeed is expected, to provide a definite answer to the interrogator's questions.[284]

Ultimately, the model predicts that "most people are open to suggestion when the necessary conditions of uncertainty, interpersonal trust and heightened expectations are present."[285] From these predictions, it can be hypothesized that "the three components, *uncertainty*, *interpersonal trust*, and *expectations* can be manipulated by the interrogator to alter the subject's susceptibility to suggestion."[286] Similarly, it can be theorized that "people who enter the interrogation with a suspicious cognitive set (e.g., those who do not trust the police or are suspicious of them) are less suggestible than those with a trusting cognitive set."[287] Gudjonsson also hypothesizes that "people with poor memory recollection and low intelligence are generally more suggestible than those with high cognitive capabilities," and that suggestibility is "related to such variables as low self-esteem, lack of assertiveness, and anxiety."[288]

Gudjonsson developed a suggestibility scale to test his interrogative suggestibility model and the hypotheses derived from it. The Gudjonsson Suggestibility Scale can be used "to assess the individual's responses to 'leading questions' and 'negative feedback' instructions when being asked to report a factual event from recall."[289] The scale employs a narrative paragraph describing a fictitious mugging, which is read aloud to the subjects. They are then asked to report all they can recall about the story, after which each person is asked 20 specific questions, 15 of which are subtly misleading. After answering the 20 questions the person is told that he or she has made a number of errors, and

---

[280] *Id.*
[281] *Id.*, p. 349.
[282] *Id.*
[283] *Id.*, p. 350.
[284] *Id.*
[285] Gudjonsson, see note 253, p. 282.
[286] *Id.*
[287] *Id.*
[288] *Id.*
[289] *Id.*, p. 283.

that it is necessary to ask the questions again. The person is also asked to be more accurate than before. Any change in the person's answers is noted as a "shift." The extent to which people give in to the misleading questions is scored as "yield." "Yield" and "shift" are typically added together to make up "total suggestibility."[290] According to Gudjonsson, two studies have shown that "it is possible to manipulate the expectations of the subjects (as described above) prior to interrogation in order to reduce or enhance suggestibility."[291]

In Gudjonsson and Hilton's study, a significant difference in suggestibility was found between three groups of people who were given different instructions about their expected performance.[292] One group of people (the "High expectation group") was told that they were expected to remember most of the story and give definite answers to all the questions. The second group was given no instructions about their expected performance. The third group (the "Low expectation group") was told that they were not expected to find a definite answer to all the questions. The most important implication of this finding for police interrogation is that interrogators "should be aware that certain expectations communicated to subjects prior to or during the interview can markedly affect the accuracy of the information obtained."[293] Gudjonsson also has noted that interrogative suggestibility "is significantly related to the coping strategies that subjects report using during the test."[294] According to his findings, subjects who proved most suggestible "tended to use 'avoidance' coping during the interrogation."[295] Gudjonsson notes that this means that they failed "to evaluate each question critically and gave answers that... seemed plausible and consistent with the external cues provided."[296] In contrast, non-suggestible subjects "were able to adopt a critical analysis of the situation which facilitated the accuracy of their answers."[297]

Section 2. Empirical Findings

Most of the recent empirical studies on confessions have been conducted in England.[298] With the exception of the 1996 study by Richard Leo discussed below, most of the U.S. studies date back to the 1960s and have largely focused on studying the effects of the *Miranda* ruling on the frequency with which suspects waive their rights and confess.

How Often Do Suspects Confess?

Research shows that many suspects interrogated at police stations confess to the crime of which they are accused and that a further proportion make

---

[290] *Id.,* p. 283.

[291] *Id.,* p. 284.

[292] Gisli H. Gudjonsson and M. Hilton, "The Effects of Instructional Manipulation on Interrogative Suggestibility," *Social Behaviour* 4 (1989), 189-93.

[293] Gudjonsson, see note 253, p. 285.

[294] *Id.*

[295] *Id.*

[296] *Id.*

[297] *Id.*

[298] Gudjonsson, see note 110, p. 130.

self-incriminating statements that fall short of a full confession.[299] Inbau et al. claim that in the United States the great majority of suspects initially deny their involvement in the offense, but, when the Reid Technique is used, about 80% of the denials change to confessions. However, there is no empirical evidence to support this claim.[300] In contrast to claims by Inbau et al., British research indicates that a confession or admission typically occurs at the beginning of an interview and the suspect usually sticks to his chosen position throughout the interview regardless of the technique used.[301] The table below lists British and U.S. studies that represent the available data on confession rates in both countries. Because Richard Leo's 1996 study stands as the only U.S. study of its kind since the 1960s, we will discuss it in further detail below.

Study	Country	Type of Data	Sample	Confession/ admission (%)	Proportion having legal advice (%)
Baldwin and McConville	England	Crown Court files	282	76	N/A
Cassell and Hayman	USA	Survey	173	42	N/A
Irving	England	Observational	60	62	10
Irving and McKenzie	England	Observational	68 (1986)	65	29
			68 (1987)	46	31
Leo	USA	Observational	182	42	N/A
Mitchell	England	Crown Court files	394	71	N/A
Moston and Stephenson	England	Questionnaire	558	59	14
Moston, Stephenson, Williamson	England	Taped interviews	1067	42	41
Neubauer	USA	Case files	248	47	N/A
Pearse et al.	England	Taped interviews	161	58	56

---

[299] *Id.,*133.
[300] *Id.*
[301] *Id.*

Study	Country	Type ofData	Sample	Confession/ admission (%)	Proportion having legal advice (%)
Phillips and Brown	England	Police documents/ questionnaires	4250	55	33
Softley	England	Observational	187	61	9
Zander	England	Crown Court files	282	76	N/A

Proportion of suspects who confess or make admission.[302]
Source: The authors; data compiled from references shown sequentially
in box below.

J. Baldwin and M. McConville, *Confessions in Crown Court Trials*, Royal
Commission on Criminal Procedure Research Study No. 5 (London:
Her Majesty's Stationery Office (HMSO), 1980).

P.G. Cassell and B.S. Hayman, "Police Interrogation In the 1990s: An
Empirical Study of the Effects of Miranda", in *The Miranda Debate,
Justice and Policing*, R.A. Leo and G.C. Thomas III, eds. (Boston,
MA: Northeastern University Press, 1998), 222-235.

B. Irving, *Police Interrogation. A Case Study of Current Practice*, Research
Studies No. 2 (London: HMSO, 1980).

B. Irving and I.K. McKenzie, *Police Interrogation: The Effects of the Police
and Criminal Evidence Act* (London: The Police Foundation, 1989).

R. Leo, "Inside the Interrogation Room," *The Journal of Criminal Law and
Criminology*, 86, no. 2 (Winter 1996): 266-303.

B. Mitchell, "Confessions and Police Interrogations of Suspects," *Criminal
Law Review* (September 1983), 596-604.

S.J. Moston and G.M. Stephenson, "Predictors of Suspect and Interviewer
Behaviour During Police Questioning," in *Psychology and Law:
International Perspectives*, F. Loesel et al. eds. (UK: Walter de
Gruyter, 1992), 212-218.

S. Moston et al., "The Effects of Case Characteristics on Suspect Behaviour
during Police Questioning," *British Journal of Criminology* 32
(1992): 23-40.

---

[302] Id., 137

D.W. Neubauer, "Confessions in Prairie City: Some Causes and Effects," *Journal of Criminal Law and Criminology* 65 (1974), 103-112.

J. Pearse et al., "Police Interviewing and Psychological Vulnerabilities: Predicting the Likelihood of a Confession," *Journal of Community and Applied Social Psychology* 8, no. 1 (1998), 1-21.

C. Phillips and D. Brown, *Entry into the Criminal Justice System: A Survey of Police Arrests and their Outcomes*, Home Office Research Study no. 185 (London: HMSO, 1998).

P. Softley, *Police Interrogation*. An Observational Study in Four Police Stations, Home Office Research Study no. 61(London: HMSO, 1980).

M. Zander, "The Investigation of Crime: A Study of Cases Tried at the Old Bailey," *Criminal Law Review* (1979), 203-219.

Even a cursory study of these data makes clear that the admission/confession rate is substantially (about 15%) lower in the United States than in England. However, Gudjonsson cautions against drawing any conclusions from this disparity for several reasons. First, he notes that generalizations from the available data may be unwise given "the scarcity of recent studies in the United States and the relatively low number of cases evaluated in each study."[303] Second, differences between England and the United States in confession rates "may relate to the greater impact of the Miranda rules on the confession rate than the restrictions imposed on British law enforcement."[304] Third, Gudjonsson suggests that many English legal representatives at police stations might be "passive and ineffectual in their role."[305] Finally, he notes that confession rate differences across nations "may be related to cultural factors influencing both police and suspects."[306] Additionally, it should be noted that the data cited in Table 2 for the most recent U.S. study (Leo, 1996) do not include suspects who made incriminating statements shy of an admission or confession. As explained below, inclusion of these figures would dramatically alter the results.

Richard Leo's 1996 study of interrogation practices in the United States involved nine months of observational work inside a major urban police department in the United States, where he contemporaneously observed 122 interrogations involving 45 different detectives.[307] Leo also viewed 30 videotaped custodial interrogations performed by a second police department, and another 30 videotaped interrogations performed by a third.[308] Generally, Leo sought to

---

[303] Gudjonsson, see note 110, p. 139.
[304] *Id.*, 139-40.
[305] *Id.*, 140.
[306] *Id.*
[307] Leo, see note 110, p. 268.
[308] *Id.*

observe and document the interrogation tactics used by interrogators and the suspects' reactions to them. For each interrogation, Leo recorded his observations qualitatively in the form of field notes and quantitatively with a 47-question coding sheet.[309] Leo noted that interrogations could yield four possible outcomes: (1) the suspect provided no information to the police that he or she considered incriminating; (2) the suspect (intentionally or not) provided some information that police considered incriminating, but did not directly admit to any of the elements of the crime; (3) the suspect admitted to some, but not all, of the elements of the crime; and (4) the suspect provided a full confession.[310] The table below displays the data from Leo's study.

Subject's Response to Interrogation	Frequency (%)
No incriminating statement	35.71
Incriminating statement	22.53
Partial admission	17.58
Full confession	24.18

Outcome of interrogations in the United States.[311]

Contrary to other authors such as Gudjonsson, who limit their scope to confessions and/or admissions, Leo operated under the assumption that an interrogation is successful "when the suspect provides the detective with at least some incriminating information."[312] Taking this assumption as given, Leo's studies reveal that "almost two-thirds (64.29%) of the interrogations [he] observed produced a successful result."[313]

However, that a substantial proportion of suspects subjected to interrogation end up confessing says nothing about the reasons behind those confessions. The next section attempts to shed some empirical light on why suspects confess.

Factors Associated with Admissions and Denials

Background Characteristics of the Suspect

Studies suggest that certain types of subjects are more likely to confess or make incriminating admissions than others. The more salient factors are:

1. *Age*: Age is often considered an indirect measure of maturity, and more mature suspects usually cope better with the unfamiliarity and demands of police interrogation than less mature suspects.[314] Gudjonsson notes that, although it

---

[309] *Id.*

[310] *Id.*

[311] As noted in the text, Table 3 contains the data from Leo's study, and is adapted from Leo; see note 110, 280.

[312] Leo, p. 280.

[313] *Id.*

[314] Gudjonsson, see note 110, p. 141.

has not been found in all studies, there is some evidence that younger suspects are more likely to confess than older suspects.[315] A 1970 U.S. study found that 42.9% of suspects under the age of 25 in Colorado made confessions under police interrogation compared with 18.2% of older suspects.[316] A 1980 British study found that 53% of suspects over 21 years of age made confessions, compared to 68% of those below the age of 21.[317] Studies in 1989[318] and 1998[319] found a difference of 10.8% and 8%, respectively, between confession rates of juveniles and adults. Gudjonsson draws two interpretations from these findings: 1) the younger the suspect, the easier it is to obtain a confession from him or her, and 2) there appears to be no clear cut-off point with regard to age, i.e., suspects do not seem to reach a ceiling of resistance after a certain age.[320]

The literature reveals several factors that could be responsible for this phenomenon. First, it might be that, due to greater life experience, older suspects are better equipped psychologically to cope with the demand characteristics of the interrogative situation.[321] Another possible explanation is that older suspects are more likely to understand and assert their legal rights during interrogation.[322] Finally, Gudjonsson suggests that temperamental differences related to age may also be important.[323] For example, factors such as neuroticism and impulsiveness, which may make some suspects confess more readily than others, are negatively correlated with age.[324] Another potential factor is that adolescents find negative feedback and interrogative pressure from interrogators more difficult to resist than adults.[325]

However, the literature does not universally demonstrate this correlation between age and willingness to confess. In a study of 248 criminal defendants in Prairie City, California, Neubauer found no significant difference in confession rates between minors (16–20 years old) and adults (21 years and older).[326] Similarly, Leo did not find age to be "significantly related to the likelihood of obtaining incriminating information from the suspect."[327]

---

[315] Id.

[316] L.S. Leiken, "Police Interrogation in Colorado: The Implementation of Miranda," 47 *Denver Law Journal* 1 (1970), 19-20.

[317] P. Softley, *Police Interrogation. An Observational Study in Four Police Stations,* Home Office Research Study no. 61(London: HMSO, 1980).

[318] R. Leng et al., *Discretion to Charge and Prosecute*, Report to the Economic and Social Research Council (UK: 1989).

[319] C. Phillips and D. Brown, *Entry into the Criminal Justice System: A Survey of Police Arrests and their Outcomes*, Home Office Research Study no. 185 (London: HMSO, 1998).

[320] Gudjonsson, see note 110, p. 142.

[321] Leiken, see note 319, p. 19-21.

[322] J. Baldwin and M. McConville, *Confessions in Crown Court Trials, Royal Commission on Criminal Procedure* Research Study No. 5 (London: Her Majesty's Stationery Office (HMSO), 1980), p. 195.

[323] Gudjonsson, see note 110, p. 142

[324] Id.

[325] Id.

[326] W. Neubauer, "Confessions in Prairie City: Some Causes and Effects," *Journal of Criminal Law and Criminology* 65 (1974), 104..

[327] Leo, see note 110, p. 291.

2. *Gender*: Gudjonsson notes that approximately 85% of persons arrested and detained at police stations in England are male.[328] However, several British researchers have found no gender differences with regard to the rate of admissions and denials.[329] Similarly, Leo found no significant relationship between gender and likelihood of confession or self-incrimination.[330] On the other hand, another researcher found a significant gender difference, with females confessing more commonly than males (73% admission rate of females versus 52% of males).[331]

3. *Ethnic Differences*: Phillips and Brown found that admission rates for whites, blacks and Asians were 58, 48 and 44% respectively.[332] Interestingly, the study also reflected that black and Asian detainees were significantly more likely than whites to request legal advice. Even when the analysis accounted for this variable, a significant difference remained between the confession rates of black and white detainees. However, Leo found no significant relationship between race and likelihood of confession.[333]

4. *Mental State and Psychological Factors*: Although the data is sparse, Gudjonsson has concluded that the only psychological/mental state factor that predicts a confession is when suspects admitted to having consumed an illicit drug 24 hours prior to their arrest.[334]

5. *Previous Convictions and Confessions*: Gudjonsson notes that suspects who have had several previous convictions are expected to be (a) more likely to know and assert their legal rights; (b) more familiar with the probable consequences of making self-incriminating admissions and confessions; and (c) more familiar with the police environment and interrogations.[335] Consistent with these expectations, Leo found that suspects with a previous felony record were four times more likely to invoke their *Miranda* rights than suspects without previous convictions.[336] Invocation of Mirada rights, in turn, implies the termination of interrogation. Consistently, Neubauer found that suspects with previous convictions were less likely to confess to the alleged offense than first offenders.[337] However, other studies have found no significant relationship between previous convictions and the rate of confessions.[338]

---

[328] Gudjonsson, see note 110, p. 143.

[329] See Moston, note 195; also see J. Pearse et al., "Police Interviewing and Psychological Vulnerabilities: Predicting the Likelihood of a Confession," *Journal of Community and Applied Social Psychology* 8, no. 1 (1998).

[330] Leo, see note 110, p. 291.

[331] Phillips and Brown, see note 322, p. 105.

[332] *Id.*

[333] Leo, see note 110, p. 291.

[334] Gudjonsson, see note 110, p. 144.

[335] *Id.*

[336] Leo, see note 110, p. 286.

[337] Neubauer, see note 326, p. 103.

[338] See Leiken, note 316; Phillips and Brown, note 319; M. Zander, "The Investigation of Crime: A Study of Cases Tried at the Old Bailey," *Criminal Law Review* (1979), 203-219.

Characteristics of the Offense

As explained previously, the more serious the offense, the greater the stakes in terms of perceived and real punishment, which most likely inhibits some suspects from confessing.[339] Thus, it might be theorized that the type and seriousness of the offense, as detailed below, of which a particular suspect is accused might influence his or her willingness to confess.

1. *Type of Offense*: Neubauer found that suspects interrogated about property offenses confessed more often (56%) than suspects of violent offenses (32%).[340] Mitchell found consistently that suspects confessed more readily to property offenses (76%) than to violent offenses (64%). Neubauer argues that the main reason for the greater number of confessions among alleged property offenders relates to the nature of the evidence that the police have at the time of interrogation.[341] In property offenses there is more often forensic evidence linking the suspect with the offense, which gives interrogators more persuasive evidence to convince suspects that denials are futile.[342] However, Moston, Stephenson and Williamson found no significant differences in confession rates between offense types.[343] Leo's findings also "do not support [Neubauer's] argument that there is a significant relationship between the type of crime and the likelihood of confession."[344]

2. *Seriousness of the Offense*: A number of studies have shown that suspects confess less readily to serious than to non-serious offenses.[345] Gudjonsson points out that the relative lack of incentive among suspects to confess to serious crimes may sometimes be compensated for by the fact that the more serious the crime, the longer suspects tend to be interrogated and the larger the number of interrogative tactics utilized.[346]

Contextual Characteristics

1. *Access to Legal Advice*: Gudjonsson notes that despite evidence that receiving legal advice influences the confession rate, access to an attorney does not appear to reduce the overall confession rate.[347] In other words, even with a high proportion of suspects being provided legal advice, suspects still confess in more than half of all cases. However, the presence of legal counsel is an important predictor as to whether or not a particular suspect will confess.[348] For example, Moston, Stephenson and Williamson (1992) found that over 50% of those who received no legal advice confessed, in contrast to less than 30% of those who had

---

[339] Gudjonsson, see note 110 p. 146.
[340] Neubauer, see note 326, p. 104.
[341] *Id.*, p. 106
[342] *Id.*
[343] Moston, see note 195.
[344] Leo, see note 110, p. 292.
[345] See R. Evans, The Conduct of Police Interviews with Juveniles, Royal Commission on Criminal Justice Research Report no. 8 (London: HMSO 1993).
[346] Gudjonsson, see note 110, p. 147-148.
[347] Id., p. 150.
[348] *Id.*

legal advice.[349] Though not directly related to the access to, or presence of, legal counsel during an interrogation, Leo's findings regarding suspects' likelihood of invoking their *Miranda* rights are illuminating, because this action usually leads to access to an attorney and the automatic termination of interrogation. Even though invoking *Miranda* is a potentially powerful tool for suspects to avoid interrogation and, thus, confession or self-incrimination, Leo found that 78.29% of his sample chose to waive their *Miranda* rights, while 21.71% chose to terminate questioning.[350]

2. *Strength of the Evidence*: The Moston, Stephenson and Williamson study provides the strongest support for the theory that the strength of the evidence against a suspect is the best predictor of the likelihood of a confession.[351] Confessions were rare (less than 10% of cases) and denials common (77% of cases) when the evidence against the suspect was weak.[352] On the other hand, when the evidence was strong confessions were common (67% of cases) and denials infrequent (16% of cases).[353] However, Leo's findings do not corroborate the theory that the strength of the evidence prior to questioning "exert[s] a statistically significant effect on the likelihood that the suspect will provide incriminating information during interrogation."[354]

3. *Interrogation Techniques*: Evidence shows that the more serious the offense, the more police use persuasive techniques to break down resistance.[355] In his study of 156 videotaped interrogations, Gudjonsson found open-ended questions in 98% of the interviews, and leading questions in 73% of the sample.[356] The most common techniques of persuasion were the introduction of allegations against the suspect, seen in 74% of the cases, and challenges to a lie or an inconsistency, seen in 20% of the interviews.[357] Other types of challenges, emphasis on the seriousness of the offense, and psychological manipulation were individually noted in less than 8% of the cases.[358] Ultimately, 53% of the suspects in Gudjonsson's study made a full confession or a self-incriminating admission (i.e., an admission of involvement in the offense, but minimizing intent or role).[359] In 97% of cases the confession or admission occurred in the first interview.[360]

---

[349] Moston, see note 195.
[350] Leo, see note 110, p. 276.
[351] Gudjonsson, see note 110, p. 150. *See also* M.L. Wald et al., "Interrogations in New Haven: The impact of Miranda," *Yale Law Journal* 76, no. 1519 (1967) (finding that suspects were significantly more likely to provide incriminating information during interrogation the stronger the evidence against them prior to questioning).
[352] Moston, see note 195.
[353] *Id.*
[354] Leo, see note 110, p. 292.
[355] See Evans, note 345; B. Irving and I.K. McKenzie *Police Interrogation: The Effects of the Police and Criminal Evidence Act* (London: The Police Foundation, 1989).
[356] Gudjonsson, see note 110, p. 69.
[357] *Id.*
[358] *Id.*
[359] *Id.*, p. 70.
[360] *Id.*

According to Leo, the number of interrogation tactics employed by interrogators in a U.S. police station was one of the only two variables that were significantly related to the likelihood of a successful interrogation.[361] In Leo's study, interrogators employed a median of 5 and a mean of 5.62 tactics per interrogation, yet used some tactics more than others.[362] The twelve tactics most commonly used by interrogators were the following (with the percentage of cases where the tactic was used in parentheses):[363]

- Appeal to suspect's self-interest (88%).
- Confront suspect with existing evidence of guilt (85%).
- Undermine suspect's confidence in denial of guilt (43%).
- Identify contradictions in suspect's story (42%).
- Use Behavioral Analysis Interview questions (40%).
- Appeal to the importance of cooperation (37%).
- Offer moral justification/psychological excuses (34%).
- Confront suspect with false evidence of guilt (30%).
- Use praise or flattery (30%).
- Appeal to the detective's expertise/authority (29%).
- Appeal to the suspect's conscience (23%).
- Minimize the moral seriousness of the offense (22%).

Leo's findings reveal that, of these tactics, the four most effective in eliciting a confession, admission, or incriminating statement were (a) appealing to the suspect's conscience (97% success rate), (b) identifying and pointing out contradictions in the suspect's denial and story (91% success rate), (c) using praise or flattery (91% success rate), and (d) offering moral justifications or psychological excuses for the crime (90% success rate).[364]

4. *Length of Interrogation*: As noted above, Leo found that the length of the interrogation, along with the number of interrogation techniques used, was the only statistically significant indicator of the likelihood of obtaining incriminating information through a confession.[365] Leo's findings reflect that the longer interrogators interrogate suspects "the more likely they are to wear the suspect down and elicit incriminating statements."[366] Successful interrogations were six times more likely to last more than one hour than unsuccessful ones (36% vs. 6%),

---

[361] Leo, see note 110, p. 292. The other variable was length of the interrogation, discussed below.
[362] *Id.*, p. 277.
[363] *Id.*, p. 278.
[364] *Id.*, p. 294.
[365] *Id.*, p. 292.
[366] *Id.*

while unsuccessful interrogations were more than twice as likely to be under 30 minutes than successful ones (58% vs. 27%).[367]

By contrast, Gudjonsson has concluded that only three variables seem to predict a confession: use of illicit drugs, prison experience, and presence of an attorney/solicitor.[368] Illicit drug use prior to the interrogation predicted the suspects' making a confession, while the other two variables were associated with suspects making a denial.[369] Gudjonsson found that the odds of a suspect's confessing were more than three times greater if that suspect had reported using an illicit drug within 24 hours of his or her arrest.[370] On the other hand, Gudjonsson also found that the odds of suspects' not confessing were four times higher for a suspect who had a legal representative.[371] With regard to prior prison experience, the likelihood of a denial was twice as great in cases where the suspect had already been to prison.[372] According to Gudjonsson's study, the greatest likelihood of suspects' making a confession occurred when there was no solicitor present and the suspect had consumed illicit drugs within 24 hours of arrest and had not been previously to prison.[373] The likelihood of a confession occurring under those circumstances was 92%, in contrast to the average confession rate of 58% for the entire sample.[374]

Gudjonsson's Self-Report Studies

One distinct method for evaluating why suspects confess during custodial interrogations is to systematically ask suspects questions about what made them confess.[375] Gudjonsson has twice administered such questionnaires, once in Northern Ireland and another in Iceland.[376] These studies revealed three "facilitative" factors and one "inhibitory" factor for confessions.[377] The first facilitative factor, *external pressure to confess*, is associated with persuasive police interrogation techniques, police behavior, and fear of confinement.[378] Fear of being confined was rated as a very important reason for the confession in over 20% of the cases,[379] while fear of the police or threats of violence were rated as important in only 5% of cases.[380] Police pressure and persuasion were rated as very important in about 20% of cases.[381] The second facilitative factor, *internal pressure to confess*, is associated with the suspect's feelings of guilt about the crime and the consequent need to relieve him/herself of the guilt by confessing.[382]

---

[367] *Id.*, p. 297.
[368] Gudjonsson, see note 110, p. 70.
[369] *Id.*
[370] *Id.*, p. 70-71.
[371] *Id., p.* 71.
[372] *Id.*
[373] *Id.*
[374] *Id.*
[375] *Id.*, p. 140.
[376] *Id.*, p. 152.
[377] *Id.*
[378] *Id.*, p. 153.
[379] *Id.*
[380] *Id.*
[381] *Id.*
[382] *Id.*

Over 42% of subjects interviewed said they had experienced considerable relief after confessing and 40% said they had confessed because they felt guilty.[383] In relation to the third facilitative factor, *perception of proof*, 55% of subjects said that they had confessed because they strongly believed at the time that the police would be able to prove they had committed the crime.[384] Gudjonsson identified *fear of the consequences* of confessing as an inhibitory factor.[385] Of the three facilitative factors, Gudjonsson concluded that the single greatest incentive to confess related to the strength of the evidence against the suspect.[386]

Section 3. Interrogation Techniques in the Literature

Turning from the theoretical and empirical literature to the practical, there are numerous guides available to the public concerning interrogation techniques. The majority of interrogation manuals, or "how-to" texts, are produced in the United States and are generally based on the practical experience of interrogators.[387] The most influential of these practical interrogation manuals is *Criminal Interrogation and Confessions*, written by Inbau, Reid, Buckley, and Jayne.[388] It is also perhaps the most comprehensive, unified approach to interrogation, laying out an overall schema for the entire interaction with the suspect. Inbau et al. take over 600 pages to describe the stages and requirements of a successful interrogation according to the Reid Technique. The Reid Technique was originally developed in the 1940s and 1950s by John E. Reid and the text has continually evolved since then, with the fourth and most recent edition published in 2004.[389] Other classic texts include Royal and Schutt's *The Gentle Art of Interviewing and Interrogation*, as well as Aubry and Caputo's *Criminal Interrogation*. A newer text that seems to be garnering some attention is Stan Walters's *Kinesic Interview and Interrogation*. These, combined with a number of other, lesser known "how-to" guides, provide a basic outline of successful interrogation. To some degree, almost all cover the same aspects of the successful interrogation: 1) characteristics/qualifications of the interrogator; 2) pre-interrogation fact gathering and analysis; 3) the interrogation setting; 4) pre-interrogation interview and rapport-building; 5) analysis of behavioral symptoms; 6) interrogation of the suspect; 7) detection of deceit; and 8) securing the confession.

While some criticize the Reid Technique and most of the other available interrogation guides as relying too heavily on overly coercive persuasion methods,[390] those critics also acknowledge that some persuasion pressure is necessary, since most suspects are reluctant to admit their crimes or often even

---

[383] *Id.*

[384] *Id.*

[385] *Id.*, p. 152.

[386] *Id.*, p. 157.

[387] *Id.*, p. 7.

[388] *Id.*

[389] Inbau, see note 109, p. ix.

[390] Gudjonsson, see note 110, p. 7.

discuss them.[391] Moreover, one can hardly imagine a custodial interrogation that is not in some way "coercive," as the interrogator "is part of a system that gives him or her certain powers and controls (arrest and detention, power to charge, power to ask questions, control over the suspect's freedom of movement and access to the outside world)."[392]

Interrogators generally use persuasive methods to convince suspects that "their best interests are served by a confession."[393] Some of the available manuals recommend strategies of deception, including concealment of police identity while trying to obtain a confession or admission, misrepresentation of the nature or seriousness of the offense during interrogation, and even trickery, such as presenting the suspect with false evidence of guilt.[394] Gudjonsson argues, however, that "the risk of false confessions is very real when psychologically manipulative and deceptive techniques are employed."[395] Thus, interrogators must be aware of these dangers. They should also recognize the three general classes of stressors that are relevant to police interrogations, so that they can both understand what a suspect is experiencing and manipulate the stressors as needed:

- Stress caused by the physical environment at the police station;
- Stress caused by confinement and isolation from peers; and
- Stress caused by the suspect's submission to authority.[396]

The following subsections summarize the various suggestions for interrogation techniques provided by the classic texts for each of the eight aspects mentioned above. The selected sources view interrogation as a method to both secure confessions and gather accurate information in a legal and ethical fashion. However, any such summary can only scratch the surface of "how-to" guides that contain hundreds of pages each. Nonetheless, we attempt to draw together those areas on which the authorities basically agree, as well as to point out some of the most salient suggestions made by each author in the various areas. We base the discussion on the Reid Technique, as it is the most widely used and accepted, and in many instances seems to be the basis for the other techniques as well.[397]

Characteristics/Qualifications of the Interrogator

All authorities agree that not just anyone can be a successful interrogator. It takes an intense dedication to the art of interrogation, years of practice and study, and certain personality characteristics, only some of which can be learned.

---

[391] *Id.,* p. 8.
[392] *Id.,* p. 25.
[393] *Id.,* p. 8.
[394] *Id.*
[395] *Id.,* p. 9.
[396] *Id.,*p. 26.
[397] Most of the discussion will refer to the interrogator and subject/suspect as "he." This is done to accommodate the texts which almost uniformly use "he," and of course is not meant to imply in any way that either party must be male.

According to the Reid Technique, the interrogator must be intelligent, with a "good practical understanding of human nature."[398] He should "get along well with others, especially individuals from varying backgrounds."[399] Patience and a "high index of suspicion" are both important attributes, as is "an intense interest" in the field of interrogation.[400] An interrogator should supplement this intense interest with continual study of "behavior analysis, related areas of psychology and psychopathology, as well as interrogation techniques. He should understand how to conduct a proper interrogation and be able to explain...the underlying concepts involved at each stage of the interrogation process."[401] An awareness of the legal regulations surrounding interrogation is also indispensable.[402] Because one individual will perform the roles of both interrogator and interviewer, the authors suggest that the interrogator needs all of the characteristics of a good interviewer: a friendly, personable, nonjudgmental, and objective manner; a genuine curiosity and concern about other people; the ability to separate the suspect from the crime; comfort in asking questions; an "easygoing confidence;" and the ability to be a good listener.[403] Beyond this, the interrogator should also have "the ability to put aside any personal feelings" about the suspect, the ability to control his emotions in all situations, comfort with "using persuasive tactics that may be considered morally offensive," and the ability to project confidence in both himself and the path of the investigation and interrogation.[404] Finally, the Reid Technique requires that the interrogator be a "skilled communicator," with the "ability to monitor a subject's behavior and respond effectively to the dynamics of the situation."[405]

The other texts hew closely to the Reid requirements. Aubry and Caputo; Aubry, Royal and Schutt, and Walters echo and flesh out some of the Reid requirements. For instance, they suggest that the interrogator "must be possessed with a strong desire to become a skilled and competent interrogator[,] and this desire must be channeled into efforts which will culminate in capability."[406] He must be confident and comfortable in his own skin;[407] "a hesitant manner, fidgeting around in the chair, stuttering and stammering, the use of profanity or vulgarity, and similar mannerisms would all be considered objectionable."[408] He must be personable and able to relate to and get along well with others from all backgrounds.[409] He should be intelligent and well-educated, and have an interest in and understanding of human nature.[410] Indeed, Walters writes that the best interrogators are those "who have

---

[398] Inbau, see note 109, p. 65.

[399] *Id.*, p. 66-67

[400] *Id.* p. 66

[401] *Id.*, p. 66.

[402] *Id.*, p. 66.

[403] *Id.*, p. 66-67, 79.

[404] *Id.*, p. 78-79.

[405] *Id.*, p. 79.

[406] Arthur S. Aubry, Jr. and Rudolph R. Caputo, *Criminal Interrogation*, 40 (1965).

[407] *Id.*, p. 40-57, 150; Robert F. Royal, Steven R. Schutt, *The Gentle Art of Interviewing and Interrogation: A Professional Manual and Guide* (Englewood Cliffs, NJ: Prentice-Hall, 1976), 65-66.

[408] Aubry and Caputo, see note 406, p. 57.

[409] Royal and Schutt, see note 407, p. 65-67.

[410] Aubry and Caputo, see note 406, p. 41; Royal and Schutt, see note 407, p. 67.

learned to observe and interpret human communication behavior, are introspective enough to know themselves, [and] have developed a broad-based understanding of other personalities."[411] Ideal experience, according to Aubry, includes years of field investigation, an "apprenticeship" as an interrogator with continual training and review, as well as studies in psychology, physiology, criminology, sociology, and basic physical sciences, literature, and English composition courses.[412] Aubry, however, concedes that a more realistic expectation is a high school diploma and at least five years of police experience, with at least two of those "spent in bona fide investigative duties of criminal violations, preferably as a Detective or Plainclothesman."[413]

Finally, the other texts point out that excellent acting ability is also a requirement.[414] The interrogator must convey numerous emotions "without affecting his judgment or revealing any personal emotion about the subject…[and must] project sincerity" to conduct an interrogation successfully.[415] He should "have developed the skill to play 'the game' in the interview room and temporarily assume any other personality."[416] The interrogator must not only be patient,[417] but also be capable of conveying infinite patience so that the suspect believes the interrogation will go on indefinitely.[418]

Pre-Interrogation Fact-Gathering and Analysis

All of the authorities agree that a thorough investigation and analysis of the facts is essential to a successful interrogation. "An interrogation must be considered as the highlight and the final act of the investigation which has preceded it."[419] The Reid Technique's "fact analysis" provides a good example of the type and extent of investigation and fact-gathering that is required before an interrogation. According to the Reid Technique, when possible, the interrogator should conduct as much of the investigation as possible for himself and should not merely read the reports of others.[420] This is not a minor or easy task, as the Reid Technique (and many of the other texts) requires that the interrogator have information on:

- *The offense itself* (including the legal nature of the offensive conduct and the exact amount and nature of the loss; date, time, and place of the occurrence in accurate detail; description of the crime area and of the crime scene itself; the way in which the crime appears to have been committed and known details of its commission; possible motives for its commission; incriminating factors regarding a particular suspect);

---

[411] Stan B. Walters, *Principles of Kinesic Interview and Interrogation* (UK: CRC Press, 1996), xi.
[412] Aubry and Caputo, see note 406, p. 51.
[413] *Id.* p. 51.
[414] *Id.*, p. 44; Royal and Schutt, see note 407, p. 65-66.
[415] *Id.*
[416] Walters, see note 411, p. xi.
[417] Inbau, see note 109, p. 66.
[418] Aubry and Caputo, see note 406, p. 60.
[419] *Id.*, p. 148.
[420] Inbau, see note 109, p. 12.

- *The suspect or suspects* (including personal background information; present physical and mental condition, as well as medical history, including any addictions to drugs, alcohol, or gambling; attitude toward investigation (such as hostile or cooperative); relationship to victim or crime scene; incriminating facts or possible motives; alibi or other statements that the suspect related to investigators; religious or fraternal affiliations or prejudices; home environment; social attitudes in general; hobbies; sexual interests or deviations, but only if directly relevant to the investigation; abilities or opportunities to commit the offense); and

- *The victim or victims* (including, for companies or other institutions, attitudes and practices toward employees and public; financial status; and for persons, nature of injury or harm and details thereof; age, sex, marital status, and family responsibilities; social attitudes regarding race, nationality, religion, etc.; gang affiliation; financial and social circumstances; physical and mental characteristics; sexual interests or deviations, but only if directly relevant to the investigation; blackmail potentialities).[421]

The investigative techniques that should be employed in gathering this information are beyond the purview of this paper, but it should be sufficient to note that gathering all of this information is no small task. In addition, all of the authors repeatedly stress the importance of this stage to ensure proper preparation for a successful interrogation.

The Interrogation Setting

Each of the authorities focuses on the physical set-up and context-construction for the interrogation. The Reid Technique suggests that "the principal psychological factor contributing to a successful interview or interrogation is privacy — being alone with the person during questioning."[422] This is based on the psychological premise that we, as humans, are more comfortable revealing secrets to only one person at a time.[423] Second only to privacy, according to the Reid Technique, is the need to minimize reminders of consequences by removing police paraphernalia from both the room and the interrogator's person.[424] Beyond this, the Reid Technique provides suggestions on, among other things, selecting proper décor ("remove all distractions"), lighting ("good, but not excessive or glaring, illumination of the suspect's face"), noise level (as low as possible), and even arrangement of chairs ("investigator and subject should be separated by about four to five feet and should directly face each other, without . . . any other object between them").[425] All of these are meant to create an environment that the authors suggest will be conducive to eliciting responsiveness from the

---

[421] *Id.*, p. 20-21.
[422] *Id.*, p. 51.
[423] *Id.*
[424] *Id.*, p. 56.
[425] *Id.*, p. 58-59.

suspect.[426] In addition, the authors recommend the use of a one-way mirror and a concealed microphone so that observers can see and hear the interrogation while maintaining the necessary privacy.[427] This allows fellow investigators to prepare themselves for later involvement by observing the suspect's behavior, protects the interrogator from false accusations of misconduct, and allows observation of the suspect when he is left alone in the room, both to evaluate his behavior and to prevent self-inflicted violence.[428]

Establishing a sense of privacy through the set-up of the interrogation room is the first recommendation of almost all authors.[429] "The removal of formal, police atmosphere, when combined with the illusion of remoteness, with quietness and the lack of sound and noise, and with privacy; can have a sudden, devastating effect upon the composure of the individual who has just come from the normal hustle and bustle of Headquarters."[430] Moreover, most authors agree on the psychological premise that it is easier to confide in or confess a secret to one other person.[431]

Aubry goes on to write that there must be a reception room adjoining the interrogation room where observers can be situated, and the only communication system between the two rooms should be a two-way buzzer, with the buzzer-button in the interrogation room out of the suspect's view.[432] "A state of quietness with an absolute minimum of sound also serves a useful purpose in helping to withdraw the suspect from his environment."[433] Like the Reid Technique, others also suggest the removal of all formal restraining agents and evidence that the suspect is in police custody, such as uniforms or shields.[434] In addition, Aubry suggests that the physical surroundings be "plain and simple," painted in a neutral shade of off-white, and with no windows that might "serve as a constant distraction and as a convenient psychological crutch upon which the suspect will lean to his own advantage."[435] Unlike the Reid Technique, Aubry recommends against the one-way mirror because it cannot be easily explained,[436] but suggests using a small picture on the wall to conceal the mirror.[437] In addition, he suggests using a sound and video recording mechanism, so long as it can be done without alerting or distracting the suspect.[438]

---

[426] *Id.*, p. 51.
[427] *Id.*, p. 59.
[428] *Id.*
[429] See, e.g., Aubry and Caputo, note 406, p. 66.
[430] *Id.*
[431] Inbau, see note 109, p. 51; Aubry and Caputo, see note 406, p. 65.
[432] Aubry and Caputo, see note 406, p. 63-65.
[433] *Id.,* p. 65.
[434] *Id.,* p. 66.
[435] *Id.,* p. 66, 67.
[436] *Id.,* p. 67.
[437] *Id.,* p. 68.
[438] *Id.,* p. 71-72.

Pre-Interrogation Interview and Rapport-Building

The Reid Technique recommends conducting an interview before beginning the interrogation to "establish a level of rapport and trust with the suspect," as well as to learn information about the suspect that will help in the conduct of the interrogation.[439] The interview, which should last 30 to 45 minutes and is conducted with "only one investigator interacting with the subject,"[440] should be non-accusatory and designed to gather information, may be conducted early during an investigation and in a variety of environments, is free flowing and relatively unstructured, and should be documented in written notes taken by the investigator.[441] Like the preparatory investigation, the interview is designed to elicit information about the offense itself, the suspect or suspects, and the victim or victims.[442] More important, however, is building rapport, defined as "a relationship marked by conformity."[443] The goals of building rapport at the beginning of the interview are: 1) give the suspect an opportunity to evaluate the investigator and ideally "conclude that the investigator is professional, nonjudgmental, and knowledgeable;" 2) allow the investigator to make an initial assessment of the suspect, such as his "communications skills, general nervous tension, normal level of eye contact, and a behavioral baseline;" and 3) allow the investigator to establish a "question-and-answer pattern" for the interaction.[444] At the same time, "efforts to establish rapport should appear natural and unassuming" so the suspect does not become "suspicious of the investigator's motives."[445] Small talk works for some suspects, while simply establishing the suspect's background information and personal history may be enough for others.[446]

All authorities agree on the importance of this initial interview, with its dual purpose of gathering information and building rapport. Indeed, according to Aubry, "nearly all interrogations which eventually fail for whatever given reason, have actually failed during the first few moments of the questioning procedure."[447] Royal and Schutt write that "resistance to the disclosure of [such] information is considerably increased if the interviewer is a total stranger, or if something is not done to establish a friendly and trusting attitude on the part of the suspect."[448] To build that rapport, they suggest the following techniques:

1. Identify yourself.

2. Begin the discussion by commenting on a topic of apparent interest to the subject.

---

[439] Inbau, see note 109, p. 9.
[440] John E. Reid and Associates, *Defending the Reid Technique of Interrogation,* at http://www.reid.com/educational_info/critictechniquedefend.html, accessed 13 March 2005.
[441] Inbau, see note 109, p. 5-6.
[442] *Id.*, p. 20-21.
[443] *Id.*, p. 93.
[444] *Id.*
[445] *Id.*
[446] *Id.*, p. 93-94.
[447] Aubry and Caputo, see note 406, p. 148.
[448] Royal and Schutt, see note 407, p. 61.

3. Establish confidence and friendliness by talking for a period about everyday subjects. In other words, have a 'friendly visit.'

4. Keep conversation informal and easy.

5. Display pleasant emotional responses and avoid unpleasant expressions.

6. Urge the subject, but never try to hurry him.

7. Do not ask questions that lead a witness or subject to believe you are suspicious of him, either by composition of the question or by method of asking.

8. Appear interested and sympathetic to his problems.

9. Do not begin the interview or interrogation until the subject appears to be quite friendly and cooperative.

10. Try to re-establish rapport at any time during the questioning if the subject appears to become reserved or hostile."[449]

Also important in building rapport is conveying the desired image of the interviewer to the suspect. The interviewer must appear sympathetic, sincere, impartial, empathetic, and firm, all at the same time.[450]

Aubry emphasizes the importance of even the investigator's entrance, writing that "he must [enter] with an intangible air which adds up to confidence, confidence in himself, and confidence in his ability to carry out a successful interrogation; he must exude this air of confidence."[451] To build rapport while maintaining this air of confidence, Aubry suggests the following techniques to be used at the initial phase of the interview/interrogation:

1. Have the suspect identify himself.

2. Use only the suspect's first or last name, and never use "Mr."

3. The interrogator should insist that the suspect call him "Mr." as this "aids the interrogator in securing and maintaining the psychological advantage over the subject."

4. The interrogator should approach the suspect with "an air of resolution and firmness" but not "be so forbidding that the subject quickly makes up his mind that the interrogator is 'out to get him at all costs.'"

5. The investigator must quickly size up the suspect, "rapidly and efficiently analyzing the personality, temperament, and make-up of the subject."

---

[449] *Id.*, p. 61-62.
[450] *Id.*, p. 65-66.
[451] Aubry and Caputo, see note 406, p. 150.

6.   Using the "size-up," the investigator should then determine the approach that will be most useful for this type of suspect.[452]

Similarly, Vrij suggests that during the interview, the investigator must "avoid guilt assumption and belief perseverance," must be open-minded and flexible, should establish rapport, and should provide little information about the case to avoid making it easier for the suspect to lie or come up with explanations.[453]

Types of Questions for the Interview

As a complement to the various interview techniques, it is helpful to consider the types of questions that an investigator should ask. Most of the authorities agree on this aspect, which is laid out most clearly by Dillon in his work on *The Practice of Questioning*. He classifies several types of questions used during the various stages of the interrogation. According to him, the questions should be prepared beforehand and written down on paper (though no other author makes this suggestion, as it would seem to inhibit flexibility).[454] The questions, according to Dillon, should be asked in the following order, by type:

1.   *Opening questions* – used at the start of the interview and designed to "get the respondent talking," these should be yes-no questions that are easy to answer and are not about the crime;

2.   *Free narrative questions* – the investigator names a topic and asks the suspect to tell what he knows about it, allowing the suspect to describe a topic in his own words while the investigator listens without interrupting;

3.   *Direct questions* – follows up on narrative questions by asking about specific items while avoiding value-laden terms such as "murder," "rape," etc. The investigator should order his questions A) from the general to the specific, and B) from the known to the unknown;

4.   *Cross-questioning* – questions designed to check and verify one answer against another, delving into problematic (i.e., contradictory or ambiguous) answers; the suspect is asked to repeat his statements "by means of questions asked in different ways and in no special order;"

5.   *Review questions* – used to confirm previous answers, repeating the information and asking 'Is that correct?' and 'What else?'[455]

---

[452]   *Id.*, p. 151-162.
[453]   Aldert Vrij, "'We Will Protect Your Wife and Child, but Only If You Confess': Police Interrogations in England and the Netherlands," in *Adversarial Versus Inquisitorial Justice: Psychological Perspectives on Criminal Systems*, Peter J. van Koppen and Steven D. Penrod, eds. (New York: Plenum, 2003), 57-79.
[454]   J. T. Dillon, *The Practice of Questioning* (London: Routledge, 1990), 82.
[455]   *Id.* p. 85-91.

At the closing, Dillon suggests again simply listening to the suspect.[456] "Their small talk often includes a casual fact or unguarded statement that contains new or different information," because they feel that the questioning is over and their guard may be down.[457]

Reviewing Dillon's five forms of questions, Walton warns the interrogator "to be aware of value-laden terms that occur in questions."[458] While he approves of the use of so-called loaded questions ("a question that contains presuppositions such that when the respondent gives any direct answer to the question he concedes certain assumptions that are at issue and that are damaging to his interests"), the interrogator must recognize when he is using these types of questions so that if the suggestive terms in the question are "incorporated into the memory of the witness" the interrogator understands what is happening.[459] At the same time, the loaded question is a key component of the Reid Technique's Step 7 ("Presenting an alternative question," see discussion below), thus showing the utility of such questions in the interrogation setting. Indeed, Walton recognizes that loaded, complex questions should be used "provided that they come in the right order of questioning in a dialogue sequence."[460]

Royal and Schutt echo this advice in their thoughts on the fundamental characteristics of good question construction:

1. Make the questions short and confined to one topic;

2. Make the questions clear and easily understood;

3. Avoid the use of frightening or super-realistic words; such as confession, murder, forger, dope addict, embezzler, etc. Use milder terms;

4. Use precise questions. A precise question is one that calls for a specific or an exact answer. It limits the requested answer to a definite item of information;

5. Use discerning questions. Discerning questions are questions designed to produce information directly bearing on the matter under discussion. They are questions that discriminate between what is relevant and what is irrelevant.[461]

Behavior Symptom Analysis

Behavior Symptom Analysis (BSA) involves evaluation of the verbal, paralinguistic, and nonverbal channels of communication to identify possibly guilty and/or deceptive suspects.[462] BSA can be considered merely a part of the

---

[456] *Id.,* p. 90.

[457] *Id.*

[458] Walton, see note 199, p. 1791.

[459] *Id.*

[460] *Id.*

[461] Royal and Schutt, see note 407, p. 32-33.

[462] Inbau, see note 109, p. 125.

pre-interrogation interview and not its own, separate stage. However, because the FBI places such emphasis on the use of BSA-like techniques (see discussion below), it is worth briefly discussing the Reid approach.

In essence, BSA evaluates a suspect's answers to interview questions not for their substance but for the manner in which the answers are given. Part of the purpose of BSA is to determine whether to move from the interview stage to the interrogation stage. The Reid Technique offers several basic principles designed to enable the investigator to conduct effective BSA:

1. Recognize that there are no unique behaviors associated with truthfulness or deception.

2. Evaluate all three channels of communication simultaneously.

3. Evaluate paralinguistic and nonverbal behaviors in the context of the subject's verbal message.

4. Evaluate the preponderance of behaviors occurring throughout the interview.

5. Establish the subject's normal behavioral patterns.[463]

These basic principles are then combined with the following generalizations about the correlation between truthfulness/deceptiveness and a suspect's attitudes when answering questions:

Truthful Suspect	Deceptive Suspect
Spontaneous	*Guarded*
Sincere ("openly expresses appropriate emotional states")	*Insincere* ("may come across as phony")
Helpful ("will openly discuss possible suspects and motives and may speculate on how the crime may have been committed")	*Unhelpful* ("reluctant to talk about possible suspects or people who could be eliminated from suspicion …may offer explanations…[or] take the position that no crime was committed")
Concerned (displays "a serious manner and pays close attention to the interviewer's questions")	*Unconcerned* ("nonchalant and downplay[s] the significance of being a suspect…may engage in levity or answer questions inappropriately")
Cooperative	*Uncooperative*[464]

---

[463] *Id.*, p. 125-127.
[464] *Id.*, p. 128-130.

The Reid Technique text then reviews various behavior symptoms that may be indicators of truthfulness and deception in each of the three communication channels.[465] While it would be duplicative to recite them all here, it is worth noting that they come with a warning to the investigator. The authors note that it is *"exceedingly important — indeed critical — that a suspect's behavior symptoms are assessed in accordance with the following guidelines:*

- Look for deviation from the suspect's normal behavior...Once normative behavior has been established, subsequent changes that occur when the suspect is questioned about the crime will become significant.

- Evaluate all behavioral indications on the basis of when they occur (timing) and how often they occur (consistency).

- To be reliable indicators of truth or deception, behavioral changes should occur immediately in response to questions or simultaneously with the suspect's answers. Furthermore, similar behavior responses should occur on a consistent basis whenever the same subject matter is discussed."[466]

BSA is unique in several respects, the most important being its emphasis on using the baseline approach to behavior evaluation. Also unique is the Reid Technique's emphasis on using BSA at a specific stage of the interrogation process. Aspects of BSA correlate with overall detection of deception suggested by other texts, but the Reid Technique uses a specific method at this stage of the interrogation — indeed, before the interrogation has actually begun — to help determine whether or not to move into the interrogation stage. The discussion below elaborates on other authors' general prescriptions for detecting deception during an interrogation.

Kinesic Analysis

The only other interrogation system that uses a similar pre-interrogation approach is the Kinesic Interrogation Technique. The process is called Practical Kinesic Analysis Phase (PKAP) and involves similar analysis of behavior to detect deception, discomfort, or unusual sensitivity.[467] Indeed, PKAP and BSA are so similar as to constitute basically the same technique. Like BSA, PKAP examines behavior related to verbal quality, verbal content, and nonverbal behavior.[468] During this phase the interrogator also develops a profile of the subject, which allows him to use a tailored interrogation approach for that subject.[469]

The basic principles of Kinesic Analysis Phase are strikingly similar to those of BSA:

1. No single behavior, by itself, proves anything.

---

[465] *Id.,* p. 130-153.
[466] *Id.,* p. 153 (emphasis in original).
[467] Walters, see note 411, p. 1-3.
[468] See generally, Walters, note 411.
[469] *Id.,* p. 2.

2. Behaviors must be relatively consistent when stimuli (such as a particular area of inquiry) are presented.

3. The interviewer must establish what is normal or baseline behavior for each subject and then look for changes from the normal baseline.

   This is done by asking non-threatening questions and observing the suspect's unstressed behavior.

4. These observed changes in the subject's baseline behaviors are diagnosed in clusters, not individually.

5. Behaviors must be timely (i.e., they must occur within three to five seconds of when the stress-provoking question is asked).

6. The subjects are watching interrogators while interrogators are watching them.

7. Kinesic interviewing is not as reliable with some groups as with the general population.[470]

The PKAP indicators of deception are also extremely similar to those listed in the BSA, and cover a range of behavioral and verbal responses.[471] As in the Reid Technique, it is only after this analysis — PKAP — and a determination that the suspect is either being deceptive or is responding to stimuli inappropriately that the investigator moves into the interrogation stage.[472]

Interrogating the Suspect

"The interview and interrogation are distinctly different procedures, usually separated by several minutes."[473] Once the investigator decides to shift from interviewing to interrogation, the Reid Technique advises investigators to "sit approximately four feet directly in front of the suspect" at the beginning; "remain seated and refrain from pacing around the room;" "avoid creating the impression that the investigator is seeking a confession or conviction;" "keep paper and pencil out of sight during the interrogation;" "not use realistic words such as 'murder,' 'rape,' 'strangle,' 'stab,' or 'steal,' except in certain situations;" "treat the suspect with decency and respect, regardless of the nature of the offense;" "not handcuff or shackle the suspect during the interrogation;" "not be armed;" and "recognize that in everyone there is some good, however slight it might be."[474] These suggestions are based on both practical necessities and psychological principles; for instance, the authors recommend not being armed not only because the suspect might seize the weapon in close quarters, but also because the interrogator should approach

---

[470] *Id.*, p. 8.

[471] *Id.*, p. 18-138.

[472] *Id.*, p. 2.

[473] John E. Reid and Associates, *Defending the Reid Technique of Interrogation, at* http://www.reid.com/educational_info/critictechniquedefend.html, accessed 13 March 2005.

[474] Inbau, see note 109, p. 79-84.

the suspect "man-to-man" rather than "police officer-to-prisoner" to create a more conducive environment for the interrogation.[475]

The Reid Technique

The heart of the Reid Technique is a nine-step approach to interrogation. The steps provide an over-arching schema that can be used to guide the interrogator through the interrogation process. It gives the interrogator signposts and helps him structure the interrogation in what the authors believe is an effective manner. The Reid Technique authors emphasize that not all of the steps are appropriate in every interrogation, and that the order in which the steps are presented is not dispositive — the investigator should carefully observe the suspect's responses and adjust his questioning accordingly.[476] Indeed, the authors suggest that different approaches are needed for the "emotional offender" and the "nonemotional offender;" the first requires tactics and techniques based on a sympathetic approach ("expressions of understanding and compassion with regard to the commission of the offense as well as the suspect's present difficulty"), while the latter requires a "factual analysis approach" (appeals to "common sense and reason").[477]

The text provides both a brief and in-depth analysis of the nine steps. Here we attempt to condense that information into an even briefer introduction to the nine steps, with a recommendation to consult the text for a deeper understanding of the Reid Technique.

Step 1 – Direct, Positive Confrontation

The interrogator confronts the suspect, asserting that he is "considered to be the person who committed the offense."[478] The suspect's verbal and nonverbal response at this point will determine much of how the interrogation proceeds, but in any event the interrogator also now offers a compelling reason for the suspect to tell the truth.[479]

Step 2 – Theme Development

"The investigator expresses a supposition [called a theme] about the reason for the crime's commission, whereby the suspect should be offered a possible moral excuse for having committed the offense."[480] The investigator should "present to the suspect, in a monologue, reasons and excuses which morally (not legally) excuse the suspect's behavior…The themes do not plant new ideas in the deceptive suspect's mind, but allow the suspect to feel more comfortable talking about his crime by allowing him to reduce the perceived consequences associated with it — both real consequences (those affecting his freedom or livelihood) and personal consequences (those affecting the suspect's self-esteem)."[481] This

---

[475] *Id.*, p. 83.
[476] *Id.*, p. 212.
[477] *Id.*, p. 210.
[478] *Id.*
[479] *Id.*
[480] *Id.*
[481] John E. Reid and Associates, see note 473.

includes creating a scenario whereby the suspect can blame either a third party, such as the victim or an accomplice, or can justify the offense based on particular circumstances.[482] The discussion below of Aubry's variations of interrogation approaches lists several of the themes that an interrogator might consider employing at this stage. Theme development is based on the argument that "in order to persuade the suspect to tell the truth, it is essential to reinforce their [sic] rationalizations for committing the crime versus focusing their attention on the possible consequences."[483] However, "at no time should the suspect be told that if he committed the crime for an understandable reason that the consequences would be less."[484]

Step 3 – Handling Denials

At this point the interrogator takes steps to discourage denials that the suspect may embark upon, and returns to the "moral excuse theme" of Step 2.[485] This stage is also important because, "depending on the nature and persistence of the denials," the interrogator "may become convinced of the suspect's actual innocence" or secondary role.[486] In general, according to the authors, an innocent person will not allow the denials to be cut off, while a guilty individual will eventually "submit to the investigator's return to a theme."[487] Thus, the investigator should cut off the denials, discourage them, evaluate the suspect's responses for indications of truthfulness, and attempt to return to the selected themes.[488]

Step 4 – Overcoming Objections

The guilty suspect, according to the authors, will now offer "reasons as to why he would not or could not commit the crime."[489] Instead of attempting to stop the suspect from voicing objections, as is done with denials, the interrogator should indulge the objections and then overcome them.[490] The technique is compared to that of a car salesman, with the interrogator "selling the suspect on the idea of telling the truth" and turning the objections around by incorporating them in the interrogation theme.[491] The interrogator must recognize the objection, reward it by acting as though the statement were expected and by not arguing with the suspect, and then turn the objection around by reversing the significance of the objection, pointing out the drawbacks if the objection was untruthful, and returning to the interrogation theme.[492]

---

[482] Inbau, see note 109, p. 213.
[483] John E. Reid and Associates, see note 473.
[484] *Id.*
[485] Inbau, see note 109, p. 213.
[486] *Id.*, p. 305.
[487] *Id.*, p. 213.
[488] *Id.*, p. 305-330.
[489] *Id.*, p. 213.
[490] *Id.*, p. 331.
[491] *Id.*, p. 333.
[492] *Id.*, p. 333-336.

Step 5 – Procurement and Retention of a Suspect's Attention

If the interrogator shows no signs of being convinced by the objections, the authors suggest the only strategy left for the *guilty* suspect who does not want to tell the truth is "to psychologically withdraw from the interrogation and ignore the investigator's theme;" according to the authors, innocent suspects will not withdraw.[493] In order to procure and retain the withdrawn suspect's attention, the interrogator should move his chair closer to the suspect, establish and maintain eye contact, use visual aids, and use hypothetical questions since "we are all conditioned to respond to questions."[494]

Step 6 – Handling the Suspect's Passive Mood

After the interrogator has gained the subject's attention in Step 5, the guilty suspect now becomes "reticent and quiet," often adopting a defiant posture, but at the same time becoming more willing to listen.[495] The interrogator should now start to distill the possible reasons for the crime presented in the theme and concentrate on the core of the selected theme.[496] This approach is supplemented by urging and advising the suspect to tell the truth, moving closer, and continuing to display understanding and sympathy.[497]

Step 7 – Presenting an Alternative Question

The interrogator now "offers the guilty suspect the opportunity to start telling the truth by making a single admission."[498] The Reid Technique suggests that it is unrealistic "to expect a suspect to suddenly break down and tell the complete truth about his crime; [instead] it is often necessary to allow the suspect to initially make a first admission of guilt and then attempt to develop the full confession."[499] The alternative question "presents to the suspect a choice between two explanations" for the crime, one much more attractive and morally acceptable.[500] At the same time, the alternative question is "loaded"; by accepting the alternative explanation, the suspect also acknowledges having committed the crime — the single admission that now leads to confession.[501] Some criticize this step as forcing the suspect to incriminate himself, but the Reid proponents point out that "the suspect always has a third choice, which is to say that neither alternative is true."[502] An example of an appropriate alternative question is, "Did you plan this out months in advance, or did it pretty much happen on the spur of

---

[493] *Id.*, p. 338.

[494] *Id.*, p. 338-345.

[495] *Id.*, p. 345.

[496] *Id.*, p. 346.

[497] *Id.*, p. 347-348.

[498] *Id.*, p. 353.

[499] John E. Reid and Associates, *Selecting the Proper Alternative Questions*, Monthly Investigator Tips, September 2004, athttp://www.reid.com/educational_info/r_tips.html?serial=1093984305141229&print=[print], accessed 13 March 2005.

[500] Inbau, see note 109, p. 353.

[501] *Id.*

[502] John E. Reid and Associates, *Defending the Reid Technique of Interrogation, at* http://www.reid.com/educational_info/critictechniquedefend.html, accessed 13 March 2005.

the moment?" with the suspect encouraged to accept the positive choice (spur of the moment). [503] An example of an improper alternative question would be, "Do you want to be charged with first degree murder, which will mean life in prison, or was it just manslaughter, where it happened [sic] on the spur of the moment?"[504]

Step 8 – Having the Suspect Orally Relate Various Details of the Offense

Even after the suspect admits guilt by accepting one of the choices presented in the alternative question, it still takes great effort, according to the authors, to draw out the rest of the details.[505] Once the suspect makes the initial admission the interrogator should move quickly toward eliciting further admissions, first through a "statement of reinforcement" and then through questions that call for longer responses and avoid emotionally charged terminology.[506]

Step 9 – Converting an Oral Confession into a Written Confession

See discussion below.

Royal and Schutt

Other authors make suggestions that are remarkably similar to the nine-step Reid Technique. However, few lay their approaches out in a similar step-by-step process that constantly moves forward toward the goal of eliciting a confession or information. Royal and Schutt come closest to an overarching schema when they suggest the following steps to a successful interrogation:

Undermine Suspect's Confidence of Success

The interrogator should "demonstrate the futility of [the suspect's] position" by "blocking all non-cooperative avenues of escape." The interrogator must detect deception, overcome alibis, and emphasize "the quality and quantity of incriminating evidence and other information derogatory to the subject."[507] In essence, the authors recommend a verbal "trap."[508]

Offer the Suspect a Mutually Acceptable Solution

"Try to convince the suspect that: 1. He is confronted with a personal emergency; 2. Since he cannot escape, he must find a way out; 3. No available solution will be pleasant; 4. Your proposal [will] result in less unpleasantness than any of the other solutions."[509]

---

[503] Id.
[504] John E. Reid and Associates, see note 502.
[505] Inbau, see note 109, p. 365-66.
[506] Id., 366-67.
[507] Royal and Schutt, see note 407, p. 119.
[508] Id.,p. 120.
[509] Id., p. 121.

Make Submission Tolerable

The suspect will be more likely to confess — which the authors suggest involves the surrender of "his very being and his own free will and destiny into the hands of the interrogator" — if the interrogator has conveyed objectivity, sincerity, and sympathy.[510]

Encourage Acquiescence and Pursue Indicators of Compliance

At the first signs that a suspect is responding to the interrogator's suggestions, the interrogator should "begin to diminish other confession-inhibiting factors and promote incentives to confess" through theme development such as that suggested by Reid (discounting fear, minimization, etc.).[511]

Consolidate Accomplishments

"When a criminal violator does submit and agrees to cooperate, the gain should be immediately consolidated and rendered as irreversible as possible."[512]

Aubry

Aubry takes a far less standardized approach to the interrogation process, and indeed presents no schema for it. Instead, Aubry's text lists the various approaches and then discusses the utility of each. Like the other authors, he observes that interrogation techniques "depend upon the subject's degree of implication and participation in the crime; the facts pertinent to his apprehension; the amount and type of evidence that links him with the crime; and the manner in which he participated in the crime."[513]

Aubry begins by listing what he calls the various interrogation approaches and explaining their respective utility. These are:

1. *Direct approach* – best "where the guilt of the subject is certain, or reasonably certain;"

2. *Indirect approach* – best "where the degree of guilt is indicated with something less than reasonable certitude;"

3. *Emotional approach* – depends on the personal qualities of the suspect — religious, emotional, etc.;

4. *Subterfuge* – "a very effective approach," but should only be used if the guilt of the suspect is "reasonably certain," the "so-called standard approaches have been tried and have failed," and the interrogator is very skilled and experienced in interrogation.[514]

The variations on these broad approaches mirror many of the themes that the Reid Technique suggests in Step 2, and include:

---

[510] *Id.*, p. 122.
[511] *Id.*
[512] *Id.*, p. 128.
[513] Aubry and Caputo, see note 406, p. 91.
[514] *Id.*, p. 75-77.

- Indifference	- Sympathy or Sympathetic
	- "Too Great a Temptation"
	- "Only Human to Have Acted That Way"
- Kindness	- Helpful
- Friendliness	- Extenuation
- Mitigation	- Shifting the Blame
- "Hot and Cold"	- Lessening the Degree of Guilt
- Magnifying the Degree of Guilt	- Minimizing the Consequences
- The "Fait Accompli"	- Bluffing
- The Stern, Business-like Approach	- Compounding Falsehoods
- Pretense of Physical Evidence	- Repetition of One Theme
- Mental Relief Through Having Told the Truth	- Perseverance
- Appeals to Decency and Honor	- "What's Your Side of the Story?"
- Tearing Down and Building Up	- "Just Tell the Truth."[515]

Each of these approaches and variations is explained in detail in Chapter 5 of the Aubry text. Aubry then lists several "general" interrogation techniques, including:

- Crumble defenses by establishing motive, premeditation, capability and opportunity of and to [sic] commit the crime.
- Establish and demonstrate intent.
- Hammer away at the subject hard and persistently.
- Nibble off little pieces of the interrogation cake. Concentrate on crumbs, don't bite off pieces too big to chew.
- Ask concise, brief questions, trim off all extra words. Be specific. Be exact. Ask questions that can be answered by simple yes or no. Practice and seek for economy of words.
- Do not ask questions which request or invite the expression of an opinion.
- Avoid leading questions as well as opinion questions because both types are weak and ineffective techniques; leading questions are, in a sense, "unfair to the subject."[516]

Aubry finally presents a list of specific interrogation techniques, with an entire chapter then devoted to the type of suspect with which each may be successful. The specific techniques include:

---

[515] *Id.*, p. 75.
[516] *Id.*, p. 104.

- The Singleness of Purpose
- The Business-like Attitude
- Calm and Matter-of-Fact
- Don't Be Shocked Whatever the Provocation
- Let the Subject Tell His Story
- Let the Subject Tell a Few Lies
- A Waste of Your Time and My Time
- You're Just Hurting Your Loved Ones
- Proven Lies So Tell the Truth
- Hammer at Right and Wrong
- How About Your Conscience?
- Establishing Motives
- Hate to Be in Your Shoes
- Things Look Awfully Bad for You
- Confusion by False Incidents
- Confession of Co-Defendant; and the Genuine Confession[517]

In many ways these lists mirror the type of theme development in Step 2 of the Reid Technique. Aubry leaves the impression, however, that despite his attempts to describe which approach or technique to use with which subject, an interrogator will only be able to choose the appropriate method after years of experience. In that sense, Aubry's list of specific interrogation techniques is in the end more descriptive than prescriptive. Indeed, as Aubry notes, "the approach (should) be adapted to the type, character, and general background of the person being interrogated; the known facts, events and incidents of the crime which has been committed; and the type, kind, nature and extent of the physical evidence available."[518] Because Aubry does not present an overarching schema for the interrogation like that of the Reid Technique, his presentation is more helpful in understanding the possible dynamics at play in an interrogation than in guiding the interrogator through the process.

Kinesic Interrogation

Like the other techniques, Kinesic Interrogation recognizes that the interrogator "cannot depend on a singular, standardized approach to the interrogation that is applied to all deceptive subjects."[519] The Kinesic Interrogation Phase is, like the Reid Technique, a continuation of the initial interview. First the interrogator makes the "interrogation attack," confronting the suspect with the accusation and

---

[517] *Id.,* p. 105.
[518] *Id.,* p. 75.
[519] Walters, see note 411, p. 2.

perhaps the evidence.[520] Rapport building, in the Kinesic Interrogation, is only necessary if the suspect has an introverted personality, while the extrovert can be confronted in a more formal, business-like manner.[521] Either way, the suspect is expected to react with one of several "ego defense mechanisms" — denial, displacement, intellectualization, rationalization, minimization, etc. — that he uses to defend against the initial accusation.[522] The interrogator must then "disarm" each mechanism in turn.[523] The interrogator is able to do this by identifying the suspect's "subconscious miscues" — verbalizations of the suspect's internal monologue.[524] The interrogator then appropriates those miscues (though not word for word), incorporating them into his questions so as to match the suspect's state of mind.[525]

It is at this point that the interrogator can "make the final push" for a confession.[526] Walters sets several rules and prescriptions for this stage:

1. An interrogator should never engage in any behavior which would force even the truthful subject to confess.

2. A false confession is most likely to have been obtained from a subject who is mentally deficient.

3. An interrogator will find that most subjects are prepared to blame alcohol or drugs for their behavior.

4. A successful attack on denial requires that the interrogator review real or circumstantial evidence with the subject every 3 to 5 minutes.

5. A successful practical Kinesic Interrogation requires the appropriate assessment and attack of the subject's primary dominant personality (i.e., introverted or extroverted, as well as subtypes of extrovert).

6. A successful practical Kinesic Interrogation requires the interrogator to correctly identify and respond to the subject's five basic stress-response states (anger, depression, denial, bargaining, acceptance). These progress in turn and the interrogator should shift techniques as each state arises.

7. Once the subject begins to break in small areas, the interrogator should begin to attack with reality-based comments.[527]

---

[520] *Id.*, p. 209.
[521] *Id.*, p. 216-217.
[522] *Id.*, p. 208.
[523] *Id.*, p. 210.
[524] *Id.*, p. 210-211.
[525] *Id.*, p. 211.
[526] *Id.*
[527] *Id.*, p. 211-217.

Good Cop/Bad Cop

One interrogation technique stands apart in the public consciousness as the prototypical approach to interrogations and so merits brief discussion here: the so-called good cop/bad cop technique ("GC/BC"). While there are few published studies of specific techniques, GC/BC has generated unique interest. Rafaeli et al. interviewed criminal interrogators and bill collectors, identifying five variations on GC/BC (the formal term they use is "emotional contrast strategies") that they use to convey "a mix of expressed positive and negative emotions in order to wield influence over target persons."[528]

1. Sequential good cop, bad cop

The suspect is first exposed to an interrogator who "consistently displays either positive or negative emotion," and then to a second interrogator who displays a "contrasting demeanor."[529] Anecdotal evidence suggests that beginning with a display of negative emotions accentuates the suspect's appreciation of the subsequent, more civilized approach.[530]

2. Simultaneous good cop, bad cop

The suspect is exposed to two interrogators, each displaying either positive or negative emotions.[531] Interrogators may "not only present different demeanors to the suspect, but also create perceptual contrast by arguing with each other in front" of the suspect about what type of treatment he deserved.[532]

3. One person playing both roles

A single interrogator "vividly displays" both emotions to a target person, alternating "between displaying a harsh, demanding demeanor and a pleasant, friendly demeanor."[533] The difficulty with this approach is that each demeanor "must appear genuine if the interrogator wishes to wield influence."[534]

4. Good cop in contrast to hypothetical bad cop

The interrogator "playing the good cop role communicates to the [suspect] that if he or she does not comply with the good

---

[528] Anat Rafaeli et al., "Emotional Contrast Strategies as Means of Social Influence: Lessons from Criminal Interrogators and Bill Collectors," *The Academy of Management Journal* 34, no. 4 (December 1991), 749-775, 752; in each variation, "good cop" refers to roles conveying positive and supportive feelings such as warmth, friendliness, approval, respect, empathy, and sympathy, while "bad cop" refers to conveying negative and unsupportive emotions such as coldness, disapproval, lack of respect, and hostility (758).

[529] *Id.*, p. 761.
[530] *Id.*
[531] *Id.*, p. 762.
[532] *Id.*
[533] *Id.*, p. 762.
[534] *Id.*, p. 762-763.

cop's wishes, a nasty, humiliating, esteem-deflating, or even dangerous interaction with a bad cop will be the next step."[535] The hypothetical bad cop need not even be mentioned explicitly, but the threat should be clear.[536]

5. Good cop in contrast to expectations of bad cop

The interrogator presents himself as warm and friendly to a suspect "who expects to encounter coldness and hostility;" this has the effect of "amplify[ing] the construed positiveness of the" interrogator.[537] This technique is most successful with those suspects who seemed scared, anxious, or suspicious of the interrogator.[538]

The strategy behind each of the variations was the same: "create a perceptual contrast for [the] targets, which is proposed to accentuate the construed positiveness of displayed positive emotions and the construed negativeness of displayed negative emotions" in order to induce compliance in the target.[539] According to Rafaeli et al., three mechanisms came into play that made GC/BC successful. First, the "accentuated anxiety" with which the suspect may respond to the bad cop leads to "accentuated relief" in response to good cops.[540] As a result, suspects may comply with the good cop's requests to escape from the anxiety or fear they feel during interactions with bad cops or expect to feel during future interactions.[541]

Second, the GC/BC contrast accentuates the suspect's perception that the good cop is kind and helpful, resulting in pressure "to reciprocate the kindness by complying with the good cop's wishes."[542] This occurs because the "actual or hypothetical contrasting unpleasant person" creates the impression that the good cop's positive feelings are "especially unusual and pronounced."[543]

Third, because the suspect develops "accentuated feelings of relief in response to [the] good cop," and (it is hoped) comes to believe he is kind and helpful, a feeling of trust develops.[544] Once the suspect believes that the good cop is truthful and "truly concerned for [the suspect's] well-being," it becomes easier for the interrogator to convince the suspect that compliance is in his own best interest.[545]

In essence, all five variations, as well as the three identified mechanisms, rely on building rapport between the good cop and the suspect, much like that

---

[535] *Id.*, p. 763.
[536] *Id.*
[537] *Id.*, p. 764.
[538] *Id.*
[539] *Id.*, p. 752.
[540] *Id.*, p. 764.
[541] *Id.*
[542] *Id.*, p. 764-765.
[543] *Id.*
[544] *Id.*, p. 765.
[545] *Id.*

suggested by Inbau et al., Royal and Schutt, and Aubry. The only difference is that the rapport is built not only on the basis of the positive interaction between interrogator and suspect, but also on the fear, anxiety, or anger caused by the actual or perceived bad cop. However, the analysis of the GC/BC technique provides a window into the workings of rapport-building, and re-emphasizes its importance in any successful interrogation.

Detecting Deception

The text describing the Reid Technique does not go beyond BSA in offering suggestions on detecting deception. However, BSA is an integrated system of analysis that can be incorporated at all stages of the interview/interrogation encounter (see discussion above). Similarly, the Kinesic approach is based on PKAP, which also can and should be integrated into the entire interrogation proceeding (see discussion above).

Traditional lie detection has focused on verbal and nonverbal communication. At various points, behaviors that were thought to indicate deceit have included speech hesitation, speech errors, changes in pitch of voice, changes in speech rate, frequency of pauses, pause durations, gaze, smiling, blinking, self-manipulations (e.g., scratching), illustration with hands and arms, hand and finger movement without the arms, leg and foot movements, head movements, trunk movements, and shifting positions.[546] For instance, in 1965, Aubry listed "flushing or paleness of skin," "pulse rate increase or decrease," and even "licking of the lips," among a generous list of indicators of deception.[547] Obviously, many of these behaviors are exhibited by individuals in everyday conversation, and some even contradict others as supposed signs of deception.

In a survey of the empirical studies on behaviors exhibited during deception, Vrij has accumulated several results that will be useful to the interrogator searching for deception. The studies, when taken together in a meta-analysis, are mostly inconclusive for the exhibited behavior, and in fact only three general trends can be found.

Verbal Characteristics

1. Liars tend to have a higher-pitched voice than truth-tellers (probably caused by stress), but the difference is so small as to be detectable only with sophisticated equipment.[548]

2. Liars seem to pause for longer when they speak than do truth-tellers.[549]

Non-vocal Characteristics

1. Liars tend to move their arms, hands, fingers, feet, and legs less than truth-tellers.

---

[546] Alberet Vrij, *Detecting Lies and Deceit: The Psychology of Lying and the Implications for Professional Practice* (New York: John Wiley and Sons, 2000), 33.

[547] Aubry and Caputo, see note 406, p. 123-134.

[548] Vrij, see note 546, p. 32-33.

[549] *Id.*, p. 33.

What is most striking about this list, according to Vrij, is everything it does not include. The findings "contradict[] the stereotypical beliefs that many people hold about non-verbal indicators of deception."[550] It turns out that Vrij's meta-analysis demonstrates that although "observers expect liars to show nervous behaviour and behaviours which indicate intense thinking," this is not the case for the majority of liars.[551] Thus, "people are usually poor at detecting lies when they pay attention to someone's behaviour."[552]

Vrij does concede, as Inbau et al. argue, that experimental studies may not be the most conducive to actually observing deceptive behavior; as he notes, it may be that the subjects "simply [are] not nervous enough during these experiments."[553] Moreover, in the majority of the studies the lie-catchers are college students who volunteer for the studies.[554] In a meta-analysis of those studies that used professional lie-catchers as observers, however, the professionals did no better than the college students.[555] One might also suggest that in the real world, where suspects are motivated to prevaricate for fear of losing their freedom, certain indicators of deception would be more obviously on display. However, not enough empirical studies of deception detection have been carried out in the field to know whether extra motivation to lie will increase indicative behaviors. Fortunately for interrogators, "it is possible to improve people's ability to detect lies."[556] Studies using various training procedures all revealed limited improvements in the ability to detect deceit, although, surprisingly, the studies show students benefiting more from the training than did police officers.[557] Vrij speculates that police officers may have scored lower because they did not believe the information they were being taught.[558]

In the end, Vrij concludes that the best hopes for lie detection are found in observing both emotional expressions and those behaviors influenced by content complexity (latency period, speech errors, speech hesitations, hand, arm, foot and leg movements).[559] He gives interrogators several "Guidelines for the Detection of Deception via Behavioural Cues:"

1. Lies may only be detectable via non-verbal cues if the liar experiences fear, guilt or excitement (or any other emotion), or if the lie is difficult to fabricate.

2. It is important to pay attention to mismatches between speech content and non-verbal behaviour, and to try to explain those mismatches. Keep

[550] *Id.*, p. 38.
[551] *Id.*
[552] *Id.*, p. 57.
[553] *Id.*, p. 39.
[554] *Id.*, p. 74.
[555] *Id.*, p. 75.
[556] *Id.*, p. 95.
[557] *Id.*, p. 94-95.
[558] *Id.*, p. 95.
[559] *Id.*, p. 97.

in mind the possibility that the person is lying, but consider this as only one of the possible reasons for this mismatch.

3. Attention should be directed towards deviations from a person's "normal" or usual patterns of behaviour, if these are known. The explanation for such deviations should be established. Each deviation may indicate that the person is lying, but do not disregard other explanations for these deviations.

4. The judgement of untruthfulness should only be made when all other possible explanations have been negated.

5. A person suspected of deception should be encouraged to talk. This is necessary to negate the alternative options regarding a person's behaviour. Moreover, the more a liar talks, the more likely it is that they [sic] will finally give their lies away via verbal and/or non-verbal cues (as they continuously have to pay attention to both speech content and non-verbal behaviour).

6. There are stereotyped ideas about cues to deception (such as gaze aversion, fidgeting, and so on), which research has shown to be unreliable indicators of deception. The actual indicators are listed in Chapter 2 [see discussion above]. These can be a guide, but bear in mind that not everyone will exhibit these cues during deception, and the presence of such cues *may* indicate deception, but does not do so in every case.[560]

Based on his research, Vrij identifies the "seven aspects [that] characterize a good liar: i) being well prepared; (ii) being original; (iii) thinking quickly; (iv) being eloquent; (v) having a good memory; (vi) not experiencing feelings of fear, guilt of duping, delight while lying; and (vii) being good at acting."[561] In theory, if the interrogator can recognize these character aspects, he can at least identify the suspect who will be better at lying, and thus can search more closely for clues to the occurrence of deception. Indeed, Vrij lays out guidelines for the interrogator who must overcome the good liar's deceit and detect the deceptions:

1. Be suspicious;
2. Be probing;
3. Do not reveal important information;
4. Be informed;
5. Ask liars to repeat what they have said before;
6. Watch and listen carefully and abandon stereotypes;
7. Compare liars' behavior with their natural behavior.[562]

Ultimately, Vrij comes to a similar conclusion as that implied by the BSA used in the Reid Technique: observe the baseline behavior of the suspect, and then

---

[560] *Id.*, p. 98, Box 3.3.
[561] *Id.*, p. 210.
[562] *Id.*, p. 222-225.

observe how that changes once certain stimuli are introduced such as challenging questions and presentation of evidence.

Securing the Confession

Step 9 of the Reid Technique covers "Converting an Oral Confession into a Written Confession." The authors recommend several techniques that lead to confessions that will stand up both to the legal and practical requirements of the judicial system: the use of readable and understandable language, avoidance of leading questions (if the confession is a question-and-answer type), use of the confessor's own language, inclusion of personal history, inclusion of intentional errors for correction by the confessor, a reading and signing of the confession with witnesses, only one written confession, and confinement of the confession to one crime.[563] Aubry recommends similar steps with no material variations.[564] Because there seems to be consensus on this point, Inbau et al.'s text can stand alone without further discussion.

Section 4. How an Interrogation Can "Go Wrong"

Finally, it is worth considering how an interrogation can "go wrong." An interrogation that has gone wrong is one that either elicits false information that the interrogator believes is true, or that has negative, long-term effects on the suspect or societal perceptions of law enforcement. Gudjonsson identifies several ways an interrogation can "go wrong," many of which echo the warnings of Inbau et al., Aubry, and Royal and Schutt's guidelines for interrogation:

- False confessions due to coercion,
- Inadmissible confessions,
- Coerced confessions resulting in resentment,
- Coercion resulting in post-traumatic stress disorder,
- Undermining public confidence, and
- "Boomerang Effect." [565]

False confessions may result where interrogators assume the suspect is guilty, either by approaching the interrogation with pre-set assumptions or placing too much blind faith in their ability to detect deception.[566] "The greater the pressure during interrogation, the greater the likelihood of false confessions."[567] Of course, a false confession is not only useless, but also actually harms the investigation, as the real perpetrator remains free and the investigation is closed. In addition, once word emerges of overly coercive interrogation techniques, public confidence

---

[563] Inbau, see note 109, p. 377-389.
[564] Aubry and Caputo, see note 406, p. 195-207.
[565] Gudjonsson, see note 110, p. 34-36.
[566] *Id.,* p. 34.
[567] *Id.*

in the police may be undermined, which, according to Gudjonsson, encourages police corruption.[568]

Coercive and manipulative interrogation techniques may not only result in false confessions, but the confessions, even if true, may also be inadmissible if obtained in violation of legal standards. An additional, unintended consequence of an overly coercive interrogation is possible long-lasting resentment and bitterness among offenders.[569] Gudjonsson points to the additional possibility of post-traumatic stress disorder in especially coercive interrogations, although no studies directly support such a relationship.[570]

Lastly, the so-called "boomerang effect" may occur when suspects "who would have confessed in their own time refuse to do so when they feel they are being rushed or unfairly treated."[571] The other possible boomerang effect is the eventual retraction of a confession by a suspect who confessed under overly coercive conditions.[572]

Section 5. Theory vs. Technique in the Literature

The interrogation techniques advocated in the literature can for the most part be characterized as one-size-fits-all. They take little account of the factors that the empirical research shows might affect a suspect's willingness to confess, and provide little or no variation for different types of suspects. While all of the technical guides point out that no single interrogation technique works with every suspect, and indeed that every suspect is different, for the most part they provide little guidance on how to adjust interrogation techniques for suspects of different ages, cultures, ethnicities, and criminal history, for crimes of greater seriousness, or for cases in which the interrogator has stronger evidence. The only factor that all of the texts cite as prompting confession is the length of the interrogation, a factor that seems to apply across the board and need not be adjusted for any particular suspect. Despite the variations discussed below, on the whole an interrogator exposed only to the "how-to" guides would have little sense of a need to adapt the techniques learned in the texts when confronting different types of suspects.

All of the texts account for seriousness of the offense and strength of the evidence, but only in indirect fashion. Reid and the other techniques are, to one degree or another, based on exploiting guilt, which for most suspects is proportional to the seriousness of the offense. While developing a theme and overcoming objections, interrogators are certain to use the seriousness of the offense as part of their "selling" of the idea of confession. At the same time, the use of minimization reflects the empirical findings that the more seriously the offense is perceived, the less likely it is that the suspect will confess. Similarly, interrogators will also use the strength of the evidence to convince suspects that

---

[568] *Id.*, p. 36.

[569] *Id.*, p. 35.

[570] *Id.*

[571] *Id.*, p. 36.

[572] *Id.*

they have few alternatives but to confess. This argument can also be used indirectly in the context of the other motivating factor behind the interrogation techniques: fear. That said, the texts do not, for the most part, offer specific techniques that the interrogator should adjust if the crime is more or less serious, or the evidence stronger or weaker; they make few, if any, explicit recommendations for how to use these factors to elicit a confession in different situations.

Aubry draws the most distinctions among various types of suspects. Like the authors of the other texts, Aubry assumes that the basic structure of the interrogation translates equally from suspect to suspect, and only the specific approach within that structure should be altered. As previously noted, he lays out specific interrogation techniques (e.g., The Singleness of Purpose, The Business-like Attitude, Calm and Matter-of-Fact, etc.) and attempts to identify the type of suspect for which each should be used. While the prescriptions do seem to take into account the confession factors that the empirical studies found statistically significant, they do so in a haphazard way that does not seem useful for the interrogator in the field. Instead of suggesting adjustments to be made based on the various factors, Aubry instead seeks to prescribe a single technique for what he apparently considers a comprehensive list of the types of suspects one might encounter. The interrogator is left to memorize the various techniques and the circumstances in which they apply, instead of learning how to adjust techniques for specific confession factors. Thus, if an interrogator were to encounter a suspect of a different sort than those listed, Aubry's text would not help him to adapt techniques to that suspect.

The Reid Technique attempts to account for some of the confession factors, but ultimately fails to provide a guide on adjusting interrogation techniques for the various statistically significant factors leading to confession. Like the other texts, the Reid Technique assumes that the basic structure of the interrogation — rapport-building, theme development, alternative question, etc. — will work across the board for a variety of suspects, regardless of the specific characteristics of the individual. Only within that structure does the Reid text offer some adjustments to make, and then only in one particular area: for emotional and non-emotional offenders, who require either a sympathetic or factual analysis approach, respectively.[573] However, it should be noted that empirical studies have not identified the emotionalism of the suspect as a factor that affects a suspect's willingness to confess. At the same time, while such differentiation may be useful, it is also very basic. According to the empirical research, age, mental state, and previous convictions/confessions are the characteristics that might affect a suspect's likelihood of confession. While the emotional/non-emotional dichotomy may reflect some of those factors, one cannot assume that they do so across the board. Moreover, the non-emotional young offender may require a different approach than the non-emotional middle-aged offender, yet the Reid text makes no such distinction. Like the Aubry text, the Reid Technique gives very few specific prescriptions for how to adjust interrogation techniques in response

---

[573] Inbau, see note 109, p. 210.

to the confession factors. Moreover, it gives no prescriptions at all for adjusting the overarching interrogation structure on the basis of the suspect's individual characteristics.

Although all the texts caution interrogators to remember that each suspect is an individual with his or her own unique traits, such generalized admonitions are practically worthless and are not reflected in the main thrust of the texts. Beyond the factors discussed above, the texts do not provide interrogators with shifts in tactics based on the traits that affect confession.[574] Indeed, they do not even acknowledge the statistically significant confession factors in any specific manner. Moreover, even when they do note that some factors may affect the interrogations (for example, Walters cautions interrogators to consider differences among cultures when attempting to detect deception), they rarely discuss specific techniques that should be tailored to the suspect. Instead, they give interrogators only general tactics without telling them how to adjust the techniques for the critical confession factors.

Finally, although the previously discussed Leo study has limited utility, the four techniques he identifies as most successful in obtaining confessions (appealing to the suspect's conscience, identifying and pointing out contradictions in the suspect's denial and story, using praise or flattery, and offering moral justifications or psychological excuses for the crime) are the same as or similar to techniques advocated in other literature. Since the texts all were written before the Leo study, it does not appear that they were based on any empirical work in the field — indeed, they make no claims that they are. However, if Leo is correct, it seems that the techniques they advocated are indeed among the most successful. An important caution, of course, is that Leo's study was conducted in a single precinct, with only Leo himself coding the interrogation techniques observed. Moreover, we do not know the specific characteristics of the suspects whose interrogations Leo observed, and thus do not know if important adjustments are necessary for success with suspects of varying characteristics.

Ultimately, empirical studies may show that there is no need to adjust to the techniques advocated in the literature on the basis of the various confession factors. Perhaps the Reid Technique in its basic form works as well for old and young, Latino and white, etc. However, as of now there is no proof that this is the case. At this juncture, we simply cannot say whether the techniques in the literature are effective across the board, or whether the confession factors that are statistically significant call for adjustments that the texts do not include.

---

[574] The Royal and Schutt and Walters texts do not provide for adjustments based on specific suspect characteristics. They instead generally point out that the interrogator should be aware of differences among suspects and should take those into account.

PART II: LAW ENFORCEMENT PRACTICES

The following sections of the paper review the interrogation training and practices of various law enforcement organizations. While not an exhaustive survey of all such organizations, the information provides a window into training available to federal, state, and city law enforcement officers in the United States. Additionally, to offer some comparative perspective, we provide an overview of interrogation training and practices in Great Britain and Israel.

Section 6. Federal Bureau of Investigation (FBI Academy at Quantico, Virginia)[575]

The FBI Academy provides training to all future FBI agents. The new agent training consists of 17 weeks of instruction totaling 643.5 hours. As part of this training program, the FBI offers 15 classes, totaling 69 hours, on interviewing and interrogation. Of this program, 9 classes are devoted to interrogation, totaling 27 hours of training. The interrogation curriculum covers, if only generally, interrogation theory and practice. The training also offers two practical exercises on interrogation, each lasting about 25–50 minutes. Finally, the training pays constant attention to the documentation and forms that agents must complete and file in connection with interrogations. According to FBI Academy staff, this last element of the training — necessary filings and documentation — represents a substantial portion of the time and attention allocated to interrogation training. Four hours of training about detection of deception are also included in the aforementioned 69 hours of general interview/interrogation training.

According to literature provided to trainees, "a successful interrogation results in a guilty or involved criminal suspect's making a confession or admitting participation in an illegal activity."[576] However, this avowed goal of obtaining confessions is downplayed by other staff members of the FBI Academy, who clarify that interrogation is best conceived of as a means to lower resistance to telling the truth. FBI Academy staff add that entering an interrogation with the sole goal of obtaining a confession means setting oneself up for failure. Whatever the ultimate objective, the FBI has adopted what it calls the Direct Accusation Approach as its chosen method of interrogation. This approach, whose elements are described below, closely tracks the Reid Technique, with the major difference being that the FBI's approach relies on confronting the suspect with the evidence available to motivate a confession.

Like Reid, the FBI training teaches agents to conduct a pre-interrogation interview. The FBI offers its agents the following eight-step process to guide them through the interview, which are the same steps followed in interviewing witnesses and victims:

---

[575] Unless otherwise referenced, the information in this section is derived from a visit to the Federal Bureau of Investigation Academy, Quantico, Virginia, 8-9 March 2005. Our host during the visit was Brian Boetig, Supervisory Special Agent in the Bureau's Law Enforcement Communication Unit.

[576] D. Vessel, *Conducting Successful Interrogations* (Quantico, VA: Interviewing and Interrogation Law Enforcement Communication Unit, FBI Academy, revised 14 October 2004), 70.

1. *Preparation*: Agents are urged to become thoroughly acquainted with the case and the subject's background prior to entering the interview room.

2. *Introduction*: Agents introduce themselves to the suspect and explain to him/her the nature of the interview.

3. *Rapport Building*: As is explained below, rapport building is the cornerstone of the FBI's entire interview/interrogation process. During this stage, investigators attempt to build a good relationship with subjects.

4. *Questioning*: The agent asks the subject questions following what the FBI calls a deductive funnel. This method of questioning starts with open-ended questions meant to foster narration on the part of the subject, followed by more closed questions such as indicator questions, identification questions, multiple choice questions, and leading (yes or no) questions.

5. *Verification*: Having concluded the questioning, the agent reviews everything the suspect has told him/her for accuracy and further recall.

6. *Catch all*: The agent allows the suspect to add anything he/she considers relevant or absent from his/her prior statements.

7. *Departure*: If the suspect will not be interrogated, arrested, or otherwise detained after the interview, the agent makes arrangements for future contact.

8. *Critique*: The agent evaluates the information obtained in light of the interview goals.

Though seemingly rigid, FBI Academy staff emphasized that this interview approach is meant as a roadmap rather than a strict list, and should be adapted as the situation requires.

FBI training emphasizes the importance of a non-accusatory pre-interrogation interview for a number of reasons. First, the interview provides interrogators with a behavioral baseline against which to evaluate the suspect's subsequent behavior and responses (both verbal and non-verbal) during the confrontational interrogation. Second, it provides investigators with the suspect's version of the events, which could later be used during interrogation to point out contradictions or lies. Finally, FBI staff noted that the pre-interrogation interview functions as the first contact between interrogator and suspect and, given its non-accusatory nature, offers a fertile opportunity to begin establishing rapport with the suspect.

After the pre-interrogation interview, the agents transition into the actual interrogation, which, as mentioned above, follows the Bureau's Direct Accusation Approach. Though not formulated as a strict step-based process, the method can be divided into a four-step plan.[577] First, an interrogator confronts the suspect with the facts and evidence that implicate him, and accuses him of committing, or being complicit in, the crime. As in the training provided by the Federal Law Enforcement Training Center (FLETC; see below), this direct accusation is meant to present a picture of overwhelming certainty that the authorities know of the suspect's involvement in the crime. Conversely, this step sets the FBI's approach apart from the Reid Technique, which does not advocate such direct presentation of the evidence in the interrogator's possession.

As might be expected, suspects usually meet these direct accusations with denials; in fact, a suspect's failure to deny involvement is treated as a strong indicator of guilt. FBI training teaches agents to cut off or stop the suspect's denials by interrupting and preventing any additional attempts at denial, and underscores that a guilty suspect's denials will weaken as the accusations continue, while an innocent suspect's will normally grow in frequency and intensity. FBI training literature notes that an effective way to cut off denials "involves interrogators repeatedly acknowledging the subject's participation in the crimes while questioning only their motivations for committing the acts."[578] FBI training literature alerts future agents to the possibility that guilty suspects will offer protests, or reasons for their innocence, in response to the direct accusations after denials have failed. Because these protests usually have some factual basis and can be defended comfortably by the suspect, FBI training urges agents to redirect and incorporate them into the following step, rather than attempting to refute them.

During the third step, interrogators engage in what practically amounts to a dialogue through which they present themes and arguments meant to persuade the suspect to confess. In essence, this theme-building step depends on the three basic tools of rationalization, projection, and minimization to achieve its ends. This is consistent with the Reid Technique and the training provided to other federal law enforcement agencies in FLETC. The interrogator derives the themes and opportunities to rationalize, project, and minimize from a combination of information provided by the suspect during the pre-interrogation interview and interrogation, and from the interrogator's own general personal experience in relation to human behavior. FBI training literature notes that "the chances of obtaining a confession increase 25 percent for every hour (up to 4 hours) of interrogation."[579] Consequently, interrogators are encouraged to have enough themes and arguments to fill three to four hours of monologue. Throughout their monologue, interrogators should seek to prevent the suspect's mental withdrawal, which is often a response to the failure of their denials and protests. One suggested tactic to prevent the suspect's mental withdrawal is to move closer to him and use his name to gain the suspect's attention. Additionally, as the interrogator rationalizes, projects, and minimizes as part of his interrogation monologue, he

---

[577] *Id.*, p. 73.
[578] *Id.*
[579] *Id.*, p. 74.

should also be attentive to signs of receptivity from the suspect. FBI training emphasizes nonverbal signs such as a drooping head, tears, and the body leaning forward. When these signs are perceived, interrogators are instructed to reduce their themes to a succinct concept and proceed to the next step.

The last step in the FBI's Direct Accusation Approach is the presentation of a bad/good option. This step of the FBI's method is identical to Reid's Step 7, "Presenting an Alternative Question." By offering the suspect two reasons for committing the crime, one of which would be unacceptable to the suspect, the interrogator gives the suspect an opportunity to make an admission. Interrogators are instructed to suggest that the suspect's actions were based on the "good" option rather than the bad, to ask the suspect to confirm this suggestion, and, if it is confirmed, to begin eliciting the confession. On the other hand, if the suspect fails to take up the good/bad option, interrogators should spend more time rationalizing, projecting and minimizing, and offering the suspect reasons to confess. Thus, it is clear that the interrogation process cannot depend solely on a strict list of steps, but must be flexible enough to adapt to the particular interrogatory situation at hand. It is equally clear that the FBI method of interrogation is extremely time intensive, and requires prolonged interactions between suspect and interrogator to work properly. Consequently, the Direct Accusation Approach might be ill-suited for time-constrained situations, such as a "ticking bomb" scenario.

With regard to detecting deception, future FBI agents are not taught to look for any specific physical or verbal signs of deception, since these can often be inaccurate and misleading. Instead, trainees are taught to consider clusters of behavior and note the context in which these behaviors arise. Additionally, students are urged to compare these behaviors with the baseline behavior shown by the subject in the non-accusatory pre-interrogation interview. Detection of deception is thus taught not as a determinative tool but as a means of helping the interview along and providing interrogators with clues to topics and themes that, if probed more deeply, might bring suspects closer to a confession.

According to the FBI Academy, rapport is the key element in motivating people to talk, be it during a non-accusatory pre-interrogation interview or an interrogation. As such, it is central to the Direct Accusation Approach that an interrogator be able not only to establish rapport with a suspect but also to maintain it throughout the interrogation. However, FBI instructors made clear that establishing and maintaining rapport is the most difficult skill to teach and learn through a standard training program. Building rapport takes time and dedication, prompting at least one instructor to recommend that his students attempt to engage with as many unknown people as possible during their free time. Additionally, FBI instructors suggested that many of the interpersonal skills necessary to build and maintain rapport might be innate, and thus highly dependent on the individual abilities of students. To paraphrase one instructor, rapport is a complex and constant dance between interrogator and suspect. This dance proceeds from information obtained through the pre-interrogation interview, common life experience, and general, sometimes intuitive, knowledge of human behavior and nature. It is common for agents to mistake rapport for facile chit-chat, which suspects often recognize for what it really is: forced and fake. Unlike forced and spurious conversation, instructors emphasized that, in essence, rapport is based on mutual respect and fostered by treating suspects with dignity and humanity. As a general matter, FBI instructors mentioned that an effective interrogator is one who has strong communication, listening, and interpersonal skills, approaches interrogations with patience, and can pay close, simultaneous attention to the facts of the case as well as to external and internal factors during the interrogation.

As may be gleaned from the information above, and as was confirmed by FBI Academy staff, FBI training in interviewing and interrogation is deliberately general. This occurs by design rather than chance. The new agent training is meant to provide individuals who, as a general rule, have had no previous law enforcement experience with the tools necessary to become competent criminal investigators in a relatively short time frame. Given the broad range of experiences and skills each trainee brings to the program, training is therefore designed to reach what instructors referred to as the lowest common denominator. As an illustration, one FBI instructor noted that he must tailor his training to a 24-year-old ex-employee of an Internet company who has spent the last 4 years of his life working in a cubicle without any significant interpersonal contact. Thus, the training is designed to provide only the skills absolutely necessary to be a competent criminal investigator.

In theory, this problem could be remedied by future, more detailed training on specialized and complex subjects such as interrogation. However, continuing education, also known as "in-training services," is sparse, and what little is available is optional and usually offered by independent contractors such as Reid and Associates.[580] The most instructors can do is provide a bibliography of books and articles on interrogation for further reading to guide future agents in their voluntary learning process. Consequently, with the exception of those who obtain additional interrogation training on their own initiative, most FBI agents rely only on their general FBI Academy training.

Like their counterparts at FLETC, FBI instructors admitted that it is unclear how much of the training agents actually apply in their interrogations, or how well they implement the techniques they employ. One instructor noted that he believed only 25–30% of agents follow what they learn during their interrogation training. FBI Academy instructors and directors have recognized this as a serious shortcoming and agreed that it is a pressing issue that requires future research.

To complicate matters further, the FBI, like all other law enforcement agencies we interviewed, lacks data as to the efficacy of the interrogation techniques it teaches. Although the instructors have a comprehensive knowledge and understanding of the literature and empirical studies, no systematic, empirical

---

[580] The scarcity of training is even more evident at the state and city police department levels. With their experience in dealing with and training police officers from around the country and the world through the FBI's National Academy, instructors underscored the fact that most police departments offer absolutely no formal interrogation training whatsoever. This observation is consistent with our own contact with the Boston Police Department and the Massachusetts State Police.

studies have tested the specific FBI approach. This lack of data may be a result of the FBI's not yet adopting a policy requiring that all interrogations be videotaped. FBI instructors noted that such recordings would serve an invaluable training and evaluative function, allowing them to learn from their mistakes as well as to monitor what agents actually do in the field.

Section 7. Federal Law Enforcement Training Center (FLETC)[581]

The Federal Law Enforcement Training Center (FLETC) provides training to agents in 81 different federal agencies. It covers all federal criminal investigators (18–11 job series federal employees) except those in the FBI, Drug Enforcement Administration (DEA), and U.S. Postal Service. It is designed to provide individuals who have no law enforcement experience with the tools necessary to become beginning criminal investigators; the specific skill-sets needed for a particular agency are then taught by that agency. It has a basic curriculum applicable to all agents and then offers more advanced or specialized training as requested, either through "add-on" programs for the specific agencies or through private contractors. The FLETC basic curriculum must be approved by all agencies and is reviewed regularly on the basis of feedback from the students and the agencies.

FLETC's primary training in the area of custodial interrogations comes in the basic Criminal Investigator Training Program (CITP). The heart of the CITP's interview/interrogation curriculum is a 10-hour lecture class titled "Interviewing for Law Enforcement Officers/Criminal Investigators." CITP also offers the course in 6- and 12-hour versions covering more or less the same aspects of interview procedures. The individual agencies choose the program most appropriate for their agents, and the 10-hour version is most commonly selected. The course is designed to "provide Federal criminal investigators (regardless of agency or position description) with foundational interviewing skills using proven questioning techniques coupled with an awareness of common behavioral responses. Emphasis is placed on planning the interview, formulating questions and following the five steps of the law enforcement interview."[582] Of the 15 objectives of the course, two focus on interrogation: #14: Identify and apply planning considerations for a confrontational interview, and #15: Identify and apply the confrontational interview technique. These objectives are covered through a two-hour lecture class. Although FLETC uses the term "interview," the confrontational interview basically amounts to an interrogation, since it is designed to elicit a confession from a party whom the agents believe to be guilty. The confrontational interview may or may not be conducted with the suspect in custody, depending on the agents' preferences for the particular situation.[583]

---

[581] Unless otherwise referenced, the information in this section is derived from a visit to the Federal Law Enforcement Training Center at Glynco, Georgia, 12-13 April 2005. Our host during the visit was Mark Fallon, Deputy Assistant Director of the Naval Criminal Investigative Service.

[582] Syllabus, *Interviewing for Law Enforcement Officers/Criminal Investigators*, FLETC Course #4162, August. 2004.

[583] The confrontational interview will hereinafter be referred to as an interrogation for simplicity and to distinguish it from other interviews.

The CITP supplements the lectures with lab exercises (ungraded) and practical exercises (graded) where students conduct interviews and interrogations with role-playing actors. The number of overall exercises in which each student participates varies somewhat by agency, but those participating in the CITP Confrontational Interview Practical Exercise spend four hours in the session, with each student conducting an interrogation and receiving personalized feedback for about an hour of that time. In addition, FLETC offers courses in basic interviewing, communication in interviewing, response analysis, cognitive interviewing technique, multiple suspect elimination technique (through interviews), field interviewing, advanced investigative interviewing, and other suspect interview techniques. The goal behind this varied program is not to tie the students to a particular regimen, but instead to give them basic interview and interrogation tools that they can use flexibly in the field.

However, FLETC does provide its students with an overarching schema for the interview/interrogation process that closely tracks both the Reid School techniques and the FBI's Direct Accusation Approach, though not necessarily by design. The goal of any interview or interrogation, according to FLETC, is to elicit useful, truthful information. In an interrogation, the goal is to elicit a truthful confession or at least a detailed lie that can be used in a later interrogation or prosecution. The major distinguishing feature of the technique taught by FLETC is the detailed presentation of the evidence to the suspect, a tactic advocated by the FBI, but rejected by the Reid Technique. According to FLETC, because the agents trained at the Center generally deal with more sophisticated suspects than do the police, it is virtually impossible to get them to confess without showing them the evidence. Thus, as discussed below, FLETC trains its agents to make a monologue presentation of the evidence to the suspect as part of the interrogation.

Before starting the interrogation, FLETC students are taught to prepare a topical outline. The outline, meant to be used both in the practical exercises in class and in the field as preparation for actual interviews and interrogations, should include the following areas:

1. Interview/Interrogation Site
2. Objectives of the Interview/Interrogation
3. Purpose Statements (to be given to suspect)
4. Rapport Areas
5. General Questions
6. Possible Themes
7. Choice Questions

The topical outline not only prepares the agents for the encounter, but also forces them to examine their preceding research and identify gaps in their information. For instance, if they cannot write down a few areas where they will be able to establish rapport, they in theory have not learned enough about their suspect. The outline is meant to be used as a guide throughout the encounter with the suspect, but agents are taught that they should be ready to throw it out if the interrogation veers off in a different direction than expected.

Once the agents have completed their topical outline, they are ready to conduct the interrogation. FLETC teaches a five-step interview/interrogation technique: 1) Introduction, 2) Rapport, 3) Questions, 4) Review, and 5) Closing. This approach is meant to be used in all federal law enforcement interviews, but has special application in an interrogation. For instance, to pass the CITP Confrontational Interview Practical Exercise, the students must "demonstrate comprehension of principles and use of skills competencies for the following:

- Introduction
    - Self
    - Partner
    - Suspect
    - Purpose
    - Credentials
- Rapport
    - Properly Established
    - Properly Maintained
- Questions
    - General Questions
    - Case Presentation — Monologue (Factual Presentation, Themes, and Choice Questions)
    - Recognize and Utilize Suspect's Nonverbal Behavior
    - Demonstrate Effective Personal Nonverbal Behavior
    - Appropriate Use of Pauses
- Summary
    - Acknowledge Suspect's Cooperation
    - Summarize Main Points from Notes
- Closing
    - Acknowledge Suspect's Cooperation
    - Contact Information — Primary, Secondary, Suspect"[584]

The case presentation step mirrors the FBI and Reid interrogation techniques, with the students taught the following: present the evidence they have gathered that implicates the suspects and thus overwhelm them with the evidence of their guilt; present the themes of rationalization, projection, and minimization, as appropriate; and then present a "choice question." The emphasis is on the students'/agents' doing all the talking in this phase of the interrogation; they are taught to cut off and overcome objections to avoid an argumentative exchange that would threaten to ruin the interrogation. FLETC instructors described the

---

[584] Syllabus, *CITP Confrontational Interview Practical Exercise*, FLETC Course # 4179, February 2005.

presentation of evidence as a sort of poker game, where the agents hold most of the cards except one (the confession) and convince the suspect that they (the agents) can win (get a conviction) even without the last card. The themes presented to the suspect are the same as those recommended by most of the texts and the FBI, although FLETC focuses only on the major three (rationalize, project, minimize). In exactly the same manner as Reid's Step 7, "Presenting an Alternative Question" (see discussion above), this section of the interrogation ends with the agent's posing a question that posits a "good" and "bad" reason for committing the crime, thus offering the suspect two choices, both of which would constitute an admission of guilt. The students are discouraged from using trickery or deceit during the monologue, both because FLETC instructors believe that more sophisticated suspects will see through it and because they believe that suspects will closely watch the investigators, who might present some of the very indicators of deception that they are trained to look for in the suspect and thus "tip their hand."

According to the instructors, the most difficult skill to teach is rapport-building, mainly because not enough time is available to spend on the subject. Moreover, many instructors believed that some of the necessary traits of a good rapport-builder are innate, while others can be taught. Because the classes are designed for a wide variety of students, the instructors must again teach to the lowest common denominator. For instance, some students have a natural ability to establish rapport with almost anyone, while others engage in forced small talk that makes the suspect uncomfortable and wary. Thus, like the Boston Police Department (see discussion below), the instructors attempt to teach the students to establish rapport through an appearance of confidence and professionalism, and through the types of questions asked. If the agents are able to engage in small talk that is ideal, but they are taught not to force the rapport through such techniques. Instructors also try to focus on so-called "rapport-busters," meaning questions or statements that break the rapport that has been established by sending a different message than that established in the rapport-building stage (e.g., "We're here to ask you a few questions."). As part of that effort, and especially in the advanced interview classes and "add-on" programs conducted for specific agencies, FLETC instructors attempt to refine the agents' questioning skills by emphasizing the use of narrative questions, as well as direct and precise questions. In addition, FLETC emphasizes a constant focus on creating an impression of confidence, patience, and persistence as a necessary component of a successful interview. Indeed, according to one instructor, confidence is the key to a successful interrogation.

The students are also taught the basics of detecting deception. According to the FLETC instructors the teaching here closely follows the literature. Students are not generally taught to look for any specific physical or verbal signals of deception, but to focus on nonverbal, verbal, and symbolic communications that occur in clusters as the result of stimuli presented in the form of questions or evidence by the investigator. Students are taught to consider the culture of the subject (although they are not taught the ways in which members of a particular culture might respond to a particular stimulus), to look for clusters of behavior that indicate deception, and to note the content of the question asked right before the cluster of behavior is observed. The curriculum emphasizes that there is no single indicator of deception, that students must observe all body language and speech presented by the subject, and that their ability to detect deception will grow with experience.

As noted, because 81 agencies are involved in setting the curriculum, and because each lecture class contains either 24 or 48 students, the instructors find that they must teach to the lowest common denominator. At the same time, many of the instructors echo the belief of other law enforcement personnel that the best way to learn is by doing and thus they place particular emphasis on the practical exercises. The exercises use role-players hired from the local community and are as realistic as possible. They are conducted in mock-up offices or other settings to give them a realistic feel, and the students are allowed to set up the furniture as they see fit. In addition, the scenarios for the various interviews are somewhat tailored to the specific agency for which the student will work (e.g., a Secret Service agent may face a scenario involving counterfeit currency); there are currently 16 different scenarios in use, each with a detailed case history, list of potential violations, and various pieces of evidence. The instructor sits in a corner of the room and silently observes the interview, while cameras overhead record the interactions from several angles. Generally one student takes the role of primary interrogator, with the other student acting as the secondary who takes notes, follows up with any additional questions, presents the summary, and in rare cases jumps in to take over the primary role if the other agent loses control of the interrogation. After the practical exercise is complete, the students receive individualized feedback from the instructor in the room. In addition, they have an opportunity to review the videotape of the interrogation and critique themselves (critiques that, according to one instructor, are usually harsher than those provided by the instructors). This allows for teaching at various levels based on individual students' needs, as opposed to the one-size-fits-all approach of the lectures.

The training provided by FLETC through the CITP and the other programs covers only the minimum requirements to be a competent federal law enforcement agent. The individual agencies then conduct "add-on" courses, either at their home facilities or through FLETC or private contractors. FLETC also provides advanced courses in interviewing and interrogation techniques. These courses are generally available to more senior agents from the various agencies on a voluntary basis, and are taught either by FLETC instructors or, more often, by outside contractors. The major contractor for many years was the Reid School, though recently FLETC has begun to use Wicklander-Zulawski and Associates. Wicklander-Zulawski, however, teaches the Reid approach as well, under a special license.

The FLETC instructors indicate that they do not know how much of the training provided in CITP and the other programs actually makes it to "the street." The only opportunity that instructors have to evaluate the efficacy of their programs (other than survey feedback from the students and agencies) occurs when former students return to FLETC for advanced training. At that point the instructors can determine how much of the initial training the agents retained. However, the number of agents who come through FLETC for advanced training is minimal compared to the number of agents who graduate from the Center's basic training program. Moreover, FLETC conducts no systematic review of the students who do return for advanced training, and therefore only anecdotal evidence of the success of the initial training program is available. Even then the students who return for advanced training are generally a self-selected group that is likely to be more interested in interrogation techniques — and thus more likely to have retained the initial training.

In addition, as with all of the other law enforcement training programs, there has been no systematic, empirical study of the efficacy of the techniques taught at FLETC; it appears that most of the support for the techniques comes from anecdotal evidence. This is in part because, without videotaping interrogations, it is impossible to determine what techniques are actually used in the field. The FLETC instructors, noting the number of studies on British interrogation techniques, indicated that they would welcome videotaping of interrogations to determine what is and is not working, and also to establish how much of their training even makes it to the street, regardless of efficacy.

Section 8. Boston Police Department — Homicide Division[585]

The Boston Police Department conforms to the general trend among local law enforcement organizations, focusing its training on the procedural aspects of interrogation. The officers and detectives receive very little, if any, formal training on interrogation techniques. The majority of the interrogation training that does occur is through the Reid School, which is offered as an option to detectives, most of whom do not choose to participate. The department has no formal manual on interrogation techniques, not even for divisions such as the homicide unit. Deputy Superintendent Daniel Coleman, who is currently in charge of the homicide unit, is putting together a protocol and checklist for interrogation techniques.

This situation can be contrasted with the issuance of guidelines and extensive training that immediately followed the decision in *Commonwealth v. DiGiambattista*,[586] which requires electronic recording of all interrogations conducted in Massachusetts and threatens a jury instruction that casts doubts on police procedures if no such recording is made. The difference results from the department's primary goal, which is to solve cases and obtain convictions, which in turn leads to an emphasis on the procedures necessary to protect suspects' constitutional rights, avoid suppression of evidence and suspect statements, and thus create the easiest path for a jury to convict. The detectives we interviewed noted that the procedures and training in place regarding interrogation are not geared toward training interrogators to elicit statements, but instead are

---

[585] Unless otherwise referenced, the information in this section is derived from interviews with Deputy Superintendent Daniel Coleman of the Boston Police Department, who is also Commander of BPD's Homicide Unit, conducted on 11 and 21 March 2005.

[586] 442 Mass. 423 (2004).

implemented to ensure that any statement elicited can be presented in a court of law. This has created a situation where few members of the department receive any significant formal training in interrogation techniques.[587] Indeed, Deputy Superintendent Coleman reports that when he moved from a uniformed to an investigational unit he received no additional formalized training. Instead, he reports that 90% of a successful interrogation is based on intuition, which can only be developed through experience, on-the-job training, and mentoring.

At the same time, the department uses many of the general techniques advocated by the Reid School and others. They focus heavily on conducting thorough pre-interrogation investigations. Detectives stress the importance of gathering all of the information on the suspect, victim, crime scene, etc., before entering the interrogation room. In addition, they try not to commence the interrogation without a clear sense of their goals and objectives. Like all other law enforcement personnel interviewed, Boston detectives believe that building rapport and conveying empathy are the keys to a successful interrogation. The homicide detectives dress in suits every day, are clean-shaven, and work in a building that one described as looking like an "insurance office"; they note the importance of removing the suspect from the police station environment. The setting contains very few reminders that the suspect is in police custody, and the officers remove all signals that could remind suspects of the consequences of their actions. The interview/interrogation room is a small, plain room, with only a whiteboard on the wall and a few chairs and a desk. The room has a two-way mirror that "no one uses" because a) any time the door opens to the room with the observers, the people standing behind the mirror can be seen, and b) every suspect knows what the mirror is and asks to have the blinds closed.

However, the detectives report that the theme-development strategy advocated by the Reid Technique does not work with most of the suspects they encounter. They postulate that this is because the strategy is based on the idea that people feel guilty when they commit crimes, but many of the suspects the homicide division encounters feel little, if any, remorse for their crimes, are not afraid of jail, and are mainly concerned with protecting themselves from retaliation on the street. Instead, the detectives find that, after establishing rapport based on kindness and professionalism (as opposed to false friendship), a straightforward, no-nonsense presentation of the situation and evidence is the best approach to secure a confession.

Despite the lack of formalized training, there is a general pattern to interrogations conducted in the homicide division. The detectives begin with the procedural requirements. When the suspect is brought in, usually from the local police precinct, the detective lets him know that he is under arrest and informs him of the charges. He advises the suspect of his right to a telephone call, and

---

[587] Supervisors in the BPD further believe that even the small amount of interrogation technique training that is provided is only somewhat useful, because it must be adapted for the various ages, cultures, and experiences of the trainees, resulting in a tendency to teach to the lowest common denominator.

then advises him of his Miranda rights. The detective then has the suspect sign a waiver of 6-hour arraignment, and informs the suspect of the opportunity to have the entire encounter recorded electronically. If the suspect elects to have the interrogation recorded, the detective re-reads the Miranda rights while the tape is recording. Even if the suspect declines to have the encounter recorded, the detectives are trained to get at least the declination on tape. According to Coleman, over 80% of suspects in general waive their Miranda rights, while only about 30% of murder suspects do so.

Once the procedural requirements are met, the interrogator moves to rapport-building. The rapport is built less on false friendship than on empathy, kindness, and professionalism. The straightforward techniques used by the department include dressing in a suit and tie to let the suspect know that the detectives are "not your average cops" and that they mean business; shaking hands with every suspect (also giving the detective an opportunity to examine the hands); speaking courteously and professionally, avoiding use of the suspect's "lingo"; keeping the conversation friendly, casual, and not overly official; offering the use of the phone in a casual manner (e.g., "Do you want to let someone know where you are and that you are okay?"); and offering food and drink. The detectives believe that this approach is effective with homicide suspects because most of them understand the situation they are in; moreover, suspects will only cooperate if they believe the detective is not hiding anything from them, and can immediately spot attempts to downplay or minimize the crime and will respond in kind by "playing" with the interrogator.

Once rapport has been established, detectives prefer not to use trickery or deceit, though they are allowed to do so under Massachusetts law. According to them, beyond just being "wrong" this is also ineffective, since it insults the suspect's intelligence and can often be exposed; it also is one of the interrogation tactics that they say can most easily lead to false confessions. At the same time, they do recommend using trickery to induce lies. This would include, for example, asking a suspect who has just mentioned a certain road about the tollbooth on the road, knowing full well that there is no tollbooth on the road and trying to catch the suspect in a lie. However, the detectives report rarely, if ever, making up evidence, witnesses, or statements that do not actually exist. At the same time, they are careful not to give the suspect any information he does not already have, saying that the entire interrogation procedure is "like a poker game." This is done both to keep the suspect from knowing what the detective knows and to prevent the suspect from appropriating the information for possible false confessions.

The more experienced detectives argue that anyone who goes into an interrogation looking for a confession is inexperienced and "an idiot." Such an approach leads to bias in the interrogation room, where what is needed is objectivity. The goal of an interrogation should be to gather information, and lies can often be as useful in an eventual prosecution as a confession. The detective should look for information that can advance the rest of the investigation, including information that the suspect does not realize might be useful for the investigation and prosecution, such as whether he is right-handed or left-handed, or even a seemingly random phone number that can then be traced or tapped. The detectives are quick to point out that while a confession is useful to have, it must still be corroborated before a prosecution can move forward.

There is no formalized mechanism for supervision of, or feedback on, interrogations conducted by the detectives in the homicide unit. Instead, Deputy Superintendent Coleman or his deputies sometimes take home the audiotapes of interrogations and listen for problems, providing feedback as necessary. Feedback is usually given only if a problem is noted, and even then many of the more experienced detectives find it difficult to change their ways. Coleman also sends his detectives to court to listen to suppression motions argued by the District Attorney's office so that they become aware of potential problems with interrogation procedures. However, these motions are usually based on legal procedural issues instead of the actual interrogation techniques. Similarly, the detectives often go to court to hear cross-examinations of detectives from their division, as well as closing arguments in cases handled by their division, so they can understand the questions and tactics used by defense attorneys and better identify possible problem areas in their interrogations. The detectives note that one of the most important skills for an interrogator, now that interrogations are recorded, is to be able to explain his techniques to a jury so that the interrogation does not appear overly coercive or tainted.

Generally the Boston Police Department does not videotape its interrogations; the Supreme Judicial Court of Massachusetts decision, like most statutes and court decisions on the subject, only requires "electronic" recording. Prior to that decision, the Boston Police Department would conduct the full interrogation, obtain the confession, and only then start the tape to obtain a recording of the suspect's confession. Deputy Superintendent Coleman noted that he initially opposed the requirement that all interrogations be taped because he was afraid that both police and suspects would act differently, that the positive dynamics established through rapport-building would be diminished, and that generally the presence of recording equipment would inhibit interrogations. His view is slowly changing as he sees the results of taping. While not fully convinced, the detectives agree that taping interrogations offers numerous benefits, but they regard videotaping as a wholly different matter. Most agree that videotaping would assist training and review, and Coleman says that certain basic tenets of interrogation could be taught more easily through the videotaping of interrogations.

At the same time, Coleman worries that because under Massachusetts law the suspect would have to be informed that he is being videotaped, the interrogation would be inhibited, less rapport would be established, and less information and fewer confessions would be obtained. Part of the worry, especially when dealing with gang members and similar criminals, is that because the tapes are discoverable, suspects will be less likely to talk for fear that the tape might get back to the street, where retaliation for cooperating with the police has spiked in recent years across the country. Nonetheless, the detectives recognize that, in general, other police departments and agencies have had positive experiences with the videotapes, and see them as the inevitable next stage in interrogation requirements.

Section 9. Case Study of One Detective[588]

Lieutenant Albert F. Pierce, Jr., currently with the Massachusetts Institute of Technology (MIT) Police Department and formerly with the Massachusetts Metropolitan Police and the Massachusetts State Police, reports a similar history. Pierce has been a police officer since 1978, working in various units and task forces on violent crimes, white collar offenses, homicides, and more. Most of his career has been spent in one capacity or another as part of the Massachusetts State Police, though he spent a significant portion of his time working on special assignment with the Suffolk County District Attorney's Office. Although he has taken classes all over the country on various policing techniques, including interrogation, the Massachusetts State Police Department does not seem to have any type of comprehensive training in interrogation techniques. Some in-service training exists, though this is provided mostly by outside experts (e.g., from the Reid School) brought in to lecture, and once in a while by more senior members of the department. The basic Police Academy training provided little, if any, information on interrogation techniques, although, as Pierce notes, this is because most police officers are not involved in conducting interrogations.

Instead, like most other law enforcement officials, Pierce reports that he learned most interrogation techniques on the job. Pierce also notes that all of the classes in the world are not nearly as useful as the skills learned in the field. His opinion should not be taken lightly, as he has participated in various interrogation training programs, including those provided by the Reid School and the New Jersey, New York, and Massachusetts State Police Departments, as well as various national academies. According to Pierce, if a young detective is lucky enough to be partnered with an experienced, successful mentor, that mentor will be the most useful source of interrogation training. As a corollary, one must assume that if the partner is not helpful or is inexperienced, young detectives will have to learn the techniques on their own. At the same time, the first thing Pierce did when he took over the MIT Police Department was send all of the detectives to the Reid School for what he referred to as Interview and Interrogation 101.

Echoing the literature, Pierce argues that it takes very special skills to be a good interviewer/interrogator. Most important among the characteristics of a good interrogator are a true liking of people, an ability to get along with people of all backgrounds, comfort in talking to people, and knowledge of how to do it. In addition, anyone who wants to be a successful interrogator needs to be a good actor: to convey sympathy, empathy, and other emotions that the interrogator does not really feel. As a young detective, Pierce would often just sit outside or in bars with his partner and observe and speak with people so that he could learn these skills and improve on whatever innate abilities he already possessed. He reports that this was one of the most useful techniques he found to build up knowledge of how people act and react in various settings. Finally, Pierce notes that the ability

---

[588] Unless otherwise referenced, the information in this section is derived from an interview with Lieutenant Albert F. Pierce Jr. of the MIT Police Department, formerly of the Massachusetts State Police, on 5 April 2005.

to know oneself and one's limits cannot be overstated; successful interrogators must have the ability to restrain their own egos and take themselves out of a situation or interrogation that they cannot handle.

Pierce argues that interrogation techniques must be individualized for both the interrogator and the suspect and are very case-specific. Some of the variables he identified included the crime committed, the suspect's education level — both formal and within the judicial system — the suspect's economic and social status, etc. At the same time, no matter with whom one is dealing or what crime the person committed, the single most important aspect of the interrogation, according to Pierce, is to establish rapport and the appearance of friendship. This is done mainly to create an environment conducive to a successful interrogation, but also to maintain the suspect's constitutional rights while minimizing the likelihood that the suspect will ask for an attorney.

The typical interrogation in which Pierce is involved proceeds as follows:

1. Conduct the pre-interrogation investigation — gather as much information as possible about the suspect, the crime scene, the victim, etc.

2. Go through Miranda and other procedural requirements.

3. Build rapport:

    a. Leave the suspect alone in a room and observe for signs of nervousness, fear, etc., through a two-way mirror or a window in the door to the room.

    b. Approach with only a few detectives.

        Pierce reports no standard procedure, but never more than three, and usually two so that one can do the questioning and another can take notes.

    c. Begin talking, offer a smoke, food, and/or drink. Never begin by "going for the throat" with a direct accusation or attempt to overwhelm with evidence.

    d. Have a two-way conversation and get to a comfort level with the suspect.

    e. Only at this point move to discussion about the crime.

Once Pierce moves into harder questioning of the suspect, the procedure seems to break down to some degree in that there is no one path to follow. Generally, open-ended questions are used to keep suspects talking, to keep them off guard, and to avoid conveying any information to them. Depending on the suspect, themes such as those discussed in the Reid Technique (minimization, rationalization, etc.) may be appropriate. All, however, require sympathy and empathy according to Pierce, who indicates that he may be using theme development without being consciously aware of it. Indeed, he reports that the most successful interrogators can make the suspect believe that the interrogator understands how the suspect feels about things, which is exactly the goal of Reid's theme development.

Pierce believes quite strongly that a good interrogator can sense deception. There are so-called "body-language schools" that teach techniques that Pierce finds effective. More importantly, however, is the ability simply to read people, and he argues that in real-world situations it is easy to pick up obvious signals that a suspect is lying if one has good people skills. At the same time, he believes it is sometimes useful for an interrogator to use trickery and deceit, such as telling the suspect that the authorities have evidence, phone records, witnesses, or statements that do not really exist. While one must be careful in using this technique, Pierce says that it is highly successful when appropriately used. Nonetheless, he reports that he never lies about the consequences of confession and tries to avoid the subject altogether, instead telling the suspect that he is just the fact-finder who writes the story, and that what happens to the suspect is in the hands of the court.

Until the recent SJC decision, the Massachusetts State Police did not use electronic recording of any kind. Pierce contends that if they had done so they would have had easier, smoother, and more successful results in court (i.e., convictions). While noting that the presence of the recording devices does affect the privacy of the interrogation, Pierce argues that the benefits outweigh the costs. Like Coleman, he finds it imperative that the detective be able to explain each technique used through the interrogation so that it does not appear overly coercive to a court or jury. In addition, he believes that recording the interrogations would aid in training; one of his chief complaints about the training he received is that it involved too much sitting in the classroom listening to lectures and not enough observation and role-playing.

Section 10. Interrogation Practices in Other Countries

Interrogation in Great Britain

General Background

Until the early 1990s, there was no national training on interrogation offered to British police officers.[589] Though the first and most recognized interrogation manual produced in Britain[590] was heavily influenced by the Reid Technique, it did not meet with much enthusiasm and does not appear to have had much impact on police training and practice.[591] According to Gudjonsson, the implicit rejection of Reid-based approaches to interrogation in Britain might be due to a combination of factors, including judicial decisions in cases involving oppressive police interrogation, research into false confessions and psychological vulnerability, and changes in police practice following the introduction of the Police and Criminal Evidence Act of 1984 (PACE) and the Codes of Practice for police officers, which

---

[589] Gudjonsson, see note 111, p. 38.

[590] J. Walkley, *Police Interrogation: A Handbook for Investigators* (London: Police Review Publication, 1987).

[591] Gudjonsson, see note 110, p. 52.

reduced the scope of coercive questioning and barred the use of deception, trickery, and psychological manipulation in interrogation.[592]

Currently, Britain has a set of national guidelines on interviewing both witnesses and suspects, composed of five distinct parts (corresponding to the acronym "PEACE"):

Preparation and Planning: Interviewers are taught to properly prepare and plan for the interview and formulate aims and objectives.

Engage and Explain: Rapport is established with the subject, and officers engage the person in conversation.

Account: Officers are taught two methods of eliciting an account from the interviewee:

- Cognitive Interview: used with cooperative suspects and witnesses.

- Conversation Management: recommended when cooperation is insufficient for the cognitive interview techniques to work.

Closure: The officer summarizes the main points from the interview and provides the suspect with the opportunity to correct or add information.

Evaluate: Once the interview is finished, the information gathered must be evaluated in the context of its impact on the investigation.[593]

The PEACE approach was based on the idea of providing officers with an ethical foundation for police questioning.[594] It focuses on information gathering rather than obtaining confessions, and it relies on non-coercive interviewing and accurate recording of the interview to achieve its goals.[595] Officers adopting "oppressive" questioning would be in breach of the national guidelines, and would presumably find judges less willing to admit into evidence statements obtained through those means.[596]

It is useful to note that an overwhelming proportion of scholarship and research on interrogation comes from Great Britain. This is mostly because PACE requires that all interrogations conducted in Great Britain be video-recorded. These recordings, in turn, allow for more research and study opportunities.

Detective Superintendent Colin Sturgeon: A Practitioner's Perspective[597]

Detective Superintendent Sturgeon of the Police Service of Northern Ireland has vast experience with interrogations both in typical law enforcement and terrorism-related investigations. During our conversation, he offered a historical

---

[592] *Id.*

[593] *Id.*, p. 53.

[594] *Id.*

[595] *Id.*, p. 54.

[596] *Id.*

[597] The information in this section is derived from a discussion with Detective Superintendent Colin Sturgeon of the Police Service of Northern Ireland during his spring 2005 visit to Harvard Law School.

perspective of interrogation in the context of terrorist investigations in Northern Ireland, which included reference to past use of interrogation tactics such as sensory deprivation, rigorous exercise, withholding of food and water, and inducing cramps through prolonged stances in certain positions. Superintendent Sturgeon noted that although these techniques proved quite successful in gaining intelligence they also alienated a vast proportion of the population and gave terrorists a broader base of support from which to operate. Eventually, outrage about these coercive interrogation techniques led to significant legal reforms in the shape of the Police and Criminal Evidence Act (PACE) and the relevant Codes of Practice.

As mentioned above, PACE and its Codes of Conduct forbid interrogators to deceive subjects or to employ any sort of trickery to gain information from them. Similarly, interrogators may not use psychological ploys common to the Reid Technique, such as rationalization, projection, and minimization. In general, the interrogator may not offer or suggest any reason to a suspect as to why he/ she should confess, but may tell a suspect that his or her cooperation would be formally made known to the judge. It is relevant to note that these restrictions on interrogation tactics apply with equal force to ordinary criminal investigations and terrorism-related investigations.

Superintendent Sturgeon noted that these legal restrictions on interrogation have made it impossible to secure a confession or incriminating admission from a suspect. In fact, he went so far as to say that he cannot recall ever obtaining a confession as a product of interrogation. Even though British law has attempted to bridge this gap by eliminating the right of a suspect to remain quiet during interrogation by allowing a judge to infer guilt from the suspect's silence, Sturgeon noted that judges rarely, if ever, exercise this discretion against suspects.

As a consequence of the legal restrictions imposed on interrogators in Britain and their resultant inability to garner confessions, interrogations are now seen as another step in the investigation process. According to Superintendent Sturgeon, the PEACE method of interrogation described above conforms well to the view of interrogations as a step in a broader investigation, and thus transforms the goal of interrogation from obtaining confessions to securing information to advance the investigation. In this context, Sturgeon highlighted the importance of thorough preparation prior to beginning the interrogation. This preparation includes an interview coordinator, whose job it is to read every document relevant to the person to be interrogated and to outline the topics that the interrogation should cover. The interrogation itself is conducted by two interrogators: the "lead," who is responsible for asking the questions, and the "sweeper," who covers anything left out by the lead. Sturgeon made clear that the *Engage and Explain* portion of the PEACE method relies heavily on rapport, which he described as being based on the concepts of reciprocity and respect. This last point is significant in that Superintendent Sturgeon sees the process of establishing rapport not as an attempt to engage in insincere chit-chat with a suspect, but as an opportunity to treat him or her humanely and with respect so as to foster some sense of reciprocity in the encounter.

Finally, Sturgeon mentioned that although videotaping interrogations in Britain has drastically reduced the number of complaints filed by subjects against interrogators, some suspects are more reluctant than others to talk when being recorded. However, British law allows for recorders to be turned off at the suspect's request.

Section 11. Videotaping Interrogations: The Law and Practice

Law enforcement officials around the country are currently debating whether or not videotaping of custodial interrogations should be required. Electronic recording of interviews and interrogations, when feasible, has been required by judicial opinion in Alaska since 1985[598] and in Minnesota since 1994,[599] although neither specifies videotaping. Illinois recently passed a statute requiring electronic recording, when feasible, of all custodial interrogations of suspects,[600] a District of Columbia statute requires it for all suspects in violent or dangerous crimes,[601] and a Maine statute requires electronic recording of interrogations for serious crimes.[602] The Supreme Judicial Court of Massachusetts recently ruled that while it would not require electronic recordings of interrogations, where such recording did not take place "the defendant is entitled (on request) to a jury instruction advising that the State's highest court has expressed a preference that such interrogations be recorded whenever practicable, and cautioning the jury that, because of the absence of any recording of the interrogation in the case before them, they should weigh evidence of the defendant's alleged statement with great caution and care."[603] As noted previously, this has led to all interrogations conducted in Massachusetts being recorded whenever feasible.[604] Various similar legislative proposals are currently or have previously been before legislatures around the country, including in New York City, Maryland, Connecticut, Oregon, and Missouri.[605]

Electronic recording of interviews is quite common in other countries. As noted, Great Britain has required it since 1984.[606] Australian police must tape-record their interrogations where feasible, and in federal prosecutions, where a contemporaneous recording cannot be made, the law requires an electronic

---

[598] *Stephan v. State*, 711 P.2d 1156 (Alaska.1985).

[599] *State v. Scales*, 518 N.W. 2d 587 (Minn.1994).

[600] 725 ILCS 5 § 103-2.1, effective 18 July 2005.

[601] D.C. ST § 5-133.20, effective 4 April 2003.

[602] Maine LD 891.

[603] *Commonwealth v. DiGiambattista*, 442 Mass. 423, 447-48 (2004).

[604] Interview with Boston Police Department Deputy Superintendent Dan Coleman, in Boston, MA (11 March 2005) [hereinafter Coleman Interview].

[605] *See Report on the Electronic Recording of Police Interrogations,* submitted jointly by the American Bar Association Criminal Justice Section and the New York County Lawyers' Association, (2002), 9, at http://www.reid.com/pdfs/NYlegalarticleonvideotaping.pdf, for a non-updated list, site access 22 April 2005) [hereinafter Report]

[606] Police and Criminal Evidence Act of 1984.

recording of the statement's being read to the suspect, with the suspect's being given an opportunity to refute anything in the written account.[607]

A 1993 study, conducted before many of the statutes previously mentioned were adopted, found that only 16% of police agencies in the United States overall, and one-third in jurisdictions with populations over 50,000, videotaped interviews, interrogations, and confessions, and that the most common circumstance in which a videotape was made was following the confession.[608] "During this process, the investigator would recap the interrogation in the presence of the suspect and continue with the formal confession being recorded."[609] This study reported that 82% of respondents said that the number of defense claims of improper interrogation techniques remained the same or decreased once videotaping of confessions began.[610] At the same time, 60% of respondents "reported no significant difference between a suspect's willingness to tell the truth whether or not the conversation was videotaped."[611] Inbau et al. argue, however, that these results are meaningless because the study did not include data on whether the agencies videotaped the entire interrogation or only the confession that resulted after a successful interrogation conducted in a private setting.[612]

Anecdotal evidence suggests that, since the 1993 study, many police agencies around the country have adopted videotaping procedures, either because it is required by local ordinances or through voluntary adoption programs.[613] Fort Lauderdale, Miami, Denver, Tulsa, San Diego, Kankakee County, and DuPage County are among the many localities that have begun videotaping interrogations.[614] Most of these agencies seem to report positive experiences with the procedure.[615] Indeed, a 2004 study of 238 police and sheriff's departments that voluntarily videotaped interrogations found that "[v]irtually every officer with whom [the authors of the report on the study] spoke, having given custodial recordings a try, was enthusiastically in favor of the practice."[616] Noted benefits included reduced defense motions to suppress statements, more guilty pleas, better evidence for use at trial, increased public confidence, and use as an interrogation-technique teaching tool for detectives.[617] In addition, the study found that recording did not inhibit rapport-building and did not result in suspects' refusing to cooperate or

---

[607] See *Australia's Third Report under the International Covenant on Civil and Political Rights*. March 1987 – December 1995, Art. 14 Par. 816.

[608] Inbau, see note 109, 393-395, and Report, 6, both citing W. Geller, *Videotaping Interrogations and Confessions, National Institute of Justice Research in Brief* (March 1993).

[609] Inbau, see note 109, p. 395.

[610] *Id.*, p. 394.

[611] *Id.*, citing W. Geller.

[612] *Id.*, p. 394.

[613] Coleman Interview; see also; "Police to Tape Suspects' 'Quizzings,'" *South Florida Sun Sentinel*, 1 February 2003, 1B; "Will the Senate seek justice?," *Chicago Tribune*, Editorial, 4 March 2003, 12.

[614] "Will the Senate seek justice?," 12.

[615] *Id.*

[616] Thomas P. Sullivan, *Police Experiences with Recording Custodial Interrogations*, presented by Northwestern School of Law's Center on Wrongful Convictions, Summer 2004, 6, at http://www.law.northwestern.edu/depts/clinic/wrongful/documents/SullivanReport.pdf, accessed 4 March 2005.

[617] *Id.*, 6-12, p. 16

confess at lower rates than those not recorded, whether or not the suspects were aware of the videotaping.[618]

The authors of the Reid Technique, however, continue to argue that guilty suspects are less likely to tell the truth and/or confess if they are electronically recorded.[619] In addition, they believe that videotaping interrogations would ultimately harm investigations and especially prosecutions.[620] They contend that unless the videotaping can be done surreptitiously (which it cannot in states that require two-party consent for electronic recording), the presence of a video recording device, or simply the knowledge that the session was being taped, would undermine the sense of privacy that is a prerequisite to a successful Reid Technique interrogation.[621] They point to a study by one of the authors, who surveyed investigators in Alaska and Minnesota and found that when the recording device was never visible the investigators obtained an 82% confession rate as opposed to a 43% rate when the device was visible.[622] This, they argue, is the foremost reason not to require videotaping of interrogations.

Inbau et al. acknowledge that videotaping interrogations may help reduce doubts as to the trustworthiness or voluntariness of the confession, help jog the investigator's memory while testifying, and defend against allegations of improper interrogation tactics.[623] They do not mention the possibility that videotaping will help in training interrogators. Ultimately, the authors argue that the costs of videotaping outweigh the benefits. They point to the possibility of "numerous occurrences where a defense expert would offer the opinion that, based on analysis of the videotaped interrogation, the defendant's will appeared to be overcome, or that in the defendant's mind he perceived a promise of leniency or a threat to his well-being (even though none was stated)."[624] They also argue that a requirement for videotaping is too great a burden for police and prosecutors, who already have a difficult time maintaining the integrity of all pieces of evidence. Defense attorneys could unfairly exploit the possibilities of the electronic device failing, portions of the recording fading or being lost due to mechanical failure, gaps because of the need to change a tape, the loss of the tape, inadvertent erasure of the tape, or the unavailability of electronic recording in a particular location to place doubts about the entire circumstances surrounding the interrogation in the minds of the judge and jury.[625]

Aubry, however, writes unequivocally that a "requirement for the interrogation room [is] an adequate and efficient sound and tape recording system."[626] He continues: "motion picture records…are exceedingly valuable" because they

---

618   *Id.*, 19-20
619   Inbau, see note 109, p. 397.
620   *Id.*, p. 393-397.
621   *Id.*, p. 397.
622   *Id.*, n.23
623   *Id.*, p. 394.
624   *Id.*, p. 396.
625   *Id.*, p. 396-397.
626   Aubry and Caputo, see note 406, p. 71.

objectively show what happened during the interrogation.[627] Such recordings, Aubry argues, "should definitely be made of the entire interrogation procedure, if for no other reason than to demonstrate conclusively that the confession was secured in conformity with legal safeguards."[628] He mentions no downside to the recording of interrogations, though he does suggest that the recording devices be hidden, perhaps indicating he would agree with some of Inbau et al.'s concerns if the suspect were made aware that he is being recorded. Similarly, the American Bar Association Criminal Justice Section and the New York County Lawyers' Association argue that it is "time the practice of videotaping complete interrogations is mandated in all state and federal jurisdictions."[629] Concerns about false confession frame their argument: worries that as interrogators convince a suspect that confession is rational and appropriate they may convince the innocent individual to confess as well.[630]

Despite Inbau et al.'s arguments, the videotaping of interrogations is coming to be seen as a positive development by both law enforcement and the defense bar. The National Association of Criminal Defense Lawyers supports the practice as "a simple procedure that would deter human rights violations, reduce the risk of wrongful convictions due to false confessions, and greatly enhance the truth-seeking process by resolving factual disputes concerning interrogation."[631] Law enforcement personnel — even those who initially opposed taping — are beginning to recognize it as an effective means of countering false allegations of misconduct and confirming the testimony of the police officers at a time when juries have increasing mistrust of police testimony.[632] They also see the tapes as an important training tool in three respects: first, they allow supervisors to review and give feedback on the interrogations; second, they enable the individuals conducting the interrogations to critique themselves; and third, because the tapes will be shown to juries, the interrogators will have to be able to explain — and thus better understand — the techniques they use to elicit confessions (e.g., theme development, presentation of alternative questions, etc.).[633]

Section 12. Summary: Interrogation Literature vs. Law Enforcement Practice

Like the practical literature on which it is based, the interrogation training provided by the U.S. law enforcement organizations consulted for this paper generally fails to incorporate the factors that, according to empirical research, might affect a suspect's willingness to confess, and provides little or no training

---

[627] *Id.*, p. 72.

[628] *Id.*

[629] Report, p. 2.

[630] Report, p. 3-4.

[631] National Association of Criminal Defense Lawyers, *NACDL Federal Legislative Priorities - 2004,* at http://www.nacdl.org/public.nsf/Legislation/Priorities?opendocument, accessed 16 April 2005.

[632] Coleman Interview.

[633] *Id.*

variation for different types of suspects. While all agencies underscored the general caution that no single interrogation technique works with every suspect, and indeed that every suspect is different, they provide little guidance on how to adjust one's interrogation techniques for suspects of different ages, cultures, ethnicities, and criminal history, or for crimes of greater seriousness or cases for which the interrogator has stronger evidence. The only confession factor that most agencies seemed to focus on is length of the interrogation. Consistent with Leo's empirical study, discussed above, the FBI training literature and the instructors at the FBI Academy noted that the length of interrogation was a determinative factor in obtaining a confession or incriminating information from the suspect.

Similarly, both FLETC and the FBI take account of the seriousness of the offense and the strength of the evidence against the suspect in their training, if indirectly. As noted, these two factors appear to be statistically significant in predicting the likelihood of a confession. Like the Reid Technique upon which they draw so heavily, FBI and FLETC training make use of theme development based on rationalization, projection, and minimization. These tactics, in turn, center on manipulating the suspects' perception of the seriousness of the crime they have committed. In addition, FBI and FLETC rely heavily on presentation of the evidence to convince the suspect that denial is futile and there is no other option but to confess. Consequently, the stronger the evidence, the more effective this FBI and FLETC interrogation step will be. These modifications to the Reid Technique notwithstanding, the agencies do not, for the most part, offer specific techniques that the interrogator should adjust if the crime is more or less serious, or the evidence stronger or weaker; they give few, if any, explicit prescriptions on how to use these factors to elicit a confession in different situations.

As noted, those officers and agents who do receive some interrogation training learn tactics that closely track those advocated in most of the literature. The emphasis in all programs is on investigating the case thoroughly prior to interrogation, projecting an air of confidence and fairness, and building some sort of rapport with the suspect. However, practice diverges from the literature in two seminal respects: interrogator qualifications and, in the case of the FBI and FLETC, the importance of confronting the suspect with the evidence against him.

Although the literature recommends that only highly skilled, motivated, educated, and specialized individuals be chosen as interrogators, the reality is that, for the most part, interrogations are conducted by law enforcement personnel of widely divergent educations and experience levels. Our research uncovered no U.S. law enforcement agencies or departments that have a dedicated cadre of interrogators to use in their counterterrorism investigations. Interrogators in U.S. law enforcement agencies and departments are not required to have any specialized training or education beyond that required to fulfill the general requirements of their respective training courses. In some of the federal agencies, interrogations are conducted by whichever team of agents happens to be investigating the case, regardless of experience or expertise. In police departments it appears that interrogations are conducted by detectives, who are by definition more experienced, but who do not necessarily have any specialized interrogation training. It thus appears that U.S. law enforcement does not perceive interrogation as a specialty, but instead as one of the many skills required by a general investigator's job.

Both the FBI and FLETC teach trainees to present suspects directly with the evidence linking them to the crime. The literature generally shies away from such an approach. Although Reid's Step 1 involves direct, confrontational accusation, it does not appear to advocate the exhaustive presentation of evidence taught by the FBI and FLETC. However, law enforcement personnel repeatedly observed that unless the authorities present the evidence in a comprehensive way, more sophisticated suspects will have no reason to confess. In an argument that appears a logical extension of Reid, they noted that theme presentation is useless unless the suspects truly believe that they will be prosecuted and convicted. The Boston Police Department's experience with gang members seems to be similar, especially because detectives note the lack of guilt or remorse among suspects. At the same time, the literature does suggest that with this type of more rational (as opposed to emotional) suspect, a straightforward presentation is appropriate. However, as opposed to the qualified application of this technique advocated in the literature, FBI and FLETC training prescribes the presentation of evidence to all suspects, regardless of their personality traits.

The reliance on presentation of evidence by law enforcement personnel points to an underlying factor in Reid and its variations that no one — either in the literature or among those conducting interrogations — seems to discuss directly: fear. Although the literature, the training, and the discussions with law enforcement personnel heavily emphasize rapport-building as the main tool for interrogators, it appears that without some underlying fear interrogations will rarely succeed. It seems that, in practice, law enforcement personnel rely on fear of prosecution and conviction as the major motivator for a confession. Perhaps this is not mentioned explicitly because it is such a basic assumption, but it is worth noting that rapport-building alone, at least in the opinion of many interrogation trainers, does not seem to convince suspects to confess unless they have some underlying fear of the consequences of refusal to cooperate.

Because of its importance both in the literature and in practice, rapport-building should be carefully examined for what it is and what it is not. Inexperienced trainees, and those who only read the classic texts, seem to understand rapport-building as an attempt to establish what almost constitutes a friendship between interrogator and suspect. This view encourages chit-chat and small talk in essence to build a relationship based on good will. The rapport-building encouraged by experienced practitioners is more often based on respect for the interrogator and on professionalism. Hence the Boston homicide investigators dress in suits and shake hands with the suspects, and FBI instructors state that they try to be one of the few decent people with whom the suspect has interacted in his lifetime. In practice, attempts to build rapport based on friendship and good will are often perceived as forced and false, and, thus, it is more useful simply to treat the suspect as an equal human being. Some texts note that many suspects will be immediately suspicious of an overly friendly investigator, but will be pleasantly surprised by the respectful, professional interrogator who does not shout at or insult them.

Another important point of tension between literature and practice lies in the concept of the purported goal of an interrogation. While the practical literature counsels against entering an interrogation with the sole purpose of obtaining a confession — advice that is echoed by instructors during training — most of the psychological studies related to interrogations focus on confession rates and confession-inducing factors. The individual interrogation techniques and training programs implicitly reinforce this focus by urging prolonged interrogations and psychological ploys meant to undo deception and obtain a confession. Although the literature occasionally refers to incriminating statements, and law enforcement officers often referred to the value of obtaining a detailed lie through an interrogation, most attention focuses on obtaining a detailed confession from a suspect to bolster the chances of a future conviction.

Currently, those law enforcement agencies and departments that teach interrogation techniques train their officers and agents in tactics that have not been proven successful through any empirical studies. Neither the FBI nor FLETC has ever studied the efficacy of its techniques in garnering confessions or incriminating statements. Generally the agencies use variations of the Reid Technique, or subcontract the training to the Reid School or its spin-off, Wicklander-Zulawski. Although the Reid School claims an 80% confession rate for those who use its techniques, no independent, empirical study has confirmed those numbers. Given the dearth of empirical evidence to support the agencies' training and techniques, it seems that reliance on them is based mostly on the reputation of the Reid approach and on anecdotal evidence of its utility. Another explanation might be the institutional inertia characteristic of most large government agencies such as the FBI and other federal law enforcement agencies.

As noted, one reason why only anecdotal information exists on the efficacy of the Reid Technique and its variations is because very little, if any, review of actual interrogations is conducted in the field in the United States. As discussed in Section 11, unlike in Britain, most U.S. interrogations are still not videotaped. Even in the minority of jurisdictions that now mandate electronic recording, most law enforcement agencies use audiotapes instead of videos. Moreover, we found no evidence that superiors systematically observe interrogations conducted by officers and agents; instead, it appears that those personnel who initially receive training in interrogation are then sent into the field with little direction or supervision, and learn the majority of their skills on the job and, if they are lucky, from more experienced officers or agents. Even the most formalized programs, like those at the FBI and FLETC, do not follow up with their students to determine the utility of the techniques taught or whether those techniques are actually being used in the field. There has not even been a comprehensive attempt to gather evidence through surveys of, or self-reports by, the interrogators and/or suspects.

At the same time, it appears that those agencies and departments that use Reid or its variations, such as the FBI and FLETC, are a step ahead of most law enforcement around the country, like the Boston Police Department, which does not train its officers and agents in interrogation techniques at all. Local law enforcement departments do not offer the training in the police academies because most officers will never conduct interrogations, and those who then become detectives or other investigators are almost never required to receive additional training in this area. Reid and other outside courses are sometimes offered as options to those who want them, requiring the officers or agents to take the initiative to pursue such training. Some individuals, such as Lieutenant Pierce, take advantage of the opportunities. However, although we hypothesize (and anecdotal evidence suggests) that the majority of investigators do not participate in such voluntary training, there has been no empirical study to determine the actual percentage of senior officers who are trained in interrogation techniques through such voluntary programs. Such training may be somewhat superfluous, however, as many senior law enforcement personnel develop and use many of the techniques used in Reid and its variations on their own. Deputy Superintendent Coleman argues that Reid does not offer anything that people with brains, people skills, and some experience could not figure out on their own. He and others note that senior investigators may not be able to identify the various steps of the interrogation but generally use the same approaches: thorough pre-interrogation investigation, rapport-building, and some sort of theme presentation. However, everyone seems to know an investigator who uses ineffective techniques (e.g., trying to overwhelm the suspect with the evidence), which suggests that, though intuitive to some, these tactics do not necessarily flow from pure logic.

In sum, the few law enforcement agencies consulted for this project that provide any training on interrogation at all do so through very general programs. Like the practical literature upon which they are based, the training programs fail to account for, or recommend adjustments in response to, the various confession-inducing factors identified by available empirical research. The training takes a "one-size-fits-all" approach and fails to instruct interrogators on how, or whether, to adapt the techniques to differences in age, ethnicity, or culture of the suspect, seriousness of the offense, or strength of the available evidence. Aside from the dearth of nuance, there is no available evidence to evaluate whether the techniques upon which training is based actually yield favorable results in practice. None of the agencies we contacted had any idea of whether the training they offered was in fact implemented by agents and, if it was, whether it worked.

PART III: RECOMMENDATIONS AND IMPLICATIONS FOR TERRORISM

Section 13. Recommendations for Future Research

Further theoretical and empirical independent study is needed in the following areas:

1. Whether the Reid Technique and its variations currently being taught to law enforcement personnel are effective;
    - Consider the confession rate and accuracy of information obtained through those techniques.
2. Whether law enforcement agents actually apply the interrogation training they receive;
3. Whether particularly effective techniques and systems for elicitation of truthful information and confessions exist in other countries;
    - Compare U.S. interrogation data with data on interrogation techniques and results in Britain, Japan, Israel, and Australia.
4. Whether the effectiveness and applicability of interrogation techniques employed by U.S. law enforcement agencies, and the theories underlying them, remain constant across cultures; and
5. Whether it would be feasible and effective to resort to a dedicated cadre of specially trained interrogators as opposed, or in addition, to training all criminal investigators on interrogation.

Such studies will be extremely difficult until U.S. law enforcement organizations begin to videotape all of the interrogations they conduct. Clearly the availability of videotapes would allow for feedback and constructive criticism by superiors, thereby breaking bad habits before they take root. Similarly, videotaping would encourage supervisors at various agencies and departments to begin more regular observations of the interrogations conducted by their personnel so as to offer feedback on their performance.[634]

Section 14. Implications for Investigation and Prevention of Terrorism

Interrogation will likely play a seminal role in the prevention and investigation of terrorist threats and incidents. It would therefore be useful to evaluate whether organizations dealing with terrorism can learn anything from current interrogation practices used by law enforcement agencies. In this context, this section raises questions and issues to be pondered and evaluated by more experienced and qualified individuals.

At the outset we note that, despite claiming the contrary, the available literature on interrogations and the related training provided by law enforcement agencies are generally geared toward obtaining a confession. In contrast to ordinary law enforcement investigations, which are predominantly reactive and preeminently concerned with obtaining a conviction, a preventive terrorism investigation has the sole objective of preventing an attack, and is thus a hybrid of intelligence collection and interrogation. Although the literature occasionally refers to incriminating statements, and law enforcement officers often refer to the value of obtaining a detailed lie through an interrogation, it is unclear how

---

[634] Additional study on the effects of videotaping on the interrogations being taped would also be useful.

well, or whether, these aims would translate into a preventive investigation. For example, in comparison to a law enforcement officer, an interrogator working on a preventive investigation would most likely have less information against which to evaluate a given lie, or even to judge whether a suspect is lying at all during the interrogation. Consequently, this potential difference in goals must underlie any assessment of the value of law enforcement interrogation practices in preventing terrorism. Similarly, all current law enforcement techniques operate under the assumption that confessions obtained must meet certain legal and evidentiary requirements. Some adjustment might be needed in purely preventive situations or when legal requirements are inapplicable.

It is difficult to arrive at any fixed conclusions about the applicability of law enforcement interrogation techniques to the terrorism context because we do not know whether they in fact are effective. As mentioned in Section 13, much research is needed into the actual effectiveness of law enforcement interrogation techniques, since individual agencies keep no statistics on confessions or any data on other measures of interrogation success. Even if the techniques prove effective, we would still have to evaluate whether they would be equally effective in the terrorism context in particular. Although law enforcement agents with experience in both regular law enforcement and terrorism investigations have noted that current techniques work well in both contexts, they also recognize that their effectiveness largely depends on having vast amounts of time to devote to the investigation and interrogation. Thus, current law enforcement interrogation techniques have little applicability to a ticking-bomb, or otherwise time-constrained, investigation scenario. Additionally, other aspects endemic to the terrorism phenomenon must be taken into account when evaluating the relevance of law enforcement interrogation techniques to that arena. For example, current interrogation techniques and training programs make no mention of, or consider adjustments for, the possibility that suspects have been trained in counter-interrogation techniques. Such training is common practice for terrorist organizations and must be taken into account when fashioning interrogation techniques to be used with terrorism suspects.

Another feature that might make both the literature and law enforcement techniques difficult to adopt in the terrorism prevention context is the conspicuous omission of any cultural adaptation. All psychological literature and interrogation techniques seem either to ignore the potential impact of culture on the outcome of an interrogation or to assume that it does not matter. Because the current terrorist threat is so intricately tied to culture and religion, failing to study the impact of those factors on the efficacy of interrogation techniques seems like a glaring oversight. Additionally, cultural awareness and adaptation would appear to be central elements of the rapport-building upon which the current techniques rely so heavily. Though by no means an exhaustive list, areas for possible study include whether culture in fact is a statistically significant predictor of the outcome of interrogations, and, if so, whether shame-based approaches to interrogation work better among certain cultures than fear- or guilt-based approaches. To this end, it may be worth bringing together interrogation experts from around the world to discuss and exchange techniques, thereby giving everyone more appropriate interrogation tools.

Finally, a note on interrogator training and qualifications. Although the literature and training agencies agree that not everyone can be an effective interrogator, the prevailing approach in practice is to train everyone, as opposed to having a dedicated cadre of interrogators. Given the heterogeneous nature of the group of people who become law enforcement agents, the few agencies that offer any training do so at a basic and general level, catering to the lowest common denominator. A different approach — employing a group of highly educated and specially trained interrogators in a counterterrorism squad and entrusting them with terrorism-related interrogations — would not be unprecedented in U.S. law enforcement. Many police departments and federal law enforcement agencies have highly trained and dedicated personnel whose sole, or primary, responsibility is to act as hostage negotiators during a hostage crisis. Given the psychological and behavioral complexity of interrogations in general, and the sensitivity of terrorism-related interrogations in particular, we think it prudent to evaluate the possibility of adopting such a model and insist on better trained and dedicated interrogators.

7
Barriers to Success:
Critical Challenges in Developing a New Educing Information Paradigm

Steven M. Kleinman, M.S.
February 2006

Abstract

The art of educing information comprises both process and content. Depending upon the circumstances, the former may unfold as inherently simple or incredibly complex (e.g., the interrogation of a cooperative, reliable source or of a source who is resistant and deceptive), while the latter may be surprisingly easy or agonizingly difficult (e.g., an interrogation that focuses on the location of a terrorist training camp or one that involves the deconstruction of a complex international financial network). Given the broad spectrum of possibilities within just these two variables, the possible permutations in outcome are essentially infinite. As a result, identifying the essential barriers to success can be an exceptionally vexing challenge.

Introduction

All intelligence products must be based on data that have been evaluated for technical error, misperception, and hostile efforts to deceive.[635]

A preliminary examination of the challenges inherent in developing and managing an effective program for educing information (EI) identifies a daunting array of barriers to success. However, systematic examination of these barriers to educing information from uncooperative sources shows that they bear reduction to three general categories:

1. Linguistic/Cultural Barriers to Success

2. Scientific/Technical/Subject Matter Barriers to Success

3. Interpersonal/Intrapersonal Barriers to Success

---

[635] Captain William S. Brei, USAF, *Getting Intelligence Right: The Power of Logical Procedure*, Joint Military Intelligence College Occasional Paper Number Two, Washington, DC, 1996, 9.

235

Linguistic/Cultural Barriers

Words perform two primary functions: they express and they interpret. Words are the packets of information we use to transfer ideas, feelings, and facts to others. To borrow from the lexicon of information technology, "expression is the push function of communications." At the same time, words shape an individual's perceptions of the external world. In the pull mode of communications, they serve as the data points upon which an internal map is generated. While these maps appear very real — and very accurate — to an individual, as the product of interpretation they may reflect only a partially correct representation of a given experience.

Just as an individual with a limited vocabulary might experience profound challenges in expressing themselves and interpreting the rich world around them, a similar phenomenon often occurs in the context of an interrogation. An intelligence officer constrained by the inability to effectively express (i.e., pose questions) and interpret (i.e., understand the source's responses) is likely to be ineffective in exploring the intelligence potential of a given source. This is, in sum, the linguistic barrier to success. While reasonably simple in concept, it can cast an insidious shadow across all EI activities.

EI operations, by definition, are uniquely language intensive. It is through words that the interrogator explores a source's knowledgeability and the nature of any resistance; it is through words that the source reveals scope of knowledge as well as the logic and methods of a resistance posture; and it is through words that the interrogator seeks to persuade the source and elicit cooperation. Clearly, such a complex and dynamic exchange cannot be effectively accomplished through a barrier of limited language skills. For the United States, which continues to struggle with a significant shortfall in its foreign language capability, this barrier can be significant.

The U.S. Foreign Language Gap

The U.S. government has established a relatively straightforward means of evaluating levels of foreign language proficiency. The scale currently in use ranges from a value of 1, termed "Elementary" ("sufficient capability to satisfy basic survival needs and minimum courtesy and travel requirements") to a value of 5, termed "Functionally Native" ("able to use the language at a functional level equivalent to a highly articulate, well-educated native speaker").[636] It is important to note that this scale reflects an exponential rather than an incremental increase in proficiency. U.S. government research has demonstrated, for example, that a Level 3 speaker could perform as much as four times more productively than a speaker at Level 2.[637]

---

[636] Technically, the scale begins at "0" ("no measurable skill").

[637] U.S. General Accounting Office, *Foreign Languages: Human Capital Approach Needed to Correct Staffing and Proficiency Shortfalls* (Washington, DC: GPO, January 2002), 5. Cited hereafter as GAO, *Foreign Languages*.

Bringing a beginning student to the needed levels of operational proficiency requires considerable time. With respect to challenging languages such as Arabic, the Department of Defense projects that at least a year of training is required to bring the student to Level 2 on the proficiency scale, termed "Limited Working" capability ("sufficient capability to meet routine social demands and limited job requirements; can deal with concrete topics in past, present, and future tense"). Given the exponential nature of this proficiency scale, it should come as no surprise that substantial training and field experience are necessary for the student to progress to higher levels of proficiency.

To support EI operations adequately, a linguist-interrogator or an interpreter must be able to function at Level 4 — "Advanced Professional" ("able to use the language fluently and accurately on all levels normally pertinent to professional needs; has range of language skills necessary for persuasion, negotiation, and counseling").[638] How quickly might U.S. foreign language training centers produce a functional linguist of this quality? According to Dr. Richard Brecht, Director of the National Foreign Language Center, a student would require approximately 6,000 hours of study to reach Level 3 or 4 proficiency in Arabic — obviously a relevant strategic language in the current war on terror.[639]

In recent years, the National Security Agency (NSA) changed its long-standing policy on the competence expected of its linguists. To fulfill the NSA's operational responsibilities, linguists must attain a Level 3 or 4. As noted above, this is a significant qualitative advance from the previously acceptable proficiency of Level 2. In a similar vein, the Central Intelligence Agency has expressed the need for interpreters to function at Level 4 (or higher), specifically to "understand the intricacies of vernacular speech: colloquialisms, slang, and multiple dialects."[640]

Linguist-Interrogators vs. the Use of Interpreters

To overcome the linguistic barrier to success, an interrogator must either possess near-native-level mastery of the source's language or be aided by an interpreter with the requisite level of ability. While the former would present the most attractive option under ideal circumstances, it may not be possible, given real-world constraints. Identifying the best approach in this critical area remains a major challenge in planning for the training of interrogators to meet future strategic requirements.

The set of countries, organizations, and personalities that may present substantial threats to U.S. national security interests is geographically — and linguistically — diverse. Given the complexity involved in educing information from uncooperative sources and the time-intensive nature of foreign language training outlined above, the difficulty of developing (through both training and

---

[638] GAO, *Foreign Language*, 5.
[639] Richard Brecht, Ph.D., "The Language Crisis in the War on Terror," address to the Eisenhower Institute, Washington, DC, 24 October 2002, URL: http://www.eisenhowerinstitute.org/programs/democracy/homelandsecurity/Whitman4report.pdf, accessed 15 November 2005. Cited hereafter as Brecht, 2002 Eisenhower Institute presentation.
[640] Brecht, 2002 Eisenhower Institute presentation.

field experience) the professional skills necessary to effectively manage high-value targets and achieve sufficient operational proficiency in a foreign language cannot be overstated.

To make matters worse, the strategic-linguistic landscape changes constantly. In 1991, for example, the focus of U.S. strategic interests shifted dramatically from the Soviet Union and Eastern Europe to the Middle East. Against this backdrop, the United States simultaneously faced challenges from narco-trafficking (requiring primarily Spanish language resources), the rise of China as a regional power (requiring Mandarin, Cantonese, and a host of lesser-known dialects), and a continuation of the decades-long surveillance and containment of an ultimately nuclear-capable North Korea. This raises a critical question: Is it even possible to train the number of operationally skilled and experienced, language-capable interrogators needed to meet such an incredible breadth of threats? If not, what role should interpreters play in helping to meet such a vexing challenge? The advantages of language-qualified interrogators over the use of interpreters in the interrogation arena are undeniable. To reap these advantages, considerable effort must go into overcoming the disadvantages noted in the following box.

Assessing the Net Value of Using Language-Qualified Interrogators Rather Than Interpreters

Advantages

- More effective use of time
- Ability to recognize and understand nuance of language (including impact of nonverbal behaviors)
- Avoids need to hire foreign nationals, which introduces security concerns
- More capable of establishing rapport with a source
- Removes time delay inherent in interpretation that can significantly impact the orchestration of specific approaches
- Interrogators have greater confidence in their ability to properly orchestrate a given approach (that is, they are able to ensure attention to all components of verbal communication)
- Words, tonality/emphasis, and body language are consistent with the intended message

---

Assessing the Net Value of Using Language-Qualified Interrogators Rather Than Interpreters(contd.)

Disadvantages

- High cost of recruiting, training, and managing a large cadre of interrogators (exacerbated by the uncertainties over what languages might be required to meet future operational requirements)
- Native or near-native language capabilities — notoriously difficult to acquire —required to support current and anticipated national security interests
- Frequent field exercises (designed to mirror challenging, real-world operations) required to avoid loss of labile skill

In looking for models that could help inform U.S. EI policy in this regard, it is difficult to find another country that faces anywhere near the same complex, diversified, and always-changing linguistic capabilities challenge. Israel, for example, while offering intriguing examples of best practices from an EI perspective, has consistently faced an enemy that, with the exception of Iran, speaks Arabic. South Korea, another country that has effectively and systematically exploited information from captured enemy personnel, continues to face an adversary (i.e., North Korea) with which it shares a native language. By way of contrast, even when considering only the Global War on Terrorism (ignoring, for the moment, the possibility of a simultaneous major regional conflict), the United States confronts a veritable Tower of Babel (see the list on the next page). It is imperative that the U.S. chart a course for resolving these imposing linguistic challenges.

Operation ENDURING FREEDOM Languages

Central Asian Languages

- **Afghanistan**
  –Dari, Pashto, Tajik, Uzbek
- **Uzbekistan**
  –Uzbek
- **Turkmenistan**
  –Turkmen
- **Pakistan**
  –Pashto, Urdu, Baluchi
- **India**
  –Hindi, Urdu, Punjabi

Southeast Asian Languages

- **Philippines**
  –Tagalog, Tausug, Cebuano, Illocano
- **Indonesia**
  –Indonesian/Javanese
- **Malaysia**
  –Malay

Source: Clifford Porter, *Asymmetrical Warfare, Transformation, and Foreign Language Capability* (Ft. Leavenworth, KS: U.S. Army Command and General Staff College, Combat Studies Institute, March 2002), 4-6. URL: http://www-cgsc.army.mil/carl/download/csipubs/porter.pdf.

As the effort to create the next generation of EI professionals moves forward, decisionmakers must carefully address the following fundamental questions:

- Is it feasible to build a cadre of highly capable interrogators who also command near-native fluency in the required languages?

- How prepared are military and civilian government personnel systems to train an interrogator in operational methodology, and also in a language that has no immediate operational requirement?

- Is it possible to develop a recognized and sufficiently compensated career field for professional interpreters who have been specifically trained to support interrogation operations?

Clifford Porter, Command Historian at the Defense Language Institute, begins to address these questions as he examines options available for the U.S. military to acquire and employ foreign language capabilities. On the basis of his extensive experience in developing and managing Defense Department foreign language programs, he offers a useful and comprehensive assessment of the advantages and disadvantages in the current range of options (see below).[641]

Military-Educated Linguists

Advantages:
- Deployable U.S. military personnel
- Top Secret/Secret clearance
- Many are careerists or join other agencies after the military (e.g., FBI, NSA)
- After career, are available for service as contractors or in Reserve Components

Disadvantages:
- Lead time to educate new linguists to the requisite skill level
- Takes time to build experience and sustain capabilities
- Military personnel system does not adequately support the retention of skilled linguists (i.e., compensation, promotions, etc.)

Reserve Component Linguists

Advantages:
- Deployable U.S. military personnel
- Top Secret/Secret clearance
- Many are careerists or join other agencies after the military (e.g., FBI, NSA)

Disadvantages:
- Lead time to plan and educate new linguists: 6 to 18 months
- Takes time to build experience and sustain capabilities
- Poorly supported by personnel system
- Insufficient time allotted to maintain/enhance language skills

---

[641] Modified from Porter, *Asymmetrical Warfare, Transformation, and Foreign Language Capability*, 12–14.

Contractors – Prior-Service Military

Advantages
- May have clearances
- Can be available on short notice for common languages
- Do not need to manage their careers

Disadvantages: Varying Quality
- Lack of quality translates into intelligence gaps
- Support affected by money, danger, etc. (may quit or strike)
- Without oversight, can be high cost and/or low quality
- Possible labor disputes: Berlitz strike in 1967 Vietnamese program
- Noncombatants and only some have clearances
- Not long-term solution for foreign language capability

Contractors – Native

Advantages:
- Available for local languages and dialects
- Do not need to manage their careers

Disadvantages:
- Lack of quality translates into intelligence gaps
- Often different political agenda and varying degrees of translation accuracy
- Opportunity for enemy intelligence penetration
- Monopoly over information
- Can quit over money, danger, politics, etc.
- Noncombatants without clearances
- Not long-term solution for foreign language capability

Heritage Speakers*/Civilian-Acquired Skills

Advantages:
- Available on short notice for local languages and dialects
- Shorter training pipeline
- Experience in language from birth
- Knowledge of culture

Disadvantages:
- Varying literacy levels in English and/or target language
- Lack of quality translates into intelligence gaps
- May not qualify for clearances
- Not enough volunteers of military age/fitness literate in target language

* Porter uses the term "heritage-speaker" to describe individuals whose foreign language skills were attained through having been born and raised abroad and/or growing up in a family where a language other than English was spoken.

Translation Using Computer Technology

Advantages:
- Powerful tool for educated and experienced linguists
- Powerful tool for experienced educators
- Powerful potential for sustaining linguists in the field

Disadvantages:
- Machine translation is inaccurate
- Programming is time consuming and costly
- Programming fails with low-literacy languages (e.g., Pashtu or Baluchi)
- Easily fooled by code terminology
- Cannot teach, must be used by experienced educator
    - Reliant on programming by experienced linguists
    - Cannot replace humans

Porter also notes that the U.S. has never had sufficient foreign language capabilities to meet wartime requirements. He recommends creating a joint language pool, as advised by the House Permanent Select Committee on Intelligence.[642]

Culture + Language = Tools for Building Operational Accord

One of an interrogator's primary objectives is to establish a level of operational accord with a source. Operational accord can be defined as a relationship orchestrated by an interrogator with a source that is marked by a degree of conformity and/or affinity and is based on a sense of understanding of, and perhaps even guarded appreciation for, respective concerns, intentions, and desired outcomes.[643]

While often difficult to identify within the complex and (at least initially) adversarial relationship between an interrogator and a source, success in gaining meaningful information of potential intelligence value is the product of an accord: the interrogator asks questions and the source provides constructive answers. Operational accord reflects a calculated effort to gain and maintain the source's cooperation long enough to satisfy existing intelligence requirements while effectively concealing acts on the part of the interrogator that might appear to the source as manipulative or exploitive.[644]

Establishing an accord of this nature can be extraordinarily difficult, with the process made even more problematic by the linguistic/cultural barrier. The interrogator who seeks to create an operational accord but who harbors cultural myopia faces a difficult path. Conversely, an interrogator whose efforts are supplemented by what has recently been termed "cultural intelligence" will conscientiously seek to build a bridge that systematically incorporates knowledge of the source's culture. Perhaps the interrogator's version of the Golden Rule might best be expressed as "Do unto others as they would have you do unto them."

In many respects, the Global War on Terror contains seeds of Huntington's "Clash of Civilizations."[645] Fortunately, the legacy of 20th-century conflict provides some powerful illustrations of U.S. forces demonstrating a positive, proactive approach to turning former enemies into allies. During World War II, the United

---

[642] Porter, *Asymmetrical Warfare, Transformation, and Foreign Language Capability*, 15.

[643] Jerry Richardson, *The Magic of Rapport* (Capitola, CA: Meta Publications, 1987), 13.

[644] The term "rapport" has been commonly used to describe an approach that employs cultural, linguistic, and interpersonal skills to establish a non-adversarial, productive relationship between interrogator and source. The term "operational accord" also incorporates such an approach while also encompassing a broader array of productive, intelligence-generating relationships. Further, "rapport," in the context of interrogation, has been so widely misused and misunderstood in recent years that its value as a relevant descriptive term is questionable.

[645] See Samuel P. Huntington, *The Clash of Civilizations and the Remaking of World Order* (New York: Simon and Schuster, 1996). Huntington's "Clash of Civilizations" theory in international relations posits that the primary sources of conflict today are fundamental differences in culture, exacerbated by the processes of globalization that bring major civilizations into unprecedented contact. Huntington divides the world's cultures into seven civilizations: Western, Latin American, Confucian, Japanese, Islamic, Hindu, and Slavic-Orthodox.

States faced the original Axis Powers: Germany, Italy, and Japan. Given the vast number of U.S. citizens who could trace their roots back to Europe, there was a degree of familiarity — cultural and linguistic — with the European enemies. Imperial Japan was an entirely different story. Few U.S. citizens at the time had traveled to Japan or possessed even a superficial understanding of such a dramatically different culture. Similarly, other than a small number of former missionaries, businessmen, and first-generation Japanese immigrants (Issei), most people perceived the Japanese language as essentially impenetrable. In essence, the challenge in 1941 was not unlike that facing America in the early stages of a new century, where an understanding of Islamic culture and the Arabic language is as rare as understanding of Japan's in the 1940s. Cultural-linguistic barriers to success were skillfully surmounted through education, innovative thinking, and an efficient exploitation of an overlooked (and widely shunned) resource: the Nisei, or second-generation Japanese Americans.[646] Cultural intelligence (although not referred to as such at the time) proved a critical factor, a point Ulrich Straus eloquently illustrated in *The Anguish of Surrender*:

> In the first years of [World War II], American interrogators found that some [Japanese] POWs remained entirely uncooperative, sullen, and arrogant, but that even they often came around to talking more freely when the interrogators had enough time to spend with them. Almost invariably, POWs reacted favorably to the good medical treatment and ample food they received. Americans realized that interrogating an enemy with such totally different cultural background had to be learned through trial and error. *Preconceptions had to be abandoned along the way for new ideas that showed greater promise.*[647] (Italics added)

Cultural Context: Knowing the Enemy

Sun Tzu is perhaps best known for his aphorism on preparing for conflict: "If you know the enemy and know yourself, you need not fear the result of a hundred battles."[648] Too often, it seems, such timeless concepts are forgotten upon entering the breach…and the cost can be staggering. As revelations of the events that had transpired at Abu Ghraib reached the public, many U.S. citizens could not grasp the Arab world's seemingly disproportionate emotional response to these actions — especially the mistreatment of prisoners in a manner that carried sexual overtones. Cultural values and traditions play no small role in determining the

---

[646]   In February 1942, pursuant to President Roosevelt's Executive Order 9006, 120,000 U.S. citizens of Japanese ancestry were moved to internment camps for the duration of World War II. A small number of the thousands of Nisei volunteers for military service during the war were selected for acceptance into the demanding U.S. Army and U.S. Navy language programs. Graduates were subsequently assigned intelligence duties involving translation and interpretation, including support to interrogation operations within the United States and at deployed locations throughout the Pacific Theater.

[647]   Ulrich Straus, *The Anguish of Surrender: Japanese POWs of World War II* (Seattle, WA: University of Washington Press, 2003), 131-32.

[648]   Sun Tzu, *The Art of War* (New York: Delacorte Press, 1983), ed. James Clavell, 2.

words and deeds that individuals or populations consider offensive. While many in the West were disgusted by the treatment of Iraqi detainees at Abu Ghraib, it deeply shocked the Arab world for reasons poignantly described by George Friedman:

> Sexual humiliation of Arabs as a means of extracting information had been practiced before — by the Ottoman Turks. As some societies treat women who are raped, Arab society holds the victim of sexual torture responsible for their fate. So taking pictures of sexual humiliation was a perfect tool of blackmail. Like a woman in nineteenth-century Sicily who had been raped, the revelation of sexual abuse could be worse than the abuse itself. No fingernails were pulled, but the spirit was broken. It was an effective means of non-physical torture.[649]

Whether the interrogator's objective is to establish operational accord, psychologically intimidate, emotionally provoke, or infer guilt, the attempt will fail if it is not orchestrated in a manner that is culturally meaningful to the target of these efforts. One cannot "know the enemy" without understanding his culture.

Breaking The Cultural Barrier — Shaping "Logical" Appeals to the Source's Belief Structure

In this heading the word "logical" is enclosed in quotation marks to denote its unique application in the context of interrogation: specifically, its use to convince a reluctant source of the merits of an interrogator's appeal. The logic used by the interrogator is not constrained by convention; rather, its purpose is to present an *apparently* logical explanation — or rationalization — for the source to capitulate. An (admittedly simple) example would be as follows:

> Interrogator: You have told me before — several times — that you believe in God. And we both agree that God would condemn acts that result in the deaths of innocent people, especially women and children. If you truly believe in God as you have said, then it is imperative that you tell me about Al Qaeda's next target so that you and I, two believers in God, can work together to prevent the tragic deaths of so many innocent people.

Resistance instructors refer to such an approach as "circular logic" and caution against underestimating the persuasive potential of this tactic. Employing this ruse in the context of interrogating a follower of Islam, however, can be problematic if not informed by the necessary cultural intelligence. Given the important differences in beliefs about the role of God in matters both prosaic and profound, interrogators unfamiliar with Islam must be cautious in the use of a circular logic approach that incorporates analogous examples of, for example, right and wrong, to persuade a source to provide information (e.g., on an impending

---

[649] George Friedman, *America's Secret War: Inside the Hidden Worldwide Struggle Between America and Its Enemies* (New York: Doubleday, 2004), 327-8.

attack). Contrasting cultural perspectives on the cause and effect associated with the attack may quickly undermine the viability of the circular logic approach. While the interrogator may try to place responsibility (and therefore guilt) on the source, the source may perceive the potential outcome of the event as strictly *inshallah*... in the hands of God.

Scientific/Technical Barriers

The rationale behind the preemptive invasion of Iraq centered on that country's suspected research and development programs involving weapons of mass destruction (WMD). The actual use of nuclear, biological, and chemical materials — from weaponizing the unstable substances to the design of effective delivery systems — involves exceptionally sophisticated activities. As a result, educing relevant information from sources with the scientific and technical expertise to support such programs requires an equally sophisticated approach: a combination of applicable technical knowledge on the part of the interrogator *and* the requisite technical vocabulary (in both English and the target language) on the part of the interrogator and/or the interpreter.

Centers of Gravity in the Global War on Terrorism

As we approach the challenge of collecting technical intelligence, we must take into account that the nature of the information sought about an adversary is as varied as the adversaries themselves. However, several constants remain within this fog of war. One of these constants is the need to correctly identify and understand the enemy's *center(s) of gravity*. This was a fundamental tenet of the strategy espoused by Carl von Clausewitz, who defined a center of gravity as "the hub of all power and movement, on which everything depends."[650]

For the purposes of this paper, it is important to note that centers of gravity in contemporary warfare often relate to technology. Therefore, interrogators must approach the task of educing information with sufficient technical competence to fully explore and exploit a given source's knowledgeability.

To use the current war on terror as an example, terrorism's centers of gravity include the ability to communicate, move, transport items, secure a safe haven, obtain financial support, and develop expertise in weapons and explosives. Examining just two of these — communications and financing — will illustrate the importance of this subset of technical barriers to success.

The information revolution, which has spawned an unprecedented array of options for communicating across town and across the globe, represents a double-edged sword in prosecuting the Global War on Terror. Wireless cellular networks, the Internet, and advanced encryption systems have made possible worldwide, real-time intelligence gathering and support to military operations. At the same time, the use of this technology — including cellular telephones

---

[650] Michael I. Handel, *Masters of War: Classic Strategic Thought* (London: Frank Cass, 2002), 54.

using SIM cards,[651] instant messaging, chat rooms, and steganography[652] — by terrorist groups in planning and staging attacks has created serious challenges for Western intelligence services. As the increasingly sophisticated face of terrorism relies ever more heavily upon the ability to communicate effectively and covertly, whether that communication involves tactical direction within an operational cell or a call to action delivered across the globe, it becomes critical for an interrogator to possess the requisite technical expertise to effectively exploit a detainee's knowledge in this vital area.

In a similar fashion, financing terrorism involves far more than simply securing money for weapons and recruits. As terrorist attacks become more complex (consider 11 September), the costs involved become substantial.[653] The ability to move large sums of money through a global system — which is now more open to scrutiny by law enforcement and intelligence agencies after decades of money laundering by international organized crime — poses challenges to the terrorist. Because terrorist organizations use both cutting-edge technology and ancient means of financing (e.g., *Hawala*, the underground, trust-based banking system that facilitates the movement of money without a trailing record of transactions), it is exceedingly difficult to identify the funding that supports terrorism against the complex background of global finance. An interrogator who lacks an understanding of how money moves across international boundaries, how currencies are transformed into digital equivalents, the nature of national and international reporting requirements, constantly evolving money laundering schemes, and the system of *Hawala*, will have little ability to leverage the potential intelligence value of a well-placed, knowledgeable source.

As challenging as these examples might be, greater challenges lie in possible future conflict scenarios involving near-peer competitors (e.g., China). The technical intelligence requirements for such a conflict would be far more complex — and far more critical to the war effort — than in any previous conventional conflict. With this in mind, the need to prepare for and overcome the technical barriers to educing information becomes self-evident.

The Challenge of Technical Support to Interrogation

Technical barriers involve far more than the *nature* of the intelligence gathered: of equal importance is the role of technology in *how* intelligence is

---

[651] The *Subscriber Identity Module* contains a small microprocessor that stores information about the phone, including the telephone number, and identifies that phone to a given network (i.e., network permissions). Pre-paid SIM cards may be inserted into a phone and used on a one-time or limited basis, which, along with encryption technology, makes it difficult to trace a call to an individual.

[652] Steganography involves the insertion of a hidden message within an image or text. Although a centuries-old practice, the advent of digital communications has presented enormous potential for employing steganography to support covert communications.

[653] The *9/11 Commission Report of the National Commission on Terrorist Attacks Upon the United States* notes that Al Qaeda operatives spent between $400,000 and $500,000 to plan and conduct the attacks. Questions about the source of sizable short-trade actions targeting U.S. airline companies in the days before September 11 remain unanswered. There has been speculation that Al Qaeda-related entities employed this strategy to exploit the financial windfall that was almost certain to occur after the hijackings, thereby funding the training and logistic support required to enable the attack.

gathered. The past two decades have witnessed an explosion in the types and quality of technology available to warfighters and intelligence officers. During this same period, however, little systematic work has gone into identifying developing, and fielding technologies in support of interrogation operations.

In this context, the search for certainty through technology has led some to place unwarranted reliance on the accuracy of the polygraph. While law enforcement agencies and intelligence services around the world routinely employ the polygraph,[654] it is certainly not the panacea some might suggest. Personality- and culture-driven factors continue to present significant challenges. For example, will the person who views lying to the enemy as an acceptable, even noble, option provide the same physiological cues that the polygraph examiner might normally read as deception?

While additional research into this and other technical means of detecting deception (e.g., voice stress analysis) should continue, other potential applications of technology also merit further examination. Audio monitoring of detainees throughout the course of their detention became *de rigueur* during World War II. Both the U.S. strategic interrogation program (MIS-Y) at Fort Hunt, VA, and the British MI-5 interrogation program at Latchmere House (Camp 020) relied heavily upon extensive recording of conversations among prisoners. In the course of conversations with cellmates, even highly disciplined German general officers and *Abwehr* intelligence operatives routinely disclosed information that they had carefully withheld from their interrogator. Twenty-first century electronic technology could facilitate an unprecedented level of surreptitious audio *and* video monitoring of detainees on a 24/7 basis.

The monitoring (and recording) of interrogations constitutes a broadly useful role for technology. The potential value of such recordings is considerable.

- They relieve the interrogator of the burden of note-taking (which can also undermine efforts to elicit cooperation from a source by serving as a constant reminder of the true nature of the exchange).

- They offer the opportunity to systematically observe and analyze psychophysical cues relating to deception.

- They provide the most accurate and comprehensive means of capturing any and all information of intelligence value presented by the source.

- They can be an invaluable tool for preventing abusive conduct on the part of interrogators as well as in investigating allegations of prisoner mistreatment.

- They can offer an unparalleled vehicle for developing the skills of new interrogators.

Despite the advent of behavioral science consultation teams, the actual interrogation has unnecessarily remained an individual pursuit. Even when

---

[654] Committee to Review the Scientific Evidence on the Polygraph, National Research Council, *The Polygraph and Lie Detection* (Washington, DC: The National Academies Press, 2003.)

subject-matter experts observe the interrogation, they can typically provide input only after the interrogation ends, unless they interrupt the process to confer with the interrogator. Off-the-shelf communications systems make it possible for an interrogator to obtain unprecedented real-time information from members of the support team without physically leaving the interrogation room. Behavioral, technical, cultural, and linguistic data and clarifications — *provided in a manner and at a pace tailored to the unique information needs and individual processing capabilities of the interrogator* — could significantly enhance the interrogator's ability to systematically explore a source's full scope of knowledgeability while reducing the potential for disrupting a productive line of inquiry that even a short break might cause.

Other promising areas of technical support for educing information are facial recognition software (a potentially powerful screening tool) and video recordings that can be analyzed for microexpressions (psychophysical cues that may occur so rapidly that they are routinely missed by casual observation).[655] Blood tests that precisely identify the geographic origins of the food recently consumed by a source could help to corroborate or disprove a source's statements regarding recent travel or claimed whereabouts.

Unlocking the considerable potential of EI operations in the context of future conflicts requires a thoughtful reassessment of the role science and technology will play in this effort. A reasonable first step would be to form a team of specialists drawn from the fields of interrogation operations, scientific and technical intelligence analysis, HUMINT technical support teams, and communications to identify a judicious way ahead.

Interpersonal/Intrapersonal Barriers[656]

> Know how to analyze a man. The alertness of the examiner is matched against the reserve of the examined. But great judgment is called for, to take the measure of another. It is far more important to know the composition, and the properties of men, than those of herbs and stones. This is the most delicate of the occupations in life: for the metals are known by their ring, and men by what they speak; words show forth the mind of man; yet more, his works. To this end the greatest caution is necessary, the clearest observation, the subtlest understanding, and the most critical judgment.[657]

---

[655] See, for example, Paul Ekman, *Telling Lies* (New York: W.W. Norton and Co.: 1992).

[656] The interpersonal/intrapersonal barrier to success suggests obvious areas of further exploration from a behavioral science perspective; however, these will be addressed here only peripherally. A more in-depth examination of those factors—with recommendations for specific areas of inquiry—will be left to the cadre of credentialed behavioral scientists involved in this EI study. Instead, the author, drawing upon his professional, operational, and academic background, limits his comments to the equally vital areas of strategy and tradecraft.

[657] Balthasar Gracian, *The Art of Worldly Wisdom: A Collection of Aphorisms* (Boston, MA: Shambala Publications, 1993), 250.

Even with an infusion of technology, EI will retain one key feature of HUMINT operations *vis à vis* other intelligence collection disciplines: cost-effectiveness. Divorced from the trappings of approach plans, questioning guides, and intelligence report writing, the process of interrogation can be effectively distilled to its underlying dynamic: *a controlled exchange of information on both an interpersonal and an intrapersonal level*. In the context of an interrogation, each side possesses information of interest to the other, and that information can be strategically disclosed at a time and a pace designed specifically to support the achievement of intended outcomes.

For the interrogator, the intended outcome is primarily the successful collection of timely, accurate, and comprehensive intelligence information. For the source, however, the intended outcome may vary dramatically from detainee to detainee. While one source may seek exclusively to stymie the collection of any useful information by the adversary (i.e., the interrogator) as part of a continued fight for "the cause," another may ultimately wish to provide information in return for specific actions/rewards/treatment (e.g., promise of expedited release, help in overthrowing a tyrant, better treatment for himself and/or his associates, etc.). The source's intended outcome will, in large measure, determine the rate at which information is offered as well as both the quality and quantity of that information.[658]

During this dynamic exchange, each side also manages a storehouse of information comprising data that can be divided into three primary categories: *what is known*, *what is believed to be true (suspected)*, and *what can only be guessed*. The interrogation itself involves a carefully controlled exchange of statements of fact and statements of supposition, liberally interspersed with an array of bluffs, feints, and ploys. This "move/counter-move" activity has been likened to the game of chess. A more accurate analogy, however, might be the ancient Chinese game of *Go*, where the number of possible combinations of board positions is estimated to be approximately 10 to the 750th power. Fortunately, interrogations — like *Go* — feature an assortment of recurring situations that, through experience, can be quickly recognized and effectively addressed.[659]

Systems Approach

To engage successfully in this exchange of information, an interrogator must possess a well-developed "talent" (whether it be an innate attribute, the product of operational training, or some combination of the two) for *systems thinking*. The

---

[658] A behavioral/cognitive approach to the interpersonal/intrapersonal barrier would pose several critical and potentially revealing questions with respect to this "controlled exchange of information." Such an inquiry might explore both the interrogator's mental construct and emotional framework as he or she approaches the interrogation as well as examine how these states might be affected by the interaction and/or over time as the operational relationship unfolds. A similar analysis involving the source might yield important insights.

[659] An important advantage that falls to the interrogator is the product of experience. While an interrogator may participate in — and be able to learn from — literally hundreds of interrogations, the source will have little personal experience to draw from, and none at all during the initial interrogation session.

systems approach recognizes interrogation as a "complex, dynamic system that is…greater than the sum of its parts." [660]

Fundamental training in interrogation views the process as a series of discrete events (e.g., approaches, questioning, termination, and bridging). Systems thinking, by contrast, requires the interrogator to adopt a perceptual framework that goes beyond a focus on discrete events to one that can rapidly identify patterns and the confluence of events that generate those patterns. This approach enables the interrogator to skillfully engage the patterns of action and reaction in ways that will "enhance or improve the situation without creating new and different problems elsewhere."[661] While the systems approach provides a uniquely helpful framework for managing complex interactions, its ultimate value rests in its ability to help propel events toward a specific outcome.

Whether or not the participants pay conscious attention[662] to the underlying dynamic, each word and every action brings with it a cascade of possible alternate scenarios. Extrapolating from studies of the application of complexity theory to intelligence analysis, it can be said that within the context of interrogation, "[i]ndividual agents within the network are constantly reassessing their need preferences and the degree to which they will compromise to bond with other agents."[663] The degree of compromise in this vein may include, among many others, acquiescence, understanding, withdrawal, defiance, or cooperation.

The Overriding Objective

Educing information from a source and negotiating the terms of agreement between two countries are arguably the micro- and macro-manifestations of the same interpersonal dynamic. Despite potentially dramatic differences in the scope of interests, the number of participants involved, and the gravity of the outcome, many of the fundamental principles involved apply in either context. This is especially true with respect to the importance of intended outcomes. Professor Roger Fisher, founder of the Harvard Negotiation Project, offers a powerful insight into this important factor, observing, "[t]ime and again, those involved in an international conflict — or in any conflict — fail to convert their goal into a decision they would like an adversary to make. Although we often think of ourselves as attempting to influence an adversary, we rarely think out just what kind of decision our side might reasonably expect of the other."[664]

---

[660] Joseph O'Connor and Ian McDermott, *The Art of Systems Thinking* (London: Thorsons, 1997). x.

[661] O'Connor and McDermott, *The Art of Systems Thinking*, x.

[662] Understanding — and preparing for — the intrinsic rules of engagement in this dynamic creates a window of opportunity for the interrogator to enhance the probability of achieving his or her own intended outcome rather than that of the source. This should be included as a fundamental objective of *third generation* interrogator training.

[663] Michael F. Beech, Lt Col, USA, *Observing Al Qaeda through the Lens of Complexity Theory: Recommendations for the National Strategy to Defeat Terrorism*, Strategy Research Paper (Carlisle Barracks: Center for Strategic Leadership, U.S. Army War College, July 2004), 5.

[664] Roger Fisher, *Beyond Machiavelli* (New York: Penguin Books USA, Inc, 1994), 95.

To capitalize on this systems approach to educing information, an interrogator must establish a lucid and unambiguous intended outcome. Such an outcome will serve as nothing less than a fundamental organizing principle around which all planning and execution of educing strategies will revolve.

Anecdotal evidence strongly suggests that the problems encountered in the course of interrogations conducted at Guantanamo Bay, Abu Ghraib, and Bagram Air Base have, at least in part, resulted from efforts to educe information from resistant sources in the absence of an operationally relevant, clearly defined, strategic outcome to effectively drive the process. Several factors have apparently contributed to the systemic failure to establish such important guideposts: improper planning, shortfalls in technical, operational, cultural or linguistic knowledge, or even frustration resulting from the high-pressure demands of combat operations.

A well-designed intended outcome would enable the interrogator to craft a thoughtful approach plan. In the context of interrogation, the intended outcome performs two vital functions:

- It should provide the interrogator with sufficient *focus* to enable him to make rational decisions when presented with unexpected challenges, and

- It should ensure the approach plan and subsequent execution of that plan will have — and maintain — *internal consistency.*

In an exhaustive study of the radical yet highly successful *Blitzkrieg* strategy employed by the German Army during World War II, Colonel John Boyd, a U.S. Air Force fighter pilot and strategist, identified the concept of *Schwerpunkt* as one of the key enabling principles. *Schwerpunkt* can be described as a concept that provides "focus and direction to the operation."[665] The profound importance of this principle is illustrated by its central role in the famed Toyota Production System, cited by many as arguably the most efficient automotive manufacturing system in the world. For Toyota, *Schwerpunkt* can be defined as "shortening the time it takes to convert customer orders into vehicle deliveries." With such a precisely defined point of focus, every member of the production team — from top manager to the worker on the assembly line — is armed with a clear and unambiguous standard upon which to base his or her actions.[666]

Focus — *Schwerpunkt* — for educing information would similarly drive the development of interrogation approaches, their implementation, and, most importantly, the decision-making of each interrogator working in an isolated, high-pressure, sometimes chaotic operational environment. This focus would empower the individual interrogator not only to glean intelligence information from a knowledgeable source more effectively, but also to do so in a manner consistent with legal, moral, and operational guidelines. In searching to identify a *Schwerpunkt* for the U.S. approach to educing information, it might be difficult

---

[665] Chet Richards, *Certain to Win* (Philadelphia, PA: Xlibris Publishing, 2004), 51.
[666] Richards, *Certain to Win*, 124.

to find a better operational exemplar than the objective established by the British MI-5 interrogation program during World War II: *Truth in the shortest possible time.*[667]

The second consideration, *internal consistency*, refers to an interrogation approach plan and questioning methodology that progress logically toward a pre-defined objective. Each action builds upon the last and sets the stage for the next. By contrast, an interrogation in which themes and/or participants constantly change in a scramble to identify a productive approach would reflect a lack of internal consistency. Internal consistency suggests far more than a beginning and an end state (although these are important factors): it requires an exquisitely detailed, yet highly accommodating, map of the course to follow between those two points. Admittedly, the complexity of any interaction between two individuals makes it unlikely that every nuance, challenge, or turn of events can be realistically anticipated. Nonetheless, an exhaustive planning effort will (1) enable the interrogator (or, better, interrogation team) to gain some measure of knowledge/expertise in the areas that are likely to surface, (2) lead to the development of an overarching strategy (as well as tactics to deal with an array of possible tangents or diversions), and (3) make it possible to devise an acceptable alternative should intractable defiance be encountered.[668]

One final note is warranted with respect to "focus." For the interrogator, effective focus implies not only a disciplined centering on the goals and objectives of the interrogation effort, but also a simultaneous awareness and consideration of *the source's* goals and objectives. Too often, interrogators intensely and aggressively pursue their operational agenda without sufficiently acknowledging that the source, too, has an agenda. In essence, the interpersonal barrier challenges the interrogator to skillfully assume multiple roles in the perceptual position paradigm that comprises *first, second, and third positions*:

> First Position – From the *first position*, the interrogator views the exchange from his or her point of view. This is a common perceptual perspective and the one naturally assumed by most individuals.
>
> Second Position – Assuming the *second position* involves an effort to view the exchange from the source's point of view. This involves not only a consideration of the source's feelings, desires, fears, hopes, etc., but also — and of equal importance — how the source might view the interrogator's approach (i.e., as compelling, helpful, threatening, etc.). From

[667] United Kingdom Public Record Office, *Camp 020: MI5 and the Nazi Spies* (Richmond, UK: Public Record Office, 2000), 109. Truth in the shortest possible time" was the objective established for the World War II MI-5 interrogation program known as *Camp 020*, which targeted suspected *Abwehr* (German intelligence) spies. This *Schwerpunkt* was based on the operational consideration that "some information in time is worth an encyclopedia out of date."

[668] In negotiation theory, this is referred to as a Best Alternative to a Negotiated Agreement (BATNA).

the second position, the interrogator is forced to consider how his or her words, tonality, and body language work congruently to generate the desired communication.

Third Position – In assuming the *third position*, the interrogator seeks to become an independent observer of the exchange. From this perspective, the interrogator is able to assess such important concerns as proxemics,[669] similarities and differences in body language, and leveraging the physical setting in support of the interrogation's objectives.[670] The third position can also be of exceptional value in the effort to objectively gauge progress toward an intended outcome. Finally, adopting this perceptual framework can be a beneficial strategy for creating the sense of emotional distance necessary when tempers flair and the exchange becomes personal. In negotiation theory, this is known as "going to the balcony."[671]

Incorporating the concept of perceptual positions into the interrogation strategy requires the interrogator to think — and act — on several planes at one time. Disregarding the source's interests can lead to unexpected and seemingly inexplicable areas of disagreement and even outright defiance. Conversely, regularly shifting among the three perceptual positions can enable the interrogator to maintain a progressive, adaptable, proactive approach plan, one governed by the overarching *focus* and enhanced by *internal consistency*. Fisher appears to advocate the value of such a paradigm from his observations of international negotiations:

> After sketching out how the choice appears to the other side and then creating an action plan to improve the situation, we need to focus next on how our action plan might become reality…[w]e fail to translate our plan into an action that someone could take tomorrow. It is time to turn a general idea into a question to be presented to the other side. What are some of the specific decisions that we might want and might reasonably expect a decision-nmaker on the other side to make. Instead of simply confronting them with a problem, we should identify one or more specific actions that we would like them to take to deal with that problem.[672]

---

[669] The study of the cultural, behavioral, and sociological aspects of spatial distances between individuals.

[670] The intrepid interrogator is mindful of the impact of the physical setting on the psychological set of the source (i.e., does the location, configuration, temperature, furnishings, and size of the room support or detract from the chosen theme).

[671] See William Ury, *Getting Past No: Negotiating Your Way from Confrontation to Cooperation* (New York: Bantam Books, 1993).

[672] Fisher, *Beyond Machiavelli*, 95–96.

Making Sense of Chaos and Ambiguity

History is replete with examples of apparently sound and carefully reasoned plans gone horribly awry as they moved from the chalkboard (or PowerPoint presentation) into the real world, where they invariably encountered a ubiquitous and implacable foe: chaos. This chaos — also known by the Clausewitzian terms "fog of war" and "friction" — is unavoidable and, in many cases, unpredictable. Incisive strategy, however, can ameliorate and even overcome fog and friction.

Chaos and ambiguity are the handmaidens of conflict. These two forces appear to remain omnipresent across the entire spectrum of conflict, from maneuver warfare on the battlefield to negotiations between multinational corporations. Rather than wish them away — or, worse yet, pretend to ignore their existence — the prudent strategist anticipates and, where possible, seeks to employ them as an advantage over a less agile adversary. Such an approach is as valid in the interrogation room as it is in other fields of battle.

The interpersonal/intrapersonal barrier to success introduces unique forms of chaos and ambiguity that an interrogator who wants to educe information from a reluctant source must recognize, understand, and address. The following are but a few examples of the intractable factors that can generate chaos and ambiguity in the course of an extended interrogation process:[673]

- The inherent complexity of personalities
- The role of changing, incompatible expectations
- The influence of life experience
- Tactics and strategies of formal resistance training
- Rapidly changing operating environment
- Rapidly changing intelligence requirements
- Introducing new and/or additional sources into the process
- Removing sources from the process.

A judicious assumption in this context is that the individual (interrogator or source) who demonstrates greater skill and adaptability in consistently responding to chaos and ambiguity, in an environment often characterized by a smog of data,[674] will ultimately prevail. If this is true, an overarching strategy for successfully navigating the conflict is essential. Fortunately, such a strategy exists…and can easily be tailored for application to the context of interrogation.

---

[673] Given the nature of chaos and ambiguity it would be practically impossible to establish a truly comprehensive list of such factors. Also, the examples above were limited to those relevant to the Interpersonal/Intrapersonal Barrier to Success. The Linguistic/Cultural and Scientific/Technical Barriers to Success generate a host of additional factors that can similarly create chaos and ambiguity.

[674] Similar to Clausewitz's *fog of war*, the smog of data represents the friction and sensory overload encountered by decisionmakers at all levels as they encounter the unprecedented volume of intelligence information generated by the modern U.S. Intelligence Community.

Decision-Making Cycles: The Importance of Agility and the Role of Ambiguity

As noted previously, a fundamental strategy for dealing with ambiguity rests on understanding how to employ ambiguity to one's advantage rather than viewing it as something to be rigidly avoided. In *Certain to Win*, Chet Richards captures the true meaning of ambiguity in a manner that has direct application to educing information from resistant sources:

> Ambiguity is a terrible thing, much more effective as a strategy than deception, with which it is often confused. Deception is correctly described as a tactic: If you are deceived, you will be surprised when you discover the truth, and it is possible that you will be led to do some things, perhaps even fatal things, that you would not have done if you had realized the truth earlier. It can be an extremely effective tactic, even though your ability to function as a thinking human being is not at risk. This is exactly what you can attack and destroy using ambiguity. There is no conflict, however, between ambiguity and deception, since the first provides the environment for the second. If something vital, such as life is at stake, losing track of a deadly threat in the fog of ambiguity can quickly lead to confusion, panic, and terror, which in turn will cause the decision-making of the less agile party to break down.[675]

Strategy, by definition, involves the effective marshalling of available resources in a manner that will achieve a purposeful outcome. The employment of strategy routinely involves the application and reapplication of resources (with each subsequent application being at levels equal to, greater than, or less than the original) in response to changes in the operating environment — be it the battlefield, marketplace, or interrogation room. Ultimately this continuous loop of action/reaction will end when a pre-determined end-state has been reached. Boyd, the fighter pilot-turned master strategist, brilliantly captured the essence of strategy as a:

> mental tapestry of changing intentions for harmonizing and
> focusing our efforts as a basis for realizing some aim or
> purpose in an unfolding and often unforeseen world of many
> bewildering events and many contending interests.[676]

Current interrogation training falls painfully short in this respect. Instead of the freeform methods necessary to meet the changing nature of the challenge (e.g., sources from different cultures, varying language requirements, rapidly evolving intelligence requirements, shifting alliances and adversaries, etc.), training and field experience too often encourages (and rewards) a rigid adherence to process. Current and emerging EI requirements can be met only with an overarching

---

[675] Richards, *Certain to Win*, 67.
[676] Richards, 84.

philosophy that advances the following foundational principle: If the adversary changes — if he learns from his experiences — the interrogator must have the capacity to learn and adapt with greater speed (what Boyd termed "asymmetric fast transients").

The ability to learn and adapt requires the interrogator to possess two critical qualities. These should permeate the methods employed and inform the decision-making cycle. The first is *sensory acuity*. This implies having sufficient situational and interpersonal awareness to recognize, understand, and make contextual sense of what is occurring. More specifically, it is the ability to make rapid — and accurate — assessments of cause and effect. This might take the form of noticing a rise in the intensity of stress-induced grooming behaviors when the source is asked questions about certain topics (e.g., the location of a training base about which the source claims to have no knowledge) and an absence of those same behaviors when he/she is asked questions about other matters. The second critical quality is *flexibility*. Flexibility — in behavior, in strategy, in choice of physical setting — ultimately means an ability to change what one is doing. The successful interrogator can quickly and purposefully change an approach plan to fit the source rather than the other way around (which, curiously, is a more common phenomenon than one might expect). Flexibility is the interrogator's key ally in the struggle against chaos and ambiguity.

Competitive Decision-Making: Applying Boyd's OODA Loop to Educing Information

Reduced to its essential nature, an interrogation can be defined as a competition between two decision-making cycles. Within this context, elements such as adaptability, speed, sensory acuity and flexibility are critical factors, with success accruing to the party that possesses and employs them more effectively. The strategy of *Observe—Orient—Decide—Act (the OODA Loop)* originated by Colonel Boyd exquisitely captures these elements and provides a unique framework for their systematic, outcome-oriented orchestration. The unique nature of this dynamic is concisely described as follows:[677]

> Knowledge of the strategic environment is the first priority. Secondly, one must be able to interact with the environment and those within it appropriately. You must be able to observe and orient yourself in such a way that you can indeed survive and prosper by shaping the environment where possible to your own ends, by adapting to it where you must. Doing so requires a complex set of relationships that involve both isolation and interaction. Knowing when each is appropriate is critical to your success. In OODA Loop fashion, one must continually observe, orient, decide and act in order to achieve and maintain

---

[677] In the context of Boyd's decision-making cycle, "knowledge of the strategic environment" can be used interchangeably with "sensory acuity," while "the ability to interact with the environment and those within it appropriately" essentially implies the same meaning as "flexibility."

freedom of action and maximize the chances for survival and prosperity. One does so through a combination of rapidity, variety, harmony, and initiative. It is these that are the core of "Boyd's Way." Rapidity of action or reaction is required to maintain or regain initiative. Variety is required so one is not predictable, so there is no pattern recognition for a foe to allow him to know of your actions in advance and thus plan to defeat them. Harmony is the fit with the environment and others operating in it. Initiative–taking charge of your own destiny— is required if one is to master circumstances rather than be mastered by them. All of course, would be focused on attaining the specified objective that is implicit in this discussion.[678]

The *specified objective* noted in this passage is a key to the *focus* addressed previously. Focus rests upon several, mutually supportive objectives that will, together, inform the OODA cycle. One fundamental objective, or *Schwerpunkt*, of the OODA strategy would have consistent and adaptable applicability to the EI process regardless of the circumstances (i.e., source, setting, intelligence requirements, etc.), and that is: *Diminish the adversary's capacity for independent action, or deny him the opportunity to survive on his own terms.*[679]

The OODA Loop and Educing Information

In considering how to apply the OODA Loop strategy (presented graphically below) to the challenge of educing information from an intelligence source, the logical first step is to examine each phase of the overall cycle individually.

---

[678] Grant T. Hammond, "The Essential Boyd," Web-Only Essay, undated, URL: http://www.belisarius.com/modern_business_strategy/hammond/essential_boyd.htm, accessed 15 January 2006.

[679] In the context of educing information, the term "survival" refers to the ability of a participant — interrogator or source — to achieve his or her specified outcomes. For the interrogator, this would mean the collection of accurate, timely, and comprehensive information. For the source, this could mean effective resistance or negotiating an attractive trade of information for a desired outcome (e.g., release, better conditions, etc.).

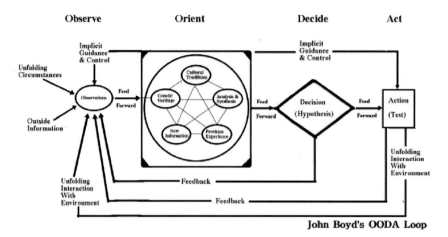

| Observe | Orient | Decide | Act |

John Boyd's OODA Loop

The OODA Loop. Source: Defense and the National Interest, URL: http://www.d-n-i.net/fcs/pdf/bazin_ooda.pdf, accessed 16 November 2006.

Observation: Observation involves gathering information via the senses. Although made possible by the physiological mechanisms of sight, sound, touch, taste, and smell, effective observation is informed by experience, training, and even intuition. Astute observation is a product of acute *situational awareness*. An experienced interrogator, by virtue of possessing the so-called "trained eye," might note a subtle gesture that a less experienced observer might miss. Boyd's research suggests that observations are both informed and influenced by *implicit guidance and control*; *unfolding circumstances*; *outside information*; and *unfolding interaction with the environment*. In a similar vein, observation systematically collects and organizes tonality, word choice, gestures, analogies, metaphors, and myriad other "observables" in a manner that enables the interrogator to move effectively to the next phase.

> **Example of Observation:** The source readily answers non-pertinent questions, seems to interact without hesitation with both the interrogator and the interpreter, and appears to be cooperative. However, when pertinent questions are posed about the location of weapons caches, the source shows observable changes in posture, speech, and ability to understand.

Orientation: Orientation involves the considered analysis and synthesis of the information gathered during the observation phase. Critical to the transition from observation to orientation is the presence of the sensory acuity described previously. Sensory acuity helps shape the mental construct necessary to effectively approach the challenge and aids in answering the important question, "What does this mean?" Orientation is enhanced through continuous refinement and training, and ultimately leads to comprehension and understanding. Boyd's concept of orientation included such considerations as *cultural traditions*, *genetic heritage*, *new information*, *previous experience*, and *analysis/synthesis*.

> **Example of Orientation:** Observable changes when answering pertinent questions open the possibility of conscious resistance. Additional questioning, research into known information about the source, and consultation with cultural and technical subject matter experts, suggest the source has useful knowledge but is constrained by concerns about the personal consequences of cooperation. Examples of the personal consequences of cooperation include guilt over the betrayal of colleagues, discomfort over feelings of appearing weak, and fear of retribution if cooperation is discovered.

Decision: Informed by both observation and orientation, one must determine the effective course of action. In the context of educing information, the decision has two aspects: (1) what *can and should* be done and (2) what *can and should not* be done. In the case of the former, the decision to act resembles a craftsman's choosing the correct implement for the job from a toolbox. By contrast, the decision regarding what actions not to take resembles the craftsman's consulting with legal, environmental, and safety professionals before beginning the job. Knowledge, the refinement of skills, perspective, the Law of Requisite Variety (see footnote[52] above), and the range of available options are major factors in the decision-making phase.

> **Example of Decision:** On the basis of observation and orientation, the interrogator considers a range of options shaped by time, tactics, and temperament. Time refers to the amount of time available for the conduct of one or a series of interrogations. Tactics refers to the approach methods and strategies that are appropriate given an assessment of not only the source's strengths and weaknesses, but also those of the interrogator. Finally, temperament refers to the selection of a lead interrogator who best matches the demographic, technical, and linguistic profile of the source.

Action: Action is the actual physical manifestation of the decision. Once the action (i.e., interrogation) begins, action is governed by the *Schwerpunkt* (e.g., truth in the shortest possible time)

Example of Action: The interrogator invests the time necessary to plan and prepare for the actual interrogation before actually encountering the source. The initial and follow-on interrogations are characterized by logical progression, internal consistency, and adaptability. The interrogator seeks to move through the OODA decisionmaking cycle more rapidly than the source, ultimately enabling the interrogator to enter and influence/control the source's decisionmaking cycle. In doing so, the interrogator limits the source's options, shapes his responses, and finally reduces/removes his ability to "survive" (i.e., effectively conceal, deceive, or resist).

The strategy described above involves a continuous cycle of observation, orientation, decision, and action, with each phase informed directly or indirectly by the others. Decisions, for example, provide direct feedback to observations, while actions indirectly inform orientation through the observation phase. The operating objective is to secure and maintain the greatest degree of freedom of action; the desired end state is survival.[680]

In unlocking the potential of any strategy, including that of the OODA Loop, an intimate understanding of the precepts must lead to their correct application in an environment defined by time, space, and mass. To navigate the OODA matrix in a manner that enables dominance of the environment — and an adversary — Boyd emphasized the need to operate with a skillful combination of *rapidity*, *variety*, *harmony*, and *initiative*:

- Rapidity: Rapidity of action and reaction is essential to gain, maintain, and/or regain the initiative. Speed in *correct* decision-making and corresponding action is critical.

- Variety: Variety – in thought and action — is required so that one is never *predictable*. Variety in action prevents the adversary from recognizing patterns of action with any degree of confidence. This, in turn, makes it impossible for the adversary to anticipate actions and craft strategies to defeat them.

- Harmony: Harmony refers to fitting or blending into the operational environment. In educing information, a great deal can be learned from the principles of the martial art *Aikido,* which places great emphasis on blending with (i.e., moving with rather than struggling against) an adversary's energy. In doing so, one creates the opportunity to subtly yet profoundly influence the movement and resulting decisions of an adversary without a costly investment of energy and resources.

---

[680] Survival in this context implies the continued viability of the educing effort. In essence, the employment of this strategy enables the interrogator to create — and take advantage of — opportunities to elicit information of relevant and timely intelligence value from a knowledgeable, albeit resistant, source.

- Initiative: Initiative – seeking out and taking control of one's own destiny — is necessary to achieve mastery of the environment and interactions with adversaries and to avoid being mastered by them.

Although Boyd's strategy began to take shape with his experiences in aerial combat during the Korean War, its application nonetheless remains unbounded by time or technology. It incorporates principles espoused by the strategist Sun Tzu over 2,500 years ago as well as those set forth by the laws of thermodynamics. Variations on this strategic theme have demonstrated their efficacy on the battlefields of World War II and in the lethality of the renowned 17th-century Japanese swordsman Miyamoto Musashi. In the following passage, Musashi, author of the classic treatise on strategy, *The Book of Five Rings*, succinctly sets forth much of what every interrogator needs to successfully educe information from resistant sources:

> [Y]ou determine [the] opponent's traditions, observe [their] character, find out [their] strengths and weaknesses, maneuver in ways contrary to the opponent's expectations, determine the opponent's highs and lows, ascertain rhythms in between, and make the first move; this is essential.[681]

Concluding Observations

> *[I]t is a paradox of the twenty-first century that, in this age of technological wonders, the threats to our lives, wealth, and order are fundamentally, crudely human. We may diagram bunkers, bombs, and entire armies, but we falter at understanding the human soul. Nor will the human heart fit into our templates. Love, fear, hatred, not machines, are the stuff of which wars are made, whether we speak of terrorist jihads, campaigns of ethnic cleansing, or conventional offensives (and do not underestimate the deadly power of love, whether felt toward a god, a people, a clan, flag, or an individual.)[682]*

Educing Information in the Last (or Current) War

With much of the nation's military, intelligence, and internal security resources currently focused on the Global War on Terror and the insurgency in Iraq, any effort to reexamine doctrine and methods for educing information can be too easily — and mistakenly — narrowed to applications within these two contexts. Although those who use terrorist and insurgent tactics have demonstrated an unprecedented mastery of leading-edge technologies, the scope and complexity of

---

[681] Miyamoto Musashi, *The Book of Five Rings*, translated by Thomas Cleary (London: Shambhala Publications, Inc., 2003), 56.

[682] Ralph Peters, *Beyond Terror* (Mechanicsburg, PA: Stackpole Books, 2002), 195.

this technology fall far short of that which would be involved in a major regional conflict or, certainly, a strategic engagement with an emerging peer-competitor such as the People's Republic of China.

The challenge of educing information from uncooperative sources cannot be overstated, but neither can the requirement for acquiring timely and accurate intelligence information that can only be obtained from human sources. Sun Tzu's observation continues to ring true in today's geopolitical environment:

> What enables the wise sovereign and the good general to strike and conquer, and achieve things beyond the reach of ordinary men is *foreknowledge*. Now this foreknowledge cannot be elicited from spirits; it cannot be obtained inductively from experience, nor by any deductive calculation.
>
> Knowledge of the enemy's disposition can only be obtained from other men.[683] (Original italics)

Toward a Third Generation in Educing Information

The effort to collect intelligence information from resistant sources can be traced back to antiquity. A review of the strategies and objectives involved suggests a sluggish evolution through just two doctrinal generations.

Through most of recorded history, prevailing political powers employed *first generation* strategies that relied heavily on physical force. In this era, the fundamental objective of terrorizing — and thereby controlling — target populations frequently took precedence over the collection of operationally useful information.

The *second generation* of educing information emerged in the closing years of World War I, when the British director of military intelligence began to examine in earnest the need to obtain timely and reliable information from prisoners of war. From that beginning, the strategic interrogation programs developed by the German, British, and U.S. militaries during World War II established, in unprecedented fashion, that a potential treasure trove of information can be obtained from a systematic, outcome-oriented approach to interrogation that relied far more on finesse than on force.

As the impetus for building on this promising beginning began to fade shortly after the conclusion of World War II, the experience of U.S. soldiers held prisoner during the Cold War — especially during the Korean and Vietnam conflicts — gave rise to a new emphasis on designing strategies for resisting coercive methods of interrogation. As a result, the preponderance of U.S. government-sanctioned interrogation research focused on deconstructing coercive methods. The objective was to develop *defensive* strategies that would protect U.S. servicemen who faced the possibility of being held in foreign governmental detention and where they would be subject to prolonged exploitation.

---

[683] Sun Tzu, 77–78.

During this same period, the study of non-coercive interrogation methods to support intelligence collection received only modest interest. Interrogation tactics, techniques, and procedures established in the Cold War era fell short in building upon the legacy of World War II strategic interrogation operations. Instead, contemporary interrogation doctrine and training curricula were developed without the benefit of formal studies of the potential efficacy of *offensive interrogation*[684] methods. In sum, a considerable portion of "what we know" about interrogation — including approach methodology, the detection of deception, and reading body language — is in fact largely unsubstantiated. Thus, when the Global War on Terror focused us anew on devising offensive interrogation methods, the product was at times adulterated by the principles of coercive interrogation drawn from studies of Communist methodologies. As this war has continued, evidence of the employment of coercive methods by U.S. interrogators has appeared with alarming frequency.

The opportunity currently presents itself to make a transition to the next generation of educing information. The strategies that will form the foundation for the *third generation* of doctrine and practice for educing information will be driven by the need to overcome the barriers outlined in this paper. The effort should be characterized by the following considerations:

- Methods will be consistent with long-standing U.S. legal and moral traditions.

- Formal research will, whenever possible, seek to demonstrate the efficacy of methods in an operational setting.

- Institutions will recognize that the complexity of challenges in interrogation is on par with those of clandestine collection operations.

- Standards of conduct and formal vetting programs will be introduced to limit recruitment to those individuals best suited to dealing with the complexities and ambiguities of interrogation.

- The long-term examination of selected high-value sources will take place under exacting standards and be subject to appropriate oversight.

- Rigorous requirements for initial and ongoing training, accompanied by an unambiguous standard of ethics and practices, will introduce a new level of professionalism into the interrogation discipline.

The barriers to success in educing information, while formidable, are not insurmountable. That these barriers still confront us reflects not necessarily the complexity of the barriers per se, but rather the absence of a systematic effort to address them. In this regard, the words of Colin Powell, former Chairman of Joint

---

[684] The Joint Forces Command of the Department of Defense has labeled interrogation operations conducted for the purpose of collecting intelligence from foreign sources *offensive interrogation*, whereas resistance to interrogation is referred to as *defensive interrogation*.

Chiefs of Staff and Secretary of State, hold true: "There are no secrets to success. It is the result of preparation, hard work, and learning from failure."

8
Negotiation Theory and Practice: Exploring Ideas to Aid Information Eduction

Daniel L. Shapiro, Ph.D.[685]
Harvard University
February 2006

Abstract

Information eduction can be viewed as a complex set of negotiations. Government officials have information needs, and sources have information they can disclose. The challenge is to determine how the government can negotiate most effectively for that information. This report describes negotiation concepts that might assist the information educer.

The Field of Negotiation

Brief Background

The negotiation field offers little in the way of direct research into the challenge of educing information (EI) in an interrogation context. However, it is worth noting that the current field of negotiation theory, like that of EI, arose from necessity and has largely been tested in the trenches of practice. Game-theoretical analyses of negotiation, such as Nobel Laureate Thomas Schelling's *The Strategy of Conflict*, sought to curb escalating tensions in the Cold War. Interest-based negotiation, typified by the Harvard Negotiation Project's 1981 *Getting to Yes*, was developed in the context of the project's negotiations in the Iranian Hostage conflict, with guerrilla forces in Central and South America, and in the Israeli-Palestinian conflict. Walton and McKersie's seminal negotiation research (1965) was developed to reduce contentious labor negotiations. The negotiation work of Mary Parker Follett evolved from dissatisfaction with the way organizations dealt with difference (Follett, 1942). Scientific research in negotiation has been a more recent development, but tends to confirm earlier, practice-based theory (Thompson and Leonardelli, 2004).

---

[685] Dr. Shapiro is Associate Director of the Harvard Negotiation Project and on the faculty at Harvard Law School and Harvard Medical School. The author wishes to thank Robert Fein, Mary Rowe, Elizabeth Tippet, Roger Fisher, and the blind reviewers who offered feedback on previous drafts of this report.

This report, then, represents an effort to offer ideas from negotiation theory and practice to those who have responsibilities for developing and carrying out EI activities. The author has selected robust concepts that show promise for successful adaptation and use by an information educer. That being said, this report is clearly exploratory. Although the author has consulted with experts in the field of information eduction and was trained by the New York Police Department in hostage negotiation, his areas of expertise are negotiation, conflict resolution, and psychology, not EI. Thus, he leaves it to the judgment and creative thinking of national security officials to consider how the following ideas might be usefully applied or adapted to EI.

Why Negotiations Fail

There are at least four major reasons why parties fail to reach a satisfactory outcome even when such an outcome is possible. First, they commonly assume that negotiation involves a "fixed pie," in which any gain by one party is a loss for the other. This assumption can quickly turn an interaction into an adversarial contest and can constrain the parties' ability to explore creative ways of satisfying their interests. Second, many negotiators fail to use the most efficient means to divide the "pie" and obtain their portion. Typically, each party tries to persuade the other via a battle of wills, which often leads to stalemate. Third, negotiators often communicate a proposal — even a promising one — in a way that fails to maximize the likelihood that the other party will agree. Finally, negative emotions — anger, shame, embarrassment, anxiety, or others — can impede the negotiation.

This report summarizes strategies that address each of these common causes of negotiation failure:

1. *Assumption of "fixed pie?"* Use methods that expand the pie.
2. *Inefficient means?* Choose an efficient process to divide the pie.
3. *Poor framing?* Craft a "yesable proposition."
4. *Emotions getting in the way?* Improve the relationship with the other side — without giving in.

Expanding the Pie

Until the early 1980s, most popular negotiation texts considered negotiation a win-lose game, in which every gain made by one side comes at the expense of the other. Negotiation was generally seen as "positional bargaining," where representatives of each side would state their position, concede only stubbornly, or demonstrate a greater willingness than the other side to walk from the negotiation table. Negotiation scholars such as Roger Fisher and Robert McKersie recognized, however, that the pie need not be fixed. In most situations, the potential exists to create opportunities for mutual gain (Fisher, Ury, and Patton, 1991; Walton and McKersie, 1991).

Seeking mutual gains is not simply an act of compassion toward the other party: it is a wise move of self-interest. One of the most important revelations of game theory is that parties who seek to gain solely at the expense of the other side often risk worse outcomes than those who search for mutual gains. Consider the scenario of the "prisoner's dilemma," where two co-conspirators who committed a crime are locked in separate cells. If each independently decides to betray his partner in order to get a better deal for himself, both are convicted. If only one defects, the other is convicted. If both stay silent, both are acquitted. To evaluate the best strategy in a multi-round version of this dilemma, researchers organized a computer tournament and invited experts to submit a strategy. The winning strategy was "tit-for-tat" (Axelrod 1984), which instructed the computer to begin by cooperating but to respond in kind if the other side defected. In this highly adversarial context, conditional cooperation best served each individual's self-interest.

Similarly, in negotiation, seeking to expand the pie can serve the self-interest of both parties. Economic theory describes the relationship between individual and joint interest using the "Pareto curve" (Raiffa, 1982), illustrated on the next page, where the y axis represents party A's satisfaction with the outcome and the x axis represents party B's satisfaction. In a traditional bargaining situation, A and B each present an opening position that exclusively serves their own interests (denoted by the circles labeled "A's Position" and "B's Position"). If A and B agree to compromise by cutting their demands in half, they end up approximately at outcome Z, but outcome Z is suboptimal. If A and B had investigated mutual gains, they could have reached an agreement lying in the grey region, where either or both would have been individually better off than at Z. The curve on the graphic represents the limit on mutual gains. Any outcome lying on the curve is a "Pareto-optimal outcome" — an agreement that cannot be improved upon by either party without disadvantaging the other.

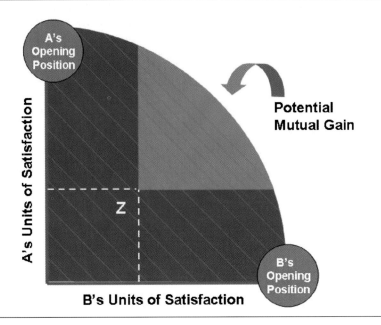

A's Opening Position

Potential Mutual Gain

A's Units of Satisfaction

Z

B's Opening Position

B's Units of Satisfaction

The Pareto Curve. Source: Roger Fisher and Bruce Patton, "The Pareto Frontier," in *Workbook for the Program of Instruction for Lawyers at Harvard Law School* (Cambridge, MA: Harvard Negotiation Project, 2006), 36.

Despite these insights of economists and game theoreticians, negotiators might persist and ask (with good reason): Why care about the *other's* interests? There are several reasons:

1. *A focus on mutual gains increases the incentive to cooperate* (Fisher and Shapiro, 2005). Parties will be less likely to cooperate if they do not see it as being in their interest to cooperate: why help the enemy?

2. *Mutual gains increase the likelihood that future interactions will be constructive* (Axelrod, 1984). Parties will be less likely to cooperate in the future if they have memories of feeling deceived or mistreated by the other party.

3. *An adversarial stance makes stalemate more likely.* If parties assume that the conflict is a win-lose situation, each is likely to stick to a position. As egos and negative emotions become increasingly involved, stalemate becomes a likely and stable outcome (Rubin, Pruitt, and Kim, 1994).

4. *"Mutual gains" does not mean giving in to the demands of the other side.* Pareto-optimal outcomes do not focus on each party's stated position, such as whether or not to give information, but on underlying interests, such as why the source does not want to give information.

In contrast to positional bargaining, "interest-based negotiation" proceeds on the assumption that negotiators often overlook opportunities for mutual gains, thereby failing to achieve the best outcome for themselves. [686] This is particularly true in negotiations that involve multiple issues, both quantitative and qualitative issues (e.g., desire for respect), and an interest in establishing a good working relationship.

Negotiation theory (e.g., Fisher, Ury, and Patton, 1991; Walton and McKersie, 1965) offers several strategies for expanding the pie.

Look beneath Positions for Interests

Positions are rigid solutions to the problems at hand (e.g., the United States should immediately withdraw all of its troops from Iraq). Interests are *why* a party wants those things (e.g., to prevent U.S. soldiers from being killed, to save money, to focus on other international threats).

In a negotiation, understanding the other side's interests enhances the power of a negotiator to persuade the other side. When one understands what the other side cares about, one can develop options that address these interests in ways that do not conflict with one's own interests. What is stopping them from cooperating? What do they care about? What do they want? Why? The author's experience in consulting for high-level governmental negotiators suggests that people often fail to consider the other side's interests sufficiently, thus reducing their power to influence their counterparts.

At first glance, an EI context would appear to be a purely positional situation. One side wants to gain information; the other does not want to disclose it. But each side has a more complex set of *interests* defining why each cares about the information. Interests for a source might include religious beliefs, a desire not to lose face within an organization, or fear of being ostracized by family, community, and peers. Interests for an educer might include national security, reputation in the local community, locating additional sources, relationships with governments, and precedent. Distinguishing between positions and interests may reveal potential sources of value creation.

Invent Options for Mutual Gain

Once parties understand each other's interests, they can invent options for mutual gain. Even where a value-creating option will not directly benefit our own interests, it increases the likelihood that the other side will accept our proposal.

Consider the recent conflict between Peru and Ecuador. The two countries disagreed over boundary issues and engaged in what the U.S. State Department called the "oldest armed conflict in the Western Hemisphere": each country

---

[686] Seven elements of negotiation comprise the essence of both hard bargaining and interest-based negotiation. These seven elements also form the basis of several of our negotiation courses at the Harvard Negotiation Project. The "Seven Elements" are a manageable number of robust concepts that one can use to prepare, conduct, and evaluate a negotiation. See the appendix for a description of each element and its contours in both hard bargaining and interest-based negotiation.

claimed that a piece of land in the Amazonian basin was legitimately theirs and theirs alone.

The Harvard Negotiation Project worked closely with President Jamil Mahuad as he negotiated a resolution to the dispute (see Fisher and Shapiro, 2005). A joint working group consisting of officials from both governments generated an option that adequately addressed each side's primary interests. The contested land would become an international park under the ownership of Ecuador and the sovereignty of Peru. No economic, political, or military activity could be conducted on the land without the agreement of both governments. This option allowed each party to reach a satisfactory resolution without giving in.

Identify Trade-offs

In a negotiation, differences are not always bad. Parties can look for different valuation of issues and trade accordingly. In its simplest form, if one person likes oranges more than apples, and the other likes apples more than oranges, a simple transfer of goods can maximize joint gains.

Parties can create contingency agreements to capitalize on differences in risk, expectations, and the like. ("If A happens, Party Y will do B and Party Z will do C.") Differences in the forecast of future events, for example, need not become stumbling blocks for agreement. Rather than fight over whose forecast is correct, parties can incorporate contingencies for each possible outcome into the agreement. Contingency agreements also can be effective if parties have different time preference or attitudes toward risk.

Unbundle One Issue into Many

If parties focus on a single issue, the negotiation risks becoming a distributional contest. Negotiation research suggests that one way to avoid a distributional contest is to "unbundle issues," transforming a single-issue, fixed-pie negotiation into a multi-issue negotiation where mutual gains can be reached (Lax and Sebenius, 1986; Thompson, 2005). For the educer, the question boils down to: How might the educer add new issues, unbundle issues, or otherwise expand the number of issues under discussion? What else does the source care about? How might those matters be incorporated into the current discussion? Putting more issues that the source cares about on the table may give the source more incentive to cooperate.

Similarly, *multiple simultaneous offers* can serve to break a deadlock (Bazerman and Neale, 1992; Kelley and Schenitzki, 1972). The offers should all be of equal value to the offering party to improve the likelihood of meeting one's own objectives without making concessions. Each offer should cover multiple issues to avoid the problem of sequential, tit-for-tat, haggling. All offers should be made at the same time, which allows the offering party to observe the other party's reaction, learn more about the other's interests, and, if an offer is accepted, reach a Pareto-optimal outcome.

Separate Inventing from Deciding

Negotiators often fear that if they invent options while the other party is present they will lock themselves into an unwise situation. For example, they may state an option that goes against their interests and the other party may hold them to the "offer." Thus, the interest-based negotiator separates inventing from deciding: both sides agree that no commitments will be made until a final package is formalized. The first task is to understand interests and invent options for mutual gain. At this stage, nothing is a commitment. Then, once a full set of options is generated, parties can refine options to best meet the interests of each side.

For example, the negotiation process used at the 1978 Camp David negotiations involved a clear separation between inventing and deciding. As mediator, the United States circulated numerous versions of a draft agreement to each side for review. Neither side was asked to make a commitment until the 23rd draft, when the United States determined that this was the best proposal that could be produced under the circumstances.

Dividing the Pie

No matter how much value parties create, they must still divide the pie to obtain what they want — whether that means land, money, or (in the case of the educer) information. The negotiation literature offers a number of strategies for increasing one's share of the distributional pie. These strategies can be divided into two categories: 1) moves that can be made at the negotiation table; and 2) moves away from the table (i.e., actions that can be taken independent of the other party). Each of these moves can influence the power dynamics of the negotiation.

Some strategies presented here might be rightly categorized as "contentious tactics" designed to get one's way at the other's expense (Rubin, Pruitt, and Kim, 1994). These strategies can provide an immediate distributional payoff, but they also increase the risk of damaging a relationship, escalating a conflict, or ending in stalemate (Axelrod, 1984; Rubin, Pruitt, and Kim, 1994). Thus, contentious tactics work best when only one issue is at stake, the issue is quantifiable, and the quality of the relationship is unimportant (Shapiro, 2000).

Strategic Moves at the Negotiation Table

Strategic moves at the negotiation table are actions intended to influence the distribution of the pie. Three such moves include drawing on standards of legitimacy, using "gamesmanship," and making threats.

Drawing on Standards of Legitimacy

Negotiations often turn into a battle of wills. Each side takes a position and demands that the other concede. This tends to lead to adversarial behavior, stalemate, or failed negotiation — even when agreement was reasonably possible for each side.

By drawing on "standards of legitimacy" (Fisher, Ury, and Patton, 1991), negotiators can improve their power to persuade and reduce the risk of a failed negotiation. Standards of legitimacy are external, objective criteria — independent of one's will or that of the other party — that can be used to persuade others that one option is more fair than another. Standards might be drawn from common practice, precedent, or the like. Rather than state "you must concede to our demands," a negotiator would offer standards of legitimacy — persuasive to each negotiator — for choosing one option over another. In the context of EI, standards of legitimacy might be drawn from religious, cultural, social, or related sources.

Using Gamesmanship

The point of gamesmanship is to "ruffle the feathers" of decisionmakers, throwing them off guard and making them increasingly willing to yield (Rubin, Pruitt, and Kim, 1994). Two such tactics include (1) changing or confusing the tempo of the discussion and (2) fostering a decisionmaker's feelings of incompetence, fluster, or personal doubt. In a classic book on gamesmanship, Potter writes about a tennis player who, after being served two or three aces running, ties his shoelace in a prolonged manner, blows his nose for an extended period, and wipes all signs of sweat off his forehead (Potter, 1948). This same tactic can, of course, be used in complicated negotiations.

The key to gamesmanship is to keep the decisionmaker blind to one's true intentions (Potter, 1948). The moment the manipulation becomes transparent, it becomes much less tactically promising. Thus, Potter wisely advises the gamesperson to "shield" his or her behavior behind a clear situational rationale. In the tennis example, the goal would be for the opponent to believe that the change in his or her fortune was due not to the change in the game's tempo, but to the player's change of racket or a variation in the wind.

Making Threats

Threats are messages about what we intend to do if the other person does not comply with our demand. The general structure of a threat is: "Unless you do X, I will hurt you."

Threats are appealing for several reasons (Rubin, Pruitt, and Kim, 1994). First, they impose no cost on the party making the threat. Indeed, as Thomas Schelling pointed out, where *brute force* may cause resistance in others, the *threat* of such force may succeed (1966). Second, threats have been experimentally shown to work — often better than promises. Experimental evidence suggests that threats are a credible form of influence (e.g., see Pruitt and Carnevale, 1993; Rubin and Brown, 1975). Third, a threat can be withdrawn without incurring cost. A person who withdraws a promise may be looked upon as untrustworthy, but a person who withdraws a threat can be seen as humane. (In either case, however, judgments still may be made about the person's credibility.)

At the same time, threats carry one great risk: the counterthreat. A threat tends to elicit reciprocal action in the other person. As early as 1960, experimental research showed that threats lead to increased suspicion, resentment, and dislike, in turn making counterthreats more likely (Deutsch and Krauss, 1960).

Actions Away From the Negotiation Table

A second class of distributional moves is conducted away from the table, independent of interaction with the other party. If used effectively, these moves can significantly enhance a negotiator's power. Two such moves include improving one's "BATNA" and making irrevocable commitments.

Improving Your BATNA

Negotiation power is largely defined by the strength of one's alternatives to negotiating. If negotiations with a counterpart should fail, what is one's walk-away alternative? The best alternative is known as the BATNA — *Best Alternative To a Negotiated Agreement* (Fisher, Ury, and Patton, 1991). The better one's BATNA, the more power one has in a negotiation. It becomes easier to negotiate with confidence, or to walk away from the negotiation without feeling confined by the other party's demands.

Negotiators can improve their BATNA by thinking carefully about it and by brainstorming possible alternatives. Ultimately, a negotiator may decide that his or her BATNA is not especially strong, an important realization that gives the negotiator additional incentive to negotiate carefully and effectively, perhaps accommodating more than would generally be wise.

Making an educated guess about the other side's BATNA can help a negotiator understand how strongly motivated the other party will be to reach agreement. If their BATNA is poor, they might be amenable to many options. If their BATNA is strong, they might decide to stand firm to reap maximal concessions. Sometimes parties overestimate their BATNA; to improve leverage in this type of situation, a negotiator might cast doubt on the strength of the other's BATNA.

Negotiators often use time pressure to influence the behavior of another party, yet this is only persuasive if the other party's BATNA would worsen after the deadline passes. If the BATNA is strong, time pressure is minimally persuasive. Negotiators who use time pressure would also be well advised to keep their own BATNA in mind, since a deadline for the other is also a deadline for themselves.

Making Irrevocable Commitments

Threats suggest a future action that one might take if the other party does not comply with one's demands. In contrast, an *irrevocable commitment* involves an action that we have already begun (Rubin, Pruitt, and Kim, 1994). To avoid being hurt by the action, the other party must change behavior. Schelling uses the hypothetical example of two drivers speeding toward one another in a game of "chicken," each testing who will swerve off the road first. A driver could throw the steering wheel out the window in full view of the other, thus creating an irrevocable commitment (Schelling, 1960).

With an irrevocable commitment, the locus of control shifts from the actor to the respondent, who now has the ability to stop an unwelcome event from happening. For this reason, it is advisable that an educer using "irrevocable" commitments actually have some way of reversing them, since it is quite possible that the other party will refuse to act. In the game of chicken, for example, the driver who supposedly threw the steering wheel out of the window might have thrown a replica — and kept the real wheel out of view of the other driver.

Crafting a "Yesable Proposition"

Even when a negotiator has developed a good proposal that creates value and distributes that value effectively, parties can fail to reach agreement because of the manner in which the proposal is framed.

The Power of Framing

Framing can have a subtle but powerful impact on how the other side perceives a proposal. For example, studies have found that negotiators instructed to "minimize losses" rather than "maximize gains" were less likely to make concessions, reach agreement, and view the resulting agreement as fair (Bazerman, Magliozzi, and Neale, 1985; Neale and Northcraft, 1986; Neale, Huber, and Northcraft, 1987).

The context in which a decision is framed can also affect how it is perceived. One study found that participants would be willing to walk two blocks to save $30 on a $70 watch, but not willing to walk that same distance to save $30 on an $800 camera (Russo and Schoemaker 1989). Thirty dollars seems like a great deal of money when compared to $70, but like a drop in the bucket when compared to $800.

The identity of the person making the offer also influences its reception. A study by Bazerman and Neale found that participants would be willing to pay more for a bottle of beer they were told came from a fancy resort than for exactly the same bottle supposedly from a run-down grocery store. Participants assumed that the grocery store beer "is an obvious rip-off" (1992). Thus, it is important to consider both who presents the offer and how it is presented.

Framing a "Yesable" Proposition

Ultimately, the question to ask is: What proposal would give the other side an option they might accept? The choice would have to address their interests sufficiently, be realistic, and be operational. By having a good sense of the other party's interests and BATNA, a negotiator can craft such an offer, which is called a "yesable proposition" (Fisher, Kopelman, and Schneider, 1994): it requires only a "yes" in response.

Rather than confronting the other party with a problem, a yesable proposition gives them an appealing offer. Consider a simple example. President Lyndon Johnson instructed his staff to attach a proposal, and a set of boxes for him to check "yes," "no," or "see me," to any memo that crossed his desk. Johnson understood the idea behind a yesable proposition: he required his staff to bring him not only a problem, but also a suggestion for what could be done.

Two tools are useful in developing a yesable proposition: the *Currently Perceived Choice chart* and the *Target Future Choice chart*.

Currently Perceived Choice (CPC) chart

The Currently Perceived Choice (CPC) chart provides an easy way to assess how the other side might perceive the offer currently on the table (Fisher, Kopelman, and Schneider, 1994). Using the chart, negotiators can clarify whom they are trying to influence, what decisions the other person faces, and the pros and cons of the decision from that person's perspective. For example, the table below illustrates how Iraqi President Saddam Hussein might have perceived his choices about whether or not to withdraw Iraqi troops from Kuwait in 1991. As the chart makes clear, there were good reasons why he refused. (Whether we agree with his motivation and behavior is another issue altogether.)

Case: Saddam Hussein, Early February 1991
"Shall I now say I will withdraw from Kuwait?"

Consequences if I say YES	Consequences if I say NO
– The bombing may continue	+ I stand up to the United States
– The blockade may continue	+ I keep my options open for better terms from the U.N
– I yield to a U.S. ultimatum	+ I can fight indefinitely and hope to outlast the United States
– Israel may still attack as retaliation for the Scud missile	+ I can always agree later
– I look weak	+ I look strong
– I lose credibility in the Arab world	+ I am a hero to many Arabs
– The United States will make new demands such as compensate Kuwait, compensate hostages, destroy Iraqi military, change the regime, accept war crimes trial	+ I can continue to defy Western will by creating more oil spills and setting the Gulf on fire
– I may be hanged as a war criminal	+ Dying a martyr is better than dying a war criminal
	BUT – The war and blockade may continue

Currently Perceived Choice Chart. Source: Derived by the author from Roger Fisher and others, "How Do You End a War?," *The Boston Globe*, 8 February 1991.

Because negotiators rarely represent only their individual interests, they must consider not only how the other side will perceive a particular proposal but also how their constituencies would view the outcome (Mnookin, Peppet, and Tulumello, 2000). Even seemingly irrational actors such as Saddam Hussein play to constituents. Framing a proposal in a way that allows the other side to save face or, better yet, improve their standing with their constituency, can increase the likelihood that it will be accepted.

Target Future Choice Chart (TFC)

A related tool, the Target Future Choice (TFC) chart, can help to identify how the other side might perceive a proposal in order to accept it. To derive such a target future choice, the negotiator must work backwards, initially defining the consequences believed to be necessary for the decision maker to say yes rather than no (Fisher, Kopelman, and Schneider, 1994). The table below illustrates the basic elements of a persuasive target future choice.

General Example
"Shall I now accept the X plan?"

Consequences if I say YES	Consequences if I say NO
+ My personal standing is secure	– I will be subjected to some criticism
+ I can easily justify the decision to my constituents	– The problem will not go away
+ I will not be seen as backing down	– It is likely to get worse
+ The action is reasonably consistent with our principles and past statements	– I will miss a fading opportunity
+ It will not set a bad precedent	
+ All things considered, it is a constructive step for dealing with this problem	
+ We still keep many of our future options open	
BUT – Some hardliners will criticize me	**BUT** + Some hardliners will no doubt support me

Future Target Choice of a Decision Maker. Source: Roger Fisher and others, *Beyond Machiavelli: Tools for Coping with Conflict* (Boston: Harvard University Press, 1994), 58. Reprinted by permission of the publisher.

A well-framed offer allows the decision maker to understand both the benefits of accepting the proposal immediately and the costs of inaction (for instance, as a result of missing a deadline by which the offer had to be accepted). An offer can be made more appealing if it is partially implemented from the outset. Car salespeople use this technique all the time when they offer a customer a car and hand him or her the keys to hold.

Improving the Negotiating Relationship

During a negotiation, negative emotions can get in the way of easy two-way communication. Negative emotions are often products of an adversarial relational structure between parties. In recent years, researchers have made significant strides in understanding the structure of negotiating relationships and how to shape those relationships to enable Pareto-optimal outcomes. As a result, negotiators have new tools to elicit emotions that can serve their negotiating purpose.

One major advance has been to link the concepts of identity and relationship. In any negotiating relationship, people care about their perceived identity vis-à-vis their negotiating counterpart (i.e., "what I think others think about me"). In this sense, a negotiator's identity is largely relational (Shapiro, 2002): people interact differently with different people. In a relationship with an aggressive person a negotiator may feel tense and resentful, and thus act in certain ways to spite the other person. In a relationship with a soft-spoken person, that same negotiator may feel emotions of connection and act in ways that support the relationship. This insight — that the structure of the interaction shapes each negotiator's identity — has important practical consequences.

One's Relational Identity Can Constrain or Facilitate a Good Outcome

One's negotiating purpose is not always served by one's "relational identity" (Shapiro, 2002). Nor is one's negotiating purpose always served by the resulting emotional, cognitive, and behavioral consequences for each party. A negotiator may fail to speak up when it would be wise to do so, or may act more cautiously than suits his or her interests.

By understanding the dimensions that comprise relational identity, negotiators can better calibrate behavior to best serve their negotiating purpose. One's "relational identity" consists of two main dimensions: autonomy and affiliation (see Shapiro 2002 for a review of research on these dimensions). *Autonomy* is the freedom to make a decision without that decision's being imposed (Averill and Nunley, 1992; Fisher and Shapiro, 2005). Research suggests that constrained autonomy leads to resistance, negative emotions, and a lack of cooperation (Brehm, 1966; Fisher and Shapiro, 2005). One explanation for why sources resist disclosing information is that they feel that demands to reveal information impinge upon their autonomy. *Affiliation* is a sense of personal connection, the opposite of rejection. A party who feels rejected is likely to resist cooperation. The feeling of rejection, in fact, stimulates the same part of the brain as physical pain (Eisenberger, N., Lieberman, M., and Williams, K., 2003), which helps to explain why trivial acts of exclusion often elicit strong emotional responses from the excluded party. Conversely, a positive affiliation tends to stimulate positive emotions and mutual cooperation.

Capitalizing on People's Emotional Reactions

Research suggests that positive emotions have particular utility in a negotiation (See Fisher and Shapiro, 2005). They improve the likelihood of a Pareto-optimal agreement; they expand people's ability to trust and to think creatively; they improve the likelihood of a stable agreement; and they make open communication easier and more likely.

How can a negotiator capitalize on the power of emotions? In the book *Beyond Reason: Using Emotions as You Negotiate*, Fisher and Shapiro offer five "core concerns" that can be used to stimulate positive emotions: autonomy, affiliation, appreciation, status, and role. These five core concerns represent a practical expansion of the relational identity framework discussed above. Each concern can be used to build rapport and stimulate positive emotions, thus encouraging cooperative behavior. The actions that correlate with each core concern are, in simple form: (1) respect the other's autonomy, (2) build affiliation, (3) express appreciation, (4) acknowledge status where merited, and (5) help parties build a fulfilling role. A significant amount of research has substantiated each of these actions (e.g., see Fisher and Shapiro, 2005).

Using Emotions Does Not Mean Acquiescing

Some people argue that enlisting positive emotions into a negotiation will put a negotiator at a disadvantage. Common fears are that the negotiator will look weak and submissive or will be more inclined to "give in" to the demands of the other party. These are serious concerns. However, these problems are reduced significantly for the skilled negotiator who uses not only emotions, but also the tools of reasoning to make wise decisions. For example, the skilled negotiator will not agree to a decision that departs from some standard of legitimacy, as discussed earlier in this paper.

Summary

This paper provides an overview of some of the key strategic approaches to negotiation that an information educer might adapt for use: expanding the pie, dividing the pie, framing an offer, and improving the negotiating relationship. The author leaves open the question of tailoring these strategies to the challenging circumstances of information eduction and would welcome the opportunity to explore such topics with experts in the field.

Appendix

Contrasting Approaches to Negotiation: Adversarial vs. Interest-based

ELEMENT	ADVERSARIAL	INTEREST-BASED
Alternatives	Threaten to inflict pain *"Talk, or else!"*	Improve your *Best Alternative To* a *Negotiated Agreement* (BATNA) Weaken their BATNA *"You have a choice. I'd like to talk openly about things with you. And I've got a colleague just outside this door waiting to go a different route. I don't want that. It's your choice."*
Interests	Debate over *positions* *"I will not tell you anything."* *"Yes, you will!"*	Look beneath positions to interests *"What's holding you back from giving us information?"*
Options	Bargain over two options: whether or not the source will tell you information	Invent multiple options without evaluating them
Legitimacy	Battle of wills "Tell us what you know." "No." "We *demand* you tell us." "NO!"	Persuade on the basis of external standards of legitimacy *The basic message:* *"There are legitimate reasons why you can reveal information to us…"*

(Continued on next page)

Commitments	Commit to telling *no* or minimal information	Consider the "4 Ps" : What is our *purpose* for negotiating, what is an efficient *process*, who are the relevant *people* to include, and what is our desired *product*? To what can we realistically and practically commit?

Commitments	Talk *at* one another
	    "We will tell you
	    what to tell us.
	    And you had
	    better tell us!"
		Talk *with* one another
		    What questions can
		    we ask to learn more?
		    How can we ask open
		    questions rather than
		    presumptive, closed-
		    ended questions?

Relationship	Treat one another as adversaries
	    From educer's
	    perspective:
	    Interrogator vs.
	    accused
	
	    From source's
	    perspective:
	    harasser vs.
	    victim
		Treat one another as joint problem solvers
		    "We have a shared
		    problem. Let's think
		    through how to deal
		    with this. The more
		    we are able to work
		    together, the sooner
		    both of us can go home."

Works Cited

Argyris, C. (1990). *Overcoming Organizational Defenses*. New York: Prentice Hall, especially 88-89.

Averill, J. R., and Nunley, E. P. (1992). *Voyages of the Heart: Living an Emotionally Creative Life*. New York: The Free Press.

Axelrod, R (1984). *The Evolution of Cooperation*. New York: Basic Books.

Bazerman, M.H., Magliozzi, T., and Neale, M. (1985). "Integrative Bargaining in a Competitive Market." *Organizational Behavior and Human Decision Process* 35 (3), 294–313.

Bazerman, M., and Neale, M. (1992). *Negotiating Rationally*. New York: Free Press.

Brehm, J.W. (1966). *A Theory of Psychological Reactance*. New York: Academic Press.

Deutsch, M., and Krauss, R.M. (1960). "The Effect of Threat upon Interpersonal Bargaining." *Journal of Abnormal and Social Psychology* 61, 181–189.

Eisenberger, N., Lieberman, M., and Williams, K. (2003). "Does Rejection Hurt: An FMRI Study of Social Exclusion." *Science* 302, 10 October, 237-239.

Fisher, R., Kopelman, E., and Schneider, A.K. (1994). *Beyond Machiavelli: Tools for Coping with Conflict*. Boston: Harvard University Press, 1994.

Fisher, R., Kupfer, A., and Stone, D. (1991). "How Do You End a War?," *The Boston Globe*, 8 February.

Fisher, R. and Shapiro, D.L. (2005). *Beyond Reason: Using Emotions as You Negotiate*. New York: Viking/Penguin.

Fisher, R. and Ury, W., and Patton, B. (1991). *Getting to Yes: Negotiating Agreement Without Giving In*. 2nd edition. New York: Penguin.

Follett, M.P. (1942). *Dynamic Administration: The Collected Papers of Mary Parker Follett*. H.C. Metcalf and L. Urwick, eds. New York: Harper.

Kahneman, D., and Tversky, A. (1979). "Prospect Theory: An Analysis of Decision under Risk." *Econometrica* 47, 263–291.

Kelley, H. H., and Schenitzki, D. P. (1972). "Bargaining." In C.G. McClintock, ed., *Experimental Social Psychology*. New York: Holt, Rinehart, and Winston, 298–337.

Lax, D.A. and Sebenius, J.K. (1986). *The Manager as Negotiator*. New York: Free Press.

Mnookin, Peppet and Tulumello. (2000). *Beyond Winning: Negotiating to Create Values in Deals and Disputes*. Cambridge: Harvard University Press.

Neale, M.A., Huber, V.L., and Northcraft, G. (1987). "The Framing of Negotiations: Contextual Versus Frames." *Organizational Behavior and Human Decision Processes* 39 (2), 228–241.

Neale, M.A., and Northcraft, G. (1986). "Experts, Amateurs, and Refrigerators: Comparing Expert and Amateur Negotiators in a Novel Task." *Organizational Behavior and Human Decision Processes* 38, 305–317.

Potter, S. (1948). *The Theory and Practice of Gamesmanship: The Art of Winning Games without Actually Cheating*. New York: Holt.

Pruitt, D.G., and Carnevale, P.J. (1993). *Negotiation in Social Conflict*. Buckingham, UK: Open University Press.

Raiffa, H. (1982). *The Art and Science of Negotiation*. Cambridge: Harvard University Press.

Rubin, J.Z., and Brown, B.R. (1975). *The Social Psychology of Bargaining and Negotiation*. New York: Academic Press.

Rubin, J.Z., Pruitt, D.G. and Kim, S.H. (1994). *Social Conflict: Escalation, Stalemate, and Settlement*. New York: McGraw Hill.

Russo, J.E. and Schoemaker, P.J. (1989). *Decision Traps*. New York: Doubleday.

Shapiro, D.L. (2000). "Supplemental Joint Brainstorming: Navigating Past the Perils of Bargaining." *Negotiation Journal* 16 (4), 409–419.

Shapiro, D.L. (2002). "Negotiating Emotions." *Conflict Resolution Quarterly* 20 (1): 67-82.

Stone, D., Patton, B., and Heen, S. (1999). *Difficult Conversations: How to Discuss What Matters Most*. New York: Viking.

Thompson, L. (2005). *The Mind and Heart of the Negotiator*, 3rd edition. Upper Saddle River, NJ: Pearson Prentice Hall.

Thompson, L, and Leonardelli, G. (2004). "The Big Bang: The Evolution of Negotiation Research." *The Academy of Management: Executive* 18 (3), 113–117.

Walton, Richard E. and McKersie, Robert B. (1991). *A Behavioral Theory of Labor Negotiation: An Analysis of a Social Interaction System*, 2nd edition. Ithaca, N.Y.: ILR Press. Reprint, with new introduction. Originally published: New York: McGraw-Hill, 1965.

9
Negotiation Theory and Educing Information: Practical Concepts and Tools

M.P. Rowe, Ph.D.
February 2006

Abstract

Negotiation theory represents a systematic way of thinking by which one can understand and plan for all human interactions – including educing information (EI). This paper offers basic tools from negotiation theory for possible discussion by those concerned with EI. We briefly present several standard ideas: a discussion of different possible strategies for EI, a brief discussion of the sources of power available to educers and sources, and then suggestions about preparation for EI. (Educers may already be using the ideas included here.)

This paper offers standard ideas generated by individuals who have extensive experience in difficult interpersonal negotiations but no experience in EI. Our overview of one way to think about preparing for EI includes:

- Taking note of the relevant parties whose interests are at stake;
- Discovering – or at least developing working hypotheses about – the tangible and intangible interests of each party;
- Evaluating the sources of power available to each side in EI;
- Developing relevant options for interrogation and "fallback" options;
- Planning strategy, style, and sequencing of tactics with the EI team;
- Planning the role of each member of a team (for example, intake and preliminary assessment, interrogation, analysis behind the scenes, integration of data into and from the relevant intelligence community database, ongoing evaluation and guidance to educers and to the users of information, and collection of records that can be analyzed for improved knowledge and practice).

Introduction

Any interaction between two or more points of view can be seen and analyzed as a "negotiation."

Negotiation includes personal and professional interactions — for example, one can theoretically even "negotiate with oneself." Applying the tools of negotiation theory can make almost all human interactions more effective. We offer some standard ideas in negotiation theory to those concerned with educing information (EI), in the hope that *these tools may help in eliciting useful and accurate information from a source.*[687]

Negotiation theory encompasses far more than the tools presented here. Other aspects that might also be pursued include the role of emotions, the role of "constituencies" on each side, the use of coalitions by each side, the use of implicit and explicit threats, the theory and practice of "sequencing" tactics, etc.

Little, if any, operationally useful negotiation literature relates to educing information from uncooperative sources. EI "negotiations" in any case fall outside the usual purview of negotiations experts. Parties involved in EI may have very different interests, sets of knowledge or lack of knowledge, and perceptions of what is important and even what is real: in short, wide differences in culture as well as language. The interaction may involve one or more translators. In some cases even the identity and first language of a source may be unknown. Each side may be away from home and under great stress. Sources may be highly dissimilar, which may add to the challenge of building expertise in EI. The patterns of power and powerlessness of each of the parties in EI interactions, as identified in "negotiations" terms below, may appear unusual for both parties. (As an example, a detained source may seem "powerless," but a source who is prepared to commit suicide has a very powerful last resort or "fallback" position. In addition, if the need for information is very urgent and the United States has a tight deadline, the U.S. interrogator has less negotiating power.)

The contributors to this paper have extensive experience with the theory and practice of negotiation, but no actual experience or firsthand knowledge of U.S. interrogation practices and activities. This paper therefore simply offers ideas from negotiation theory and experience for possible discussion by people concerned with EI activities and EI research.

The paper does not prescribe any one "negotiation strategy" for EI. It sets forth a "negotiations way of thinking" about EI: a way of thinking that, in fact, considers many strategies. (This way of thinking may — or may not — have been used intuitively by individuals in intelligence, military, or law enforcement communities who conduct interviews and interrogations with detained persons.) We present some standard tools in negotiation theory and then apply them to the

---

[687] We will use the term "sources" (or "detainees") to indicate persons from whom information is sought, and use male pronouns on the assumption that most are male.

idea of preparation for EI, in the hope that the ideas may help in eliciting useful and accurate information.

This paper addresses three imperatives, each discussed in a separate section.

- **Consider *Multiple* Strategies**: It would appear that U.S. interests require preparing to use more than one "strategy" in EI. A single strategy, like trying physically to force a source to talk or trying only to buy information, is not likely to be effective in negotiations. Tactics and strategies can be developed *uniquely for each source, with a menu or sequence of options relevant to that person*, rather than "trying" tactics on an unplanned basis. This section lays out a way of thinking about strategies.

- **Analyze Sources of Power**: Analysis of the "sources of power available to each party in negotiations" may be helpful. As mentioned above, sources may have considerable, sometimes unanticipated, power in an EI negotiation. The United States, however, may be able to develop power in EI, for example, by pulling together many sources of information, by preparation and expertise in interrogation, by building credibility, and even by "recruitment" of sources who can provide information.

- **Prepare, Prepare, Prepare — for Each Source**: In this section we apply the theoretical ideas presented earlier. Negotiation theory suggests that it would be important for an educer to learn as much as possible about 1) specific information needed by the United States, and also the interests of relevant persons on the U.S. side, and 2) the individual source, his likely knowledge and sensibilities, and how he might contribute, and also about his individual interests. The interests of each side will include *tangibles* and *intangibles*.

Strategies in Negotiation

To lay the groundwork for thinking about negotiation and EI, we discuss a range of negotiation strategies. Some of these strategies are intended positively; others are punitive. Positive strategies include both competition and collaboration (which is a search for "joint gains"). Punitive strategies, on the other hand, intend injury to another person or intend injury to oneself. The distinction is important for EI. The goal of EI is to get accurate and useful information to serve U.S. interests, which may often be possible with "positive" strategies. The immediate goal of negative strategies is to injure the other party, which is not the goal of EI.

Positive Strategies

Negotiation theory has traditionally included a scheme of five possible strategies for conduct of interpersonal and business interactions: competition, collaboration, accommodation, compromise, and avoidance. We call these strategies "positive" because none is specifically intended to harm another person. In teaching about negotiations, these strategies are often introduced with a famous (imaginary) situation in which two persons, A and B, are fighting over a single orange. Both take the "*position*" that they must have the whole orange. We are first told that A and B have construed the interaction as a zero sum game, where the gain of one is the loss of the other. For readers who think graphically, this situation is illustrated by the following graphs.[688]

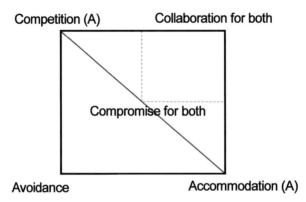

Competition (A)   Collaboration for both

Compromise for both

Avoidance   Accommodation (A)

The graph is labeled to represent the perspective of person A. At the *competition* point, A gets the whole orange. At A's *accommodation* point, B gets the whole orange. (A's accommodation point would be B's competition point if the graph were labeled from the perspective of B). The orange is split equally between the two at the *compromise* point (see dotted lines showing how much of the orange goes to A and how much to B).

To illustrate the meaning of the *collaboration* point, the story changes to illustrate that *two people may not actually want exactly the same thing.* We are now told that A in fact wanted the orange peel for a cake, and B wanted the juice of the orange; therefore, both could get all of what they wanted once they dropped their *positions* and discovered their real "*interests.*" In negotiation theory the word "interests" has come to mean the whole set of tangibles and intangibles that an individual actually wants in an interaction. *Interests are both short-term and long-term in nature, and they may also change in the course of a negotiation.* It is rare for two sides to consider only "one and the same" interest, so there is often room for some degree of collaboration. Collaboration may work for both, *whether they like each other or not.*

Tangibles

Negotiation strategies are often wrongly presumed to be only about "tangible things" of value, often discussed as a "pie." (Will I try to take the whole pie? Can I expand the pie by finding things in addition to the pie on the table — things that

---

[688] The first and second graphs which follow are adapted from the work of Kenneth W. Thomas, "Conflict and Conflict Management," in the *Handbook of Industrial and Organizational Psychology*, ed. Marvin Dunnette (Chicago: Rand McNally, 1976). The specific construction of these graphs and the adaptation included as the third graph are the work of the present author. The seminal work on strategies in negotiations that underlies the presentation in this paper is that of R.E. Walton and R.B. McKersie, *A Behavioral Theory of Labor Negotiations: An Analysis of a Social Interaction System* (New York: McGraw-Hill, 1965).

will be of value to the other person — and thus be able to share more value? Give up the pie? Split the pie 50:50?) Negotiations are sometimes inappropriately seen as a "game" or as "war," therefore about winning and losing — and about winning or losing things.

Intangibles

In fact many negotiations are about respect, information, the wish to be "heard," expertise, access to friends or colleagues, the long-term reputation of a person or country, etc. The interaction between the negotiators itself often becomes — for good or ill — an intangible "part of" a negotiation. For example, a person may feel respected or disrespected in a way that influences the outcome in a first encounter and over the long term. In an EI case, the educer could possibly prompt more cooperation by invoking intangibles, and can certainly make matters worse by arousing more hatred. (The educer could make the situation worse in the short term, with one source, or in the long term, with everyone who identifies with the source.)

It follows that in planning an EI strategy negotiators might also wish to plan their *style*. Because negotiators may exhibit a style that is interpreted differently than they intend, this topic requires planning as well as training, self-discipline, and practice as a negotiations professional.

One might sometimes plan a style that is not the same as the strategy. For example, the negotiator might feel very unfriendly toward a given source but decide to treat the person with "strategic" or "purposeful" respect. In fact, much training in negotiations emphasizes the importance of preparing to behave strategically in a way that conveys respect (or behaving in a way that is perceived as respectful), which is seen as an "intangible" interest of likely value to the recipient and one that the negotiator can offer at little or no cost.

It is in fact hard to imagine circumstances where it is theoretically sound to plan to humiliate a source, at least if there is ever to be more than one meeting with that person. Negotiation theory and practice suggest that deliberate humiliation is a potent cause of destructive and vengeful motivations and behavior — for an individual source and for all those who identify with him. Thus, even where the strategy is that of "forcing" a source, or putting him in fear, it does not follow that it is wise to do so disrespectfully or in a manner calculated to humiliate him. *Humiliation is not the same as forcing someone to do something.* Experience suggests that humiliation causes many people to develop deeper rage and hatred than physical pain does. *Before considering authorization of humiliation as a tactic in EI, it would be worthwhile to find out if any convincing research evidence attests to the effectiveness of this tactic.*

Interests vs. Positions

The story of the orange illustrates the reality that the "*interests*" of different people, as opposed to their "*positions*," may differ in ways that permit collaborative solutions that benefit both A and B more than the results of pure competition. As another example, A and B might each present the same initial "*position*" about a house, namely, that they want to settle, by June 1, on A's sale (and B's purchase) of A's house. If they share their *interests* about the timing of the sale, and discover that A wants to move the furniture on September 1 and that B does not really want to occupy the house until September 5, they can find a collaborative solution that is better for both of them than a June 1 purchase and sale. Each has the security of an agreement that the house will be sold (or available), and each will be happier during the summer. Each has gained something tangible and something intangible, *whether they like or dislike each other.*

On the graph below, the dotted line box includes solutions that are better than a compromise for *both* A and B in a negotiation between them. These include possible trade-offs between things that A wants and some different things that B wants. *Collaborative solutions, where there are "joint gains," depend on A and B wanting somewhat different things so that the negotiation need not be a zero sum (win-lose) game.* Most human interactions are not a zero sum (win-lose) game, indeed not a "game" at all. In the realm of EI, for example, the United States wants information. There may be tangibles or intangibles of interest to the source that would permit a trade for information, *whether we like or despise this person.*

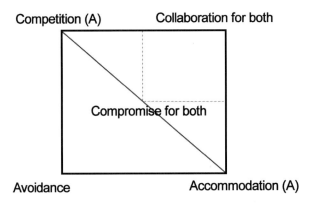

Competition (A)　　　　　Collaboration for both

Compromise for both

Avoidance　　　　　Accommodation (A)

Moving Among the Positive Strategies

Negotiation theory suggests that A may interact with B in any — *and often all* — of five ways in any one negotiation. Much of negotiation theory and considerable research have focused on these five strategies, sometimes looking at them separately (e.g., *Getting to Yes* or *Win All You Can*). However, there are very few negotiations where one would choose — or even be able — to employ only one strategy. Most well-planned negotiations include a mix of strategies.

Most negotiations involve elements of *competition* (I want to stake out my requirements early here and I may demand a bit extra for "bargaining room"), some *collaboration* (I would like to hear your interests and see if there is some way to meet them), some *avoidance* (Some conflicts are not worth thinking about, at least not right now), some *accommodation* (I am happy just to let you have what you want on that point) and a good deal of *compromise* (At the end of the day, let us just split the difference). Much theoretical work in negotiation centers on managing the important tension between competition and collaboration (Do I want to try to get as much as I can in just one brief encounter, or is there short- or long-term value in building some degree of credibility for future, operationally useful interactions with the other person?)

In most negotiations, as in most human interactions, it is important to have the ability to move back and forth from collaborative phases to competitive phases and vice versa. The circumstances in which one might rationally pursue a *purely competitive* strategy would be:

- One knows one will never see the other person, or anyone from his "tribe," again, and

- One believes that it is actually possible to meet one's own interests, using only competitive tactics, in one interaction or time period, and

- There is nothing else that might later be gained in future interactions with the person or his "tribe."

These circumstances are rare. In real life one usually sees the other person again, or one sees his fellow countrymen. It is rare to have no long-term interests and to obtain all of what one wants in one interaction. Pure (win-lose) competition on its own is usually not "rational"; one needs to be able to combine and move among strategies.

We can look at the task of EI through this lens. The purpose of EI is for one party — the United States — to gain accurate and useful information from the other party — the source. If the source does not want to give part or all of this information (a point that the interrogator cannot know before the negotiation begins) then this EI appears to be a *competitive* situation. It might, however, be possible to begin with some *compromise* elements, for example by asking first about matters that are relatively easy for the source to discuss. Moreover, the source might be willing to give information that does not threaten his own interests — an *accommodative* possibility on his part that should be explored early and throughout the process of EI. And we have just begun the analysis.

May there be something to trade, such as creature comforts, the circumstances of the EI, "respectful listening," or plans for release? Are there large or small *collaborative* possibilities involving the source's family, friends, or future plans? Can the United States possibly recruit this source for the future?

We will not know unless we begin to learn the relevant interests of the parties — a task which is required *for all strategies*. Some information about the interests of the source may be available from a central database. Learning the interests of a source on the spot is most likely to happen through a process that negotiation theory calls "building trust" or "relationship." In the context of EI this might mean building a "strategically useful connection," credibility, and believability, perhaps by members of the EI team as well as by the individual educer.

Negative Strategies

The practice of negotiation can also involve negative strategies, which include the intention to injure the other person. U.S. interests in EI are to *obtain information, rather than to harm* the source. However, the real interests of the source may be to harm the United States and its representatives — and in so doing he might even accept injury to himself or even affirmatively *wish* to be harmed.

Dealing with the possibility that an individual source intends harm to the United States is particularly complicated, in part because we do not know what a specific person intends until we design and implement a plan to find out — or until the person acts. But even where the source is focused on harming the United States, it does not follow that a reciprocal, negative strategy on the part of the United States will be an effective way to acquire useful information from him.

There has been little research on how to convince an individual B, who wishes to injure A, to become willing to collaborate (especially when B is willing to accept or even seek injury to himself). Convincing a person to relinquish vengeful interests, or to override the desire for revenge, is difficult. This is in part because the wish to injure often derives from *intangibles,* and especially from perceived humiliation. (*My people and I have been humiliated. The United States is a sinful state that must be brought to its knees. God wishes me to take revenge on His enemies.*)

Tangible losses can sometimes be dealt with more easily, by providing tangible incentives to cooperate. If someone is "tangibly" harmed (*I hit his car*) it may be relatively easy to negotiate a restitution with money. If someone is *emotionally* harmed, or believes that someone close to him has been harmed or humiliated, the path to dealing with that person's "real interests" may be more complicated, and it may be impossible to "buy him off" with money or creature comforts.

In addition, much of negotiations research has dealt with "tangible things of positive value," whereas wanting to injure someone or a nation is an intangible (hard to see, understand, label, discuss, and quantify) and lies in a negative zone. Thus, convincing a vengeful person to cooperate may require a change of attitude on his part, all the way from very negative to positive, and may call for offering intangibles of value. The next figure illustrates this graphically:

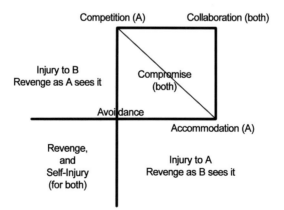

Nevertheless, we know anecdotally that it is not impossible to convince another person to change at least a little, even from a negative strategy, usually by causing that person to doubt much of what he thought he knew (in this case before capture). This would make it all the more important for the United States to use trained educers who could plan (with their team) strategies that would be as effective as possible in changing some of the source's views about offering information. Part of this plan might involve offering intangibles to try to make things better and at least not make them worse.

Sources of Power in Negotiation Theory

Different theorists have compiled slightly different lists of "sources of power" in negotiation, but they are all short lists. That is, there is only a finite number of kinds of negotiation power. Some sources of power explored in this section are associated with potential collaboration: building respect or at least credibility, using charisma and moral authority effectively, and offering rewards. Some sources of power are associated with competition: taking away alternative options from the other person, using sanctions, and employing commitment power (persistence in the negotiation until the source gives in). Some are associated with punitive strategies: the use of force or putting someone in fear, extreme use of commitment power, and attempts to deprive the other person of any alternative options.

Many questions about the ethics of negotiation relate to uses of power, and people disagree profoundly about when and how various sources of power should be used. It is not the purpose of this paper to discuss the ethical issues. However, with respect to all controversial EI methods it would seem reasonable at least to know if any of the controversial methods can be proven to be more *effective*, compared with other methods, in eliciting accurate and useful information. Any known use of any sources of power in EI, especially in cross-cultural EI, might therefore be studied for short- and long-term effectiveness.

Legitimate Authority

Legitimate or positional authority recognized by the other person is a commonly acknowledged form of power. However, in EI, a detainee might not recognize his captor as a legitimate authority for the purposes of sharing information or for any other purpose. He might see a relevant religious leader as a source of legitimate authority, which may hurt the interests of the United States if the leader speaks against the United States, or might help if a relevant religious leader were to condemn terrorism. A detainee might also recognize another highly placed detainee as a legitimate authority, which may hurt the interests of the United States, or might conceivably be used to help the process of EI if that highly placed source became willing to cooperate. In order to sow doubt in the mind of a source about previous beliefs it might be helpful to consider any possible "legitimate authority" that might help to persuade him to share information.

An attempt to *presume* "legitimate authority" can be used against the interests of the United States. For example, if sources believe they are being held "unjustly" their beliefs about the "illegality" of their confinement might stiffen their resolve not to talk.

Rewards and Sanctions

Rewards and sanctions are used very commonly, and in many contexts, as sources of power in eliciting information. In EI, many tangible and intangible rewards and sanctions could be explored, from the beginning to the end of the EI process. These might include rewards and sanctions that affect the conditions of detention, the reputation and status of the source, positive and negative effects on the source's family and friends, and respect for religion.

In negotiation theory, and in many cultures, an important element of rewards relates to reciprocity. We know that many people expect a concession to be reciprocated by some other concession: if we offer something the other person "should" reciprocate, and vice versa. Thus, if the source offers information the educer "should" consider reciprocity. EI might therefore include planning for reciprocal rewards (and sanctions). For example, the *process of negotiation itself* might be seen as a "reward" to the source — a positive gesture that costs little or nothing. It could begin with apparently small tangibles and intangibles: where will the EI discussion take place? Will there be food, and time for religious observance? How will the discussions be conducted? And, especially, could these points be negotiated with the source in a manner that might, in and of itself, help to build some credibility, some "connection," and a sense of "strategic respect?"

Force, and Threats of Force

Interrogators around the world have used force, and threats of force, as sources of power, probably achieving occasional short-term and long-term gains. The use of force by the United States may also have caused short and long-term *damage* to U.S. interests and credibility, some of which may not be known.

Negotiation theory would suggest that threats should be planned strategically: threats should be appropriate to the task, appropriately timed, and believable. It would seem that the use of force or threats of force might best be used only as part of careful strategic planning, with careful attention to possible positive and negative consequences — for getting accurate and useful information, and for the long-term interests of the United States. *It is hoped that any such use would be evaluated for effectiveness.*

EI may be an unusually difficult task to accomplish by physical force. It appears easier to *stop* someone by force from talking than to *compel* speech — especially accurate and truthful speech. (The nature of the "negotiation" of forcing someone to talk is inherently problematic, unless the interrogator knows enough facts to know when the source is lying or that his information is inaccurate.)

Using force, with the intent to stop the use of force if and when a source is willing to talk, might present difficulties for both parties in understanding what the other party may do. How would the educer know when to stop? What does the use of force do to the judgment of the person who uses it? On the other side, a source might worry about "How much is enough?" and "Can I trust this interrogator to stop hurting me if I agree to talk?"

In fact, the interrogator who uses physical force may lack believability for any other strategy. The very nature of the use of physical force would seem to undermine the likelihood of useful connection with a source beyond the immediate sessions. It might also increase a source's hatred of the United States and interest in suicide or willingness to be killed. So-called "restrained forcing" might be worthy of study in EI.

The *fear* of injury, and implicit and explicit threats of the use of force against a source or his family and friends, could also be problematic. (Putting a person in fear may be *interpreted* as intending harm, even though it may in fact be intended as an alternative to actual harm.) However, careful research might show that fear is sometimes effective.

Sources may have received training to resist EI, but the training might not necessarily "take hold" immediately after capture, especially for an unsophisticated captive. There may be a period after capture when fear of injury and/or disorientation (keeping someone "off base") might lead a source to begin to talk. A source might even be able to save face among his peers if he could later claim that he was immediately in great fear of injury. (Educers might consider using "good cop/bad cop" [or, more accurately, "bad cop/good cop"] tactics with those who have just been captured.)

Educers must remember that the use of physical force against sources — especially forms of coercion that are claimed to be illegal — may also be used against the United States. For example, others might then find it easier to mistreat our own troops.

Information Power

Accurate information, especially information about the real interests and knowledge of the specific source, appears essential in every strategy. All strategies require checking of educed information for accuracy and usefulness. *Information power may be the most important source of power in EI.*

Negotiation theory suggests that it is vital for educers to learn even small things about the individual source before interrogation so that they can plan a strategy and the uses of various forms of power. For example, data may be available from a central database, or "intake" members of the EI team might be able to learn something about the interests of a source (theory suggests that the real "negotiation" with the source will begin at the first meeting with the first member of the team). Negotiation practice would also suggest the importance of (seen or unseen) observers and analysts available to peruse the results of every interrogation session — in part to integrate what is learned, in part to affirm established ethical guidelines, in part to monitor effectiveness, and in part to prepare for the next EI session.

How and when an interrogator would share information with a source is likely to be important, partly in building a "strategic connection" and believability, and partly in encouraging honesty and forestalling deception. "Sequencing" is therefore another issue that deserves further study. Bluffing and deceiving (the source) are two classic topics of negotiation theory that EI research could evaluate. Another topic deserving study is any past use of imparting information or *mis*information to a source who was set free.

In thinking about EI, one would imagine getting information from a source to send *to some central agency* where the information can be combined with information from other sources. A negotiations theorist would also assume that information should continuously come to the educer *from other agencies* to keep improving the EI process.

Negotiation theory has for decades examined the pivotal role of the "constituencies" behind the parties. How information is communicated from the EI team to the final user, and from the intelligence community that collates many sources of information back to the EI team, would therefore seem to be an important topic for review. How information is communicated (if at all) among the source and fellow detainees and fellow countrymen would also be important if this could be studied.

Information power is of course widely used against the interests of the United States, for example, if terrorists effectively prepare sources to resist EI tactics. Sources may also plan, or be instructed, to use *mis*information against U.S. interests.

Expertise

Expertise, especially expertise in the language, values, culture, ways of thinking and interests of the source and his people, would seem essential as a source of power. For example, such expertise is probably vital to the ability to convey respect for the source's religious beliefs. To change somebody's mind about giving information — in negotiation theory, moving his point of resistance to giving information — the educer may need to "sow doubt" in the source's mind as to the validity of his views about talking. An EI team also would need expertise about the beliefs of a source to assess the effectiveness of various EI tactics in persuading sources to give useful information.

Expertise in the *process* of EI will be vital to plan and implement a course of action appropriate to each source. Expertise and preparation in resisting EI may also be widely used against U.S. interests, and educers should therefore understand the techniques that might be used.

Elegant Solutions

Elegant solutions are a source of power in which a negotiator who has come to understand the real interests of a source or a group of sources crafts deals in which certain information may be exchanged for certain benefits — deals to which the source and the United States can both say "yes." For example the deal might require the source to offer information in return for a reliable agreement to conceal the source's identity or to provide certain things of value to that person or his family. (Note that this kind of deal requires the United States to be able to build a certain kind of credibility; namely, that the United States can be trusted to honor the deal.)

Commitment Power

Commitment power is the power of persistence in negotiation. In an extreme form, it means that the interrogator will never relent, in the hope that the source will "give up," cede control over his life, and then provide information (*Abandon hope, all ye who enter here.*) Commitment power may sometimes be effective, or appear effective, in getting people to say *something*, but it carries with it a possible downside: taking away options from people may also incite rage, recalcitrance, and a permanent rejection of more positive tactics that might later be used. (This is one of the many reasons to consider negotiating over apparently small details, such as where and how EI sessions will be conducted, in order to mitigate the source's pain of feeling that he has lost control over his life. It might motivate an educer to "let up" sometimes in an interrogation, and just to listen.) Pragmatically speaking, some uses of commitment power might also pose legal difficulties for the United States.

Commitment power can of course also be used against the interests of the United States. For example, a source may simply refuse to speak, or may provoke someone to kill him. The source who uses commitment power against the educer may at the least incite weariness, acute frustration, and rage.

There is a classic negotiations question about dealing with mistakes in use of commitment power: how to help the other person, or oneself, give up a commitment, or change one's position, without losing face. This would appear to be an essential element of EI — how to help the source give information and still save face. It could also happen that the educing team fails badly in some tactic, but the negotiation must continue. How might the United States proceed without losing face?

As noted above, one possible way for a source not to lose face is for him to be able to convince his peers that he was in extreme fear. (It does not follow that he need actually have been injured.) However, there is also a classic list of alternatives, which includes discovery of "new facts," a change in the "rules," appeal to a new "authority," or the appointment of a new negotiator. These methods might occasionally be useful if an educer needs to reposition the discussion — to use "new facts hitherto unknown to the source," or to declare that some aspect of EI has changed "due to new orders," or to send in a new interrogator (for apparently extraneous reasons but actually to improve the "chemistry" between educer and source).

Another classic method to help a source save face is simply to ignore a previous commitment as if it had never existed. For example, the educer might behave as though the source had never taken an oath that he would never talk; this tactic might work if the source will not be returned to a camp with other detainees. Another classic method is for the educer to appeal strategically to a fairly good "connection" at an appropriate point ("I am hoping that you might be willing after all these weeks to tell me X, for the sake of our relationship — if I have to tell my boss I have failed, I will be in serious trouble.") and for the educer then to grant something of value to the source, "because of our relationship."

Relationship Power

Emotions, like all sources of power, can play positive or negative roles with respect to the interests of the United States. Making enemies, especially needlessly, may worsen the situation of the United States with the individual source and with his countrymen. In fact, educers should always consider the possibilities for building some "chemistry" or a "strategic connection." In this mode the educer would think of "recruiting" the source. Establishing some minimum respect between educer and source would likely be a prerequisite for elegant solutions and deals and also for recruiting agents, changing the mind of the occasional source, building an atmosphere where sources let down their guard with people planted in their midst, and so on.

Negotiation theorists and experienced interrogators could be misunderstood when they use terms such as "relationship," "trust," "interpersonal chemistry," "positive emotions," or "rapport." These terms seem to imply making friends with an enemy. *Nevertheless, the "strategic connection" between a particular source and a particular interrogator is likely to be essential to effective EI.* Strategic respect and building credibility may be important, especially in those cases where there could be some on-going interactions or where saving face for the source or the United States is at issue. Believability is important for the use of rewards or threats.

Moral Authority and Charisma

Moral authority and charisma are important sources of power in the present conflict with terrorists. Consistently and effectively conveying respect for the customs and religion of a source might on occasion be a prerequisite to sowing doubt in the source's *political* belief system. As noted previously, moral authority may also be used with great effect against the interests of the United States: to recruit people willing to use violence, persuade sources not to speak, and so on.

Best Alternative to a Negotiated Agreement (BATNA) or "Fallback Position"

Having a BATNA is a source of power, and the lack of a BATNA is a source of weakness, in the present conflict. The fallback position for each side is *What will happen if this negotiation does not succeed?* Beliefs about "what we will do if this does not work" would define both the U.S. resistance point (where we would give up trying to educe information from a specific person) and the resistance point of the source (when he might decide to give information, or alternatively seek to commit suicide, suffer injury that would prevent him from talking, or provoke his being injured or killed). To shift the resistance point — to change the source's mind about talking — the interrogator would wish to sow doubt in that source about whether he can and wants to maintain silence or maintain his cover story. The source, in turn, would want to sow doubt in the mind of the interrogator as to whether he knows anything useful and whether he will ever speak.

In an emergency situation there might be very little time to try to change someone's mind; in trying to educe information against a tight deadline (the "ticking bomb" scenario) the United States would have no fallback position. In negotiations terms, the BATNA power of the source would be great and that of the United States correspondingly weak. Alternatives in this situation would depend on knowing or guessing what matters to the individual and using that information according to a strategic plan. In such a situation it might be especially important to focus on the goal (*obtaining accurate and useful information*) without such "distractions" as the wish to vent frustration or punish the source.

In the war against terrorism any person willing and able to commit suicide would have a near-perfect BATNA — the strongest in the world in resisting the use of *force*. The United States would need to build a fallback position. Even in the face of detainees' willingness and ability to commit suicide, many sources of power might yet be effective if there were time to use them: for example, mobilizing any imam who opposes the use of violence or citing a fatwa that does so, applying rewards and sanctions judiciously, instituting a tenacious and long-term effort to win friends for the United States, and "building community" (a careful long-term plan to gain — and deserve — moral authority).

For Effectiveness: Prepare, Prepare, Prepare

Several basic tasks seem essential for effectiveness in every strategy in an EI negotiation:

- Taking note of the *relevant parties* whose interests are at stake;
- Discovering – or at least developing working hypotheses about — the *tangible and intangible interests* of each party;
- Evaluating the *sources of power* available to each side in EI;
- Developing relevant *options* for interrogation, *and "fallback" options*;
- Planning *strategy, style, and sequencing of tactics* with the EI team;
- Planning the *role of each team member* (for example, intake and preliminary assessment, interrogation, analysis behind the scenes, integration of data into and from the relevant intelligence community database, on-going evaluation and guidance to educers, and the users of information, and collection of records that can be analyzed for improved knowledge and practice).

The first two tasks need special care.

Preparing with Respect to U.S. Interests and Personnel

Effective negotiation in every strategy requires consideration and understanding of the interests on both sides. An educer would thus first consider the short-term and long-term goals of the United States. The short-term interests are to obtain as much useful and accurate information as possible, as fast as possible. Longer-term interests could include improving the image of the country, the possibility of sowing doubt in the mind of a potential enemy, the importance of planting information in a person or a group who will be released, and the possibility of recruiting a secret agent or source.

It may not be a simple task for the U.S. side to understand the various interests of the different people involved, let alone build a coherent or effective EI team. However, planning and preparing a team approach for each source would be important.

As an example, one party whose interests are at stake is the U.S. interrogator. In a given EI situation the interests of the United States are not necessarily the same as those of the educer(s). Imagine an untrained, frustrated interrogator who is angry with "terrorists," loathes his or her job in a detainee camp, and feels great pressure to "get results." This person, or the EI team, might have an interest in "taking it out" on a source in a way that will not be in the short- or long-term interests of the United States. A poorly trained interrogator or one who lacks self-discipline might try to show off to co-workers in unfortunate ways, without understanding the possible damage to U.S. interests. An interrogator who has just arrived on the scene might not know what he or she needs to understand about U.S. operational goals, and might therefore act according to his or her own interests.

There might also be multiple agencies, or agents from multiple countries, interested in information from one source. It may sometimes be helpful, *as part of a thoughtful strategic plan*, for different people to try to educe information from the same source, together or separately. However, theory suggests that the presence of known observers and multiple parties is likely to change the dynamics of a negotiation. Multiple educers could also be quite damaging — the presence of more than one educer or educer team might make any of the parties less cooperative. The involvement of more than one educer might sometimes interfere with establishment of a "connection" with a source. Planning the roles of each member of the EI team would seem essential.

Preparing with Respect to the Interests of the Source

What are the interests of the source and relevant persons who support the source and/or his position? The characteristics of each individual source might be important. Some sources may not be bitter enemies of the United States. Some may not know anything of value. Some may be willing to trade (for example, they might trade information for reputation, family benefits, money, or something else of value). Some may be affected emotionally in predictable ways, for good or for ill, by the way they are treated. Some might be "turned" and become willing to provide information because of an interest in freedom and opportunity for themselves and family members. Some might occasionally want their viewpoint to be "heard," or become lonely in detention, and tell more than they originally intended. Some may be motivated by false information that can be refuted. Some may be trained to resist certain sources of power that might be used in EI, but understanding the training methods may indicate ways of sowing doubt in that training.

Another reason to know the interests of a source is to understand what negotiation theory refers to as a "resistance point": a point at which the source changes his mind in an important way about dealing with the educer. This could be the point at which the source will stop dealing with his captors and seek other alternatives, such as trying to injure himself seriously, persuade someone else to injure him, or commit suicide. A source might have a resistance point of a different kind; that is, a point at which the source *will* decide to share — or appear to share — important information. The educer would obviously benefit from discovering this latter resistance point in order to try to move it toward cooperation. (The educer might endeavor to lower the resistance point by causing the source to doubt his own assessments, either about the United States or about his interests.)

To identify something to trade the educer would need to know what the source would value: for example, changing aspects of the EI sessions, conditions of custody, contacts with family, or time of release. EI interactions might present numerous opportunities to offer something of value — tangible or intangible — that involves little or no cost to U.S. interests. And if the source accepts something of value, this might also mean that he now might stand to lose something if he were to stop being helpful.

Few sources would be unique: each belongs to a religious group, a political group, and an ethnic culture. He may belong to an extended family. How one interacts with an individual source may be, de facto, part of a much larger "negotiation" with all the others in his immediate group, and potentially with all the people around the world who identify with the source. Members of the source's ethnic or religious group may also be at the site of the negotiation, which means the question of "negotiating with the constituency" is close at hand. The willingness of a source to give information might depend in important ways on the attitudes of a group of sources and might require that the source be separated from other sources. Alternatively, a group of sources might include people from different backgrounds whose interests at least initially differ. Such differences among the sources might advance U.S. interests if the United States could develop a coalition with one or another group.

The Need for Research about Negotiations and EI

The founders of modern-day negotiation theory, Walton and McKersie, developed their theory by studying records of negotiations.[689] This type of study could easily be extended to EI. Existing records of EI sessions, including debriefs

---

[689] Richard Walton and Robert McKersie, *A Behavioral Theory of Labor Negotiations* (Beverly Hills, CA: Sage Publications, 1965).

from the past, could be coded and analyzed with regard to the preparation, strategies, tactics, different uses of negotiation power, and different team configurations employed. Any available EI records from any country could be analyzed in negotiation terms.

Perhaps the most important reason for establishing an on-going research team would be not just to evaluate tactics "today," or in a single time period, but for continuous improvement of EI. Further study seems especially important with respect to cross-cultural interactions; for example, building a strategic connection and credibility and understanding success in identifying and changing the resistance points of sources. Gender, nationality and religion of educer and source would seem especially important in cross-cultural interactions.

Many different areas of negotiation theory may be important. For example, research could:

- Investigate coalition theory, and the importance of the "constituencies" behind the educer and the source, to help U.S. educers who are part of an extended intelligence community work with sources who are part of a group or come from different groups;

- Examine the effects of having a team of educers in the room in comparison to having one person conduct the negotiation;

- Study well-known tactics such as "good cop/bad cop" and "restrained forcing";

- Track the sequencing of imparting information to a source to test the accuracy of information provided by a source;

- Evaluate the usefulness of planting information and misinformation; and

- Track the *use* of information, from the EI team to final user, and from central databases to the EI team.

EI practitioners might explore the possibility of bringing together a few negotiations theorists who have analyzed hundreds of negotiations to prepare a protocol for analysis of records. They might either obtain clearances or train analysts with security clearances to study old EI records from a negotiation perspective. By the same token, it might be useful to bring negotiations experts together with EI experts simply to discuss best practices and continuous improvement.

10
Options for Scientific Research on Eduction Practices

Paul Lehner, Ph.D.
The MITRE Corporation
November 2005

Abstract

Eduction practices are methods, techniques, procedures, strategies, etc., employed as part of interviews and interrogations to draw out information from subjects, some of whom may initially be unwilling to provide information. Obviously educed information can provide an important source of HUMINT. Surprisingly, the last forty years have seen almost no scientific research examining eduction practices. Rather, our current knowledge is based on feedback and lessons learned from field experience. The "interrogation approaches" taught in standard interrogation training (e.g., Army Field Manual 34-52) have remained largely unchanged since World War II.

This paper argues two points: first, that scientific investigation of eduction practices is needed to supplement lessons learned from field experience, and second, that various research venues are available to examine these practices. Research approaches could include both retrospective analyses of data about past interrogations (including those that used harsh methods) and new studies that relate different eduction practices to the value of information obtained.

Need for Scientific Investigation of Eduction Practices

As noted above, current knowledge of eduction practices is based on experience. However, considerable historical and scientific evidence suggests that expertise and experience provide an insufficient basis for determining the effectiveness of practices *when experts subjectively evaluate their own practices.* To illustrate, consider the case of a procedure to alleviate psychiatric disorders that emerged from the medical community in the 1930s. According to one early study, 121 out of 133 patients either "improved" or "improved somewhat"; in another 153 patients improved, while 73 remained the same or got worse. On the basis of these encouraging results the procedure gained in popularity; it was used until the late 1960s to treat thousands of patients. The pioneer of the procedure received the 1949 Nobel prize in medicine. The procedure? Lobotomy.

After drilling a small hole in the temple on each side of the skull, the surgeon then inserts a dull knife into the brain, makes a fan-shaped incision through the prefrontal lobe, then downward a few minutes later. He then repeats the incision on the other side of the brain.... The patient is given only local anesthetic at the temples — the brain itself is insensitive—and the doctors encourage him to talk, sing, recite poems or prayers. When his replies to questions show that his mind is thoroughly disoriented, the doctors know that they have cut deep enough into his brain.[690]

How could this procedure receive rave reviews? Apparently, the flaw in these early studies was simply that physicians who provided these treatments also rated the results. We know of no evidence to suggest that these physicians were intentionally biased or deceitful; or that they had anything other than the best interest of their patients at heart.

For a more contemporary example, consider the presumed ability of law enforcement interrogators to evaluate their subjects. Professional interrogators view nonverbal cues as important for detecting deception. Such cues include level of eye contact; movement of legs, feet, head and trunk; shifting body positions; "covering gestures" such as a hand over the mouth while talking; ear tugging; etc. All of these have been tested; *none* is substantiated as an indicator of deception.[691] A similar result occurs when interrogators are asked to determine (on the basis of case summaries and interrogation videotapes) whether a confession is true or false. Most studies show that trained and untrained evaluators (e.g., police officers and college students) are equally poor at distinguishing between the confessions of guilty and innocent study subjects, even when viewing videotaped interviews from law enforcement situations. Often, however, law enforcement personnel have more confidence in their abilities than untrained subjects — even though their detection capabilities are no better.[692]

Associated with such examples is an extensive scientific literature on human judgment. We will not review this literature here, but simply note that the examples noted above should not be considered atypical.[693] Natural human judgment biases, such as the *Law of Small Numbers* (the tendency to jump to conclusions on the basis of too little data) and the *Confirmation bias* (the tendency to underweight or ignore evidence inconsistent with current beliefs), are very strong. These biases

---

[690] This description of the history of lobotomy was drawn from R. Dawes, *House of Cards: Psychology and Psychotherapy Built on Myth* (New York, The Free Press, 1994).

[691] Research on detection deception is summarized in G. Hazlett, "Detection of Deception Research Review," prepared under the auspices of this ISB study.

[692] See S. M. Kassin, Meissner, and R. J. Norwick, "I'd Know a False Confession If I Saw One": A Comparative Study of College Students and Police Investigators. *Law and Human Behavior*, 29 (2005), 211-227.

[693] For review of this research see R. Hastie, and R. Dawes, *Rational Choice in an Uncertain World: The Psychology of Judgment and Decision Making* (Thousand Oaks, CA: Sage Publications, 2001).

are quite resistant to "knowing better"; they often prevail even when experts are fully aware of them and explicitly endeavor to mitigate their effect.[694]

These findings have a clear implication for the assessment of eduction practices: it is imprudent to base assessment only on the subjective feedback of interrogators. Interrogators are professionals, and are certainly committed to providing the most honest evaluations they can. However, unless they differ greatly from other experts, their judgments and memories will be biased in favor of the effectiveness of the practices they employ. Information gleaned from field experience constitutes a critical source of knowledge, and without question many of the lessons learned from such experiences are valid. But, equally without question, many are invalid. Which is which? Only objective, scientific research can help to distinguish between them.

Feasibility of Scientific Investigation of Eduction Practices

Researchers have substantial opportunity to investigate eduction practices scientifically in ways that pose no ethical or political problems. The paragraphs below outline some alternative study designs for these scientific investigations.

Venue 1: Objective Analysis of Contemporary Interrogations

As noted above, considerable evidence indicates that experts overrate the effectiveness of their own practices. This occurs particularly when experts do not receive frequent, objective feedback on the results of their practices — precisely the circumstance in which interrogators usually find themselves. Although they know whether or not a subject "talked," they do not receive substantial feedback on the accuracy or usefulness of the information educed. This can cause problems, because a subject who has decided to feign cooperation would probably choose to "reveal" two types of information: information that is accurate but useless and information that appears useful, but is inaccurate.

Solving this problem requires independent, objective assessment of the information educed. Fortunately, straightforward approaches exist for acquiring such assessments. In essence, analysts should rate the usefulness, accuracy, and timeliness of the information distributed from interrogations. To ensure objectivity, the analysts performing these ratings should not know the source of the information. Furthermore, these ratings should be delayed until after any actions taken to follow up on the educed information are complete, because the

---

[694] For a concrete example to which the reader can relate, have you ever seen a professional basketball player on a "hot streak," "in the zone," etc.? In fact, you haven't. A detailed analysis of shooting behavior in almost every venue imaginable has yet to find a single professional player who exhibits streaks beyond chance. The chance of making the next shot is simply independent of the results of recent previous shots. In fact, shooting behavior is *maximally inconsistent* with the "hot streak" hypothesis. Nevertheless, anyone who watches a game, including those of us who understand statistics, "sees" streaks. The hot streaks are completely obvious and completely illusory.

accuracy and/or usefulness of educed information may not be known until the follow-up activities occur.

Objective feedback would provide a wealth of information about eduction practices. At a minimum, the accuracy, usefulness, and timeliness of the educed information could be correlated with:

Eduction strategy. Objective feedback may shed light on the effectiveness of different strategies. It would certainly provide data for an objective inquiry into claims about the effectiveness of alternative approaches to eduction, such as building rapport, use of coercion and stress, indirect eduction using stooges, etc.

Interrogator characteristics. Interrogators with certain backgrounds or training may be especially effective. It may also be that certain interrogators are simply better. If researchers can establish, objectively, that some interrogators are better than others, they can begin to investigate the defining characteristics of better interrogators.

Interrogator assessments. Can interrogators actually distinguish between subjects who cooperate and those who feign cooperation? It is important to understand the extent to which, in general, one can rely on the EI practitioners themselves to predict the value of the information they distribute.

Subject characteristics/behaviors. Different subjects react differently, and collecting data that relates subject characteristics to EI results will offer considerable guidance for future EI.

Field testing of new methods. Of course, as new eduction methods are introduced into the field, the objective assessment of interrogation results would also provide objective feedback about the effectiveness of the new methods.

Venue 2: Objective Analysis of Historical Interrogations

Consider the following (paraphrased) claims:

"The initial goal of an interrogation is to break the subjects' will. Once that is accomplished, the subjects will tell you everything they know."

"Torture is a poor interrogation technique. The information you obtain from the subject is unreliable."

Researchers cannot ethically investigate claims such as these by conducting experiments, either in an academic setting with students as subjects or with detainees in U.S. custody. However, they may be able to evaluate these claims by drawing on the considerable historical data available. A principal data source would be historical POW records and post-detainment debriefings. Unfortunately, torture-based methods were commonly practiced against U.S. POWs, so a wealth of such data exists.

POW records can be objectively analyzed by following five steps:

Step 1: Develop specific criteria for determining, on the basis of verbal descriptions, the eduction practices employed. This step should be completed before the records that will be part of the formal analysis are examined.

Step 2: Partition each record into three sets of statements
S1: Statements about the eduction practices employed
S2: Statements about the information educed
S3: Statements not related to either method or information.

To the extent possible, the timing of the S1 and S2 statements should be noted to indicate when the event occurred. With POW data such timing information will be approximate at best (e.g., "This happened during the first few months after I was captured."), but it will still be useful.

Step 3: Analyze S1 statements and apply the criteria in Step 1 to determine the eduction practices employed. This assessment must be performed by individuals who were not involved in Step 2 or Step 4 below. This will ensure that knowledge of the information educed does not influence the determination of the method employed.

Step 4: Analyze the S2 statements. This should be done by an analyst or historian who is asked to rate information statements for *accuracy*, *usefulness*, and *completeness*. Step 4 must also be executed by people who were not involved in Steps 2 or 3.

Step 5: Analyze the statistical correlation between the eduction practices employed and the accuracy, usefulness, and completeness of the information educed. The person performing the statistical analysis need not be informed of the content of the S1 and S2 statements.

Using these data sets and analysis procedures, it should be possible to test some of the claims about the efficacy of eduction practices that the United States does not now employ. For example, the claim that subjects can be "broken" implies that subjects will reach a point where they will simply "tell all." The independent assessments resulting from Step 4 may shed considerable light on whether this is true. Similarly, the claim that torture results in unreliable information is equally testable, provided we have an independent evaluation of the information educed.[695]

While an objective analysis of historical data is unlikely to generate definitive results on many questions of interest, it will provide some scientific feedback on the validity of claims about coercive techniques. These data should be exploited.

---

[695] We believe it may be possible to acquire North Vietnamese records of POW internments.

Venue 3: Experiments with SERE Students

The U.S. military puts several hundred students through survival, evasion, resistance, escape (SERE) training annually. SERE students receive resistance training under conditions that are made as stressful as practical. They provide an excellent subject pool for investigating eduction practices involving stress: both practices intended to induce stress and methods that do not induce stress but may lead to results that differ from those obtained under non-stress conditions.

Unlike the objective analyses described above, research with students undergoing SERE training provides an opportunity for controlled experimentation where the effect of an EI practice can be carefully separated from other variables. This will be particularly useful for evaluating individual techniques intended to have immediate impact or results, such as detection of deception, interpretation of behaviors, behavioral tricks, etc.

However, since the SERE program only lasts a few weeks, research with SERE students would not help in assessing practices based on building certain longer term relationships with the subject. For example, the general claim that rapport-based approaches are superior to coercive methods cannot be tested in this setting.

Venue 4: Experiments with Other Military Personnel

Eduction practices that do not involve coercion or stress could be tested in the general military population. Experiments with military personnel would be particularly appropriate for research on practices whose effectiveness depends on the subject's ignorance of the specifics of the technique. For example, subjects could defeat questioning strategies that derive information from what a subject does not say, or the manner in which a subject responds to a question, if they knew which behaviors the interrogators were seeking.

Venue 5: University Research

While ethical or secrecy concerns preclude university research on some practices, many eduction practices are entirely benign and open. Research into new and innovative approaches to educing information could and should proceed in a traditional university setting. Indeed, as some of the reviews in this study have documented, a wealth of ideas and approaches have already been investigated in this setting.[696]

Venue 6: Research with Foreign Personnel

The extent to which culture and language influence the efficacy of various eduction practices remains an open question. It is not at all clear, for example, whether any behavioral indicators of deception cross cultural boundaries. As new techniques are developed, researchers must test them with people from diverse

---

[696] In particular, see G. Hazlett, "Detection of Deception Research Review," and R. Borum, "Approaching Truth: Behavioral Science Lessons on Educing Information from Human Sources," both prepared under the auspices of this ISB study.

cultures. To some extent this can be achieved through university research within the United States or through field tests. However, both of these approaches have limitations. Foreign-born students in U.S. universities are somewhat acclimated to U.S. culture, so the ability to generalize from this research may be limited. Opportunities to perform field tests with subjects under U.S. custody will be sparse. This suggests a need to develop cooperative research arrangements with other nations to engage in this research in their university and perhaps military settings.

Summary of Venues

The table below summarizes this discussion by showing how different types of eduction practices can be investigated in different venues. Eduction practices vary by whether they seek tactical, short-term results (e.g., immediately detect deception) or strategic, long-term results (e.g., build rapport). They also vary according to the degree of coercion employed or stress induced. As the table shows, the different venues are appropriate for examining different categories of eduction practices.

	No Stress	Low Stress	Moderate Stress	Extreme Stress
Tactical/ short-term results	University Research; Military Research; Foreign Research	Military Research; SERE Students; Contemporary Interrogations	SERE Students	No Research Venues
Strategic/ long-term results	University Research; Military Research; Foreign Research	Contemporary Interrogations	POW Records	POW Records

Research venues appropriate for different types of eduction practices.
Source: The author.

Taken together, the diversity of research venues suggests that researchers have substantial opportunities to assess scientifically many, if not all, of the eduction practices that the United States might employ. They can also conduct substantial retrospective scientific inquiries into practices the United States does not employ.

Conclusion

Experience and lessons learned offer a necessary, but insufficient, basis for determining the effectiveness of eduction practices. A program of scientific research on eduction practices is both necessary and highly feasible. Researchers have diverse venues available to investigate eduction practices. Such a research program should combine experimental research with a substantial effort to perform independent and objective analyses of specific interrogation results.

11
Educing Information Bibliography

Theresa Dillon
The MITRE Corporation
February 2006

This selected, annotated bibliography accompanies the Intelligence Science Board Study on Educing Information. It includes the most useful items in English covering the theory, research and pragmatics of interrogation over the past 50 years. Deception detection, persuasion, and compliance research as well as legal and military doctrine are not covered in this bibliography.

Interrogation Best Practices

Biderman, A. D. (1960). "Social Psychological Needs and 'Involuntary' Behavior As Illustrated by Compliance in Interrogation." *Sociometry* 23 (2), 120-147.

> Drawing on a study of former Korean War U.S. Air Force POWs, Biderman presents a social-psychological framework to explain why prisoners yield during interrogation, with emphasis on the inability of most POWs to remain silent during interrogation. Silence is inconsistent with the prisoners' need to maintain a viable social role and positive self-esteem. Also considered are the effects of frustration, hostility and guilt.

Bowden, M. (2003). "The Dark Art of Interrogation." *The Atlantic Monthly*, October, 51-76. http://www.theatlantic.com/doc/200310/bowden [Accessed 5/8/2006]

> Bowden provides an in-depth account of the debate over torture via case studies and interviews. The author traces the history of U.S. interrogation and presents best practices as reported by expert interrogators from Israel's General Security Service, the New York Police Department, and the CIA.

Johnson, W. R. (1986). "Tricks of the Trade: Counterintelligence Interrogation." *The International Journal of Intelligence and Counterintelligence 1*(2), 103-113.

This essay presents lessons that the author learned as an interrogator during WWII. Johnson discusses why torture does not work; characteristics that make a good interrogator; and how to handle hard cases involving sociopaths, veterans of torture and professional intelligence officers.

Lelyveld, J. (2005). "Interrogating Ourselves." *New York Times Magazine*, 12 June.

This essay reviews legal issues surrounding "torture lite." The author reports on interviews with high-profile interrogators about best practices in interrogation; reviews the Kennedy School and Harvard Law School project that proposes legislating standards for the application of torture lite; and examines what the United States can learn from interrogation practices in Israel.

Meltzer, M. L. (1958). *Power and Resistance in Interrogation.* DTIC – AD220464. Washington, DC: Georgetown University Medical Center. Distribution authorized to U.S. government agencies and their contractors.

Meltzer examines different types of power employed by interrogators, including reward power, coercive power, expert power, attraction power, and legitimate power. Citing supporting research studies, the author details when each approach should be used and the psychological forces at work.

Moran, S. F. (1944). *Suggestions for Japanese Interpreters Based on Work in the Field.* San Francisco: Division Intelligence Section, Headquarters, First Marine Division, Fleet Marine Force. The original source document is located at the Alfred M. Gray Research Center (USMC Archives) of the Marine Corps University in Quantico, Virginia. Link: http://www.mcu.usmc.mil/MCRCweb/

This letter report by Marine Major Sherwood Moran highlights the importance of attitude and language skills for a successful interpreter. He rejects strong-arm tactics in favor of rapport building. Interpreters should exhibit sincerity and sympathy and be good salesmen. Idiomatic language skills and cultural knowledge are also recommended. Having spent 40 years in Japan as a missionary prior to WWII, Moran draws on his knowledge of language and culture in this timeless report.

Stanton, G. (1995). "Defense against Communist Interrogation Organizations." In H. B. Westerfield (ed), *Inside the CIA's Private World: Declassified Articles from the Agency's Internal Journal, 1955-1992.* New Haven, CT: Yale University Press, 415-436.

Originally published in 1969 and classified CONFIDENTIAL, this manual instructs undercover agents on how to prepare themselves in advance for communist interrogation. The article outlines what to expect and how to behave at each stage from arrest to interrogation. It also describes arguments and tactics used to make suspected spies talk and suggests effective resistance strategies.

Toliver, R. F., and Scharff, H. J. (1978). *The Interrogator: The Story of Hanns Joachim Scharff, Master Interrogator of The Luftwaffe*. Fallbrook, CA: Aero Publishers.

During World War II, Hanns Scharff served as master interrogator of the Luftwaffe. He questioned captured U.S. fighter pilots of the USAAF Eighth and Ninth Air Forces. Through analysis of pocket litter, detailed files on pilots and squadrons, and transcripts of radio communication, Scharff could convince a captured pilot that he already knew everything. After the official interview ended, Scharff would induce soldiers to reveal military secrets through conversation rather than coercion. His technique included befriending the captured pilots and showing respect for rank.

Zimmer, H., and Meltzer, M. L. (1957). *An Annotated Bibliography of Literature Relevant to the Interrogation Process*. DTIC – AD220465. Washington, DC: Georgetown University Medical Center. Distribution authorized to U.S. government agencies and their contractors.

Covering the fields of psychology, sociology, anthropology, physiology, psychiatry, and medicine, this bibliography, published in 1957, pulls together unclassified scientific literature related to the interrogation process. Complete with abstracts, the bibliography is broken down into the following sections: interpersonal observation and evaluation; deception and the accuracy of reported information; communication and interaction between two persons; communication and interaction methodology; authority and its internalization; reactions to coercive pressures; manipulation of the source's conscious controls; ideological compliance, conformity, and conversion; morale in combat and captivity; and the group as a source of support or conflict for the individual.

Interrogation Case Studies

Bond, M. (2004). "The Enforcer." *New Scientist*, 20 November.

Michael Koubi worked for Shin Bet, Israel's security service, for 21 years and was its chief interrogator from 1987 to 1993. In this interview, Koubi discusses best practices and provides details on the interrogation of Sheikh Yassin, the former leader of the Palestinian group Hamas.

Bond, M. (2004). "The Prisoner." *New Scientist*, 20 November.

> After interviewing Michael Koubi, Michael Bond interviews a
> Palestinian woman about her interrogation by Koubi after she was
> arrested while trying to smuggle sensitive photographs across the
> border. She describes the techniques Koubi used to try to get her to talk.

Hoffman, B. (2002). "A Nasty Business." *The Atlantic Monthly*, 289 (1), January,
49-52.

> A terrorism expert, Hoffman illustrates the complexity of gathering
> human intelligence from insurgents. He uses the Battle of Algiers and
> Tamil Tigers in Sri Lanka as case studies.

Mackey, C., and Miller, G. (2004). *The Interrogators: Inside the Secret War
against Al Qaeda*. New York: Little, Brown.

> In this memoir, a senior interrogator details the U.S. Army interrogation
> operation, including interrogation training at Fort Huachuca, language
> training at the Defense Language Institute, and deployment as an
> interrogator in Afghanistan. This narrative covers interrogation
> strategies and case studies; collection priorities and findings; report
> writing and analysis; and the relationships between military intelligence
> services, and domestic and foreign civil intelligence agencies. The
> motivations of detainees from different ethnic groups are also examined.

Pribbenow, M. L. (2004). "The Man in the Snow White Cell." *Studies
in Intelligence*, 48 (1).
http://www.cia.gov/csi/studies/vol48no1/article06.html
[Accessed 5/8/2006]

> Nguyen Tai, the most senior North Vietnamese officer captured in the
> Vietnam War, was interrogated by both the U.S. and South Vietnamese
> using a variety of strategies. He spent the last three years in a white
> cell, lit around the clock by bright lights, and kept at cold temperatures.
> This case study provides a history of Tai's capture and interrogation as
> well as his remarkable strength in concealing his knowledge of North
> Vietnamese operations.

Pryor, F. L. (1994/1995). "On Reading My Stasi Files." *National Interest*, Winter.

> From 1959 through 1961 the author lived in West Berlin, writing his
> doctoral dissertation for Yale University on the foreign trade system of
> the Soviet bloc, using East Germany as a case study. While traveling to
> East Berlin, he was arrested and charged with espionage and released
> five months later. With the fall of the Berlin Wall, the Stasi files became
> open. The author reviews his files, examining the motives of the Stasi
> and the methods used in his interrogation.

Saar, E., and Novak, V. (2005). *Inside the Wire: A Military Intelligence Soldier's Eyewitness Account of Life at Guantanamo.* New York: Penguin Press.

Saar, an army linguist deployed for six months at Guantanamo Bay's Camp Delta, shares his experiences of working in both the Joint Detainee Operations Group (JDOG) and the Joint Intelligence Group (JIG) from December 2002 to June 2003. With the JDOG, he served as an Arabic translator on the cell blocks, translating between detainees and the military police (MP), medics and psych teams. With the JIG, he supported interrogators from the U.S. Army, civilian intelligence agencies, and civilian contracting firms. Problems include a loose command structure, training gaps, morale issues, and intra- and inter-group hostilities. He describes treatment of the detainees by the MPs, organization of detainees on the cell blocks, and what happens in the interrogation room.

Van de Velde, J. R. (2005). Camp Chaos: U.S. Counterterrorism Operations at Guantanamo Bay, Cuba. *International Journal of Intelligence and Counterintelligence, 18,* 538-548.

The author, who had been stationed at Guantanamo Bay (GTMO) as both a naval intelligence officer and later as a contractor, reviews the GTMO operation and highlights its shortcomings. While Army SOUTHCOM is in charge at GTMO, the camp falls victim to the competing interests of the CIA, the FBI and the DoD. GTMO is plagued by an ill-defined mission and the lack of standard procedures for producing and distributing intelligence products. The intelligence that is gathered is not properly analyzed or viewed in a larger context. Military interrogators are reservists who spend only 6-8 months at the camp. They tend to clash with civilian contractors with longer tours of duty and higher pay.

Zagorin, A., and Duffy, M. (2005). "Inside the Interrogation of Detainee 063." *Time Magazine, 165,* 25, 20 June.

Based on secret interrogation logs, this article details the interrogation of Guantanamo Bay Detainee 063, Mohammed al-Qahtani, widely thought to be the 20th hijacker in the Sept. 11 attacks.

Interrogation Policies, Practices and Research

Communist Interrogation, Indoctrination and Exploitation of American Military, and Civilian Prisoners, 84th Congress, 2nd Sess. (1956).

These 1956 U.S. Senate subcommittee hearings delve into Communist interrogation and indoctrination of U.S. prisoners of war. They provide a good review of Army, Air Force, and Marine Corps research into

Russian and Chinese methods and their application during the Korean War.

Biderman, A. D. (1956). *Communist Techniques of Coercive Interrogation.* DTIC – AD0098908. Randolph Air Force Base: Office for Social Science Programs, Air Force Personnel and Training Research Center. Distribution authorized to U.S. government agencies and their contractors.

This report describes the coercive techniques employed by the Communists to undermine resistance and induce compliance. Techniques include isolation; monopolization of attention; induced debilitation and exhaustion; cultivation of anxiety and despair; alternating punishments and rewards; demonstrating "omnipotence" and "omniscience" of the captor; degradation; and enforcing trivial and absurd demands. Physical violence and torture are not an essential part of the Communist repertoire. The author also comments on the effectiveness of self-inflicted pain and ideological appeals, as well as the role of "mind reform" in inducing compliance.

Biderman, A. D. (1957). "Communist Attempts to Elicit False Confessions from Air Force Prisoners of War." *Bulletin NY Academy of Medicine* 33 (9), 616–625.

Based on research on repatriated U.S. Air Force POWs captured in Korea, Biderman's article describes how Communists shaped compliance and elicited false confessions. The objective of the Communists was not merely to get the captor to confess to certain acts but, rather, to behave as if he actually committed the confessed crimes. Two useful charts are provided, one outlining the eight coercive methods used by the Communists, including their effects and specific forms, and another detailing the range of POW behaviors in response to coercion, from complete resistance to complete compliance.

Biderman, A. D., and Zimmer, H. (1961). *The Manipulation of Human Behavior.* New York; London: John Wiley.

This out-of-print book reviews scientific knowledge in the field of interrogation, focusing on attempts to elicit factual information from an unwilling subject. It includes the following papers: Lawrence E. Hinkle Jr., "The physiological state of the interrogation subject as it affects brain function"; Philip E. Kubzansky, "The effects of reduced environmental stimulation on human behavior: A review"; Louis A. Gottschalk, "The use of drugs in interrogation"; R. C. Davis, "Physiological responses as a means of evaluating information" (this chapter deals with the polygraph); Dr. Martin T. Orne, "The potential uses of hypnosis in interrogation"; Robert R. Blake and Jane S. Mouton, "The experimental investigation of interpersonal influence"; and Malcolm L. Meltzer, "Countermanipulation through malingering."

Biderman, A. D. (1963). *An Annotated Bibliography on Prisoner Interrogation, Compliance and Resistance.* DTIC – AD670999. Washington, DC: Bureau of Social Science Research.

This bibliography contains about 200 items from the unclassified literature that appeared in 1953–1963 on prisoner interrogation, compliance and resistance.

Blagrove, M. (1996). "Effects of Length of Sleep Deprivation on Interrogative Suggestibility." *Journal of Experimental Psychology: Applied* 2 (1), 48-59.

Blagrove investigates whether loss of sleep can cause people to acquiesce to leading questions as well as change their answers in subsequent interviews. In this study, subjects listened to two taped short stories and later, after one or two nights without sleep, answered a set of leading questions on information not contained in the stories. Using the Gudjonsson Suggestibility Scale, a standard measure of interrogative suggestibility, participants were scored on how many affirmative answers they gave to leading questions and on how often they changed answers after negative feedback. The study reveals that sleep-deprived individuals are more suggestible than control groups, due to lowered cognitive ability and the motivation to acquiesce.

Cunningham, C. (1972). "International Interrogation Techniques." *Journal of the Royal United Services Institute for Defence Studies* 117 (3), 31–34.

Cunningham, former Senior Psychologist, POW Intelligence, UK Ministry of Defence, discusses the object of interrogation and reviews the three methods of interrogation: direct, indirect, and clandestine. This article was written in response to the UK's 1972 Parker Report, which recommends authorized procedures for the interrogation of suspected terrorists.

Goldberger, L. (1993). "Sensory Deprivation and Overload." In L. Goldberger and S. Breznitz (eds.), *Handbook of Stress: Theoretical and Clinical Aspects*, 2nd ed. New York: Free Press, 333–341.

This brief chapter provides an overview of research on sensory deprivation and overload by reviewing the major studies and findings since the 1950s. The practical application of sensory research to a variety of domains is discussed.

Hinkle Jr, L. E., and Wolff, H. G. (1956). "Communist Interrogation and Indoctrination of 'Enemies of the States'." *AMA Archives of Neurology and Psychiatry* 78, 115–174.

This comprehensive report provides a detailed analysis of the structure and practices of the Russian KGB and the state police in Communist China in the 1950s. On the basis of input from field experts, the study of former Communist prisoners, and published literature, Wolff and Hinkle provide a window into Communist arrest and interrogation systems from investigation to "trial."

Hoare, O. (ed). (2000). *Camp 020: MI5 and the Nazi Spies: The Official History of MI5's Wartime Interrogation Centre*. Richmond, Surrey: Public Record Office (UK). Originally published in 1947 as TOP SECRET by R. W. G. Stephens and titled, "A Digest of Ham."

This book captures MI5's official history of Camp 020, Britain's WWII spy prison. The introduction reviews the events that led to the establishment of Camp 020, including the public hysteria over a supposed Fifth Column of German agents working behind Western lines; outlines the organization of WWII British intelligence services; and paints a picture of Lieutenant-Colonel R.W.G. "Tin Eye" Stephens, Commandant of Camp 020. Volume One deals with interrogation techniques, trends in enemy espionage, and the various phases of Camp 020's development. Volume Two provides case histories, including how agents were "broken" and the resulting intelligence yield.

Kleinman, S. M. (2002). *The History of MIS-Y: U.S. Strategic Interrogation during World War II*. Unpublished master's thesis, DTIC Document ADA447589. Washington, DC: Joint Military Intelligence College.

This thesis captures the essence of the MIS-Y strategic interrogation program and the challenges of obtaining intelligence through the interrogation of German prisoners-of-war in support of the Allied war effort. MIS-Y operated from 1942–1945 at Fort Hunt near Washington, D.C., and was a carefully guarded secret. This study examines the key elements of the MIS-Y strategic interrogation mission, including program organization; procedures for screening, selecting and handling POWs; training for interrogators; methods of interrogation; Allied information requirements; and intelligence collected.

Lifton, R. J. (1956). "'Thought Reform' of Western Civilians in Chinese Communist Prisons." *Psychiatry* 19, 173–195.

Lifton, formerly a psychiatrist at Walter Reed Medical Institute, interviewed Western civilians released from Chinese Communist prisons in 1955 and 1956. In this account, he provides a window into Chinese penal "thought reform," citing the experiences of individual prisoners. Chinese Communist "thought reform" seeks to annihilate identity, establish guilt, and create internal conflict. The interrogator demands more and more information and the prisoner develops an increasing need to meet those demands. The struggle continues back in the cell where "reformed" cellmates harass the prisoner. When the prisoner has reached the "breaking point," captors adopt a policy of leniency or calculated kindness that rewards cooperation. Coached by his interrogators, the prisoner gives in to the compulsion to confess to real and fantasized actions, ultimately writing a well-crafted final confession. With reeducation, the prisoner spends most of his waking hours in study group sessions transferring his guilt for confessed crimes to major elements of his identity. He begins to interpret his past life as evil and completely identifies with the aggressor. Lifton maintains that the Chinese Communist prison is "probably the most thoroughly controlled and manipulated group environment that has ever existed."

MacDonald, H. (2005). "How to Interrogate Terrorists." *City Journal.* http://www.frontpagemag.com/Articles/ReadArticle.asp?ID=16572. Accessed 5/8/2006.

This controversial piece discusses the consequences of the Abu Ghraib scandal for military interrogation practices and defends the use of stress techniques. Case studies from Afghanistan and Guantanamo Bay and interviews with interrogators are included.

Mayer, J. (2005, 14 February). "Outsourcing Torture." *The New Yorker.*

The United States established an "extraordinary rendition" program to transfer terror suspects to foreign countries for interrogation. Mayer documents the rendition program's history, identifies shortcomings, and provides case studies.

McCoy, A. W. (2005). "Cruel Science: CIA Torture and U.S. Foreign Policy."
New England Journal of Public Policy 19 (2), 209–262.
http://www.mccormack.umb.edu/nejpp/articles/19_2/CruelScience.pdf
[Accessed 5/8/2006]

This lengthy essay provides a history of the CIA's psychological
interrogation methods over the past fifty years from secret research into
coercion and human consciousness in the 1950s and 1960s to renewed
interest in CIA techniques after September 11. It surveys the MKUltra
project, CIA's mind-control research program, profiling major efforts
and researchers. It includes case studies of the dissemination of CIA
methods to Uruguay, Iran, and the Philippines. Finally, it examines
the record of the Bush administration and recent U.S. policy on harsh
interrogation.

McGuffin, J. (1981). *The Guineapigs.* 2nd ed. San Francisco: Minuteman Press.
http://www.irishresistancebooks.com/guineapigs/guineapigs.htm.
Accessed 5/8/2006.

This book documents the British Army's use of sensory deprivation
torture on fourteen Irish political prisoners in 1971. First published
in 1974, this book sold out on its first print run and was then abruptly
taken off the market following pressure from the British Government.
The updated 1984 second edition is now out of print and available
online only.

Merton, V., and Kinscherff, R. (1981). *The Court-Martial of Bobby Garwood:
Coercive Persuasion and the "Culpable Mind."* Garrison, NY: Hastings
Center Report, 5-8.

This article examines the court martial of Bobby Garwood, a POW who
collaborated with the Vietnamese after indoctrination. Merton addresses
learned helplessness and the victim's identification with the aggressor
and poses the question whether coercive persuasion is a valid defense.

Piper Jr, A. (1993). "'Truth Serum' and 'Recovered Memories' of Sexual Abuse:
A Review of the Evidence." *Journal of Psychiatry and Law* 21 (4),
447–471.

This article outlines the amytal interview process and reviews the
literature on the accuracy of information obtained while a subject is
sedated with amytal. Studies reveal the following weaknesses in the use
of amytal as an interview tool: increased patient suggestibility; ability
to lie during sedation; possibility of induced hypnosis; and disturbances
in mental process that can result in unreliable information.

Ruscio, J. (2005). "Exploring Controversies in the Art and Science of Polygraph Testing." *Skeptical Inquirer* 29 (1), 34–39.

> The polygraph test is used to investigate specific incidents and for screening. The Control Question Test (CQT) and the Guilty Knowledge Test (GKT), two distinct types of polygraph, are reviewed. The author examines the validity and utility of the CQT and the GKT in different scenarios.

Schein, E. H. (1961). *Coercive Persuasion: A Socio-Psychological Analysis of the "Brainwashing" of American Civilian Prisoners by the Chinese Communists*. New York: W. W. Norton.

> Between 1950 and 1953, the Chinese Communists imprisoned U.S. civilians who were later repatriated with altered attitudes, values, and beliefs brought about through thought reform. The Chinese program emphasized confessions for rehabilitation and reform and relied on coercive persuasion. In this book, the behavior changes of a sample of these U.S. prisoners are examined from a socio-psychological viewpoint. The historical and political context of the Chinese thought reform program and the relevant psychological, physiological, psychiatric, and sociological theories at work are outlined.

Straus, U. (2003). "The Interrogations." In *The Anguish of Surrender: Japanese POWs of World War II*. Seattle: University of Washington Press, 116-149.

> Japan indoctrinated soldiers with the belief that death was better than the dishonor of becoming a POW. With the shame of capture, Japanese POWs were without a country and held no hopes of returning to Japan. Cultural norms regulate the giving and receiving of favors in Japanese society. Americans did not simply spare the lives of the Japanese POWs, they also gave the prisoners cigarettes, food, and medical treatment. The POWs, in return, gave answers to seemingly innocuous questions. Humane treatment combined with knowledge of Japanese culture and language was effective in getting POWs to talk. In addition to describing the psychology of the Japanese POW of WWII, this chapter documents the use of Nisei (second-generation U.S. Japanese) linguists and reviews both tactical battlefield interrogations and interrogations at Camp Tracy, a secret facility focused on technical and strategic information gathering.

Weinstein, H. (1988). "Supply and Demand." In *Father, Son and CIA*. Halifax: Formac Publishing Co. http://www.serendipity.li/cia/c99.html. Accessed 5/8/2006.

A psychiatrist chronicles the decline of his father, who was subjected to mind control experiments funded by the CIA. This chapter provides the history of mind control in the United States and surveys the major research programs and scientists involved.

Winter, A. (2005). "The Making of 'Truth Serum'." *Bulletin of the History of Medicine 79*, 500-533.

This essay gives a history of "truth serums" such as scopolamine, focusing on the social and cultural forces that led to their acceptance in the 1920s and 1930s. Mesmerism and hypnotism set the stage for belief in a confessional state. Psychology, as an emerging discipline, was vulnerable to unproven ideas, including the reliability and permanence of memory. The general public, concerned about crime and corruption and swayed by the power of scientific discovery, was eager to embrace "truth serums" as scientifically sound.

Wolff, H. G. (1960). "Every Man Has His Breaking Point." *Military Medicine* 85-104.

This report debates whether every man has a breaking point and examines U.S. government policies on POW behavior. It reports on the frequency of collaboration and resistance in the WWI, WWII, and the Korean War. It discusses why prisoners talk and compares combat-related breaking points to psychological POW breaking points. In addition, it highlights the role of character and commitment to resistance behavior.

Interrogation as Dialogue

Walton, D. (2003). "The Interrogation as a Type of Dialogue." *Journal of Pragmatics* 35, 1771-1802. http://io.uwinnipeg.ca/~walton/papers%20in%20pdf/03interrogationdialogue.pdf. Accessed 5/8/2006.

This analysis examines the methods and techniques of argumentation that are used in interrogation. Interrogation is classified as a hybrid type of dialogue employing both deliberation and information-seeking. Characterized by both deception and coercion, it is asymmetric in nature as one party has power and the other is passive. A normative model of interrogation is presented.

Captivity Dynamics

Biderman, A. D. (1961). *Cultural Models of Captivity Relationships*. BSSR
Research Report 339-4, DTIC – AD257325. Washington, DC: Bureau
of Social Science Research.

The behavior of captives depends in large measure upon their
conceptions of what social roles are appropriate to the unfamiliar
situations they encounter. These situations are also shaped in important
ways by cultural conceptions of the captor regarding the status of his
captives. This report reviews some of the historical and traditional
elements of the cultures of captor and captives that have important
direct effects on these role conceptions. The report was prepared as part
of a critical review of studies of prisoners of war, concentration camp
prisoners, and political prisoners.

Biderman, A. D., Heller, B. S., and Epstein, P. (1961). *A Selected Bibliography
on Captivity Behavior*. DTIC – AD253964. Washington, DC: Bureau of
Social Science Research. Distribution authorized to U.S. government
agencies and their contractors.

This bibliography lists over 600 titles focused on the extremely
deprivational captivity experienced by U.S. POWs during the Korean
War. It was prepared to accompany a report titled *The relevance for the
social sciences of knowledge derived from studies of stressful captivity*,
written by Biderman and Schein.

Farber, I. E., Harlow, H. F., and West, L. J. (1957). "Brainwashing, Conditioning,
and DDD (Debility, Dependency and Dread)." *Sociometry* 20 (4), 271-
285.

The authors examine the states of debility, dependency, and dread
(DDD) that POWs were subjected to in Korea. Debility was induced by
conditions such as semi-starvation, fatigue, and disease. The captor's
control of the POW's basic needs created dependency. Dread was
marked by the POW's intense fear and anxiety. Some of the behavioral
principles explaining the effects of DDD derive from instrumental
learning and classical conditioning. DDD alters self-concept and
results in the primitivization of thinking. The intermittent nature
of DDD served to keep hope alive. POWs get much-needed social
communication through interrogation and indoctrination sessions. The
authors conclude that resistance to the consequences of DDD is a matter
of degree and may be modified by physical health and initial anxiety,
albeit not indefinitely.

Hinkle Jr, L. E. (1963). *Notes on the Physical State of the Prisoner of War As It May Affect Brain Function*. DTIC – AD671001. Washington, DC: Bureau of Social Science Research.

This short report notes the deprivations of captivity, their possible effects on brain function, and the implications for POW and captors. Hunger, pain, signals of danger, and other sensory input are, of themselves, not toxic to the brain. Instead, it is the reaction of the individual to these inputs that can affect brain function. By contrast, isolation, sleep deprivation, and fatigue are intrinsically adverse to brain function and the individual's reaction is only one factor in determining how long these effects can be withstood. The author cautions, however, that disturbed brain function does not allow an interrogator to extract information at will.

Obedience to Authority

Haney, C., Banks, C., and Zimbardo, P. G. (1973). A Study of Prisoners and Guards in a Simulated Prison. *Naval Research Reviews*. Accessed 5/8/2006.

The infamous Stanford Prison Experiment simulated a prison environment with college students divided into groups of guards and prisoners. Participants conformed to assigned role types, with guards exhibiting aggressive behavior and prisoners acting submissive and docile. This study provides insights into the power of social contexts to influence behavior.

Milgram, S. (1963). "Behavioral Study of Obedience." *Journal of Abnormal and Social Psychology* 67, 371-378.

In this classic study on obedience, 40 subjects were instructed to administer increasing levels of shock to a volunteer victim in the context of an experiment on learning and memory. Without knowing that the shock generator was a fake, 26 out of the 40 subjects obeyed the experimenter's commands to the end, ultimately delivering the highest level of shock available. Milgram's experiment reveals that an individual who is commanded to obey by a legitimate authority usually complies.

Law Enforcement Tradition

Gudjonsson, G. H. (2003). *The Psychology of Interrogations and Confessions: A Handbook*. John Wiley and Sons.

> Gudjonsson, an expert on false confession, examines various aspects of investigative interviewing and highlights the accuracy and completeness of the information gathered during police interrogation. This book covers the theoretical, research, and practical aspects of interrogation and confession in the United States and Britain. In addition, it addresses reasons why suspects confess, false confession, and suggestibility, as well as English and U.S. law regarding confessions.

Inbau, F. E., Reid, J. E., Buckley, J. P., and Jayne, B. C. (2004). *Criminal Interrogation and Confessions*. 4th ed. Boston: Jones and Bartlett Publishers.

> First published in 1962, this book is the classic text for the Reid Technique, the standard U.S. law enforcement approach to interview and interrogation.

Kassin, S. M. (2005). "On the Psychology of Confessions: Does Innocence Put Innocents at Risk?" *American Psychologist* 60 (3), 215-228.

> Confession evidence plays a part in 15% to 25% of wrongful convictions. What causes innocent people to make false confessions? In pre-interrogation interviews, investigators make judgments about guilt that influence the entire interrogation process. Innocent suspects waive their Miranda rights in the belief that their innocence will exonerate them and are subjected to coercive interrogation designed to elicit confession. Police, judges, and juries cannot distinguish between uncorroborated true and false confessions. The author proposes reforms to current interrogation practices including videotaping interrogations as a means of protecting innocent suspects.

Kassin, S. M., and Gudjonsson, G. H. (2004). "The Psychology of Confessions: A Review of the Literature and Issues." *Psychological Science in the Public Interest*, 5 (2), 33-67.

> This comprehensive literature review surveys major research on confession. It examines the pre-interrogation interview; the impact of Miranda; modern police interrogation methods; the problem of false confessions; and the consequences of confession evidence. It also discusses detection of deception, social influences, why people waive their Miranda rights, and why people confess.

Leo, R. A. (1992). "From Coercion to Deception: The Changing Nature of Police Interrogation in America." *Crime, Law and Social Change* 18, 35-59.

> Over the past 50 years, methods of police interrogation have shifted from the use of physical coercion to psychological deception. Coercive interrogation, or the "third degree," is characterized by physical violence, torture, duress and threats of harm. Deceptive interrogation includes misrepresenting the interrogation as an interview; downplaying the seriousness of offenses; playing sympathetic roles to manipulate suspects; offering psychological excuses or moral justifications for actions; making promises; concealing the interrogator's identity; and fabricating evidence. Leo describes and explains the changes in police interrogation as driven by police professionalization, changing public attitudes, and court-driven legal doctrine.

Leo, R. A. (1996). "Inside the Interrogation Room." *The Journal of Criminal Law and Criminology* 86 (2), 266-303.

> Based on fieldwork involving 182 cases, this study describes and analyzes police interrogation practices in the U.S. criminal justice system. Findings indicate that the number of interrogation tactics employed and the length of the interrogation contribute to successful interrogation. The most successful tactics include appealing to the suspect's conscience; identifying contradictions in the suspect's story; using praise or flattery; and offering moral justifications or psychological excuses. Successful interrogations are defined as those interrogations that elicit incriminating information from suspects.

Ofshe, R. J. (1989). "Coerced Confessions: The Logic of Seemingly Irrational Action." *Cultic Studies Journal* 6 (1), 1-15.

> An expert in false confessions, Ofshe uses the case study of Tom Sawyer, a man coerced into confessing to murdering his neighbor in 1986, to illustrate how police can manipulate certain vulnerable suspects into confessing to and even believing they have committed crimes of which they have no memory and which evidence proves they could not have committed.

Ofshe, R. J., and Leo, R. A. (1997). "The Social Psychology of Police Interrogation: The Theory and Classification of True and False Confessions." *Studies in Law, Politics and Society* 16, 189-251.

> Ofshe and Leo, leading researchers in false confession, present a social-psychological model of police interrogation that describes both tactics that interrogators use to influence the interrogation and factors that

guide suspects' behavior. They also propose a classification system for statements made during interrogation.

The Torture Debate

Arrigo, J. M. (2004). "A Utilitarian Argument against Torture Interrogation of Terrorists." *Science and Engineering Ethics* 10 (3), 543-572. An earlier version of this paper presented at the Joint Services Conference on Professional Ethics is available online at: http://www.usafa.af.mil/jscope/JSCOPE03/Arrigo03.html. Accessed 5/8/2006.

Drawing from criminology, organizational theory, social psychology, the historical record, and interviews with military professionals, the author explores the potential of an official U.S. program of torture interrogation of suspected terrorists from a practical viewpoint. Three models of how torture interrogation leads to truth are examined. In the animal instinct model, suspects give up information to escape pain or death, with the prototype here being the "ticking bomb" scenario. The cognitive failure model maintains that, due to physiological and psychological stress, suspects are unable to maintain deception and comply with the interrogator. This model is associated with the torture of fanatics, martyrs, and heroes. To obtain reliable information, the data processing model analyzes a large amount of data from indiscriminate torture interrogation of many detainees. The dragnet interrogation of terrorist suspects and their associates employs this model. The article highlights special institutional requirements of and major hindrances to each model and outlines the societal and political costs of torture interrogation.

Casebeer, W. D. (2003). *"Torture Interrogation of Terrorists: A Theory of Exceptions"* (With Notes, Cautions, and Warnings). Paper presented at the Joint Services Conference on Professional Ethics, Springfield, VA, 30-31 January. http://www.usafa.af.mil/jscope/JSCOPE03/Casebeer03.html. Accessed 5/8/2006.

When is it morally permissible to engage in torture interrogation? The author attempts to answer this question using the three major tools of moral analysis: utilitarianism, deontology, and virtue theory. Walzer's "Supreme Emergency" doctrine is applied to the justification of torture interrogation. The author concludes that while torture might be permissible in certain theoretical circumstances, these circumstances will never arise in practice.

Krauthammer, C. (2005, 5 December). "The Truth about Torture: It's Time To Be Honest about Doing Terrible Things." *Weekly Standard*, 11 (12).

> In response to the McCain amendment, this essay debates not whether torture is permissible, but when. The real argument should be what constitutes legal exceptions to a torture ban. Although torture may not provide reliable information, it may be useful in some situations and should not be taken off the table. According to the author, we may be morally compelled to torture in a ticking bomb scenario and with low-fuse, high value terrorists such as Khalid Sheikh Mohammed.

Rejali, D. (2004, 18 June). "Torture's Dark Allure." Salon. http://archive.salon.com/opinion/feature/2004/06/18/torture_1/index.html Accessed 5/8/2006.

> Rejali argues that torture during interrogation does not yield better information. He discusses the nature of pain in the context of torture, the effects of torture on the torturer, the incremental nature of brutality, and the reliability of information gleaned through torture.

Rejali, D. (2004, 21 June). "Does Torture Work?" Salon. http://www.salon.com/opinion/feature/2004/06/21/torture_algiers/index.html Accessed 5/8/2006.

> An expert on torture, Rejali debunks the claim that the Battle of Algiers was won through the use of torture. He argues that the French won the Battle of Algiers through force, not by superior intelligence gathered by torture. He also outlines and counters arguments made by torture apologists.

Sullivan, A. (2005, 19 December). "The Abolition of Torture: Saving the United States from a Totalitarian Future." *The New Republic*.

> Sullivan responds to Charles Krauthammer's essay condoning torture in certain scenarios. By legally sanctioning torture, U.S. values are undermined and our relationship with foreign countries as well as our ability to get actionable intelligence is jeopardized. Once allowed, torture cannot be contained.

INDEX

A

Abu Ghraib, 130, 245, 253, 319

Accuracy, 4, 17, 19, 31, 32, 34, 35, 37, 46, 65-68, 70, 71, 73, 82, 83, 85, 107, 111, 137, 150, 163, 205, 231, 242, 248, 295, 302, 305, 307, 313, 320, 325

Affiliation, 117, 178, 279, 314

Agility, 257

All-seeing eye approach, 126

Alternative question methodology, 110, 111, 148, 183, 189, 190, 202, 207, 212, 224

Ambiguity, 102, 129, 134, 256, 258

Appreciation, 195, 244, 280

Approach avoidance, 22, 110

Army Field Manual 34-52, 6, 18, 126, 127, 303

Attitudes, 21, 22, 29, 33, 37, 47, 64, 107, 114, 116, 147, 150, 152, 178, 180, 184, 193, 202, 272, 292, 301, 312, 321, 326

Authority, 23, 36, 110, 116, 120, 151, 172, 175, 293, 297-299, 313, 324

Authority principle, 105, 112, 126

Autonomy, 279, 280

B

Barriers to success, 3, 6, 115, 235, 236, 244, 247, 248, 250, 265

BATNA (Best Alternative To a Negotiated Agreement), 254, 275, 276, 281, 298, 299

Behavioral indicators, 5, 45, 46, 52, 308

Behavioral science, 1, 3, 4, 10, 17-19, 104, 249

Behavioral symptoms, 142, 174

Behavioral cues, 47, 48, 113

Biderman, Albert D., 33, 98, 132, 139, 311, 316, 317, 323

Bind-strain theory, 110

Body language (see Body movements)

Body movements, 47, 68, 118, 122, 146, 213, 220, 238, 255, 265

Book of Five Rings, 263

Boston Police Department, 142, 144, 212, 214, 217, 228, 230

Boyd, Colonel John, USAF, 253, 257, 258, 263

Brain activation patterns (see Electroencephalography (EEG))

Breaking point, 30, 319, 322

Bush Administration, 320

C

Camp 020 (MI-5), 318, 249, 254

Camp David negotiation, 273

Case study, 144, 218, 314

Casual empiricism, 10, 11

Centers of gravity, 104, 247

Chaos, 134, 256, 258

CIA (Central Intelligence Agency), 5, 75, 96, 106, 237, 311, 315, 320, 322

Cialdini, Robert B., 23, 105, 112, 119, 126, 128

Circular logic, 246

CITP (see Criminal Investigator Training Program)

Clash of Civilizations, 244

Classes, 204, 212, 218

Coercion or coercive methods, 9-14, 19, 24-27, 35, 36, 96, 98, 102, 106, 114, 120, 123, 124, 130-133, 136, 137, 149, 174, 200, 201, 221, 222, 264, 306-309, 313, 316, 320-322, 325, 326

Coleman, Daniel, 214-217, 220, 230

Commitment (see also Irrevocable Commitments), 24,25, 36, 54,117, 125, 154, 273, 275, 282, 293, 297, 322

Communications (see also Non-verbal Communication), 13, 19-21, 26, 34, 36, 45, 46, 48, 104, 106, 118, 121, 136, 140, 147, 151, 177, 180, 183-185, 197, 208, 210, 212, 236, 238, 247-250, 255, 279, 280, 313, 323

Compliance, 17, 20, 22, 24, 25, 33, 35-37, 102, 103, 105, 109, 110, 114, 116, 119, 124, 126, 128-131, 137, 191, 196, 313, 316, 317

Confession (see also Oral Confession; Securing the Confession), 5, 6, 18, 39, 74, 99, 100, 110, 111, 118, 142, 144, 145-152, 155-159, 163-175, 183, 186-191, 193, 194, 200-204, 207, 209, 210, 212, 215-217, 220, 222, 224, 225, 227-232, 256, 304, 316, 319, 321

Confidence (see also Interviewer Confidence), 16, 47, 49, 85, 107, 111, 112, 119, 123, 172, 176, 181, 190, 200, 212, 224, 227, 238, 262, 275, 304

Confirmation bias, 304

Confusion, pressure caused by, 29, 129, 134

Consistency (see also Consistency principle and Internal consistency), 24, 36, 171, 185, 253-255, 262

Consistency principle (see also Consistency and Internal consistency), 112, 128

Consultation teams, 249, 261

Contentious tactics, 273

Contingency agreement, 272

Controlled exchange of information, 250, 251

Cooperate, 1, 13,

Core concerns, 280
Criminal Investigator Training Program, 209-211, 213
Criteria-based content analysis, 48
Culture, 15, 17, 23, 35, 36, 51, 52, 68, 84, 109, 117, 134, 201, 203, 212, 227, 230-232, 243-246, 248, 257, 286, 294, 296, 301, 308, 309, 312, 321, 323

D

Debility, 32, 37, 97, 130, 132, 137, 323, 324
Deceit, 79, 142, 149, 174, 197-199, 212, 216, 220
Deception, 3, 5, 27, 45-53, 63-85, 114, 121-123, 145-148, 175, 184-186, 190, 197-204, 207, 212, 213, 220, 221, 229, 249, 257, 265, 296, 304, 308, 309, 311, 313, 322, 325-327
Decision-making cycles, 257, 258
Deconstructing, 116, 264, 104, 117, 235, 264
Deforest, Orrin, 106, 119
Denials, 5, 22, 142, 145-149, 152, 164, 167-173, 188, 194, 203, 206, 227
Dislocation of expectations, 134
Dividing the pie, 273, 280
Duress (see also Debility)

E

Educement, 1-7, 10, 12, 17-28, 31-39, 46, 119, 128, 133, 139, 140, 235-237, 247, 248, 252, 253, 257, 258, 264-267, 271-275, 282, 285-302, 305-308
EEG (see Electroencephalography (EEG))
EGG (see Electrogastrogram (EGG))
Electroencephalography (EEG), 34, 46, 75, 76, 80, 82, 85
Electrogastrogram (EGG) 64, 66, 67, 82
Emotions, 102, 176, 177, 195, 196, 218, 268, 270, 279280, 286, 298,
ERP (see Event-Related Potential (ERP))
Event-Related Potential (ERP), 75, 76
Expectancy effects, 49
Eye blinks, 64, 66, 67, 69-71, 77, 82
Eye contact, 48, 180, 189, 304

F

Facial expressions (see also Microfacial expressions), 48, 64, 68-70, 82
Fact-gathering, 177
Fatigue (see Debility)
FBI (see Federal Bureau of Investigation (FBI))

Fear, 11, 24, 25, 29, 33, 36, 68, 69, 85, 97, 102, 116, 118, 132, 138, 145, 155, 157, 173, 174, 191, 196-199, 202, 217, 219, 228, 232, 245, 254

Federal Bureau of Investigation (FBI), 75, 142, 144, 184, 204-212, 227-229, 244, 315

Federal Law Enforcement Training Center (FLETC), 142, 144, 206, 208-214, 227-229

Fisher, Roger, 268, 270, 271, 277, 278, 280

Fixations, 64, 69-71, 82

Fixed pie, 268, 272

FLETC (see Federal Law Enforcement Training Center (FLETC)),

Flexibility, 100, 106, 109, 182, 258

fMRI (see Magnetic Resonance Imaging (MRI))

fNIRS (see Functional Near Infrared Spectroscopy (fNIRS))

Focus, 49, 100, 110, 112, 252-255, 257, 259, 270-272

Follett, Mary Parker, 267

Foreign language, 15, 101, 110, 117, 134, 200, 236-247, 257, 286, 296, 308, 312, 314, 321

Framing, 112, 143, 268, 276, 277, 280

Functional Magnetic Resonance Imaging (fMRI), (see Magnetic Resonance Imaging (MRI))

Functional Near Infrared Spectroscopy (fNIRS), 80-82

G
Game theory, 268

Gamesmanship, 273, 274

Gaze aversion, 48, 199

Gender, 169, 302

Geneva Convention, 11, 74, 98

Gestures, 47, 48, 69, 118, 140, 260, 304

Getting to YES, 267, 290

Going next door approach, 124, 138

Good cop / bad cop, 29, 195, 196, 295, 302

Great Britain, 142, 144, 204, 220, 221, 223

Guantanamo, 3, 107, 117, 253, 315, 319

H
Harmony, 259, 262

Harvard Negotiation Project, 252, 267, 271

Hawala, 248

Heart rate, 46, 65, 67, 118, 159, 249

Heritage speakers, 243

Hinkle, Lawrence E., 137, 139, 316, 318, 324

Hostage negotiation, 268

How-to guides, 174

Human Intelligence (HUMINT), 1, 8, 18, 45, 52, 101-103, 122, 138, 139, 250, 303, 314

HUMINT (see Human Intelligence (HUMINT))

Huntington, Samuel P., 244

I

Initiative, 133, 259, 262, 263

Innocent, 50, 66, 108, 158, 188, 189, 206, 226, 246, 304, 325

Intended outcome, 251-255

Interests, 21-24, 36, 68, 103, 155, 172, 175, 237-239, 252, 255, 267, 270-281, 285-301, 304, 315

Internal consistency, 253-255, 262

Interpersonal intelligence, 101

Interpreters, 52, 108, 237, 247, 260, 312

Interrogation (see Interrogation approaches ; Kinesic Interrogation ; PEACE-British Interrogation Techniques; Pre-interrogation ; Strategic interrogation ; and Tactical interrogation)

Interrogation approaches, 6, 9, 142

Intimidation, 10, 11

Intrapersonal intelligence, 101

Ireland, 142, 173, 221, 222

Irrevocable commitments, 275

Isolation, effects of, 97, 135-138, 156, 157, 175, 258, 316, 324

Israel, 12, 15, 53, 144, 204, 231, 239, 267, 277, 311-313

Israel High Court of Justice, 12

Ivan is a dope approach, 126

K

Kinesic analysis and interrogation, 174, 185, 186, 193, 194, 197

Knowing the enemy, 245

Knowledgeability, 99, 103-105, 107, 108, 112, 117, 122, 125, 128, 136, 137, 139, 236, 247, 250

Kreimer, Seth,

KUBARK,

L

Language (see also Foreign language) (for Body language see Body
movements), 20, 21, 27, 36, 47, 81, 123, 134, 200
Law of requisite variety, 109, 124, 261
Law of Small Numbers, 304
Legal traveler, 97
Likeability, 23
Lobotomy, 303, 304
Logical appeals, 246
Loudness, 49

M

Magnetic resonance imaging (MRI), 46, 53, 75, 77-82, 85
Magnetoencephalography (MEG), 75-77, 82
Maximization, 149
McCain Amendment, 13, 328
McCoy, Alfred W., 96, 320
McKersie, Robert, 267, 268, 271, 301
MEG (see Magnetoencephalography (MEG))
Memory, 31, 32, 34, 50, 76, 77, 79, 81, 139, 161, 162, 183, 199, 225, 322, 324,
326
Microfacial expressions, 51
Minimization, 149, 191, 194, 201, 206, 211, 219, 222, 227
Miranda, 163, 165, 166, 169, 171, 216, 219, 325
MIS-Y, 3, 108, 111, 249, 318
Monitoring, 46, 48, 49, 113, 249
Motivation, 22, 24, 25, 28, 29, 31, 32, 34, 36, 50, 52, 79, 85, 97, 101, 102, 125,
146, 157, 198, 202, 204, 206, 207, 227, 228, 275, 277, 289, 297, 301, 314, 317
MRI (see Magnetic resonance imaging (MRI))
Multiple simultaneous offers, 272
Musashi, Miyamoto, 263
Mutual gains, 268-273

N

Narcoanalysis, 64, 73, 82, 83
Negotiation (see also Best Alternatives to a Negotiated Agreement (BATNA);
Camp David negotiation; Harvard Negotiation Project and Hostage negotiation;
Hostage negotiation; and Seven Elements of Negotiation), 4, 6, 20, 36, 103, 108,
233, 237, 252-256, 259, 267-302
Neurolinguistic Programming (NLP), 26, 27, 36

New York Police Department, 268, 311

NLP (see Neurolinguistic Programming (NLP)),

Nobody loves you approach, 25

Non-coercive method or model, 102, 114, 123, 124, 130, 221, 265

Non-verbal cues or communication, 47, 49, 51, 118, 120, 140, 151, 183-185, 187, 197-199, 205, 207, 211, 212, 238, 304

Non-vocal (see Nonverbal cues or communication)

Nutritional Deprivation (see Debility)

O

Objections, 188, 189, 201, 211

Objective analysis, 305-307

OODA Loop, 258-262

Operational accord, 103, 244

Oral confession (see also Confession), 190, 200

Outcomes, 27, 29, 33, 119, 120, 143, 151, 152, 167, 232, 235, 244, 246, 251-259, 264, 268-272, 277, 279, 289

P

PACE (see Police and Criminal Evidence Act of 1984 (PACE))

Pain, 25, 33, 34, 35, 37, 68, 81, 97, 116, 130, 133, 135, 279, 281, 289, 297, 316, 324, 327, 328

Paradoxical Intention, 30

Paralinguistic cues, 47, 49, 51, 183, 184

Pareto curve, 269, 270, 272, 279

Pauses, 49, 70, 197, 211

PEACE - British interrogation technique, 221, 222

Perception, 15,21,25, 31, 34, 48, 76, 147-151, 158, 174, 196, 200, 227, 236, 286

Perceptual positions, 75, 115, 195, 196, 254, 255

Personality characteristics, 11, 24, 49, 101, 103, 105, 106, 108, 110, 116, 117, 120, 125, 134, 136, 142, 175, 177, 181, 194, 228, 249

Persuasion (see also Subliminal persuasion), 5, 17, 21, 23, 25-28, 35-39, 105, 128, 143, 147, 153, 171, 173, 174, 237, 311, 320, 321

PET (see Positron Emission Tomography (PET))

Physical setting, 97, 110, 119, 135, 255, 258

Pierce, Albert F., Jr., 141, 218-221, 230

Police and Criminal Evidence Act of 1984 (PACE),

Polygraph, 5, 52, 63-68, 71-73, 75, 78, 82-85, 97, 118, 123, 248, 249, 316, 321

Porter, Clifford F., 240-243

Positional bargaining, 268, 271

Positions (see also Perceptual positions), 20, 21, 25, 95, 107, 164, 254, 255, 268-271, 273, 288, 289, 293, 297-300
Positron Emission Tomography (PET), 75, 77, 78, 82
Posture, 47, 69, 112, 116-118, 124, 128, 131, 133, 189, 236, 260
Pre-interrogation, 185
Pressure, 11, 13, 25, 26, 28, 32, 35, 36, 112, 114, 116, 118, 120, 123, 128-133, 136, 150, 151, 156-159, 168, 173, 174, 196, 200, 253, 275, 300, 313
Prisoner's dilemma, 125, 269
Proficiency, 236-238
Prosecution, 99, 159, 210, 216, 217, 223, 225, 228
Psychological assessment, 105, 125
Psychological set, 97, 104, 105, 119, 135, 255
Psychophysiological measures, 66, 84
Pupillary dilation, 48

Q
question design, 121

R
Radar Vital Signs Monitor (RVSM), 64, 67, 68, 102
Rapidity, 259, 262
Rapport, 22, 26, 27, 102, 112, 114, 120, 121, 135-138, 142, 174, 180-182, 194, 196, 197, 202, 205-212, 215-222, 225-232, 238, 280, 298, 306, 308, 309, 312
Reality monitoring, 48, 49
Reciprocity, 13-15, 24, 36, 122, 222, 294
Recording, 48, 67, 70, 76, 77, 113, 144, 179, 209, 214, 216, 217, 220-229, 249, 250
Regression, 109, 130-132
Regulatory depletion, 30
Reid Model or Technique, 142, 145-148, 155, 157, 164, 174-180, 183-193, 197, 199-206, 210, 215, 219-222, 225, 227, 229, 231, 325
Rejection-then-retreat scenario, 128
Relational identity, 279, 280
Rendition, 3, 319
Repetitive Transcranial Magnetic Stimulation (rTMS), 82
Research venues, 6, 303, 309
Reserve component, 241
Resistance, 2, 17, 19, 25, 26, 28-33, 35-37, 52, 95, 98, 99, 110, 112, 114-117, 119, 120, 123-129, 132-134, 138, 145, 149, 158, 168, 171, 180, 204, 236, 246, 256, 261, 274, 279, 296, 298, 301, 302, 308, 312, 313, 316, 317, 322, 323

Resistance training (see also Resistance), 26, 99, 117, 134, 256, 308

Response latency, 49

Richards, Colonel Chet, USAFR, 257

rTMS (see Repetitive Transcranial Magnetic Stimulation (rTMS))

Rule of law, 11-13

RVSM (see Radar Vital Signs Monitor (RVSM))

S

Saccades, 64, 69-71, 82

Sampling, 50, 51

Scharff, Hanns, 102, 313

Schelling, Thomas, 267, 274, 275

Schwerpunkt (see also Focus), 253

Screening, 52, 66, 75, 85, 101, 107, 118-123, 134, 250, 319, 321

Securing the confession, 142, 174, 200

Sensory acuity, 258, 260

Sensory Deprivation, 32, 34, 37, 222, 318, 320

SERE (see Survival, Evasion, Resistance and Escape (SERE))

Setting, 37, 39, 45, 47, 50, 63, 67, 73, 74, 83, 85, 97, 103, 107, 110, 115, 119, 124, 133-135, 142, 174, 178, 183, 213, 215, 218, 224, 255, 258, 259, 265, 277, 306, 308, 309

Seven Elements of Negotiation, 271

Shock of capture, 111, 133-135

Shock the conscience, 12

Situational awareness, 260

Skin conductance, 46, 66, 75, 76

Sleep Deprivation, 32, 37, 137, 317, 324

Social biases, 49

Social proof principle, 119

Social Validation, 24, 36

Specificity principle, 100

Speech rate, 197

Stalemate, 268, 270, 273

Standards of legitimacy, 273, 274, 281

Starvation (see Debility)

Statement Validity Assessment, 48, 49

Status, 23, 24, 74, 84, 108, 178, 219, 280, 294, 323

Strategic interrogation, 9, 108, 134, 249, 264, 265, 318

Strategic-linguistic landscape, 238

Strategy, 12, 20, 21, 26-29, 32, 100, 101, 116, 119, 123, 128, 134, 138, 139, 189, 196, 215, 247, 253-259, 262, 263, 267, 269, 285-295, 299, 300, 306

Stress, 17, 19, 32, 35, 50, 64, 66, 67, 71, 72, 85, 98, 109, 115, 123, 126, 129, 134, 151, 157, 160, 175, 186, 194, 197, 258, 286, 306, 308, 309, 318, 319, 323, 327

Sturgeon, Colin, 221-223

Subjective evaluation, 303

Subliminal Persuasion, 26, 27

Suggestibility, 34, 97, 148, 159-163, 317, 320, 325

Sun Tzu, 116, 245, 263, 264

Survival, Evasion, Resistance and Escape (SERE), 2, 98, 99, 101, 117, 120, 129, 308, 309

Systems approach or thinking, 251, 252

T

Tactical interrogation, 9, 115, 134

Target future choice chart, 276, 278

Technical intelligence, 247, 248, 250

Technology, 1, 46, 52, 53, 66-75, 78, 81, 113, 243, 247-250, 263, 264

Terrorism, 4, 6-15, 18, 45, 46, 54, 74, 103, 104, 115, 117, 127, 130, 134, 138, 143, 144, 221, 222, 227, 230-235, 239, 247-249, 252, 263, 296, 298-300, 314, 315, 317, 319, 327, 328

Thermal imaging or photography, 46, 64, 72, 73, 82

Threats, 9, 10, 15, 17, 18, 25, 28, 29, 66, 85, 97, 98, 107, 127, 149, 154, 155, 173, 196, 225, 231, 232, 237, 257, 263, 271, 273-275, 281, 286, 294, 295, 298, 326

Ticking bomb scenario, 9, 103, 207, 232, 299, 327, 328

TMS (see Transcranial Magnetic Stimulation (TMS))

Torture, 9-14, 33, 35, 133, 134, 246, 306, 307, 311, 312, 316, 319, 320, 326

Tradeoffs, 7, 16, 272, 290

Training, 2-4, 6, 11, 18, 22, 26, 30, 45, 47, 53, 54, 82, 98-106, 114-117, 121, 125, 126, 128, 132, 134, 139-144, 177, 198, 204-209, 213-220, 225-235, 237-239, 240, 251, 252, 256-261, 265, 289, 295, 301, 303, 306, 308, 314-316, 319

Transcranial Magnetic Stimulation (TMS), 75, 81-83

Trickery (see Deceit)

Truth serums, 63, 64, 73, 74, 82, 83, 322

Types of questions, 182, 183, 212

U

Uncertainty, 49, 157, 159-162

V

Veracity, 45, 46, 49, 66, 73, 104, 122, 138

Verbal cues, 47, 48

Videotaping, 69-71, 143, 144, 179, 214, 217, 221, 223-226, 229, 231, 249, 250, 304, 325

Voice pitch/tension, 49

Voice Stress Analysis (VSA), 49, 64, 71, 72, 82, 123, 249

VSA (see Voice Stress Analysis (VSA))

W

Walzer, Michael, 327

War crimes, 14, 277

Y

Yesable proposition, 268, 276